Durkheim and modern sociology

Durkheim and modern sociology

✧✧

STEVE FENTON

with

ROBERT REINER *and* IAN HAMNETT

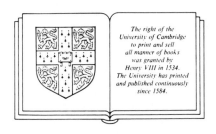

The right of the
University of Cambridge
to print and sell
all manner of books
was granted by
Henry VIII in 1534.
The University has printed
and published continuously
since 1584.

CAMBRIDGE UNIVERSITY PRESS

Cambridge

London   New York   New Rochelle

Melbourne   Sydney

105447

Published by the Press Syndicate of the University of Cambridge
The Pitt Building, Trumpington Street, Cambridge CB2 1RP
32 East 57th Street, New York, NY 10022, USA
296 Beaconsfield Parade, Middle Park, Melbourne 3206, Australia

First published 1984

Printed in Great Britain at the University Press, Cambridge

Library of Congress catalogue card number: 83–26248

British Library Cataloguing in Publication Data

Fenton, Steve
Durkheim and modern sociology.
1. Durkheim, Emile   2. Sociology
I. Title   II. Reiner, Robert
III. Hammett, Ian
301   HM22.F8D8

ISBN 0 521 25923 1 hard covers
ISBN 0 521 27763 9 paperback

Contents

Acknowledgements

Although writing the 'acknowledgements' section comes at the end of the very hard business of writing a book as one of the 'small' tasks one must do, I actually very much welcome the chance to say my thanks to scholars and friends whose help and support I have had. And I have no doubt at all about whom I should mention first and above all others. To put it very simply and briefly, I am deeply grateful to Edward Tiryakian for years of friendship, counsel and intellectual inspiration.

Others have helped me with particular chapters. I am of course, very thankful for the contributions made by Robert Reiner and Ian Hamnett and they have both helped me in ways which have gone beyond the particular chapters they wrote.

Theo Nichols splattered red ink over several drafts of chapter 2 and forced me to clarify the arguments.·

Sandra Acker helped a great deal by taking me through much of the terrain in the sociology of education, and commenting with great skill on drafts of chapter 5.

Sue Allen Mills and Francis Brooke of CUP have earned my thanks too.

And finally I want to record a heartfelt public thank you to Jackie Bee, Pauline Tilley and Sue Palmer.

Introduction

Wherever students of society are introduced to sociological traditions of thought, it is likely that the work of Emile Durkheim features strongly in the initiation. Durkheim's name is so firmly planted in the heartland of sociology's classical tradition that the reiteration of his importance has become something of a ritual performance. In a certain orthodoxy he is credited with conferring distinctiveness on the discipline, founding its method, and with defining a set of facts eminently social, and, as such, distinguishable from the 'facts' drawn from a psychological, biological, economic or utilitarian understanding of man and society. By the quality and volume of his own work, he has earned his place of importance, and through the inspiration of others he has brought forth a sociological literature of merit and substance. At the same time his work has been subjected to many criticisms, some justified, and to a number of misleading interpretations which have led to his work being neglected by some and turned aside by others. In early American sociology his writings were seen as granting an undue realism to social phenomena, and were thus believed to be antagonistic to America's individualistic and voluntaristic tradition.[1] In France his school of thought suffered an eclipse after the 1914–18 War, and through the 1930s; only recently has there been, especially in the pages of the *Revue Française de Sociologie*,[2] what amounts to a quite remarkable revival of interest in his method. In Britain the identification of Durkheim with a conservative image of society, and the linking of his concern for 'solidarity and the conservation of societies' to the general functionalist model, led to his work acquiring the unpopularity reserved for all functionalist thought, as Marxist and quasi-Marxist models were revived in the late 1950s and 1960s.[3]

The last decade has seen a clear revival of interest in his work, signalled by several English, French and American works,[4] and by the publication of special 'Durkheim' issues of the French *Revue*. But it should not be taken as a symptom of a renascent conservatism in sociological thinking. On the contrary, the revival has been marked by a distinct move away from past

1

interpretations of Durkheim as the cornerstone of sociological conservatism, and, whilst the new work has not shed all scepticism about Durkheim's
weaknesses as a sociologist, it does see these weaknesses in a new light.
Recent interpretations have provided a more finely balanced estimation of
Durkheim's sociology, and a sharper view of how Durkheimian thinking
may be evaluated. We are now required to take more seriously the claim
that Durkheim ought to be regarded, in some senses, as a radical critic of the
developing industrial society he observed, and, instead of dismissing him as
reactionary, set out to assess the nature and quality of this 'radicalism'.

The renewal of interest in and reinterpretation of his work deserves our
attention, especially since the new commentaries have not been written by
scholars wholly antagonistic to his mode of thinking, nor by scholars
unreservedly sympathetic. John Horton pointed the way when he spoke of
alienation and anomie, central concepts in Marx and Durkheim, as
'metaphors for a radical attack on the dominant institutions and values of
industrial society'.[5] Joseph Neyer and Melvin Richter, in a 1960 collection of
essays, did much to undermine the established orthodoxies about his
theories.[6] But it was not until later works, and especially that of Lukes and
Giddens,[7] began to make their impact that a new view of Durkheim's
sociology began to penetrate widely into sociology. It is this new current of
thought which has, in large part, provided the occasion for the present
book.

This book attempts to draw together and crystallize a singular interpretation of Durkheim's work and hold it up to critical examination. In doing so
we have had to remind ourselves of the power of fashion in sociological
thinking and guard against allowing the pendulum to swing too far in a
different direction; we have had to temper enthusiasm with caution. But we
have tried to do more than this, because this volume attempts to do more
than reinterpret Durkheim's writings. As well as presenting to the new or
returning student the major elements of Durkheimian sociology, as well as
trying to evaluate the view of him as a 'radical' ('a socialist of sorts' as
Lukes has described him) – we have also tried to free consideration of his
writing from narrowly scholarly treatment. This is not because such
exegesis is not valuable – without it the task could not even begin – and in
any case most of the now available exegesis is of a very high quality. But we
have tried to expand our consideration of his work away from pure exegesis
simply because the next task – the consideration of his value as a
sociological guide to concrete substantive areas of analysis – demands to be
undertaken anew in the light of the enriched understanding of his general
ideas. So, in this book, we have also concentrated on demonstrating the
actual impact of Durkheim's thinking on important substantive areas of
sociological inquiry – the state, the division of labour and class conflict,

religion and ideology, race and society, education, and the problems of law and deviance. We hope that because of this, sociologists will be able to broaden their appreciation of his work, and new students will have an entrée into his theories which goes beyond methodological debates and formal treatment of him as a 'founding father'.

This volume sets out to provide 1) a basic introduction to Durkheim's thought; 2) a consistent view or interpretation of his sociology and political philosophy and 3) a practical introduction to his thought as applied to areas which are commonly part of current sociological inquiry. This last intention, carried through in the bulk of chapters 2 and following, naturally includes the discussion of more recent writers who have been directly or indirectly influenced by Durkheim's work.

An outline of the present book

In the first chapter we present a guide to his written work and his life and public career. Considerable space is given to an account of French society and politics of the period 1870–1920, especially as they formed the setting for his sociological thinking, and indeed as they formed the stage on which he acted out his practical reforming concerns. Choices of emphasis have to be made, and we have set out to evaluate the continuing relevance of Durkheimian thought; therefore correspondingly less space is given to the intellectual antecedents of Durkheim. Readers are directed to good reading on this subject. Chapter 1 also contains the broad interpretive thesis of the book, conveyed by way of a critique of Nisbet's view that Durkheim's work is motivated by profoundly conservative impulses and constitutes the very foundation of sociological conservatism.[8] Without denying the importance of his concern with 'solidarity' and the conservation of societies, we have found good cause to support the view that there is an important strand of radical criticism in his work, backed by a secular reforming spirit. This theme – or at least the tension between conservatism and radicalism in his thought – is pursued in the substantive interests of the later chapters.

Chapter 1 does aim to stand as a general introduction to his major works, but it should be noted that rather less space is given to those topics which are naturally taken up in greater detail in the following chapters. For example, we mention his work on education in the first chapter, but more detailed attention is given in chapter 5; *Suicide* is discussed in rather more detail in the opening chapter because it does not have a single 'home' in the later chapters. The reader should also make a mental note of similar dispositions in regard to the treatment of major writers who have been influenced by Durkheim. Merton's elaboration of the concept of anomie has obviously been very important.[9] In this book, the concept of anomie is discussed at length in the chapter on the division of labour – the context in which Durkheim himself developed the idea to a great extent – whereas Merton's work is discussed most fully in the chapter on deviance and the law, again the area in which it most naturally falls. Similarly the work of Lévi-Strauss has a clear *general* importance in the development of Durkheimian themes, but detailed discussion of Lévi-Strauss is here reserved for the chapter on religion (7) and on race (4).

It is the chapters on the division of labour and class conflict (2), the political state (3), education (5), the law and deviance (6) and, to a lesser degree, race and primitive mentality (4) which provide the best opportunities for extending the interpretive arguments of chapter 1. In the fields of economic organization and education particularly, there is abundant evidence of Durkheim's practical reforming ideas and these can be readily judged in the light of subsequent developments. It is less immediately apparent in his work on religion, but the sociology of religion played such an important part in the corpus of his writings, that a book on Durkheim would be seriously incomplete without a discussion of it. The reader will note that five chapters and the introductory and concluding remarks have been written by one author who has tried to achieve consistency of theme and argument. Since we are not only concerned with Durkheim's writings, but also with fields of contemporary interest, especially where influenced by Durkheimian ideas, the chapters on religion and law and deviance have been contributed by different authors who not only have an understanding of Durkheim, but also have great depth of knowledge in these specialist fields. They were asked to contribute these chapters because of their specialist knowledge of these substantive fields and they were not expected to guarantee that everything they wrote adhered to the main author's ' party line '. Most readers will probably not discover striking contradictions, but differences and difficulties will remain and readers are warmly invited to explore them. Indeed we hope that all the chapters will occasion renewed discussion and debate. For example, in the field of education the revival of serious interest in Durkheim's work is at a very early stage, compared with, say, his influence on the sociology of religion.

We have written this book persuaded that the central themes or argument advanced by Durkheim concerning solidarity, the division of labour and the state are central to the general appreciation of his sociology. Therefore these ideas are introduced in chapter 1, and advanced in detail in chapter 2. To some degree they can be taken as understood in later chapters, but their very centrality has meant that it has been impossible to avoid some reiteration. Whilst we expect that the book can best be read in the order in which it is set out, readers with a special subject area interest may find their needs met by reading chapter 1 followed by that substantive area chapter.

Chapter 4 on race and primitive mentality requires some special comment. In all other areas treated it is not difficult to uncover Durkheim's own interests, nor to trace the hand of his influence in current sociology. In the case of race and society this is transparently not so. But there are at least three good reasons for including this chapter. The first is that we believe that a reading of it will demonstrate that there is much more to be said on 'Durkheim and race' than many would have suspected. The second is that it shows that Durkheim did place very great importance on his arguments *dismissing* the significance of race in sociological understanding; he thus formed an early part of a sociological orthodoxy which conceptualized race in biological terms and ejected it from sociological thinking. Since this orthodoxy *and* continuing vital interest in race and society both persist, this raises intriguing questions about the adequacy of sociological attitudes to race. The third reason is that direct Durkheimian influence was not the only criterion for our selection of substantive areas; we were also influenced by the current importance attached to areas of inquiry in subsequent sociological writing.

One final comment should be made here, and this concerns the evaluation of Durkheimian sociology and its importance in contemporary work. The present volume is neither a hymn of praise nor a catalogue of condemnations. If we overlooked what we see to be the weaknesses, small and large, in Durkheim's approach, we would be misleading the reader. If, conversely, we had found little or nothing of value in his writings, it is most unlikely that we would have embarked on this project. In the matter of specific areas of inquiry, there are clearly many where his insights have been influential and continue to provide a profound stimulus – one can turn for example to the sociology of law, of religion and of suicide. There are others – and I suspect the sociology of education is one – where much of worth remains to be tapped. In the matter of the broader sociological philosophy – the Durkheimian meta-sociology if you like – his work, correctly seen as the writings of a man of conservative temperament with a broad vision of necessary social reconstruction, deserves to be evaluated in just that light. There is nothing new or startling in the observation that all sociology of any substance or breadth contains within it implicit or explicit political and social values, and embodies assumptions and presuppositions about the nature of man and society, particularly with regard to change and changeability. Some social philosophies maintain that societies are natural orders in which men intervene at their peril; others that societies are torn by internal contradictions which are transcended in the birth of a new order.

We have suggested in chapter 1 that present day sociology contains within it an opposition between reformist and revolutionary thinking, between thinking predicated on the assumption that social pathologies are 'treatable' broadly within the existing structure of property relations and the disposition of democratic power, and thinking predicated on the assumption that most social pathologies are finally traceable to the central contradictions of contemporary society and can only be overcome in the transcendence of that society. That is not the only, nor necessarily the most central, opposition in contemporary sociology, but it is evident and important. Durkheim clearly believed that modern society was troubled by profound pathologies; that people could, should and would impose themselves on the natural process of social change towards greater complexity and individualism, in an effort of social reconstruction. He also quite explicitly rejected social revolution as a means of approaching the social ideal. One of his most explicit statements of this position occurs early in *Professional Ethics and Civic Morals*:[10]

Let us suppose that by a miracle the whole system of property is entirely transformed overnight and that on the collectivist formula the means of production are taken out of the hands of the individual and made over absolutely to collective ownership. All the problems around us that we are debating today will still persist in their entirety.

The possibility of the transformation of property did not escape his attention, nor did the proposals for revolutionary change. Rather he gave reasons for rejecting these ideas. He contended that change through class conflict incurred more social harm than good; that the regulation of economic activities was a moral question as much as a question of power and interest; and he was also guided by his belief that radical socialist proposals for change entailed the danger of an over-powerful state organ. Settlement of these arguments has not been achieved; they cannot be set aside.

Since differences between Durkheim and other sociologists on this kind of issue are as much matters of presupposition as matters of sociology, it follows that any discussion of his work is bound to remain substantially within his own terms. Those terms need not and may not be accepted. But the challenge is to remain within his terms long enough to push his sociology to its limits and then reach our judgement of where the strengths and weaknesses lie. This is, on the whole what we have tried to do. But there are significant exceptions and this is so because there are areas – particularly with regard to the state and class relations – where Marxist analysis looms so large that it would be unwise to neglect it.

I do not think that Durkheimian theory provides a wholly sound basis for sociological theory; I do believe that it provides a consistent theory, of depth and imagination, yielding up a theoretical challenge which must be met. It also seems clear to me that in specific areas of inquiry his work contains insights of continuing value. And I am convinced that there is some fundamental truth in his understanding of the moral quality of social life which cannot be discarded. In the chapter on Durkheim's political sociology I have tried to show, through a discussion of authority and obligation as against coercive power and interest, how deeply this 'moral' conception of social facts penetrated into Durkheim's thinking. In his own terms this is thoroughly consistent. Stepping outside of his terms, it does appear to lead to his underestimation of power, coercion and interest. He does not offer a theory of how capitalism works, he does not incorporate into his sociology an explicit 'economic' theory of land, labour and capital. But then we return to the point that capitalism was not, for Durkheim, the focal category of analysis. Some of the difficulties this entailed can best be seen in his discussion of property; his view of changing property relations has been seen above. In several passages a discussion of the distribution of property (and possible changes in it) glides imperceptibly into a discussion of the moral attitudes and regulations surrounding property. If there is something wrong with theorizing about property relations without considering the moral elements of economic behaviour, there can equally be something wrong with conceptualizing property relations as if they were wholly or mostly moral relations. In fact some of his commentary on property, inequality and inheritance strongly implies the need for quite radical changes in the distribution of property and regulation of property relations, but this is discussed without any systematic acknowledgement of the resistance likely to be met when property rights and privileges are challenged. The loosely sketched out reasons for the expectation of a gradual 'evolutionary' change in property relations seem inadequate.

I am not, then, a Durkheimian. The strengths, and the limits of his work, in my estimation, are exactly as I have expressed them above and are developed in the body of this book. My distance from Durkheim will not always be readily apparent in the pages which follow and this is partly because, in devoting time and effort to his works, I have acquired a curious kind of sympathy – perhaps that minimum necessary for being able to appreciate his thought – but a sympathy which falls short of endorsement.

1

Durkheim's life, public career and sociological thought

Social crisis and sociology

Durkheim was but twelve years old when France registered the double shock of defeat in the Franco-Prussian war, and the upheaval of the Paris Commune of 1870–1. But these events made their mark on him, as they did on most people of his generation, the first being a severe blow to national pride and self-confidence, the second dramatizing the potential for violent class conflict in a society which was becoming markedly more industrial, even if the pace of change in France was slower than in other European societies. Durkheim grew up in a France which was openly concerned with the question of national purpose and solidarity, and was faced with new and growing symptoms of social division, as the urban working class began to realize its strength. On the one hand, therefore, Durkheim had some ready awareness of a 'social question' which formed part of the social consciousness which influenced his sociology. In lectures and discussions he speaks freely of the divisive force of inequality, and the generality of class conflict in industrial societies.[1] On the other hand, the 'national question' greatly affected him too. The struggles of the Third Republic to establish its authority – against both reactionary and revolutionary forces – dominated his adult experience of political life. He had, like other nineteenth-century intellectuals, a sense of crisis, manifested variously as the loss of moral certainty, the spectre of social dissolution, of social division and class conflict, and as the problem of political authority. His sociology was very largely concerned with his understanding of this 'crisis', of its historical roots, its present manifestations and the paths to social reconstruction.

But a persistent oversimplification in interpreting Durkheim and other nineteenth-century writers has been to suggest that somehow they shared a sense of crisis, that they shared an understanding of social dissolution, and therefore founded their sociologies on the same basic intellectual impulse – the desire to find a way of preserving society. This is so vague and general a formula that it explains everything and nothing. Many writers of the period did have a deep sense of crisis, a sense that the whole basis of social life was being transformed at such a rate and in such ways that it not only reduced the lives of many people to misery, uncertainty or moral despair, but also threatened to bring an end to even the merest modicum of social order and political continuity. But the actual nature of the appreciation of this 'crisis', the diagnosis of its causes, and the prescription of a cure – these specific elements of different writers' ideas – varied so much that to trace them all to the same vague sense of crisis is to leave much unexplained and unexplored. This is especially true of the interpretation of Durkheim's sociology. We have been too readily persuaded by the bland argument that Durkheim lived in a society in which the 'problem of order' was paramount and thus founded his intellectual constructs on the perceived need to preserve its integrity. Some knowledge of both his life and of French society of the time is a prerequisite to the task of reshaping our appreciation of his sociology.

Durkheim's life, politics and the social context of France

Durkheim was born in 1858 in Alsace-Lorraine into a Jewish family which came to expect young Emile to become a Rabbi. He died in Paris in 1917, broken in spirit by the death of his son in the war, and worn out by academic work and by the public duties occasioned by the war effort. When Durkheim was a teenage boy the shaky structure of the Third Republic, which was to endure throughout his life, was beginning to emerge from the ruins of the upheaval of 1870. Because, despite its precariousness, the Republic did endure, and because, in broad terms, this period of forty odd years was 'peaceful' and relatively prosperous, it may appear to have been a period of some calm, interposed between its stormy beginnings and its tragic close. Indeed the latter two decades have sometimes been referred to as *la belle époque*, when, following their ultimate victory in the Dreyfus affair, the Republican forces had better secured their ground, and a kind of prosperity, particularly of the middling classes, had settled on France. Henri Peyre has described the Third Republic as 'the most stable of all French regimes' and has painted a picture of a nation – in the 1890s – 'enjoying unprecedented prosperity' at the heart of which Paris was 'the glamorous metropolis' frequented by pleasure-loving men and women who 'flocked to light comedies and Offenbach's frothy music'.[2] Such a picture may well be taken to sit uneasily with those brief quasi-historiographies which have described Durkheim's work as being written against a backdrop of grave crisis, and as preoccupied with order. To get closer to the truth we must abandon this simplistic equation which purports to explain his thinking, and relinquish characterizations of the period evoking a monotone of either crisis or calm prosperity. Peyre himself, though more inclined than others to speak of a stable prosperous regime, is fully aware of another side to his story; his frothy Paris is a description which betrays some of the fragility and superficiality, and he adds that this life was 'for the happy few and the foreign visitors'.[3] To Durkheim's stern eye they did not, in all probability, even appear to be happy. In any case the life of Paris was not the life of France. Its cosmopolitan enclaves were not very distant from a different Paris which fostered a serious radical and communist citizenry. Those like Durkheim who came from the provinces were never likely to mistake Paris, notwithstanding its dominance, for the nation.

Social pathologies were never far from the surface, and were to be found, in periodic crises, right on the surface. In the first place, the stable regime, the Third Republic, was, for the first twenty years of its life at least, far from stable and far from securely founded. The Constitution of 1875 which consecrated the Republic, is described by Coser as having been 'framed by Monarchists who expected the Republic soon to give way to a return of the Bourbons'.[4] The word 'Republic' was inserted in the Constitutional laws 'almost by chance', and these laws were only barely passed by the two assemblies. Coser describes the first crisis of the fledgling Republic:

> After the Constitution was adopted, the Republic was plunged into a new crisis. The President of the Republic, Marshal Marie de MacMahon, tried to establish a strong presidential system of government largely independent of parliament and with a weak cabinet, that could be recalled at will. In the course of the ensuing struggles, the President dissolved the Chamber of Deputies for the only time in the history of the Third Republic. His actions pitted the Church, the landowners, the upper bourgeoisie, and the forces of law and order against the Republican left, which was mainly composed of the lower middle classes, the anti-clericals among the educated and a working class weakened by the blood-letting of the Commune. In 1879 the Republicans decisively defeated MacMahon after he had dissolved the Chamber, and thus put an end to his dictatorial ambitions.[5]

Durkheim was, by this time, twenty-one years of age. He had left his native Épinal, in the eastern province of Lorraine, and had come to Paris. He had been outstandingly successful (and, as in the rest of his life, serious, studious and hardworking) at the Collège D'Épinal and, heartily recommended, had entered the Lycée Louis le Grand in Paris, a stepping stone to the École Normale Supérieure, the 'training ground for the intellectual elite of France'.[6] He was not altogether happy at this school and showed his distaste for the emphasis on literary and aesthetic pursuits, which he saw as being at the expense of moral concern and scientific inquiry. Noted for his seriousness, nicknamed 'the metaphysician', and out of tune with his professors, he was placed near the bottom of the list of successful aggregation candidates in 1882.[7] But his graduation was a necessary and important step for one with growing ambition for a career of study, and he met many brilliant contemporaries at the École. The names of some of them were to become as prominent as his own – Henri Bergson was at the École at this time, as was Jean Jaurès, the future Socialist leader, who became and remained a close friend of Durkheim.

At this point, 1882, Durkheim's own life and the life of the nation came notably closer together. Durkheim left the École for a five year period of teaching philosophy in Parisian schools, and gradually acquired the credentials, experience and personal contacts necessary for his later climb to the peaks of higher education in France. At the same moment the very shape, spirit and content of education in France was being placed under close public scrutiny, and was the immediate object of reform. Defeat in the Franco-Prussian war had provoked a general questioning of French national institutions and, as Terry Clark's account argues, 'educational institutions were felt to be singularly outdated and a major factor in the French defeat. A programme was put into effect, reorganizing the system from primary school through graduate and research institutions.'[8]

The more vigorous German universities were, up to a point, seen as a model, and Durkheim was one of several young teachers and scholars (others were Bougle, Halbwachs and Davy – Durkheimians-to-be) sent on scholarships to German institutions with a brief to enlarge their own experience and to convey reports and reform proposals back to the French Ministry of Education. Amid all the search for greater efficiency and 'modernity' in French education lay the overwhelmingly important question of the participation of the Catholic Church, whose institutions and precepts had so long dominated French education, and as such formed the backbone of civic and moral education.* It was in 1882 that the Primary Education Law was passed 'providing free, obligatory, non-religious education for all children from ages six to thirteen' and included in its provisions measures to weaken the Church's grip on moral and practical instruction.[9] The moderate Republicans in power during this period had, it seems, been heartened by the defeat of McMahon and his Rightist supporters in the Church and among the landowners, and had now taken the opportunity to strike a blow at clerical power. Though resisting the demands of the more radical anti-clerical lobby, they had begun the process

---

* It is of course too simple to say that the Roman Catholic and the French reactionary Right were one and the same thing: French Rightist inclinations had other ideal and material foundations, beyond the Catholic Church. And there were among Roman Catholics those who combined a desire for reform, of Church and society, with Republican sympathies. But on the whole anti-Republican ideals of the Right found inspiration in traditional religion, and the more radical Republicans were the strong voice of anti-clericalism. See also chapter 7 where Ian Hamnett discusses whether the secular study of religion undermines religious faith.

of secularizing education, and had therefore thrown open the question of what was to replace the traditional religious precepts as the basis for civic morality.

The Church's loss, the Republic's gain, were, most interestingly, Durkheim's opportunity. A young and ambitious teacher, a man of Jewish family origin, but one who had already relinquished traditional Judaism in favour of the secular scientific spirit, he stood not at all distant from the centre of these grand social changes:

The debating of Catholic orthodoxy – the prior foundation for moral and civic training in the schools – created a void that educational administrators actively sought to fill during the 1880s and 1890s. Several accounts report that Louis Liard, Director of Higher Education, had a conversation with Durkheim in 1886 in which he learned of Durkheim's ardent Republicanism and desire to formulate a secular morality based on science. The next year a fellowship from the Ministry of Education financed Durkheim's study with Wilhelm Wundt at Leipzig and at the University of Berlin. Then, after Durkheim published an impressive series of articles on the new scientific morality in Germany, Liard appointed him, in 1887, to teach social science and pedagogy at the University of Bordeaux.[10]

At Bordeaux he completed his theses, published *The Division of Labour in Society*, *The Rules of Sociological Method*, *Suicide*, and established a grand enough reputation to be promoted in 1896 to a full professorship in social science; in 1902 he left Bordeaux for the Sorbonne where he was to become first Professor of the Science of Education (1906) and, in 1913, Professor of the Science of Education and Sociology. In this way Durkheim's fortunes can be seen to have been closely linked with the fortunes of the Third Republic; he rose as it rose, the prophet of many of the causes it espoused, and, as such, a man inevitably identified as an enemy by those Catholics, Rightists and Monarchists who saw this liberal, secular and scientific spirit as the poison of the French nation.

Having avoided disaster in 1879, and having begun to push through educational reforms, the Centrist Republicans appeared to be solidifying their position; but they were not to be free of further threat. The Right *and* the radical Left made gains at their expense in the elections of 1885 and these emboldened Georges Boulanger, Minister of War, to manoeuvre himself into a position to make a coup d'état. He failed ignominiously but 'the Republic had a close call'.[11] To an increasing degree the Centrist Republicans had to be aware of a threat from the Left as well as from the Right, especially since the latter threat had been muted by the Pope's call for loyalty to the Republic. Much of the Republican support came from the middle and lower-middle classes, and had not fully accommodated the growing voice of the urban proletariat. France, indeed, had been comparatively slow in developing 'full-blown' industrial capitalism, remaining a country in which the peasantry persisted materially, and continued to be a force to be reckoned with politically. Economic historians have agreed that France lagged behind England and Germany in this respect, and have reached some agreement on the underlying causes. The traditional political regard for the importance of the peasantry meant that measures which may have hastened their decline were delayed, and economic forces tending to aggregation were stifled. In business and commerce the spirit of the petit bourgeois, and pride in the small family business inhibited the growth of corporate capitalism, as did the slow development of a banking system which could have supported such a growth.*

But the signs of the growing importance of an urban industrial proletariat were beginning to show, as those living on the land dropped to below half of the population, and those employed as industrial workers or artisans rose from 23% in 1870 to 39% in 1914.[12] For this reason the voices of socialism began to be heard in French politics, representing a growing constituency in the French nation. For reasons which I have already hinted at (and more fully explained later),[13] Durkheim was never at home with the radical Left of French politics. But the voice of 'socialism' was not (then as now in France) a unified voice and, to the extent that some of their views could be accommodated on the Left of the Republican spectrum, and to the extent that a number of Durkheim's views on the need for planning and social reconstruction merged with those of the non-revolutionary socialists, his opponents, and the opponents of the Republican sentiments with which he was most closely identified, could mark him as a 'socialist' and attempt to vilify him as such. Unmoved by the niceties of political theory, the ideologues of the Right blithely grouped together secularism, free-thinking, liberal reconstructionism, sociology and socialism as but minor variants of the same dangerous doctrine and programme.

Whilst the Republican Left could absorb some of this pressure, in 1893 socialist deputies were elected to parliament for the first time, Durkheim's friend Jaurès being prominent among them. This parliamentary wing of the socialist movement could, on most occasions, be counted upon to support the Republic and in later crises, most notably the Dreyfus affair, they were to play a crucial role. It is recorded that in the Dreyfus affair, Durkheim called upon his friend Jaurès to rally socialist support for the Dreyfusard position.

---

* This retarding of industrial capitalism in France was to be reflected in Durkheim's writings – especially in *The Division of Labour* – in so far as he appeared to write from a view of industry composed of still comprehensible and moderate units, apparently not fully aware of the dynamic expansive capacity which international capitalism contained. He recognized, and wrote of, the unprecedented growth of commerce and industry, and was greatly concerned about its social consequences; and yet he did not seem to grasp the immensity of the forces which made further 'unplanned' expansion so likely in the long run. See my discussion in chapter 2.

The thoroughgoing Marxist wing of the socialists (the Guesdists after their leader, Guesde) eschewed parliamentary politics, as did the syndicalists and the small army of anarchists who, from time to time, disturbed the calm of French politics, these last being, no doubt, most distasteful to a man of Durkheim's temper.

Although it is probably true to say that the last two decades of the Republic were founded on greater stability than the first two, they were not immune from disturbance, as we shall see. But first let us recall that it was this period of relative stability and solidification of the Republic which formed the backdrop to Durkheim's maturing scholarly progress and his notable public career. It was the period in which he moved from his late twenties to his mid-fifties, from Paris teacher to Bordeaux Professor to Paris Professor, a position in which he was to have such an immense influence stretching beyond his acknowledged centrality in the shaping of French sociology to his influence on French higher education, and on French public education in general. This included curriculum reforms at many layers of French education, organizational changes, further trimming of the influence of the Catholic Church in the wake of the Dreyfusard victory early in the new century; it also included the more direct influence he was able to wield as a gifted lecturer, teaching cohorts of trainee teachers who passed through his classes in Paris.

After the Boulanger debacle had passed, it was not long before a new crisis erupted, this time a revelation of bribery and corruption in the construction of the Panama Canal – the great Panama scandal. But this was later to appear minor by contrast with the public controversy, breaking in 1896, which was to dominate French public and political life for a decade at least. The Dreyfus affair both uncovered and exacerbated all the major social antagonisms in the French polity. The outline of the case is relatively simple. A French officer, Esterhazy, was discovered to have been selling information to the Germans, but by subterfuge was able to transfer suspicion and blame to Captain Alfred Dreyfus, a man of lower military rank and a Jew. Anti-Semitism was only one of the reasons which led to Dreyfus's conviction – and sentence to life-imprisonment on one of France's notorious convict islands – but it was an important one. And anti-Semitism bound the anti-Dreyfusards together when subsequent investigations began to cast doubt on Dreyfus's guilt. Several Frenchmen in prominent positions (including Durkheim) were first doubtful of his guilt, then convinced of his innocence. But the affair took such a deep hold on the public imagination that it became much more than a simple question of the Captain's actual guilt or innocence. Many of the same representatives of the Right which had threatened the Republic in its early days were ranged among the anti-Dreyfusards – the Church, the army and a growing anti-Semitic nationalist

Right. Similarly, liberal and radical forces rallied in defence of Dreyfus.

The significance of the Dreyfus affair, in France's life and in Durkheim's life, is such that we shall come back to it several times in this volume.* Some of the major points should be noted straight away. First it must be simply recorded that Durkheim was unequivocally aligned with the Dreyfusard forces. He was publicly visible as an enemy of the anti-Dreyfusards and, by association, of all the things which they represented. Perhaps most strikingly he was attacked as an 'intellectual', as a leading representative of the intellectuals and their corrosive liberal doctrines. One such attack spurred Durkheim to write his 'Individualism and the intellectuals', an article in which he defended the virtues of intellectual inquiry, spelled out his commitment to justice, liberty and the rights and dignity of the individual, at the same time as dissociating his own conception of individualism from the 'disruptive' or 'unrestrained' individualism with which his accusers associated him.[14]

Of competing importance is the light which the affair throws on Durkheim's own relationship to his 'Jewishness'. Despite his early abandonment of the Jewish faith, the influence of his early life and family origins cannot be lightly dismissed. Jews were becoming progressively assimilated into French life but the fact of Jewishness had not lost all its grip, among Jews themselves or in the minds of non-Jews; Jewish 'ethnicity' had not, as Durkheim thought it was destined to, disappeared without trace. The extent of assimilation prompted Durkheim to write of anti-Semitism in French life as a passing manifestation of a deeper malaise; it was not endemic or traditional as he suggested it was in Russia. For all this, it was and remained a powerful force. Yet in the Dreyfus affair Durkheim insisted on distinguishing his position from one of a 'mere' defence of Jewish rights. The defence of Jewish rights was a defence of all men's rights and liberties. Friends have recalled that he refused to see the affair as a singularly Jewish matter.[15] This corresponds neatly with the view that Durkheim, having turned away from Judaism, never paraded his renunciation, and never made great play of his position as a secular agnostic Jew. It has been speculated – and it can only be speculation – that despite the break he made with it, his early Jewish life provided him with a lifelong model of a disciplined, solidary, moral community; that his relinquishment of one moral community made him all the more urgent in his quest for the foundations of another, not so much for his own integrity, but for the integrity of a society which, having transcended the social conditions

---

* It is discussed in chapter 3 where I pay particular attention to his article 'Individualism and the intellectuals'; and in chapter 4 (concerning race and racism) where I examine his views on anti-Semitism.

capable of sustaining traditional moral certainties, stood all the more in need of a new morality supported by a reconstructed social order.

Such are the bold outlines of the links between the life of a man and the life of a nation. And Durkheim was pre-eminently a Frenchman, steeped in French intellectual traditions,[16] perhaps the preponderant part of the intellectual history of his thought can be traced to French writers.* Although Auguste Comte undoubtedly influenced Durkheim, first place should be accorded to Comte Henri de Saint-Simon (1750–1825) who had lived through the revolution and had devoted much of his life to social and philosophical study.[17] Three main ideas appearing in Durkheim can be traced to Saint-Simon: 1) the idea of the evolution of society through stages, and the possibility of uncovering laws of progress; 2) the importance attributed to science in the modern age and the possibility of creating – and applying – a science of society and 3) the belief that the modern order is, above all, an *industrial* order, complex and differentiated, but capable of yielding an organic (interdependent and peaceable) and rational social order. New social classes emerged in industrial society but they were capable of being organized into an interdependent system, because they were all 'producers' joined together in the task of industrial production. Nonetheless, for this new order to become stable, gross inequality and poverty must and could be eradicated. (The idea of antagonistic classes and the argument that inequality and private property must be abolished – these were developed by later socialist Saint-Simonians.)[18] These thoughts were all reflected in Durkheim's work – the aim of creating a scientific sociology capable of guiding social reconstruction, the evolution from mechanical to organic societies, the centrality in modern societies of the industrial economic activities and above all the argument that the division of labour was destined to be the basis of social solidarity in differentiated societies. In 1895–6 Durkheim produced a series of lectures on socialism, and a great deal of these were devoted to an examination of Saint-Simon's writings; they are now available as a single volume, *Socialism*, and in it Durkheim gives clear precedence to Saint-Simon, over Comte, as the founder of sociology. In two important respects Durkheim clearly diverged from Comte. He does not accept Comte's emphasis on the need for value

---

* This should not be overstated. He visited Germany, was impressed by works that he read there, and continued to review German writers (for example, Ferdinand Toennies) in the pages of the *Années Sociologiques*. And he may have been more influenced than is apparent by writers whose ideas he set out to criticize – for example Herbert Spencer and William James (see Lukes, *Emile Durkheim*, at p. 82 and p. 485); the emphasis on critique may disguise what he shared with them. He certainly began his explorations into religion by looking well beyond French sources (see chapter 7). But he was inclined to believe, it seems, that certain foreign seeds could not be planted in French soil; there is nothing of the German dialectic in Durkheim's sociology.

consensus in modern societies, and he does not accept the view that the division of labour is inherently socially divisive. Far from seeing Comte as Durkheim's chief mentor, Gouldner has portrayed Durkheim's first major work as a 'polemic against Comte' on precisely these points of argument.[19]

French social philosophers of the nineteenth century were bound to take a stance towards the French revolution. Durkheim, a good historical sociologist, knew that the events of a year (1789) did not alone constitute a break from one social order to another; they were historical markers in a long process of social transition. He viewed the revolution, as Edward Tiryakian has aptly put it, as neither calamity – as it was viewed by the Right – nor as a sham – as it was viewed by the Left – but as an index of a work of social and civic reform begun but not yet completed.[20] Not only had the civic liberties and virtues preached by the revolutionaries to be realized and extended, the work had also to be pressed further into the achievement of real material conditions of justice and greater equality.

He was, then, distinctively French in his intellectual consciousness, but was nonetheless sensitive to the growing 'universality' of modern industrial cultures. He observed that both intellectual culture and the broader culture of societies were destined to transcend national boundaries. The emerging civic morality of France rested on a process of social change which was not confined to France, and we know that he looked ahead to the formation of a supra-national European community.[21] But that stage of development had not yet been reached, and for the moment he believed that France had a leading role to play. Scientific sociology was a distinctively French intellectual product:

Everything has predestined our country to play this role . . . sociology could only have been born and developed where the two conditions which follow existed in combination: first, traditionalism had to have lost its domain. Second, a veritable faith in the power of reason to dare to undertake the translation of the most complex and unstable of realities into definite terms was necessary.[22]

France, he believed, was the site of this necessary combination.

Herein lies the true quality of his regard for his country and it should not be mistaken, as it has been, for a blind love of nation.[23] If he loved France it was because he believed that France sheltered or was capable of realizing the civil morality which was his faith. In this light we can understand his public patriotic commitments when his beloved France was drawn towards the tragedy of the Great War.[24] Deeply dismayed he threw himself into public works with great vigour. But the war carried away his very own son, and this loss all but extinguished the vitality of his soul. He died in 1917 at the age of fifty-eight.

The major writings of Durkheim

In his youth – having rejected the idea of training for the Rabbinate – he steadily developed a secular scientific view of the world, dedicating himself to philosophy and history, and eventually to the task of laying the theoretical, methodological and empirical foundations of the science of society – sociology.

Because his early studies were conducted in an academic world which did not recognize the discipline of sociology, it is vital to understand that he directed so much of his effort to 'emancipating' the study of society from metaphysics, and establishing the social level of study as distinct from psychology, biology or the utilitarian precepts of economists. His insistence that sociology proceeded by the study of *social facts* contained two emphases, one that we are concerned with *social* facts, the other that we are concerned with social *facts* – consider social facts as things, he wrote, 'comme les choses'. The facts observed by sociologists were social, supra-individual and irreducible to individual elements; they were also observable in concrete form without recourse to philosophical conjecture. Social facts contained within them 'subjective experience and ideas' but these took on external qualities or objective form which made them accessible to observation. Thus he tried to sweep away the prejudice that social development, laws and morals could not be studied by the scientific method. This is not to say – as we point out later – that he satisfactorily resolved the tension between individual and collective realities, or between forms of organization and symbolic representations. But he wrote with great certainty on these matters – almost as if he were trying to convince himself – and certainly provided himself with a set of guidelines for a rich life of sociological study.

His first major publication was *The Division of Labour in Society*, published in 1893, which contained his account of the evolution of society from simple to complex, primitive to modern, with special emphasis on what he saw to be the critical issue – social solidarity.[25] He characterized the solidarity of simple societies as 'mechanical' and based on 'resemblances', meaning that such was the simplicity of material and social life, and such was the absence of social differentiation, that moral ideas growing out of social life were correspondingly simple, and were shared by all members of society whose individual consciences were barely distinguishable from the collective conscience. Solidarity – the stable life, the integrity – of society was based on the homogeneity of moral belief. As social differentiation increased, so the social basis of a simple shared moral culture was undermined and gradually lost.

Having said this much, the rest of the book is concerned with the question

– what replaces mechanical solidarity? What is the source of solidarity in societies whose division of labour has become so complex – and in which social life has become correspondingly complex – that moral solidarity founded on the sharing of moral convictions is no longer possible? The dissolution of simple homogeneous societies created greater scope for individual differences, the freeing of men and women from social and moral restraint of an 'automatic' kind, from being tied directly to the moral 'centre' of society and thus produced what he described as moral and social polymorphism. By that he meant a kind of social 'many-sidedness', of many forms rather than a single form – more concretely a society with many and varied social milieux, these different milieux forming the basis or centre of the moral life of the individual.

The process of development from simple to complex, from primitive to advanced, was, for the individual, a process of emancipation. Greater freedom for the individual, and greater variation in social and moral forms, were inseparable from societies based on a highly advanced division of labour. What, in these societies, was to replace the solidary force of the shared moral culture? Durkheim could be said to have given three answers: 1) the advanced division of labour created a great amount of interdependence in society and these links of interdependence, coupled with a moral awareness of men's dependence on each other, were the new bases of solidarity.* 2) The separate social milieux of a differentiated society themselves fostered particular moral cultures which became a new kind of moral and social 'home' for the individual, an immediate sphere of social contact and common culture, and created a link between the individual and society as a whole. 3) The *social* changes which fostered greater individuality, necessarily fostered a great *faith in* the individual and therefore gave rise to those moral beliefs which protected his rights and dignity. Paradoxically this code, this cult of the individual, is the chief manifestation of a moral belief diffused throughout the whole society and is therefore a new and significant basis of solidarity itself.†

This solidarity, characteristic of modern societies, he termed 'organic solidarity', a term which he does not appear to have used after this first work; but the basic analysis remained unchanged. As Giddens stresses:

> Durkheim continued in his later thinking to base his works upon the distinction between 'mechanical' and 'organic' solidarity; . . . the existence of solidarity deriving from the division of labour was always conceived by Durkheim to be the most distinctive feature of contemporary society as opposed to traditional

---

* One translation of 'solidarité' is 'interdependence'.
† This is consonant with his argument that what remains of collective morality in a complex society is progressively vague, general and 'indeterminate' i.e. made up of generalized values not in themselves guides to specific actions.

societies; . . . and 'the kinds of society, constraint, and solidarity' dealt with in all his later works have everything to do with the attributes of contemporary society as formulated in the *Division of Labour*.[26]

After *The Division of Labour* Durkeim's work took him through an impressive array of different fields, but the underlying questions – the nature of solidarity, the basis of the attachment of the individual to society, the relationship between social institutions and morality, the character of law, morality, crime and religion – remained the same. His chief works were, after his first volume, *The Rules of Sociological Method* (1895) in which he spelt out the claim for sociology's distinctive and scientific nature; *Suicide* (1897) in which the problem of the attachment of the individual to society, and the social causes and consequences of that link being weakened, were explored through the analysis of the incidence of suicide, an act which he took to be the culminating expression of dissociation from the social order; *The Elementary Forms of the Religious Life* (1912) in which he sought to establish the nature of religion by examining it in its 'simplest' condition; and some posthumously published works, especially those now known as *Moral Education* (1925), *Socialism* (1928), and *Professional Ethics and Civic Morals* (1950).[27] Despite the importance of *The Elementary Forms of the Religious Life*, which was based on evidence from 'primitive'* societies, his main concern remained with the problems of modern societies. His central argument was that the social and moral forms destined to replace the 'mechanical solidarity' of simple societies had not fully developed and therefore modern society was experiencing a crisis of morality in a period of transition. The term which he used to capture this crisis of morality – and for which he is best known – is 'anomie' now commonly used in that form in English, but frequently in a vague and general manner which loses the original sharpness. The basis of the term is the Greek word *nomos* with a negative prefix, i.e. an absence of law, moral order or regulation, for which the cumbersome but nevertheless precise 'de-regulation' is perhaps the best phrase capable of escaping the vagueness which has come to surround 'anomie' in English usage.

Two aspects of his argument should be emphasized.

1 That the problem of anomie stemmed from the *transitional* nature of modern society, in particular from the rapid growth of economic functions and the division of labour which had outstripped old forms of control of economic activity, such as the ancient guilds, without developing more than the mere beginnings of new forms.

2 The ever-present Durkheimian argument that the social and the moral realms were intimately linked, this indicating that de-regulation would

---

* For a discussion of his view of 'primitive mentality', see chapter 4.

be replaced by regulation not through a resurgence of morality, but through the parallel development of morality *and* social institutions and agencies of law and regulation.* Since morality grew in collective life, the 'cure' for anomie lay in the fostering of those nascent forms of collective social and institutional life which promised to provide a meaningful collective context for individual existence and social rules. Since the development of modern society necessarily involved the growth of the state as a separate organ of society, a critical problem was the role to be played by the state in this process of reconstruction, especially the co-ordination of state action with the functions of secondary groups in society (i.e. of groups intermediate between the individual and the state). The value of the state was its ability to see the social canvas in its entirety; its danger lay in its remoteness from the decentralized milieux of individual and collective life; the values and dangers of the secondary social milieux in promoting social and moral reconstruction were exactly the converse.

The source of, and the image of a social malaise in the work of Durkheim and his followers was, thus, similar in some respects to that of socialist and Marxist writers, but it was understood from an entirely different perspective which led to very different conclusions:

According to our regular image of modern society, we might draw out two principal aspects, otherwise bound up with each other, of French society: the socio-economic structures which have presided over the industrial development in the second half of the nineteenth century (which Marxists look upon as the emergence of 'advanced capitalism'); the predominance of a social philosophy of laisser-faire of individualism and utilitarianism, which was one of the principal targets of Durkheim and his group. In this regard the socio-economic milieu is seen as important not only for the understanding of *The Division of Labour in Sociology*, but also the researches undertaken by the members of the group who specialised in economic studies and constructed a critique of laisser-faire capitalism, on which they blame the destruction of the social fabric.[28]

A concern with 'the social question' remained with Durkheim throughout his life, even when it was expressed through his study of subjects apparently remote from it. His direct interest in the division of labour, the state and the regulation of economic activity did not end with the 1893 publication. He continued to lecture on the topic, in the late 1890s he gave a series of lectures on socialism and communism (focussing on Saint-Simon), and in 1902 he published a lengthy new preface to a second edition of *The*

---

* The application of the idea of anomie to the analysis of the economic order is discussed in chapter 2; its application to the study of crime and deviance is examined in chapter 6 (Robert Reiner).

Division of Labour, in which he extended his thoughts on the role of occupational groups in the social and moral structure of modern societies.

Methods of inquiry

In the immediate period after the publication of *The Division of Labour* he turned his attention to establishing the basis of sociological study, firstly in *The Rules of Sociological Method* (1895) and secondly in the ambitious study *Suicide* (1897). The forthrightness of language and pioneering zeal of *The Rules* may have caused misunderstanding. What was an emphasis on 'the social' as a rejection of biological and psychological reductionism* has been taken to be a thorough reification of society†; what was an emphasis on the external observability of social facts has been taken to be a thorough neglect of subjective meaning and inner consciousness. When we allow for his zeal, much of what he claims is quite unremarkable. His assertion of a special social level of facts was not a great deal more than a matter of drawing attention to the circumstance that each individual is born into a social milieu – a society – in which common practices, established and sanctioned, already exist.[29] He attacked psychological reductionism, not psychology *per se*; his enthusiasm for the sociological may have led him to underestimate *his own* attention to inner experience, but he never did deny the importance of psychological explanation.

In *The Rules of Sociological Method* he addresses most of the questions which have since persisted as the central vexing questions of sociological methodology or the philosophy of social science. These included, as we have mentioned, the *definition* of social facts (the quality of facts which are properly considered social, distinguished from the non-social, the individual or the merely general), the *observation* of social facts (the difficult questions of observability, the nature of the intervention of the observer, and the distinguishing of scientific categories from lay categories) and the *explanation* of social facts (the nature of functional explanation, and the questions of causation and causal priority). Two other questions, to which he devotes considerable attention, are infrequently discussed today. These are the 'rules for distinguishing the normal from the pathological' and the classification of social types. The latter task has receded in sociology as the general evolutionary view of societies has receded; Durkheim's view of types of society was closely tied to his view of a general historical development from the simple to the complex. 'We shall begin by classifying

---

* Reductionism (psychological): explaining the social by direct reference to the non-social. 'Reducing' the understanding of a level of facts to another 'more fundamental' level of facts.
† Reification: granting society a concreteness, a status as a real 'thing', which it does not possess.

societies according to the degree of organization they present, taking as a basis the perfectly simple society or the society of one segment.'[30] Furthermore the former question – the identification of the moral and the pathological – can be seen to have presupposed a system of classification since he defined a social fact as normal 'in relation to a given social type at a given phase of its development, when it is present in the average society of that species at the corresponding phase of its evolution'.[31] In the analysis of a particular instance one can take a step further by attempting to show that 'the generality of the phenomenon is bound up with the general conditions of collective life of the type considered'.[32]

The evolutionary view of society has faded partly because the sheer amassing of evidence has cast doubt on one evolutionary schema after another, partly because of greater specialization and narrowness of scope in social research, and partly because of the perceived 'internationalization' of the world in which societies are seen as, not so much developing entities, but as part of an inter-related world system. But schemes of classification of types of social system have not disappeared, and Durkheim can be regarded as an important figure in the encouragement of comparative studies. More markedly, the notion that sociology could determine which social phenomena were healthy, and thus move from analysis to prescription, has declined in the face of an acknowledgement of relativism in regard to what is socially desirable, and of the way in which desired consequences are tied to particular sections or interest groups in society. Implicit in Durkheim's thinking was the view that it was possible to determine scientifically what promoted the health of the collective social order. However, a narrower prescriptive sociology has not disappeared, sociologists being willing to say 'assuming you wish X as a consequence' these or those social arrangements are likely to produce it. This would be to accept or take for granted certain ends as socially desirable; Durkheim believed that the desirable could be scientifically determined.

The questions of the nature of the social, observability and explanation are still with us. Durkheim did not resolve them, but it is to his credit that he recognized them so clearly. Consistent with his style and temperament, his answers to these questions are stated with great precision and apparent finality, despite the contradictions which remain – and which, if the evidence of his substantive work is examined, he probably recognized. That there are social facts distinguishable from other orders of facts is perhaps the least problematic – as we suggested, Durkheim is, to a degree, only pointing out what most sociologists would accept. Roles, institutions, forms of social organization, and common beliefs exist and have a shape beyond their individual manifestations – they are, as Durkheim put it, external to the individual and exercise a certain constraint on him or her. Nor is it remarkable to argue that social facts can be observed – laws are recorded, social statistics are gathered, patterns and relationships can be detected – as, say, between Protestant affiliation and the rate of suicide in a community. But the problem of the true quality of the social fact – the relationship between its interior and exterior qualities – and the problem of the relationship of material social organization to its symbolic representations – these problems are never finally resolved. These unresolved difficulties weaken the bases of his whole methodological position in its formal expression. He sometimes seems to see forms of 'material' social organization as a prior order of social fact, within, around and upon which ideal reflections are built. He sometimes seems to argue that every way of acting is necessarily accompanied by a symbolic, regulatory or normative component and that the ideal representation can be taken as an index of the social fact. And he also can be found arguing that social facts are essentially ideal, that is that the moral or collective representations are the basic observables of the sociologist.[33]

On more practical matters of methodology Durkheim has little to say in *The Rules*, but of course his substantive work provides plenty of evidence. In general his study of suicide is regarded as displaying undue trust in public statistics, and his studies of religion – especially of totemic religions among Australians – as relying on unreliable anthropological sources.* He certainly did not engage in field work in the more modern accepted sense, nor did he use the survey or interview methods of later sociologists. How much this was attributable to conviction is difficult to say. We can be sure, however, that his empirical studies – *Suicide* in particular – pressed further than had ever been pressed before the idea that social phenomena were susceptible to systematic scientific study and explanation. Keeping in mind our earlier remark – that Durkheim's writings were produced in the face of a potentially hostile and unreceptive audience – he achieved, through these applications of his method, more than could be expected of one man.

Suicide

His next publication became his most famous application of his method, taking a phenomenon which appeared to be so eminently 'psychological' in all its bearings, and treating it sociologically. In *Suicide* he argued that sociologists could study variations in the *social rate* of suicide by studying those characteristics of societies which were likely to cause suicide – i.e. the study of suicidogenic social formations. The two most important causes which he elaborated were 'egoism' and 'anomie', or, more precisely, persistent social conditions which he described as 'egoistic' and 'anomic'.

* See chapters 4 and 7.

Thus *Suicide* afforded the opportunity for the most extensive elaboration of the important concept 'egoism' (social isolation, detachment of the individual from collective life) and for further application of the term 'anomie' (the loss of force of moral ideals, the breakdown of moral control). His audacity in choosing the rate of suicide as an object of study has provoked many later students to accuse him of overstepping the mark, by arguing that this study provides ample evidence of the way in which his insistence on the social led to a neglect of individual meanings and sensibilities. Some of these commentators may not have read *Suicide*. Whilst his chief insistence was on the ability of the sociologist to isolate the varying rate of suicide as a social fact, and to attribute variation in the rate to characteristics of the social and moral quality of life, in particular types of social and collective settings, it is also clear that he had pondered much about the so-called individual psychology of suicide. His description of egoistic suicide, for example, shows how he contemplated the effect on the individual of the social conditions which he believed to be crucial to the aetiology of this type of suicide. Those who claim that Durkheim neglected the meaning of acts for actors, and spoke of the causes of suicide without mentioning meaninglessness, despair, sadness, indifference or melancholy, may consider the following passage, in which he elaborates the notion of egoistic suicide as provoked in a condition of society in which men become detached from association with any group life:

Social man necessarily presupposes a society which he expresses and serves. If this dissolves, if we no longer feel it in existence and action about us and above us, whatever is social in us is deprived of all objective foundation. All that remains is an artificial combination of illusory images, a phantasmagoria vanishing at the least reflection; that is, nothing which can be a goal for action. Yet this social man is the essence of civilized man; he is the masterpiece of existence. Thus we are bereft of reasons for existence; for the only life to which we could cling no longer corresponds to anything actual; the only existence still based on reality no longer meets our needs. Because we have been initiated into a higher existence, the one which satisfies an animal or child can satisfy us no more and the other fades and leaves us helpless. So there is nothing more for our efforts to lay hold of, and we feel them lose themselves in emptiness . . . If life is not worth the trouble of being lived, everything becomes a pretext to be rid of it.[34]

In truth, the book *Suicide* is filled with references to melancholy, despair, indifference, the sadness of bereavement, of personal catastrophe, mental torture and disgust with life. His study of suicide is not unassailable, but it readily resists the most common charges laid against it – charges which have provided a pretext for the rejection of his work.*

* The most recent work on Durkheim and suicide, Steve Taylor, *Durkheim and the Suicide*, Macmillan, London, 1982, gives some support to this view of the psychological aspects of Durkheim's work.

But there is another aspect of the study of suicide which is of greater importance for the general argument of this book. That is the unmistakable repetition in *Suicide* of all the central themes of *The Division of Labour*. The emphasis on *Suicide* by later commentators has frequently been a means whereby they have sought to substantiate the argument that he saw modern society as the scene of social dissolution and moral collapse and that this vision, unqualified in any way, was the dominating inspiration of his sociology. But his diagnosis was not a *general* assertion of some human need or attribute like 'a need for belonging', and anomie was not a *general* notion of man's need for moral restraint – each of these 'needs' unsatisfied in a fragile social order. Rather he argued that egoism and anomie were *particular* historical products of a new phase of social development, and that anomie was seen to be characteristic especially of *economic* life:

If anomie never appeared except in intermittent spurts and acute crisis, it might cause the social suicide rate to vary from time to time, but it would not be a constant regular factor. In one sphere of social life, however – the sphere of trade and industry – it is actually in a chronic state. For a whole century, economic progress has mainly consisted in freeing industrial relations from all regulation . . . religion has lost most of its power. And government, instead of regulating economic life, has become its tool and servant.[35]

At several critical points throughout *Suicide*, especially in the discussion of anomie, and for most of the last thirty pages of the book, he reiterates and elaborates all the major themes of *The Division of Labour*, devoting much space to the discussion of occupational groups. The detachment of the individual from contexts of group life (egoism) and the absence of moral, legal and institutional regulations of mens' desires (anomie) were the central themes of *Suicide*; they were not social conditions ahistorically conceived, but were expounded as specific features of the developing industrial society of modern France, in a manner wholly consistent with the social, political and economic arguments of *The Division of Labour* which we outlined in the earlier part of this chapter.

Religion

The *Elementary Forms of Religious Life*, along with *Suicide* and *The Division of Labour*, has played a leading part in establishing Durkheim's reputation and has become the starting point for a whole genre of social anthropological and sociological studies of religion and the social production of beliefs, thought and knowledge (since *Elementary Forms* also contains the outlines of Durkheim's sociology of knowledge). In it, the core of his method and theory is extended and applied, signified by the insistence on treating religion as a social fact not reducible to (for example) psychic needs of the individual, and by the insistence of explaining the collective facts which underpin religious ideas:

The general conclusion of this book is that religion is something eminently social. Religious representations are collective representations which express collective realities; and rites are a manner of acting which take rise in the midst of the assembled groups and which are destined to excite, maintain or recreate certain mental states in these groups.[36]

Religious phenomena, defined by Durkheim as 'consisting of obligatory beliefs united with definite practices which relate to objects given in the beliefs', are rooted in 'the nature of the societies to which they relate', and thus changes in the character of religion are traceable to the process of social evolution.* The underlying sentiment of religion, as experienced by the individual, was a kind of awe, respect or sense of dependence, and the only thing capable of inspiring this sentiment is society. 'The state of perpetual dependence in which we are towards society inspires us with a sentiment of religious respect for it'.[37] Since the key elements of religious life were 'collective representations' (ideals and beliefs) founded in the conditions of collective existence, his analysis naturally extended to a sociology of knowledge – the elaboration of the hypothesis that categories of thought, and (in an evolutionary perspective) the growth of science, were founded in the conditions of social life. The sociologists' attention was thus drawn towards an examination of these conditions themselves and away from a purely idealistic level of analysis – i.e. examination of the contents of beliefs *per se*. His close study of religion was a great test of his methodological convictions. In one respect we can see that the foundations of his method were unmoved – in his insistence that the nature of religious phenomena is rooted in the nature of social organization. This 'social structure – ideal superstructure' view had been most evident in *The Division of Labour*, where he had argued that population changes caused social organizational changes, which in turn caused moral changes. Later, in *The Rules of Sociological Method*, he made the following remarks:

Man cannot live in an environment without forming some ideas about it according to which he regulates his behaviour. But, because these ideas are nearer to us and more within our mental reach *than the realities to which they correspond* [my emphasis], we tend naturally to substitute them for the latter and to make them the very subject of our speculations. Instead of observing, describing, and comparing things, we are content to focus our consciousness upon, to analyse, and to combine our ideas. Instead of a science concerned with realities, we produce no more than an ideological analysis.[38]

---

* For further discussion of the definition of religion see the opening passages of chapter 7 (Ian Hamnett).

In the same year Durkheim wrote a review of a Marxist publication and in this review he commented on the degree of common ground to be found in his own and Marxist methodology:

We regard as extremely fruitful this idea that social life must be explained, not by the conception of it held by those who participate in it, but by profound causes which escape consciousness; and we also think that these causes must be sought chiefly in the way in which the associated individuals are grouped.[39]

But the study of religion had also convinced him of the great importance of religious phenomena, describing religion as the most primitive of all social phenomena 'the source of all other manifestations of collective activity'.[40] Collective representations formed the very stuff of social life, and in *The Elementary Forms of the Religious Life* he came to speak of them as 'partially autonomous realities which live their own life'.[41]

As well as becoming the starting point for much subsequent sociology of religion and sociology of knowledge, *The Elementary Forms* has also attracted criticisms, some points of which are particularly relevant here. Durkheim based his conclusions about 'primitive religions' on studies of societies (especially Australian aboriginal societies) which he had never visited, and relied, perhaps naively, on seemingly unreliable sources, so much so that one later commentator has judged that 'the idea which Durkheim has derived of "simple societies" is entirely erroneous'.[42] Critics were particularly harsh on his assumption that he had found examples of typical 'simple societies' whose material and social modes of existence differed dramatically from complex modern societies.* The idea that repressive law – which is characterized by the predominance of repressive sanctions (punishments for transgression of a 'simple' moral order) – is typical of these societies, and that restitutive law – aimed at restoring a condition prior to a breach of moral or formal law (e.g. contractual adjustment) – develops predominantly in the evolution of modern societies has been particularly strongly challenged.† His portrayal of 'primitive men' gripped by blind adherence to custom is now seen as understating the importance of moral and social forms structured around exchanges and reciprocity in so-called primitive societies. Indeed the work of Malinowski and others has done much to undermine thoroughly the ideas of 'primitive and modern' implicit in Durkheim's work, as our section on race will demonstrate.[43] But this is less critical for Durkheim's general analysis of modern societies than at first would appear to be the case, especially because the importance of an evolutionary perspective in his work was

---

* For further comment on Durkheim's attitude to evidence and 'the facts' of religious life see chapter 7.

† This controversy is fully discussed in chapter 6.

progressively weakened. The elucidation of the character of modern societies *by way of contrast* with the primitive is questionable to the extent that the view of the primitive is erroneous, but it is not to be dismissed for that reason alone. *The Division of Labour* contains the most explicit evolutionary model in that he *did* see modern solidarity developing from pre-modern forms, and believed that the emergence of social institutions, appropriate to the fostering of solidarity in complex societies, was largely an evolutionary process. But he gradually discarded this emphasis, and came to stress the ways in which men, particularly through the active agency of the state, should seek out the social means of reconstructing society.

Furthermore, the crucial argument, that *The Elementary Forms* illustrates Durkheim's belief that some form of (religious) unifying moral order is fundamental to *any* society, is a misconception, at least in the way in which it has been presented. Anthony Giddens has discussed this question and cited the critical passage: 'the importance we attribute to the sociology of religion does not in the least imply that religion must play the same role in present day societies that it has played at other times'.[44]

For more detailed discussion of Durkheim's sociology of religion and his influence on this field, the reader should turn to Ian Hamnett's contribution, chapter 7 of this book.* My own view – expressed above – is that Durkheim's enthusiasm for 'religion' has been misinterpreted; this, coupled with a tendency to see *Suicide* as a generalized diagnosis of social dissolution, has contributed to an unduly 'conservative' estimation of the import of his work.†

Durkheim's conservatism

The association of Durkheim with a loose notion of 'conservatism' has appeared in so many guises that it is next to impossible to extract a single theme and likewise difficult to construct a single counter-argument. The emphasis has been, variously, on what have been seen to be the fundamental impulses of his life work, his personal and political temperament, the imagery of his sociological language, the construed consequences of his understanding of 'the social malaise', looking back to supposed

---

* In particular Hamnett argues that the key elements of Durkheim's analysis of religion *do* pertain to primitive society and are scarcely, if at all, applicable to modern states.

† We have discussed religion at some length here despite the fact that it is treated in great depth in chapter 7. This is because an understanding of his posture towards religion is central to one of the main themes of this opening chapter – the alleged 'conservatism' of his sociology. It is also important in opening up discussion of Durkheim's methodology – and we have confined explicit discussion of method to this introduction. His sociology of education, which also illustrates his practical concerns and his view of morals, has been mentioned (see above on his career) but is more fully discussed in chapter 5.

conservative antecedents and forward to supposed reactionary developments. In all, this is a disparate collection of commentary and interpretation
which has linked his name with the nineteenth-century 'reaction', with
romantic solidarism and nationalism, with corporatism and fascism, and
methodologically with anti-individualism, reification of the social, and
association with the alleged ideological bias of sociological functionalism.
This broad band of commentary varies in emphasis, but it also varies in
quality – from interpretation of substantial subtlety and scholarship, to ill-
informed suggestion and sweeping attributions. As a consequence the task
of countering these arguments is sometimes a relatively simple matter of
refuting something demonstrably incorrect, but in other instances, a much
more intricate task of suggesting a certain undue emphasis, or of arguing
for some redressing of balance in interpretation. Finally, of course, it should
be recognized that no interpretation can be conclusive since in important
respects the motives and meanings of a past author must always remain
partially hidden and we will be forced to conclude, inconclusively, that
support can be found for conflicting interpretations of his work. The present
effort is then directed towards achieving a balance which is at present
lacking.

Disinterested 'scholarly' motives aside, it is not easy to answer the
question of why such an argument should be undertaken, but if, for the
moment, we allow a distinction between scientific sociological interests and
meta-sociological political interests, two reasons can be adduced.
Durkheim's sociology has unquestionably become very influential, and, for
those who regard an objective science of society as a realizable aspiration, a
proper appreciation of his work is necessarily important. For those who
regard sociology as inseparable from political theory and action, it is
likewise important to locate Durkheim's work correctly in the meta-
sociological ideology of social science. There is a tradition, in the
interpretation of Durkheim, which associates him with a kind of reactionary, medievalist glorification of authority, religion and hierarchy – a
thoroughgoing anti-modernism – which, as a matter of both sociology and
politics, is effectively dead.

To consign Durkheim to this position as an anachronism, is to avoid
considering his actual modern relevance as a sociologist who accepts
modern society, diagnoses both its healthy and sickly features, and envisages a future of reconstruction and consolidation. And he did not only
distinguish his position from that of the ultra-conservatives. It is important
to remember – when contrasting Durkheim's sociology with a 'revolutionary' sociology which distrusts reform – that Durkheim also gave
his reasons for warning against revolutionary aspirations. He expressed this
view with some force:

Man's intelligence should precisely have, as its overriding aim, the taming and muzzling of these blind forces, instead of letting them wreak destruction. I am quite aware when people speak of destroying existing societies, they intend to reconstruct them. But these are the fantasies of children. One cannot in this way rebuild collective life: once our social organization is destroyed, centuries of history will be required to build another. In the intervening period, there will be a new Middle Ages, a transitional period, in which the old departed civilization will not be replaced by any other, or at least will only be replaced by a civilization that is incipient, uncertain and seeking to find itself. It will not be the sun of a new society that will rise, all resplendent over the ruins of the old; instead men will enter a new period of darkness. Instead of our hastening the advent of that period, it is necessary to employ all our intelligence so as to forestall it, or, if that is impossible, to shorten it and render it less sombre. And to do that we must avoid acts of destruction that suspend the course of social life and civilization.[45]

This argument is important simply because so much contemporary sociological argument has circled around the question of 'reform and revolution'. Of course, if one were to cast the net wide enough, one could find sociology of many varieties: the profoundly conservative, the administrative sociology of authoritarian states, or the pursuit of social measurement and social accountancy. But, outside of these forms, there is a large corpus of sociological work which, at the meta-sociological level – looking beyond the analysis to the implicit vision of social and political change – revolves around a debate about the possibility of social structural reform and the nature of institutional change.

Broadly speaking, the 'revolutionary' sociologist perceives modern (bourgeois) society as contradictory, as torn by divisions and oppositions which are inherent in its nature. The manifest social evils are only to be overcome in a more or less total, and more or less dramatic, transformation of society's current foundations. The reformist or 'liberal' sociologist may well acknowledge many of the same evils but holds on to the view that more gradual, institutional change can eradicate or minimize them. Precisely *how* radical this institutional change need be remains an open question. Indeed much contemporary sociology in the 'liberal' context is faced with the internal contradictions of reform itself. The sociologist who, by training, is conscious of the web-like inter-relatedness of social phenomena may well conclude that planned changes, designed to remove the pathologies of a given institutional sphere, fail because it is impossible to control all the forces which affect that sphere. (Creating equality or equality of opportunity in educational institutions would be a good example.) The sociologist's training also attunes him to the unintended consequences of human actions, a sensitivity which may lead him or her to despair of revolutionary and reforming change alike. These are some of the foundations of liberal sociological pessimism.

But if, at this point, the sociologist shrinks from the conclusion that nothing but a revolutionary transcendence of the current social order promises a real change in individual and collective destinies, he either condemns himself to a permanent liberal pessimism or stretches to advocating ever more 'radical' or far-reaching reforms of the current order – in spite of his instinct that sociological inertia or concentrated power prevent this. There are also, of course, revolutionary social scientists whose own debate with gradualist reform has come to an end, even when they too are pessimistic and frustrated by the seemingly endless resilience of bourgeois society. But there are yet others who have never quite closed the door on non-revolutionary change, and for whom the resolution of a *particular* question of sociology and social action continues to present both difficulties and potentialities. If Durkheim's work is rescued from its supposed reactionary setting, then it can become the basis of consideration of this question of institutional change.

Nisbet's thesis: the conservative foundations of sociology

Durkheim's conservatism has been construed, not from his active political engagements, but from an interpretation of the force of his sociological argument. The best-known exponent is Robert Nisbet, who has claimed that a fundamentally conservative impulse underlies the very origins of the sociological imagination.[46] The crux of his argument is that Durkheim progressively and dramatically modified his view of modern society, as expressed in the *early part* of his first major work – *The Division of Labour*. Durkheim, we recall, had written of organic solidarity emerging in advanced societies to replace the mechanical solidarity of simple societies. Nisbet summarizes this as 'the general emergence of individuality from the restraints of the past' so that 'it becomes possible for the first time in history for social order to rest, not on mechanical uniformity and collective repression, but on the organic articulation of free individuals pursuing different functions but united by their complementary roles' – an accurate enough résumé of one part of Durkheim's unfolding argument. Rather than allowing for Durkheim's elaboration of this argument – in both the early and later sections of the book – Nisbet focusses on the emphasis of the later sections and claims to find in them a 'reversal of argument'.

He concludes:

The kinds of society, constraint, and solidarity dealt with in all his later works have nothing whatsoever to do with the attributes he had laid down for an organic and (presumably) irreversibly modern society in the *Division of Labour*. On the contrary, society – in all its guises and functions and historical roles – becomes for Durkheim, a compound of social and psychological elements that he had at first relegated to folk or primitive society. Not only is normal society founded, he would ever after declare, on such traits as collective conscience, moral authority, community, and the sacred, but the only appropriate response to modern conditions is the strengthening of such traits.[47]

This is the very crystallization of the argument which presents Durkheim, not as a critic of the excesses of modern society, but as a principled anti-modernist for whom all manifestations of progressive social change are repugnant; and these are held up for scrutiny, not against an ideal of a reconstructed advanced society, but against an image of a solidary folk society. Quite apart from the political implications of such an interpretation, we can examine the strength of the 'reversal' claim itself.

Nisbet cites the following as the 'crucial passage' in *The Division of Labour:*

The division of labour can only be produced in the midst of pre-existing society. There is a social life outside the whole division of labour, but which the latter pre-supposes. That is indeed, what we have directly established in showing that there are societies whose cohesion is due to a community of beliefs and sentiments, and it is from these societies that those whose unity is assured by the division of labour have emerged.[48]

Nisbet sees Durkheim here to be acknowledging 'the continuing necessity in modern organic society of sinews of stability that are mechanical in character' (i.e. that the basis of solidarity in modern societies must also be founded upon a deep inculcation of a shared moral culture). He finds the watershed of Durkheim's thinking in his attack on Spencerian sociology – on the view that society could be understood as an aggregate of utilitarian exchanges. Contracts may bring men into contact, Durkheim argued, but they do not bind men and society in and of themselves. In truth all contracts contain non-contractual elements, specifically they contain moral elements. Thus if I agree (contract) to do x for you in return for you agreeing to give me y, there is, superadded to this material exchange – the x for the y – a moral concept, such as the idea of what constitutes a just agreement, or the trust and honour which exists between parties.

What can be made of this thesis? In the part of the book preceding Nisbet's mid-point (p. 277) Durkheim has concentrated on distinguishing solidarity based on moral and material resemblances (the collective conscience of mechanical solidarity) from solidarity based on interdependences in the division of labour. As collective life becomes more complex, the possibility of a uniform collective conscience being sustained and governing society progressively recedes. Where moral rules do emerge they tend to govern select spheres of social activity rather than the whole. Durkheim certainly never abandoned these two arguments. It is wrong for Nisbet to find in Durkheim's historical analysis a moral past and an amoral present or future. The moral quality of social life is constant; its nature changes.

Durkheim also contended that, given this type of social change, the repressive law of simple societies gives way to the restitutive laws of complex societies. But restitutive law *is* law; it represents society's, interest in individual transactions:

> Although these rules are more or less outside the collective conscience, they are not only solely interested in individuals. If this were so, restitutive law would have nothing in common with social solidarity, for the relations that it regulates would bind individuals to one another without binding them to society.[49]

Though specialized in their function by contrast with uniform legal rules, these laws also create agencies of control – consular tribunals, councils of arbitration, administrative tribunals of every sort (see *The Division of Labour*) – these forming a model of the modern mechanisms of social regulation which appear and reappear throughout his works. He always rejected the notion that the mere links created by contracts are sufficient for social solidarity (see *The Division of Labour*, pp. 114, 211) by arguing that contracts presuppose a social and moral force, and that the power of contracts to bind men derives from society (p. 114). The famous phrase 'tout dans le contrat n'est pas contractuel' – all in the contract is not contractual, i.e. there is a moral element in every contract – actually reinforces this point (at p. 211). Restitutive law is characteristic of societies in which contractual arrangements are common – because restitutive law is that kind of law which is designed to maintain or restore proper balance between contracting persons, as distinct from repressive law which is concerned with enforcing a uniform moral code. And we see above that restitutive law is seen as doing much more than binding individuals to other individuals. In short the Nisbet thesis rests upon a misplaced emphasis in the interpretation of Durkheim's arguments in the early part of the book, as well as on his over-enthusiasm for the notion of a radical 'shift' in the book as a whole. The misplaced emphasis of Nisbet lies in his tendency to see Durkheim's early argument as being one that opposes a society held together by morality, to a society held together by interdependence based on a multitude of contacts. He is actually opposing a society which is simple enough in its structure to be governed by a uniform moral code, to a society which is so complex in its structure that the collective moral code is weakened, or recedes both in strength and importance. In these advanced societies a kind of collective conscience remains, but one which is quite different in character; it is more abstract and general and less of a guide to the direct moral sanctioning of each action by each individual. Moral order in advanced societies rests upon the action of this different kind of collective conscience, and upon the new form of moral regulation which develops in and around the interlocking social relations of a society with an advanced division of labour.

Part of the difficulty in getting the emphasis right in this matter lies in the way in which sociologists use what we would now call the ideal typical method and then apply it to a process of long historical change. In creating an ideal type a sociologist selects out certain prominent features of what he sees to be a distinctive form of social organization; he may then select out certain features of a second distinctive form of social organization and contrast the first ideal type with the second. The sociologists always tries to make it clear that he is creating abstractions; he is drawing out what he sees to be critical, and critically different, features of two forms of social organization. He will also point out that the ideal type is not the historical reality but a constructed type against which the historical reality is examined. If he is arguing that type 1 changes towards type 2 he will acknowledge that all societies contain elements of both types, that in the transition period features of both are combined, and that the movement is from a preponderance of one to a preponderance of the other. If we understand that this is what Durkheim is doing in contrasting mechanical and organic solidarity we will not mistake his meaning:

In the first, what we call society is a more or less organized totality of beliefs and sentiments common to all members of the group. This is the collective type. On the other hand, the society in which we are solidary in the second instance is a system of different special functions which definite relations unite. These two societies really make up only one. They are two aspects of one and the same reality, but nonetheless they must be distinguished.[50]

This clarification appears quite early in the text as does his assertion that the collective conscience does not disappear in advanced societies. That he is clear on this point confirms what we have said – that Durkheim was not opposing a moral order to an amoral system, – but analysing the change in the *nature* of the moral order.

This is not to say that the common conscience is threatened with total disappearance. Only, it more and more comes to consist of very general and very indeterminate ways of thinking and feeling, which leave an open place for a growing multitude of individual differences. There is even a place where it is strengthened and made precise; that is the way it regards the individual . . . the individual becomes the object of a sort of religion.*

Durkheim continues to make it clear that he is not arguing that morality disappears. All societies are moral orders in some fashion, and what he calls a 'sociological monstrosity' is a society in which individuals tend to become socially and morally dissociated from each other and from any moral centre. 'It is wrong', he writes, 'to oppose a society which comes from a

* This passage occurs at p. 172, uncomfortably early for Nisbet's view. It foreshadows his later analysis of the cult of the individual which Nisbet tends to neglect.

community of beliefs to one which has a co-operative basis, according to the first a moral character, and seeing in the latter only an economic grouping.'[51]

If, then, Durkheim has never envisaged a society of transacting individuals lacking in any collective morality, it is wrong to suggest that his continued elaboration of the nature of morality in advanced societies constitutes a new recognition of the need for moral order in all societies. Durkheim sometimes stresses that economic activities in the division of labour take place *within* a moral and social context; sometimes that these activities and contexts *give rise to* moral and social bonds. What he emphatically rejects is the model of society in which dissociated individuals simply come together to pursue their individual interests. 'Interests', he argues, 'never unite men but for a few moments, contracts are mere truces in a continuing antagonism. Nothing is less constant than interest. Today it unites me to you; tomorrow, it will make me your enemy'.[52] This presents a stark contrast to the view of shared interests as the basis of 'solidarity' or the model of contemporary society as composed of interest based associations.

The incomplete realization of organic solidarity

Although we shall return from time to time to the conservative interpretation of Durkheim, we have dealt sufficiently with the 'reversal of argument' thesis. 'The truth of the matter', Giddens has said, 'is almost completely the reverse of the view suggested by Nisbet.'[53] But to understand sympathetically his continued interest in modern morality, we have to appreciate that his interest was always spurred on by the realization that organic solidarity was a model of the potential stability of modern societies and not something which had been achieved. The natural corollary of his argument that economic activities in the division of labour assumed ever increasing importance in society – displacing the family and religious spheres – was that the *lack* of moral regulation of the economy was supremely damaging to social solidarity. As occupational groups replace tribe, clan, village, territorial groupings and the family, they must become the centre of social and moral life. In looking for moral regulation to emerge from economic actions he argues in two ways. On the one hand he argues that regular contact *per se* is sufficient, that these regular contacts must assume or be granted a moral character; on the other hand he argues that these contacts fail to give rise to morality *because* they are insufficiently regular.*

---

* This is an important difference, the implications of which he never fully confronted. The first view suggests either that 1) regular contact will gradually promote moral regulation (the more people engage in exchanges, the more they will construct forms of moral restraint to

In his diagnosis of the moral failure of modern economic life, he argued that economic activities were anarchic, subject to constant interruption and breakdown. They had developed rapidly in scope without a parallel growth of regulatory institutions. The precise arguments as to how *political and economic* problems (as facets of the general problem of solidarity) were to be understood and 'cured' are illustrated in further sections of this book.† Suffice to say that the theme of state intervention in the promotion of agencies of regulation of the economy, and the development of the moral and legal character of occupational groups, are constantly repeated. If there was a significant change in Durkheim's view it lay, not in the basic outline of his understanding of organic solidarity, but in his gradual abandonment of what Lukes has called his 'evolutionary optimism', in favour of a view which suggested the urgent need for the state to take an active part in the task of social reconstruction. The virtual tendencies of the division of labour were apparent; but it may take some strenuous effort to bring them to fruition.

In *Suicide* he ponders what could be the source of solidarity necessary to prevent the individual from feeling so strongly his lack of integration. The notion of a return to a folk society's collective morality is firmly rejected. Political society, the individual's connection with public life as a whole, is too weak to have this force. Religion too has lost its power over individuals: 'We are only preserved from egoistic suicide in so far as we are socialized: but religions can socialize us only in so far as they refuse us the right of free examination. They no longer have and probably will never again have enough authority to wring such a sacrifice from us.' [54]

The family too is turned aside as unsuited for this role and he returns once more to occupational groups composed of 'individuals devoted to the same tasks, with solidary or even combined interests. No soil is better suited to bear social ideas and sentiments. Identity of origin, culture and occupation makes occupational activity the richest sort of material for a common life.' [55]

Egoism and individualism

These two terms appear often enough in Durkheim's work for it to be wise for the student to be as clear about them as is possible. Confusion is

govern these exchanges – a natural evolutionary view) or that 2) regular contacts of an economic kind are so clearly important that people must consciously create forms of control (the interventionist, legalistic, state guidance view). The second view suggests that much of the problem resides in the chaotic nature of the economy itself and by this he meant crises in production, failures in business, overproduction and scarcity, etc. This implied the need for a planned economy, not just the moral regulation of existing economic activity.
† See chapters 2 and 3.

particularly likely because he did not use them in recognizably conventional senses. Failure to distinguish properly between them – as, we may note, Nisbet did – can lead to misunderstanding. An initial rough guide can be acquired by seeing Durkheim's category 'egoism' as denoting a pathological development – the sickly dissociation of the individual from society, the social isolation of individuals, moral and social detachment – and the category 'individualism' as denoting a healthy development – the changes in social structures which permit increased individual differences, but more particularly the accompanying moral code which preaches liberty and justice and the dignity of the individual, 'the glorification not of the self but of the individual in general'.[56] It should readily be seen that if Durkheim is viewed as not only condemning the former – egoism – but also the latter – individualism – his sociology appears to be profoundly anti-progressive and illiberal.

The question of the relationship of the individual to society had been dominant in his mind from the outset:

As to the question which gives rise to this work, it is that of the relations between the individual personality and social solidarity. What explains the fact that, while becoming more autonomous, the individual becomes more closely dependent on society? How can he simultaneously be more personally developed and more socially dependent?.[57]

His answer to this question is complex. He argued that the same social processes which fostered increased individuality also were capable of creating new forms of collective life and moral regulation, especially in the spheres of occupational groups and public and semi-public agencies of social control. This is the argument elaborated in *The Division of Labour*, in the Preface to the second edition, in the later pages of *Suicide* and in *Professional Ethics and Civic Morals*; these arguments we have just introduced. They constitute an analysis of new forms of *social organization* which are seen to replace those pre-modern forms destined to fade in importance. But in the essay 'Individualism and the intellectuals'[58] he pays particular attention to an elaboration of the argument that the division of labour also produces new *ideological* forms which have a crucial role in reconciling the inevitable, and socially produced, progress of individuality with the need for solidarity. In this paper he draws out his analysis of the 'cult of the individual' – that powerful social creed which simultaneously dignifies individual liberties and forms a distinctively new type of collective conscience – an analysis which we have seen foreshadowed in *The Division of Labour* itself.

By contrast the concept of egoism is developed, in *Suicide* especially, to capture *pathological* forms of detachment of the individual from any source of collective life. To the extent that new modes of social organization, capable of replacing the integrative functions of pre-modern collectivities, have insufficiently emerged, to this extent men and women are exposed to social isolation and its debilitating effects. Thus egoism is a conceptualization of a pathological tendency in societies undergoing transition from an ancient to a modern order; individualism is a virtual tendency capable of, itself alone, or in association with related developments, giving rise to elements of solidarity.

Nisbet's writings provide a good example of an interpretation of Durkheim based on a failure to distinguish the pathologies of social isolation (egoism) from the virtues of the creed of the dignity of the individual (individualism). Since Durkheim saw the march of individualism to be inevitable, such an interpretation naturally causes Durkheim to appear profoundly pessimistic about modern social orders:

> The specter of modern man's isolation from traditional society hovers over all of Durkheim's work . . .

> Not self-discovery but self-fear, not confident optimism but excessive melancholy and anxiety: these for Durkheim are the consequences of the modern history of individualism . . .

> The essence of modernism is the devitalization of that sense of society which alone can maintain individuality . . .

> Comte's obsession with individualism as the 'disease of the Western world' is no less vivid in Durkheim . . .[59]

Durkheim's view of individualism is wrongly equated with Comte's view, and Nisbet completes the elision of the two phenomena by illustrating Durkheim's view of '*individualism*' with quotes from his exposition of egoism: 'Human personality necessarily presupposes a stable social order. If this dissolves . . . whatever is social in us is deprived of all objective foundation.'[60] (Nisbet is here quoting from Durkheim on egoistic suicide.)

The outcome is that individualism is seen as the disease of modern societies, *par excellence*: 'It is individualism itself that is the cause of suicidal currents in society and of all the other manifestations of disorganization and alienation. For individualism by its very nature is separation from the norms and communities that are the sinews of man's spiritual nature.'[61]

Nowhere does Durkheim cite individualism as a cause of suicide: the last sentence is almost the opposite of Durkheim's argument and intentions.

The generalization of the 'conservative' argument

We have challenged Nisbet's view of Durkheim's sociology at several critical points: 1) the interpretation of the early sections of *The Division of Labour in Society*, 2) of Durkheim's estimation of the role of the collective conscience in advanced societies and 3) of Durkheim's separate analysis of egoism and individualism.

We argued that the early sections of *The Division of Labour* do not warrant the conclusion that Durkheim envisaged a modern society integrated, spontaneously and solely, by the links formed in individual transactions and exchanges. He consistently recognized the need for these links to be surrounded by new forms of moral and legal restraint. To point to later examples of Durkheim's insistence on the need for moral regulation in the modern division of labour does not, therefore, indicate a 'shift'; it indicates a consistent elaboration of the same argument. The emphasis on *some* form of collective conscience persisting in advanced societies is likewise not a reversal; he never said that collective moral ideas would disappear, rather that they would change their nature.

In his 1914 lectures on 'Pragmatism and sociology'[62] he can be found still grappling with the question of the character of collective representations in modern societies. If, in the simple societies of the past, social myths had functioned to provide societies with an ideal image of themselves, it might be thought that objective scientific knowledge would steadily replace these myths. But Durkheim was not so enthused by *social* science, to believe that this process was nearly complete, or would ever be completed, nor did he accept that men in society could proceed on scientific knowledge as far as it stretched, and consign the remaining realms to intellectual doubt. He did, therefore, recognize that in modern societies collective ideas and moral images would persist and that these would bear greater resemblance to ancient myths than to modern science. They would constitute grand moral ideas endowed with great force and authority, relatively closed to discussion – such as 'democracy', 'progress' and 'the class struggle'.

There is, there always will be, in social life, a place for a form of truth which will be expressed perhaps in a very secular form, but which will still have a mythological and religious basis. For a long time yet there will exist in all societies two tendencies: a tendency towards objective and scientific truth, and a tendency towards truth perceived from within, towards mythological truth.[63]

But once we have recognized that Durkheim never expected the collective conscience to disappear in advanced societies, we can understand his later writings as a continuing attempt to discern the form that collective representations might take in a modern social order. From his earliest explorations of the notion of the cult of the individual, we can see that he returns to the question of the importance of such grand ideas as 'liberty', 'human dignity', 'democracy' and 'progress'. In the 'Pragmatism' discussions we can see that he did not expect the mythological function of these ideas to be lost in the advance of social scientific understanding. At the same time it cannot be expected that these powerful abstract ideas could perform the same function in modern societies as did the close-woven moral concepts of a simple society.

The unduly conservative interpretation of Durkheim's sociology has encouraged the unduly conservative interpretation of his politics, and much of the rest of this book will, directly and indirectly, be concerned with restoring the balance and placing the emphasis where it belongs. We will briefly outline here some of the more common of these interpretations.

One common 'political' extrapolation has been the linking of Durkheim with 'nationalism', the suggestion that his work laid the foundations for apologia of nationalistic excesses of the twentieth century. An examination of the essay 'Individualism and the intellectuals' shows that there is scant justification for this view, as Steven Lukes has pointed out:

> Durkheim's article is of considerable interest. It offers a conclusive refutation of a certain interpretation of him as fundamentally anti-liberal and anti-individualistic, as a right-wing nationalist, a spiritual ally of Charles Maurras and a forerunner of twentieth century nationalism, even fascism – an interpretation that relied on a selective misreading of certain of his writings and, in some cases, a mistaken importation into his centralized guild socialism of the connotations of fascist corporatism. Here, in effect, is a Dreyfusite manifesto and an eloquent defence of liberalism, stated in the categories of Durkheim's sociological theory.[64]

Durkheim argued that, in general, our attachment to the political state defined by national boundaries is weak, and necessarily and properly so. Economic and social life in contemporary societies increasingly spreads across national boundaries, and, whilst we have a proper sense of loyalty to our country, the importance of this is increasingly diminished by the strengthening of supra-national spheres of action. Durkheim believed that 'national loyalties were real and valuable, but they should not be exclusive and they should be extended in an internationalist direction'. He came to speak of a kind of 'European community' superseding in some respects the national sources of identification: 'Doubtless we have toward the country in its present form . . . obligations which we do not have the right to cast off. But beyond this country, there is another in the process of formation, enveloping our national country; that of Europe or humanity.'[65]

The supposed sympathy with Charles Maurras, the propagandist of *Action Française*, is even more unlikely. Maurras was fiercely anti-Republican, by contrast with Durkheim's reputation as one of the leading ideologues of the Third Republic. Maurras's advocacy of the monarchy and, equally, his anti-Semitism make him an unlikely 'ally' of Durkheim. As regards Durkheim and the earlier conservative reaction, his practical political postures towards the Church and his sociological attitude to traditional religion are evidence contrary to the view of him as having close affinity with such as Joseph de Maistre.[66]

Again, his views on the role of occupational groups are much more consonant with the Guild Socialists than they are with corporate fascism. Whilst fascism seeks to subject labour unions and occupational associations to the will of the state, Durkheim saw occupational groups as serving to protect individuals against arbitrary state power. Nor can he be seen as a proponent of a powerful state: although he came to attribute greater importance to the role of the state in the task of social reconstruction, he retained his suspicion of the over-powerful state and consistently opposed those political programmes which, in his view, gave the state powers which it was unfit to exercise.*

A note on methodology and 'conservatism'

We should, finally, take note of a vein of commentary which on the one hand takes Durkheim as the principal inspiration of modern functionalist thinking, and on the other portrays functionalism as a decidedly 'conservative' sociology.[67] At a glance this appears to be a reasonable view; on closer examination it can be seen to be in need of considerable modification. The first point to make is that there have been many varieties of functionalism; in some hands the functionalist methodology is no more than an assumption of 'inter-relatedness', that is a standard sociological understanding that elements of a social system must be viewed in their interdependence with other elements.[68] As Cohen has pointed out this could even be taken to be a view with 'revolutionary' implications since, if 'everything is bound up with everything else' in a social system, one could be forgiven the conclusion that piecemeal institutional change is virtually impossible.[69] The truly 'conservative' implications of functionalist thought are most apparent only when certain assumptions are made: that all parts of a social system contribute positively to the functioning of the whole, or that there is an enduring tendency towards equilibrium on social systems. When societies are viewed as stable and self-regulating systems, there may also be a relative neglect of historical process and endemic conflict. These assumptions or 'models' cannot be found in Durkheim's work. He cannot be charged with a neglect of history,[70] the analysis of conflict – however flawed – was, as we shall see in chapter 2, a major preoccupation; and it is precisely because he viewed order as being problematic in modern societies that he devoted his energies to an understanding of the sources of social integration.

Something of the same may be said about Durkheim's relationship to some of the subsequent conceptualizations of role theory and the process of

* Further discussion of the state appears in chapter 3.

socialization. It was the American writer Dennis Wrong who, in discussing tendencies in role theory in American sociology, coined the phrase 'the over-socialized conception of man'. He had two tendencies in mind: 1) sociologists writing about role behaviour had slid into the assumption that conformity to role expectations is normal, automatic or 'to be assumed', and 2) the emphasis placed by many sociologists on the wish to conform, or the search for acceptance, as the motive force in individual behaviour. With regard to the first of these, a central question is whether we regard the moral code of a society as an external constraint on individual behaviour, or see moral norms as constitutive of the individual.[71] Durkheim certainly saw moral norms as having a certain externality, but also suggested that when the individual absorbs the constraints into his self, these constraints are scarcely felt. But he did not regard this process as being automatic, and, as we shall see in chapter 5, he argued that in modern societies there is increasingly a rational or conscious element in the acceptance of constraints. More strikingly, the very fact that Durkheim devoted so much attention to 'egoism' and 'anomie' (social conditions of disassociation and moral breakdown – see chapters 2 and 6) clearly indicates that he did not view conformity as unproblematic. Indeed he developed a conception of change and innovation which suggested that crime or deviance may be viewed as 'normal' in an advanced society. This issue is discussed again in chapter 6. The second theme is characteristic of post-war American sociology when it was argued that men and women searched for social identities in a society which was open and changing but which at the same time exerted strong pressures to conformity. As a specific sociological argument it has no real counterpart in Durkheim's writings.

Dennis Wrong concludes, correctly, that the excesses of role theory are not of Durkheim's making.[72]

Durkheim the radical critic of contemporary society: the proponent of social reform and reconstruction

In these final pages of our introductory chapter we shall leave aside the mistaken conservative interpretations of his work and concentrate upon specifying an alternative, and more accurate, estimation of his politics and sociology. In so doing we will briefly contrast his position with a Marxist analysis but this is not intended as comparative evaluation because there are limits to what can be gained by stretching across these two frames of reference. As we discuss in chapter 3, on the sociology of politics, Durkheim's definition of sociology's problematic and his categories of understanding exclude consideration of social phenomena as phrased by the categories of the Marxist problematic. Equally, excluded from Marxist language is the consideration of what was central to Durkheim – the relationships between the structure and quality of human association, and the moral and spiritual quality of life in society. Small bridges may be constructed between the two languages – where apparently similar questions are addressed – but the traffic on these bridges will be light.

Although the question of locating Durkheim politically is not to be solved by finding the right terminology, there are a number of labels which can be usefully clarified. These would include 'radical', 'reformist', 'Centrist', 'liberal' and 'social reconstructionist'. Steven Lukes has ventured to describe Durkheim as a 'socialist of sorts' but there are so many sorts that this is clearly not intended as definitive. But all of the above terms – except possibly 'liberal' – fit Durkheim tolerably well – but only when we consider the shade and context of meaning. 'Liberal' fits least well because of its dual associations, with the guarding of civic liberties and with economic liberalism. Durkheim may qualify on the first set of associations because of his forthright defence of individual liberty and human justice but we have seen that his definition of individualism was unique and departed from the classical defences of individual freedom as an absolute value as espoused by, for example, J. S. Mill. For Durkheim, true freedom was to be found within a context of moral restraint; his analysis of 'moral autonomy', discussed in chapter 5, illustrates this best. More pointedly, he quite clearly rejected the doctrine of economic liberalism; we have already seen that he turned every argument available to him against the notion that the greater good flowed from permitting the utmost freedom in economic transactions. The charge of illiberal conservatism is ill-founded – but the term 'liberal' sits uneasily too.

The term 'radical', in political analysis and prescription, has the connotations of attention to fundamentals, of a concern with the very roots of the social order, and of a depth and breadth of scale and scope of the political imagination. Once we grasp that Durkheim was concerned with 'moral and social structure' as he understood them – and not with political economy in the Marxist sense – his analysis can be quite readily recognized as radical. His analysis of individualism – discarding what he saw to be its wrongful representations and promoting its healthiest forms – was an analysis which took him to the fundamentals of modern social structure. His rejection of bourgeois individualism and of the pursuit of wealth – his total questioning of the supposed virtues of 'material progress' – show that his critique of contemporary society was far more radical than a passing distaste for greed or excess. In this he was more radical than the Marxists, not sharing with them any of the enthusiasm for the energies and adventurous achievements of capitalism. In his political prescriptions he may appear to be a man of the Centre – partly because he never ventured to outline a programme; partly because his caution drew him to the Centre; and partly because his sociological convictions led him to reject the solutions of both Right and Left.

Reform too is a term with multiple connotations and its import will depend on the scope of reforming measures intended. Reform measures or proposals may indeed be quite radical, but the word is often intended to convey a sense of limit, or a sense that what is being proposed is 'mere' reform and fails to get to the 'root' of the pathology in question. Durkheim did envisage a re-formation of society because he believed that older and obsolete forms of social regulation had disappeared without their being adequately replaced. If we 'stretch out' his tentative sketches of social reconstruction, we see that they imply a programme of radical reconstruction – in the laws of property and inheritance, in the creation of a wide range of judicial and quasi-judicial bodies of political and economic governance, and in such central institutions as the family and educational system. This is not a matter of endorsing his reforming proposals, rather it is a matter of distinguishing his ideas from reform which could more justly be described as piecemeal or as narrow social engineering.

This intermediate position of Durkheim is best illustrated in his view of the economy and the division of labour. He did not accept, despite his sense of a deep malaise, that class struggle preceding a revolutionary transformation of property relations was a necessary or desirable course. Intellectual conviction and temperament alike led him to oppose the idea that social change of a positive kind could emerge from the prosecution of the war between classes. Class conflict was, for him, a symptom of a deeper malaise (the profound absence of regulation of economic activities and appetites) and it seemed impossible that intensifying the symptom could promote a cure. And yet if the concept of anomie is recognized as his diagnosis of the malaise of industrial societies, it can be seen that he was speaking of a deep rooted malaise which demanded a radical cure. For he saw that moral and social disorganization was in evidence above all in the sphere of trade and industry, in commerce – in short in economic activities. Therefore the monumental task of social reform and social reconstruction involved, more than anything else, bringing economic activities under legal, moral and institutional control. The subsequent steps in Durkheim's analysis and proposals for reform are discussed in detail in chapter 2. The key point is that he believed that it was possible – and necessary – to achieve, through progressive social reform, a grand amelioration of all the prominent symptoms of economic anarchy – the term he occasionally reserves for an economy based on the unrestrained pursuit of individual interests.

In passages that we shall discuss in detail later, we shall see that his analysis went further to include an attack on material inequality. His somewhat remote, but nonetheless urgent, appreciation of the discontents of 'les classes ouvriers' at least permitted him to see that the gross inequalities of industrial societies themselves prevented the fostering of social solidarity; therefore the process of social reform presupposed an attack on 'external inequality' in the division of labour, an inequality which meant that contracts were *ipso facto* never truly just, and that social mobility – or the process whereby individuals found the social task most suited to their capacities – was never truly 'spontaneous'. When Durkheim expresses this view he comes very close to all those liberal and radical critics of the bourgeois notion that capitalist society is just (or 'fair') simply because it is 'free'. Opportunities must not only be abstractly free, they must be actually equal. This is impossible when structured inequalities persist. Consonant with this is his contention that the work of the French revolution was not the source of modern difficulties – rather it was unsatisfactory because its work was incomplete. To political liberty had to be added real equality and fraternity, an interesting convergence with the idea that formal liberties are limited in value when unaccompanied by real changes in the social substratum.

Durkheim's concordance with a broad band of reformist thinking is further exemplified by his view of the state. We know that he distrusted proposals for granting undue power to the state but that he also acknowledged that the state had a role to play so long as it was circumscribed by the power of secondary groups. This view necessarily presupposes a conception of a general interest, and supposes that the state is capable of recognizing, representing, protecting and furthering the collective interest. It is this very view – that the state was somehow above class conflict, and that the state could transcend the divisions of civil society – that Marx had attacked in his examination of Hegel.[73] Marx argued that the state did not stand above the divisions of civil society, rather it was the latter which dominated the former. The state therefore was to be seen as a reflection of class interests and not as the transcendence of them. This analysis necessarily projects the question of why and how can the state in a capitalist society be capable of transcending sectional or class interests.

In Durkheim's terms part of the answer lies in the fact that his sociology *did* permit him to conceive of a common good or common interest; part stems from his belief that laws are formalizations of the collective interest and morality; the state which creates and administers laws does so as the true representative of the common good. It is also apparent that Durkheim has an affection for all types of 'fonctionnaires' – public officials, whether they be teachers, lawyers, judges, administrators, direct or indirect agents of the state. He would have hesitated to call them a class (a middle class) but in many respects Durkheim places his faith in their good will, their conciliatory functions, their understanding and their 'neutrality' in enabling them to carry out the functions of the state as arbiters of common good.*

This question of the nature of reconstruction and sociology is not the only theme of Durkheim's work – or of this volume – but it is an important one and it will recur in several guises, in practical areas of contemporary substantive sociological inquiry outlined in the following chapters of this book. His view of the state, power and coercion, and of bureaucracy, is treated in chapter 3; chapter 2 deals with the social organization of the economy and examines the reforming ideas in recent applications of the concept of anomie; chapter 4 treats the question of racism and the depth of its roots in contemporary society; chapter 5 examines Durkheim's sociology of education – perhaps the best example of his practical reforming interests; chapter 6 deals with the application of Durkheimian theory to the problems of law and deviance; and chapter 7 explains his understanding of religion. We shall see that his radical diagnosis of the modern malaise often appears to stretch further than his tentative sketches of social reconstruction. But Durkheim was far from being a mere technician of social engineering.[74] The extent to which the reforming optimistic cast of mind is bound up with a specialized or limited social analysis is clearly a matter of degree, and Durkheim's work demonstrates that it is possible to contain the reforming mentality within a highly generalized and broad-reaching analysis of society and historical process. His radical mind presented difficulties for his cautious soul but his analysis shows that the reformist sociological imagination can be broad and deep in scope.

* This view of the state (and its servants) as the 'brain' of society contains a form of elitism common to much social reformist thinking, i.e. the belief that men *en masse* may not realize or recognize the common good (or even their own best interests), but those upon whom experience and position have conferred a broader appreciation of social needs *do* have such an understanding.

2

꤮꤮꤮

The division of labour, class conflict and social solidarity*

To become a free seller of labour power, who carries his commodity wherever he finds a market, he (the labourer) must have escaped the dominion of the guilds, from their rules for apprentices and journeymen, and from the impediments of their labour regulations. Hence the historical movement which changes the producers into wage workers appears on the one hand as their emancipation from serfdom and from the fetters of the guilds, and this side alone exists for bourgeois historians.

Karl Marx, Capital, Vol. 1, p. 752.

For a whole century, economic progress has mainly consisted in freeing industrial relations from all regulation.

Emile Durkheim, Suicide, p. 254.

Marx and Durkheim are here speaking about the same historical process – the reshaping of the relationship of producers to their product, to their fellow producers, through the expansion of labour markets in which the 'free' contract between the labourer and the hirer of labour is the defining relationship. Neither saw this as a genuinely free condition. They shared the view that the conditions of the contract meant that the relationship was not freely entered into; those who sold their labour power were *compelled* to do so and therefore this multitude of individual contracts could not be said to be the basis of a free and just society.

Marx argued that this 'economist's' view of freedom was an ideological and bourgeois view because it was contained within the constraints of a society dominated by the bourgeois class. Durkheim rejected the utilitarian view that mere assent to contracts could be a basis of justice and solidarity. Both agreed that this process of 'emancipation' produced a spurious freedom, Marx insisting that it was merely bourgeois freedom under conditions of class domination, Durkheim arguing that freedom from regulation was no freedom at all. True freedom, in Durkheim's view, was to

---

* The introductory chapter has set out many of the main themes of *The Division of Labour*. A reading of the first chapter is presumed here, but certain points are repeated where they are necessary to the flow of argument and exposition.

be found in willing and conscious assent to social forms of regulation under conditions of greater equality.

The economists, Durkheim argued, seek to justify this 'freedom' by seeing it as necessary to the expansion of human effort and the production of greater wealth. He himself could not accept that the sole historical purpose of the division of labour was to create wealth in which all could share:

Judged in this way, productive output seemed to be the sole primary aim in all productive activity. In some ways it might appear that output, to be intensive, had no need to be regulated; that, on the contrary, the best thing were to leave individual businesses and enterprises of self-interest to excite and spur on one another in hot competition, instead of trying to curb and keep them within bounds.

Such an ordering of affairs is to permit chaos in the productive centre of society, and to lay the foundations of perpetual discontent:

Production is not all, and if industry can only bring output to this pitch by keeping up a chronic state of warfare and endless dissatisfaction among its producers, there is nothing to balance the evil that it does. Even from the strictly utilitarian point of view, what is the purpose of heaping up riches if they do not serve to abate the desires of the greatest number, but, on the contrary, only rouse their impatience for further gain? . . . Society has no justification if it does not bring a little peace to men – peace in their hearts and peace in their mutual intercourse.[1]

Durkheim did not accept the virtues of ever increasing material production. Marx, by contrast, retained some admiration for the productive energies which capitalism released, whilst seeing the class relations which brought them into existence as fundamentally irrational and contradictory; the releasing of men's truly productive energies for *social* needs would be the achievement of socialism.

In Durkheim's analysis little attention is paid to any possible explanation of *why* industrial activity, production, and markets for commodities continually expand. He frequently *describes* it – this unprecedented and rapid expansion of economic activity – and sees in it a major reason for the pathologies of modern society. He speaks of an uncontrolled, unplanned, haphazard, even 'anarchic' development – but offers few clues as to its source. In Marx's case an explanation of the roots of economic anarchy is central to the theory of capitalist development. It was a law of capitalist modes of production that capital must always expand. Capital must always seek new fields, and new and more intensive ways of extracting profits from co-operative labour; capitalists must always accumulate or be extinguished.

As well as writing about the macro-social effects of the division of labour, Marx and Durkheim also discuss the consequences of the sub-division of tasks and routinized specialization as they impinge on the daily experience of the labourer. When they describe the indignity of minutely divided work, there is a broad similarity in the language they use. They speak of the creative worker being reduced to detail labour, becoming a 'crippled monstrosity' (Marx), and a 'mere cog in a machine' (Durkheim) repeating routine tasks with no conception of the whole productive activity. Marx saw this as a necessary feature of the division of labour in a capitalist society, Durkheim saw it as an excess which could and should be restrained.

For Marx the division of labour was the capitalist division of labour, a means whereby the bourgeois class extended its dominion over workers; it was a tool in the hands of a class who were compelled to extract the maximum surplus value from the organized energies of wage labour. Durkheim saw the division of labour less as a historically specific form, and more as an evolving generalized feature of advanced societies. Excesses which Marx saw as inescapable in a *capitalist* society, Durkheim saw as undesirable in a complex *industrial* society. Far from seeing the pathological features of the division of labour as 'necessary', Durkheim viewed them as aberrations (as abnormal forms) capable of being reformed and re-constructed, thus paving the way for the division of labour to realize its true function in modern societies as the very foundation of truly co-operative interdependence, that is of solidarity.

Finally Marx understood inequality of wealth and power as part of the nature of capitalist society. Durkheim believed that the gross inequalities of wealth – which were as he phrased it, 'external' to the division of labour itself – were a hindrance to the realization of solidarity; but he also believed that these external inequalities could be removed, or at least sufficiently reduced for this hindrance to be overcome. We have, therefore, in these two thinkers the classical confrontation between the belief that inequality is inescapable in capitalist social relations, and the belief that – however drastic the measures of redistribution may have to be, and however much property rights may need to be curbed – they *can* be reformed by institutional means.

The division of labour in society

In Durkheim's language, modern European societies were not described as capitalist societies but as advanced industrial societies, advanced in the progress of social evolution, and industrial in their dominant institutions. The master process in social evolution was the progressive elaboration of the division of labour, the major consequence was social and structural differentiation. Rapid industrialization had occurred in the late eighteenth and throughout the nineteenth centuries, its main features being the

Type of society

	Simple (primitive or lower)	Modern (advanced, complex)
Division of labour	Simple	Complex, high degree of structural differentiation
Law*	Repressive	Restitutive
Basis of solidarity	The common conscience (mechanical)	An abstract moral code, co-operative interdependence, different group moralities (organic)

*A full discussion of repressive and restitutive law can be found in chapter 6.

growth in scale of production, the national and international expansion of markets, and, social structurally, the inevitable demise of the ancient guilds which had controlled production in an era when industry and markets had been on a smaller scale. How or why this expansion and this differentiation takes place is not fully explained in Durkheim's work; he relies chiefly on the argument that population increases promote richer contacts between previously disparate social groupings, and these contacts themselves give rise to new moral and social arrangements. We have seen in chapter 1 that most of his argument was concerned with the *consequences* of social differentiation, especially with its consequences for moral consensus, and with the disorderly and incomplete nature of the transition to modernity.

To restate his position very briefly, we saw that Durkheim argued 1) that the common moral culture of mechanical societies was replaced by a more abstract collective conscience constituted by the reverence for the individual, liberty, democracy and justice, 2) that organic solidarity grew out of the web of interdependent links formed in the advanced division of labour and 3) that occupational groups formed the basis of a system of different moral and social milieux. The process of development from simple to advanced society was also marked by the decline of repressive law – in which punishment is exacted for transgression of a common moral code – and the preponderance of restitutive law, in which the emphasis is upon the restoration of relationships obtaining prior to the breach of an agreement. Durkheim's evolutionary scheme can now be illustrated in the above table.

Once the outline of Durkheim's evolutionary theory has been understood, we can turn our attention to his prolonged concern with the process of transition from the ancient to the modern order. The 'healthy' tendencies of social evolution are interrupted by imperfections and imbalances, and 'de-regulation' has occurred without the moral certainties of the old order being replaced by new forms of constraint. Hence the absence of regulation – anomie – is a prevailing characteristic of modern societies, nowhere more so than in economic life.

The great rapidity of social and economic change is, in Durkheim's work, the main explanation of why contemporary societies are morally confused, disrupted by sectional and class conflicts, and of why individuals are subjected to new social and psychological pressures. Added to this the growth of the modern solidary society is obstructed by the perpetuation of unjustified and unprincipled inequality, i.e. inequality which cannot be justified to men by reference to an understood and accepted set of principles. He does, from time to time, hint at some more proximate causes of social malaise. For example he comments that the great cities where commercial and industrial activities are concentrated are chiefly made up of migrants and immigrants, that is of people, uprooted from one milieu, who have not formed lasting ties in a new one. This comment focusses upon the inadequacy of group life in a period of growth and transition, a profoundly sociological argument which has been particularly attractive to American sociologists as they reflected on the social lives of immigrants massed in growing American cities.[2]* Another proximate cause of discontent – something which he mentions rather than 'analyses' – are those industrial crises where markets are over-supplied and under-supplied, where production is interrupted and production and consumption are ill-co-ordinated. (By implicit contrast with a stable situation where goods are locally produced for local markets.) Such ill-co-ordination may occur because producers and consumers are insufficiently in contact with each other when market operations expand in distance and scale. Arguments like this show that Durkheim recognized the way in which crises in market relations may surface in social life, but we can also see how he places primary emphasis on *social* disintegration – on the inadequacy of group life and the social and moral insufficiency of contacts in the market place – rather than on systemic difficulties in the operation of markets themselves.

Indeed this provides an interesting contrast with Marxist interpretations of crises of production, in which intermittent over-supply and under-supply are seen to be endemic in a capitalist society, where production is oriented to profit rather than social need. In the Marxist argument, commodities which are needed but cannot be produced profitably are under-produced; and profitable commodities are produced in great abundance until over-supply creates a crisis of over-production. The Marxist view implies the need to

* The best-known elaboration of the concept of anomie is to be found in Merton's paradigm of means and goals, applied to the analysis of deviance, and this is discussed in chapter 6.

transcend capitalist relations of production; the Durkheimian view implies the need for rational guidance of production – the planned economy.

Evidently, a concern with 'pathological' or 'anomic' forms in advanced society occupied much of Durkheim's attention. Since we have outlined his theory of social development, and contrasted his views with Marxist analysis, we shall turn now to Durkheim's analysis of anomie in the division of labour – and subsequently to the way in which later writers have utilized his approach.*

Conflicts, crises, strikes: pathologies in the division of labour

The optimistic evolutionary view of the division of labour is altogether balanced by his portrayal of pathologies – what he called abnormal forms of the division of labour – and the balance is such that we must always keep in mind a distinction between what Durkheim saw to be the ideal state of advanced societies and what he saw to be the actual state of affairs. In addition to market dislocations, Durkheim describes industrial crises in the form of strikes, disputes between employers and employees, the breakdown and failure of businesses, bankruptcies, and so on: all symptoms of a pervasive anarchy in the economy. His detailed account of abnormal forms of the division of labour appear in the latter part of *The Division of Labour in Society*, and are treated under three headings: anomic forms, the forced division of labour and imperfect co-ordination.

Anomic forms of the division of labour

The essence of the idea of anomie as applied to economic behaviour is that relations between men, or groups of men engaged in commercial and industrial enterprises, are devoid of regulation by shared moral beliefs or by formal legal rules. Although he commonly refers to men engaged in economic activities as 'producers' (irrespective of class position), it is evident that he plainly accepts, in some sense, the existence of classes and the regularity of class conflict. It is an exaggeration to say that Durkheim ignored the existence of classes or of class conflict. But such conflict was not seen as the 'central dynamic of capitalism' but as a series of disputes and clashes which resulted from the absence of agreed conceptions of justice and proper rewards. There are passages in which he makes open acknowledgement of the class struggle – 'la lutte des classes' – using precisely that phrase,[3] and, whilst he sometimes uses the classless phrase 'producers', he also speaks of those 'forced to sell their labour' as distinct from 'employers'

---

* This is discussed in chapter 6 on law and deviance.

and 'entrepreneurs'. Referring to class conflict in one moment, he next speaks of an industry, corporation or sphere of economic activity as a milieu shared by those engaged in it, and therefore capable of producing a solidary moral force. It is this milieu of joint activity which dominates men's lives, rather than the class division within a particular industry, or across all industries. In these milieux moral codes develop:

And thus the peculiar characteristic of this kind of morals shows up . . . we see in it the decentralization of moral life. Whilst public opinion, which lies at the base of common morality, is diffused throughout society, without our being able to say that it lies in one place rather than in another, the ethics of each occupation are localized within a limited region. Thus centres of moral life are formed which, although bound together, are distinct, and the differentiation in function amounts to a kind of moral polymorphism.[4]

Although he cites the example of professional associations, such as lawyers' organizations, which create professional ethics governing their work, he says that for the most part these occupational groups have not evolved in the way they should, and business industrial and commercial life is 'anomic':

If we were to attempt to fix in definite language the ideas current on what the relations should be of the employee with his chief, or of the workman with his manager, of the rival manufacturers with each other and with the public – what vague and equivocal formulas we should get.[5]

Later in the same volume Durkheim writes of the absence of law governing relations between capital and labour:

The relations of capital and labour have, up to the present, remained in the same state of juridical indetermination. A contract for the hire of services occupies a small part in our Codes, particularly when one thinks of the diversity and complexity of the relations which it is called upon to regulate.[6]

In modern terms, the heart of the matter is the insufficiency of industrial law; many of the things which he seems to have had in mind have since become commonplace. He does not appear to have been thinking about the problem of 'wage-restraint' (suggesting rational collective bargaining procedures, or pay boards, arbitration boards, and the like – although he may well have approved of some of these) so much as conditions of work, and contractual conditions of employment. This suggests forms of employment protection, and legislation aimed at ensuring safety, healthy conditions of work and the replacement, as he saw it, of rule by unequal power by rule of law. Each industry was expected to create a kind of self-governing institute, empowered to administer codes of conduct binding on all those engaged in the occupational sphere. These institutes – 'les corporations' – would each be linked with the state; excessive decentralization of power led to anarchy but the corporations could equally protect their members against arbitrary state intervention.[7]

This was not, as we and others have pointed out, a recipe for corporate fascism, rather it came closer to the ideas of the British Guild Socialists.[8] But his attitudes to trade unions are not easy to discern since the occupational groups and corporations of which he writes are not unions in the accepted sense. His anti-revolutionary position meant that he envisaged some form of incorporation of the collective agencies representing occupational groups into the structures of the state; on a Marxist reading this is bound to read like some form of institutionalization and collaborative incorporation of the labour union movement. But when he does directly discuss wage demands and labour unions[9] his tone is not aggressively anti-union. Anomie is rooted in the insatiable appetites of manufacturers or entrepreneurs as much as, if not more than, in the unlimited desires of workers. (Later in the chapter we shall see that this contrasts with recent applications of the concept of anomie to industrial discontents, in which inflationary and unrestrained wage demands are taken to be the core of 'the problem'.) But to leave the organization of the economy to the syndicates themselves would be to replace individual selfishness by collective selfishness, since competing representative groups could not overcome the anarchy of the economy.

Durkheim's attitude to *les syndicats* (trade unions)[10] was formed by his opposition both to administrative syndicalism (the decentralizing and anti-statist and anti-socialist philosophy of the middle class unions) and to revolutionary syndicalism found among the militants of the Confédération Général du Travail. Rejecting both these ideals he advocated the progressive strengthening of corporations or 'groupes professionels' to regulate each sphere of work life.

As Durkheim elaborates his idea of the corporation governing the activities in an industrial sphere, we naturally become curious as to how such corporations are expected to overcome class divisions or conflicts of interest. In the closing passages of *Professional Ethics* he briefly raises the question of the part to be played by employer and employee in these groups:

Such a body could only carry out its functions provided that it included both these elements. However one is forced to wonder whether a distinction would not have to be made at the base of the structure; whether the two categories of industrial personnel would not have to nominate their representatives separately – in a word, whether the electoral bodies would not have to be independent, at all events when *their respective interests were obviously in conflict* [my emphasis].[11]

Durkheim recognizes the possibility of a conflict of interests between employer and employee, without seeing this as an insuperable obstacle to making these corporations, in conjunction with the state, the cornerstones of solidary economic, social and political life. In discussing the sharing of duties between corporations and the state, he gives some indication of the kind of functions he envisages them performing:

From the legislative point of view, certain functions have to be classified according to the industry, such as the general principles of the labour contract, of salary and wage remuneration, of industrial health, of all that concerns the labour of women and children, etc. and the state is incapable of such classification. The provision of superannuation funds cannot be made over without danger to the funds of the state, over-burdened as it is with various services, as well as being too far removed from the individual. Finally the regulation of labour disputes, which cannot be codified as laws on any hard and fast principle, calls for special tribunals.[12]

Finally, he acknowledges again that 'some recasting of the laws of property is to come about' and he may have had in mind the transference of property rights from the family or individuals to the occupational group.[13] He foresees a process of evolution in which property ceases to be a private privilege and becomes a collective resource.[14] But he also concludes that it is hardly likely that the day will come when 'nothing remains of the old rights of property, when the position of employer will no longer exist and when all the rights of inheritance will have been abolished'.[15]

Large scale industry: the loss of craft skills

There are two other important strands in Durkheim's discussion of the anomic division of labour. Firstly he clearly believes that sheer agglomeration, the greatly expanded size of industrial and commercial enterprises, militates against solidarity. In what, in retrospect, looks like a rather naive passage, he dwells upon the virtues of the small factory in which all producers are continuously in contact with one another, and thus engender a solidary moral atmosphere. It appears naive because in his regard for the small firm – shared by fellow Frenchmen – he does not envisage a return to it, nor does he exhibit any understanding of the economic logic which encourages large scale production. Along with these comments are similarly wistful remarks on the decline of craft skills.

As the market extends, great industry appears. But it results in changing the relations of employers and employees. The great strain on the nervous system and the contagious influence of great agglomerations increases the needs of the latter. Machines replace men; manufacture replaces hand-work. The worker is regimented throughout the day. He lives always apart from his employer, etc. These conditions of industrial life naturally demand a new organization, but as the changes have been accomplished with extreme rapidity, the interests in conflict have not yet had time to be equilibrated.[16]

This passage nicely illustrates the tone of his argument about the rapidity of change; but there is no convincing explanation of why 'markets extend and great industry appears'. We should note that, at this point, Durkheim adds an important footnote, writing 'This antagonism is not entirely due to the rapidity of these changes, but, in good part, to the still very great inequality of the external conditions of the struggle. *On this factor time has no influence'* (my emphasis). We are not told what Durkheim thinks *will* influence this factor.

Following on this, Durkheim elaborates his condemnation of the effects on the worker of routine mechanized work:

> In fact if the individual does not know whether the operations he performs are tending, if he relates them to no end, he can only continue to work as a matter of habit. Every day he repeats the same movements with monotonous regularity, but without taking any interest in them and without understanding them. He is no longer anything but an inert piece of machinery, only an external force set going which always moves in the same direction and in the same way. Surely no matter how one represents the moral ideal, one cannot remain indifferent to such debasement of human nature.[17]

Durkheim's approach to industry could not be described as 'managerial sociology'; his critique went much deeper. But passages such as these cited have been used in support of social engineering, of promoting the loyalty of the worker to his firm, or of altering work routines to enhance work satisfaction. Durkheim's 'abnormal forms' are 'excesses' or 'deviations', abnormal because they do not lead to solidarity. Georges Friedmann has remarked that Durkheim would have been forced to consider 'abnormal' 'most of the semi-skilled jobs that are actually performed today in offices, industry, commerce, and even agriculture'.[18] He correctly points out that Durkheim fails to distinguish between craft skills and dexterous routines, more evidence that Durkheim's acquaintance with industrial production was slight.

The forced division of labour

It is under the heading 'the forced division of labour' that Durkheim discusses those social structured inequalities which undermine solidarity, and, in so doing, shows that he does not perceive the pathologies of the division of labour as a wholly moral matter: 'It is not sufficient that there be rules, however, for sometimes the rules themselves are the cause of the evil. This is what occurs in class wars.'[19] Durkheim explicitly recognizes that class inequalities restrict the opportunities of the lower classes and prevent the realization of abilities. Resentment accumulates and men are led to think revolutionary thoughts:

> Doubtless we are not from birth predestined to some special position: but we do have tastes and aptitudes which limit our choice. If no care is taken of them, if they are

ceaselessly disturbed by our daily occupations, we shall suffer and seek a way of putting an end to our sufferings. But there is no way out than to change the established order and set up a new one.[20]

Durkheim here emphasizes 'thwarted aspirations' rather than 'unlimited desires', another indication, perhaps, that for him the anarchy of capitalism was rooted in the 'greed' of entrepreneurs as much as in the insatiable demands (wage claims?) of workers (compare my discussion later in this chapter). He is ambivalent about the notion of natural talents and abilities, speaking of them as both inhering in the nature of the individual and as being socially moulded; no doubt, as a scientist, he regarded the questions of heredity and environment as unresolved. It is clear that he does not regard revolution as a tolerable solution to the problems of industrial civilization. Rather he advocates broad measures of social equalization designed to promote what modern social democrats would call equality of opportunity. He shows *some* hesitation in this regard in that he seems anxious to distinguish equality as a broad ideal from 'sameness' or uniformity. Where equality means uniformity it is incompatible with modern societies, indeed it is a characteristic of simple undifferentiated societies; the master trend of modern societies is differentiation, the production of social differences through the division of labour. But modern societies do also elevate the ideal of equality in the more abstract sense of granting equal dignity to all men, and in coming to regard all hereditary material inequality as being arbitrary and as such having no moral justification. Modern society can no longer tolerate such external inequalities:

If one class of society is obliged, in order to live, to take any price for its services, whilst another can abstain from such action thanks to resources at its disposal, which, however, are not necessarily due to any social superiority, the second has an unjust advantage over the first at law. In other words, there cannot be rich and poor at birth without there being unjust contracts.[21]

The removal of conditions which create 'rich and poor at birth' is necessary for the realization of justice in contracts and of social solidarity. This diminution of arbitrary inequality is implied in a process of social evolution in which social progress overwhelms 'natural inequalities':

Domestic life itself, with the heredity of goods it implies and the inequalities which come from that, is, of all the forms of social life, that which depends most strictly on natural causes, and we have seen that these inequalities are the very negation of liberty. In short, liberty is the subordination of external forces to social forces, for it is only on this condition that the latter can freely develop themselves. But this subordination is the reverse of the natural order. It can, then, realize itself progressively only in so far as man raises himself above things and makes laws for them, thus depriving them of their fortuitous, absurd, amoral character; that is, in so far as he becomes a social being. For he can escape nature only by creating another world where he dominates nature. That world is society.[22]

This is a very interesting passage because it indicates a view of the relationship between 'nature' and 'society' which, in exegesis of his writings has been relatively unexplored. It might be compared with Claude Lévi-Strauss's writings on nature and culture.[23] Certainly Durkheim here equates the 'natural' with the fortuitous and arbitrary, and portrays nature as something which is transcended by society. The passage also shows that he took the question of property very seriously; his rather cloudy vision of how property relations might be modified is discussed in chapter 3.

Failure of co-ordination

Lack of co-ordination in work routines is dealt with very briefly by Durkheim in his final remarks on abnormal forms. It seems to amount to little more than an argument that men are ill at ease when their work is interrupted and poorly co-ordinated; it comes closest to confirming Georges Friedmann's suspicion that Durkheim would have approved Frederick Taylor's[24] emphasis on management's role in co-ordinating work operations. Durkheim makes a casual reference to Marx's phrase about the division of labour 'contracting the pores of the working day', and some assorted references to scattered sociological observations of men at work. It is a passage in which he relies, most irritatingly, on vague analogies with the functioning of organisms – analogies which he undoubtedly took very seriously. But it says little to his general theory of the division of labour, and merits little attention, except perhaps as another indication of his slight knowledge of working life in industry.[25]

Durkheim's analysis applied to the study of class conflict and industrial relations

Having reviewed Durkheim's own writings we turn now to some illustrations of the uses of his ideas by later sociologists. Naturally some adaptations of his ideas are more faithful to their origins than others. But all those whose works we examine – Mayo and the human relations writers, Wilensky and the industrial sociologists in America, and Fox, Flanders and Goldthorpe in British neo-Durkheimian writing – have cited Durkheim with enthusiasm. Whilst the former (American) group focussed on the notion of group integration, the latter group's concern with anomie in industrial relations and with inequality may be seen as pressing further Durkheimian ideas. Of course Durkheim's writings – and the concept of anomie in particular – had a *general* impact on sociology; but in this chapter we are concerned with industrial sociology and with classes and the division of labour.[26]

American industrial sociology

Elton Mayo's work was particularly influential in the 1930s and 1940s, the period when American industrial sociology took shape; a decade or so after this Harold Wilensky had established himself as a leading figure in this sociological tradition. Both lay strong claims to the Durkheimian heritage.

In the broadest possible sense Mayo's work was founded on a premise with a distinctively Durkheimian ring. For he began, as Durkheim did, with a critique of the utilitarian model of man and society, arguing that the chief weakness in our understanding of economy and society lay in the acceptance of the economists' assumptions. When Mayo, working as investigator and consultant in the famed Roethlisberger–Dickson studies of productivity and industrial relations in an American industrial plant, claimed to have discovered empirically the importance of informal social groups in forming attitudes and practices at work, he believed that he had uncovered a principle of general significance for industrial studies. That is he converted the particular finding that informal associations influenced men's working attitudes, into the general principle that industrial be-haviour should be understood through its social contexts. The chief error, he argued, of management theory was to believe that the behaviour of men was largely a matter of self-interested material motives and sheer physical co-ordination. Human behaviour, he continued, was not wholly nor even predominantly rational and logical and the assumption that it was could be a great obstacle to further understanding. 'The desire to stand well with one's fellows, the so-called human instinct of association, easily outweighs the merely individual interest and the logical reasoning upon which so many spurious principles of management are based'.[27]

In the *Social Problems of an Industrial Civilization* he draws on Durkheim's evolutionary model to elaborate his own distinction between 'established' and 'adaptive' societies, and cites *Suicide* to characterize the decay of established groupings and the failure of a restless modern civilization to create alternative bases of social life. In simple societies the individual is *solidaire* with his group; in industrial society 'the family tie is weakened and, more often than not, no new or developing group relation is substituted for it'. From this point it was a relatively simple step to advancing the argument that the industrial firm or business enterprise could supply that necessary social milieu capable of engendering a sense of belonging and identification.

Mayo gives us instances where industrial administrations have succeeded in making factory groups so stable in their attitudes of group co-operation that men in the groups explicitly recognized that the factory had become for them the stabilizing force around which they developed satisfying lives . . . Thus industry itself effectively substitutes for the old stabilizing effect of the neighbourhood. Given stable employment, it might make of industry (as of the small town during most of our national life) a socially satisfying way of life, as well as a way of making a living.[28]

Reflections of Durkheim's arguments can be seen here, but some significant divergences are already apparent. In Mayo it is *the firm* which is seen as providing a source of social identity and belonging, foreshadowing personnel policies designed to heighten the identification of the worker with his employer's enterprise. In Durkheim it is the occupational or professional group, or the totality of those engaged in a specific industry who are seen as sharing a co-operative milieu. For these to become the basis of social solidarity presupposes the reform of industrial relations and of the relations between labour and employer which goes far beyond anything which Mayo envisioned. What in Durkheim is a profound conception of the social quality of all social life and culture, is reduced in Mayo to a mere assertion of the importance of the 'motive to associate'. Translated into 'reform' Mayo's work points in the direction of the manipulation of attitudes, recommending the scientific training of 'interviewers' skilled in relating to workers, and the creation of a corps of personnel managers on whose shoulders would fall the major burden of harmonizing industrial relations. Trained in psychiatry himself, Mayo was much given to 'psychoanalytic' interpretations, particularly when it came to explaining 'disruptive' behaviour and 'the disruptive mentality'. He ventures to suggest that eventually, the fire of Marx's radicalism will be seen to have derived from some personal maladjustment, traceable to an emotional grudge in his personal history.[29] Many of the 'treatments' of factory radicals which he records are of a clinical psychiatric kind, as in the case of one such radical worker satisfactorily 'cured' by a physician: 'He drifted into the hands of a medical colleague . . . made a good recovery and discovered to his astonishment that his former political views had vanished.' This particular worker even graduated into the middle class. 'He had been a mechanic, unable to keep his job although a good workman . . . After recovery he took a clerical job and held it; his attitude was no longer revolutionary.'[30] What appears to be a stress on the sociological descends into frail psychologism centred upon individual modes of adjustment and the notion of a sociative motive. Quite outside of Mayo's purview are those problems of industrial capitalist societies to which Durkheim refers – crises of production, the anarchy of markets and external conditions of inequality. Durkheim's analysis of the division of labour recognizes their occurrence and his prognosis of reconstruction presupposes their amelioration. Mayo's 'blinkered intensiveness' produced studies which 'made no mention of trade unions and little mention of unemployment – although the period covered was that of the great depression and was also one of the most disturbed in the history of management–labour relations in America'.[31] Durkheim's career as a stern and serious scholar may have shielded him from many of the realities of industrial work, business and commerce, but his milieu did not foster in him any uncritical sympathy with the bourgeois individualism of the capitalist class; on the contrary many of his ideas were antagonistic to that ethic. This is evident not only in his broadly 'liberal socialist' outlook, but also, as we have seen, in his fashioning of the concept of anomie into a diagnosis of a general malaise in contemporary industrial organization. By contrast, as a management consultant, Mayo lived easily in the world of corporate managers, their problems were his problems, and there was little of significance about which they would have disagreed. In his hands the notion of anomie – and this is true of much American sociology, as Horton has pointed out – became little more than a vague characterization of unease, unrest and dislocation in a changing society.

American sociology and the theme of belonging: the human relations approach

The dilution of the concept of anomie into a general term for social disestablishment and for the individual's unsatisfied 'need for belonging', became typical of American sociology, but was particularly influential in the Mayo-inspired human relations tradition in industrial studies. In a 'technical' sense this loose usage came closer to Durkheim's idea of *egoism* than it did to his own conception of anomie. The notion of egoism, given fullest expression in *Suicide*, is virtually inseparable from the notion of anomie, especially since he argues that moral life (the absence of which constitutes anomie) and group life (the absence of which constitutes egoism) depend upon each other; but he does make an analytical distinction which he regards as important:

anomic and egoistic suicide . . . have kindred ties. Both spring from society's insufficient presence in individuals. But the sphere of its absence is not the same. In egoistic suicide it is deficient in truly collective activity, thus depriving the latter of object and meaning. In anomic suicide, society's influence is lacking in the basically individual passions, thus leaving them without a check rein. In spite of their relationship, therefore, the two types are independent of each other. We may offer society everything social in us, and still be unable to control our desires; one may live in an anomic state without being egoistic, and vice-versa.[32]

The concept of egoism focusses on the strength (or weakness) of *social integration* of individuals into solidary groups. (And this *is* a central theme in

Durkheim's sociology reflected in both American and British industrial sociology. Durkheim's mention of economic crises and market failures does not really match Lockwood's distinction between social integration and system integration, although Gilbert, see below, has suggested that it does.) When society is strongly integrated, we find 'in a cohesive and animated society, a constant interchange of ideas and feelings, from all to each and each to all, something like a mutual moral support, which leads, . . . the individual to share in the collective energy, and support his own when exhausted'.[33] And if the essence of egoism is disintegration, the essence of anomie is *de-regulation*, most marked in economic life where relations in trade and industry have been 'freed from all regulation'. In stressing the former rather than the latter there has been a tendency in American sociology to neglect some of the force of Durkheim's characterization of economic life as anomic, that is as suffering from a chronic and pervasive, if not endemic, malaise. The emphasis has not been so much on economic anarchy, or on the absence of regulation of economic activities and appetites, but on the disruption of social routines in general and on the disruption of social arrangements of work life in particular. Breakdowns of trade, recessions and crises in the economy, the failure of business enterprise and the conflict between capital and labour – all, as we have seen, given *some* prominence by Durkheim – remain wholly peripheral to the work of Mayo and others of his school.

In emphasizing the purely *social* (as opposed to the *economic*) needs of men, Mayo found the pathologies of adaptive societies in the lack of solidary groups in which men might achieve a sense of belonging and thus satisfy their natural sociative motive. Equating anomie with the absence of solidary groups and the individual's loss of a sense of place, some form of *personal* dissatisfaction is thus identified as the root of the problem, this dissatisfaction having its origins (variously) in failures of communication, the disruption of established social routines, disharmony between workers and management, and a lack of identification with corporate purposes and institutions. Manipulative prescriptions flow naturally from this type of analysis. To the extent that North American sociology has been concerned with 'the problem of belonging' it has, despite appearances, been more concerned with something like egoism than anything like anomie. Although this is an understandable projection of an element of Durkheim's thought, its elaboration and extension at the expense of equally important themes in Durkheim's work, has produced an unbalanced application of his analysis.

Social integration and the division of labour: Wilensky's approach

In the more recent work of Harold Wilensky, the author speaks of the relationship 'between the division of labour and social integration' and examines the variable degree to which work situations and labour force experiences encourage participation in, and integration into, secondary social groups. 'If we give a man some college' he writes, 'put him on a stable career ladder, and top it off with a nice family income, he will get into the community act.' [34] If Wilensky is simply concerned with the measurable social correlates of work experience, i.e. the empirical relationship between work and non-work life, this might be unobjectionable; but 'getting into the community act' bears little relationship to anomie as Durkheim understood it. As Dennis Wrong has pointed out, this exemplifies how the idea of the importance of solidary groups to social integration, and the corresponding psychological notion of the importance for personal integrity of attachment to these groups, have, in fact, become major theoretical assumptions in sociology. It is a kind of 'Americanization of Durkheim' in which the proposition that men seek status in the acceptance of others has become the guiding psychological assumption in social research.

Wilensky clearly presents his hypothesis, that stable experience in the labour market leads to social integration, as a test of 'Durkheim's ideas'. He argues that men with orderly careers have contacts with kin, friends and neighbours that are at once 'more integrated, wide-ranging and stable'; their occupational community is stronger. He adds 'if our interest is in the integrative potential of social ties, we must note too the participation pattern of miners, longshoremen, and others who are surrounded by men like themselves, and who, in lodge and union, at home and at the bar, reinforce their common alienation and isolation'. [35] Not all group integration is solidary! Indeed, in the above passage, the *integration* of these workers very quickly becomes their *isolation*. And yet they are patently not isolated from their occupational group. What then are they isolated from? The only possible answer to be derived from the rest of Wilensky's analysis is to say that they are isolated from 'the mainstream of social life'. This mainstream begins to take on the appearance of a middle class stream. The model is the banker with overlapping obligations and role definitions at work, in the country club, the family and the Republican party. [36] Furthermore, this overlapping integration is the solution to the problem of social control, the problem of anomie, as well as the problem of egoism. 'It is assumed that these roles, that are most integrated, are most effective in social control; from the viewpoint of the person such roles reduce conflict and choice and make for an easy falling in line.' [37] An 'easy falling in line' and 'getting into the community act' have become the keys to the problem of social control. But what disqualifies the overlapping ties of miners or longshoremen to union, bar and family from being equally integrative? Since in *form* they are analogous to the overlapping ties of the banker, the crucial unspoken difference must be in the *content* which in the model banker's case is unexamined; in the case of miners and longshoremen these common ties, in Wilensky's words, 'reinforce common alienation'. These unresolved difficulties in Wilensky's analysis come in part from a distorted application of 'Durkheimian' ideas, and from a facile identification of social participation with social integration, and of social integration with social control.

Conclusion

The identification of Mayo and later industrial sociologists with Durkheim, may, with regard to understanding Durkheim, be misleading. Their psychologistic and social psychological assumptions clearly mark them off from some of the fundamentals of Durkheim's sociology. As a general characterization of social disorganization and the disruption of established patterns of behaviour, the concept of anomie was imported into sociology; it became part of the language of industrial sociology but in a way which evaded a characterization of economic behaviour as such as anomic. American industrial sociology adopted the term anomie (reduced in Blau's definition to a 'state of feeling isolated and disoriented')[38] but was not inclined to use it as a point of departure for a critique of economic individualism. The sociologistic and psychologistic strands in industrial sociology, which had their origins in a critique of the asocial assumptions of economics, replaced a non-social economics with a non-economic industrial sociology.

The sociology of occupations and professions

The Durkheim-influenced sociology discussed so far in this chapter could be loosely grouped under a heading like 'the sociology of work and industry'. A literature has developed, with an interest in the world of work, but with a rather narrower emphasis, and that is the sociology of occupations and professions. Some of its roots go back to the early days of Chicago sociology, represented in the studies of typically 'disreputable' jobs, the curious milieux of the hobo, the taxi dance-hall girl and the professional thief. It was one of the central figures in that tradition, Everett Hughes, who elevated the study of the world of work, to a major stream of sociological inquiry.[39]

In Hughes's work, and in that of later writers, we can identify two strands which bear clear marks of Durkheimian inspiration: 1) a consistent interest in the way in which work experience becomes the central life experience of the modern citizen and 2) in the way in which modern occupations do, or do not, take on the moral and organizational characteristics of 'professions'. The precise nature of different occupational milieux and the spread of 'professionalism' have become empirical questions for recent sociologists; Durkheim rather tended to assume that occupations had or would increasingly develop those moral characteristics which gave them their crucial role in social solidarity. The fact that he wrote of the condition of anomie to be found in the world of work and industry is only another indication of the ideal and the actual in his writing. In *Suicide* he repeatedly suggests that the occupational group is destined to take over many of the social and moral functions of the family. 'Identity of origin,' he writes, 'culture and occupation make occupational activity the richest sort of material for a common life.' This was not seen merely as a formal organizational setting of everyday life, but as a living 'community'. He wrote of the occupational milieu as a milieu of friends 'nurtured by shared activity in the division of labour . . . (whose) aim it is to cause coherence among friends and stamp them with its seal'. The occupational group was a reassuring circle with a life of its own, and with simultaneous moral effects: 'it is a source of life *sui generis*. From it comes a warmth which animates its members, making them intensely human, destroying their egotisms.'[40] The way in which he envisaged this natural social equation of occupational likeness and moral solidarity is best illustrated in his preface to *The Division of Labour*:

When a certain number of individuals in the midst of political society was found to have ideas, interests and sentiments, and occupations not shared by the rest of the population, it is inevitable that they will be attracted towards each other under the influence of these likenesses. They will seek each other out, and thus, little by little, a restricted group, having its special characteristics, will be formed in the midst of a general society.[41]

This is Durkheim's conception of the substratum of communal life which develops in the world of work. Beyond this, as I have described above, he looked for emergent forms of legal and administrative institutions creating a guild-like organization of industry with regulatory professional bodies as the model of the occupational group. It is evident that the model fits best to the likes of medical and legal professions, occupations in which we do see a degree of self-regulation, whilst the fit with other occupational groups is problematic.

There are two significant differences between these ideas as they appear in Durkheim's work, and their representation in recent studies in the sociology of occupations and professions. Firstly, the modern sociological studies of occupations have often been narrower in scope, ethnographies of particular work milieux, rather than cast in a broader conception of the division of labour and society.[42] Secondly they have been more directly empirically based. Thus they have investigated rather than assumed the degree of occupational community and professionalization evident in various spheres of work. This has also meant that alternative modes of organization of work and involvement in work, relatively neglected by Durkheim, have been conceptualized, specifically the phenomenon of alienation from work – sometimes reflected in the concept of privatization, and the 'bureaucratic' form as distinguished from the professional and entrepreneurial forms. We shall touch upon privatization and bureaucratization later (in the last part of the present chapter and in chapter 3) but we can readily see that these were two themes which were scarcely prefigured in Durkheim's work. The tendency to locate purpose, meaning, sociability and identity in the 'private' sphere of life – coupled with an instrumental or indifferent attitude to work life – is virtually the opposite of Durkheim's conception. Likewise the theme of bureaucratization – as well as creating an image of a dry, administrative, neutral and circumscribed orientation to work – suggests 'loyalty' to an organizational structure which may compete with loyalty to the professional or occupational group.[43] This is one of the themes of Gouldner's well known article 'Cosmopolitans and locals', the local moving in a sphere in which the important loyalties are to the particular organization and community, the cosmopolitan being oriented to a wider definition of his or her calling.[44] In a university the distinction might be between the lecturer devoted to his students and teaching, and providing services finely tuned to his particular college, and the scholar or scientist whose horizons are set by his profession, an international community of researchers or writers.

The findings and arguments in this sub-field of sociology have been various, with some reasserting Durkheimian themes, but perhaps the preponderant number suggesting that if occupational communities and professional structures have developed they have only done so in some specific cases, and nowhere producing in the society as a whole the organic effects that Durkheim envisaged. Everett Hughes began by suggesting that 'a man's work is as good a clue as any to the course of his life, and to his social being and identity' and that the 'ordering in our society is very much a matter of man's relation to the world of work'. But these became the questions which framed investigation – 'to what extent do persons of a given occupation "live together" and develop a culture which has its subjective aspect in the personality? What part does one's occupation play in giving his life organization?' – and the studies yielded variable answers.[45] Work may be a matter of great indifference or of fleeting and changing contacts; equally, where occupational solidarity does emerge, it may not be based on occupational identity *per se*, but on the contingent shared ethnic origin – where particular ethnic groups command a specific occupational sphere, or on shared place of residence or class sentiment such as may be found in mining villages or the dockland and fishing industry areas of great ports.[46]

Hughes did argue that 'professionalization' is a growing feature of modern work: 'The profession aims and claims to be a moral unit. It is a phenomenon of the modern city that an increasing number of occupations are attempting to gain for themselves the characteristics and status of professions.' But he saw this in rather a different light from Durkheim, suggesting for example, in his comments on American realtors, that professionalization is a strategy whereby established practitioners of a trade protect themselves against upstarts and competitors.[47] Researchers have found a high degree of occupational community among some professional groups, and Goode has spoken of the professions as a 'community within a community', but even here contrary evidence is found, for example among dentists who have been portrayed as being largely dissociated from their co-professionals, and even alienated from their work itself.[48] A study of nurses has suggested that social solidarity among nurses is not uniform, but that where it does occur there is much less evidence of alienation from work.[49]

One theme that has received continued attention is the argument that the structures of modern society progressively weaken the particularistic ties of family, ethnic origin and religious group. Durkheim clearly believed these 'primary' loyalties to be associated with pre-modern society, destined for dissolution in the contemporary world. (See our discussion in chapter 4.) Not surprisingly, it is Wilensky who has most faithfully reflected this image of the modern society:

Modern workplaces – and the social and training institutions that feed them – are therefore great mixers of the races, religions and ethnic groups. In so far as corporate and occupational communities flourish, they undermine those minority based primary relations which shape courtship and marriage patterns – that is they subvert ethnic-religious endogamy.[50]

The literature on immigration and assimilation may well, on balance, suggest that this is not far from the mark.[51] But certainly where specifically racial or racist definitions have been at work, the persistence of social separateness and racial identity has been quite marked. Even where this is not so much the case, some recent writers argue that earlier sociologists had overestimated the propensity for ethnic identities to decline or disappear.[52] In the sociology of work, occupations and professions we have a literature which has, then, been considerably influenced by the questions which

Durkheim raised, but one in which the empirical findings have challenged several of his leading assumptions.

The 1960s and 1970s: British neo-Durkheimian economic sociology

Everything that we have said in the middle passages of this chapter indicates that a broad vein of industrial sociology, particularly in the United States, has courted some of the shadows but little of the substance of Durkheim's analysis. It is common enough for European social scientists to point to the consequences of American sociology's longstanding neglect (with notable exceptions and less true today) of the Marxist tradition of thought; and in the 1950s, a period of unprecedented growth of the discipline in America, that neglect was none too mysterious. It has been less commonly observed that many sociologists, in adopting Durkheim's ideas, equally evaded the radical elements in this evidently non-revolutionary figure.

In the 1960s, sharpened social divisions forced an awareness of deep-rooted conflict upon American sociology, but since, in overt political terms, these conflicts were 'non-economic' in outline, the spectre of irreparable social division was not immediately apprehended in terms of economic class conflict. Rather, the problems of the War in Vietnam, of civil rights and racial justice at home, and the shattering collapse of faith in the honesty and authority of government, were perceived in the main in moral and political ways. By contrast in Great Britain the social divisions that repeatedly surfaced in the sixties and seventies had their roots in, and were seen as having their roots in, the unnerving appearance of cracks in the earlier sense of prosperity. Later, there was a downright sense of crisis as commentators, politicians and British people in general registered the signs of apparently insoluble economic uncertainty and decline. Understandably, under these conditions, Marxist traditions of thought, which had already sent down some roots in British social science, experienced a flowering and a vibrant expansion into new and re-newed areas of inquiry – the incidence and nature of industrial strikes, the organization of workers on the shop floor and throughout industries, the international ramifications of periodic crises in capitalist economies, the analysis of bourgeois ideologies, the examination of the role of the state in the containment of conflict, the question of the new middle classes, and a revival of interest in Marxist conceptions of the division of labour and the labour process.

But, remaining within a non-Marxist and non-revolutionary tradition, there was also a revival of interest in Durkheim's analysis of economic anomie, especially as 'the crisis' was in many quarters seen as a problem of planning, co-ordination, radical institutional reform, equality and social justice, and as a *moral* question of anarchic desires and the reconciliation of sectional demands with the collective good.

Given this latter broad definition of the 'social question', the ground was prepared for the re-entry of Durkheim's conception of society and the division of labour. Equally, given the intensity and depth of a sense of social malaise, the piecemeal applications of his ideas in industrial sociology and the related managerial schemes of social adjustment (designed to foster unity, participation and identification) were seen to be patently inadequate, and the radical elements of his analysis were rediscovered. This is not to say that this later application of Durkheim did not also suffer from a certain selective attention to his work, nor did it transcend all the difficulties of the earlier Durkheimian sociology, or the difficulties inherent in Durkheim's own analysis. But there are two reasons why the later Durkheimianism was broader-based and as such provided a more faithful reflection and 'test' of his theories: 1) the new Durkheimians wrote against a backdrop of a generalized sense of social malaise and 2) the questions were phrased as problems of national policy rather than as problems of management strategy.

The revised analysis of 'anomie' was not confined to the academies; the reformist industrial sociologists, in some notable instances, struck responsive chords in the agencies of government and the directors of social and political policy. This was especially true in the Labour Party and during the Labour governments of 1964–70 and 1974–9, as attempts were made to reconcile the trade unions to the measures seen to be necessary to economic survival. (In this particular economic and political climate 'anomie' acquired a new emphasis. For the neo-Durkheimians, 'anomie' was commonly seen as the problem of unrestrained wage demands (unlimited appetites) causing wage-led inflation. This, we have seen above, is not wholly consistent with Durkheim's work.) The Labour Party, laying claims to the traditions of social reform, equality, social justice, and socialist reconstruction, found itself presiding over a new crisis of the capitalist economy, and was compelled to search along every avenue of possible cure – from voluntary and compulsory pay restraint, legal and institutional reform of collective bargaining, frail programmes of economic planning and national ownership, to the Social Contract with its far-reaching extension of the co-optive incorporation of the established trade union movement into the management of capitalism. The broad failure of these measures, culminating in the so-called 'winter of discontent' of 1978–9, heralded the return of an aggressively 'free-enterprise' government in the spring of 1979, led by a party whose leadership and supporters had, with increasing success, poured scorn on 'socialist' efforts to solve the crisis of British capitalism. There emerged a sense of the end of an era, the passing of which was marked by a comprehensive re-writing of the political agenda. Before it ended an interesting chapter in the academic history of industrial sociology and social policy had been written; one which provides an opportune occasion for further examination of the idea of anomie applied to the discontents of industrial societies.

Restraint, inequality and distributive justice: the neo-Durkheimians

In 1978 Michael Gilbert provided a commendably neat summary of those writers who had found renewed inspiration from Durkheim's *Division of Labour, Professional Ethics* and *Socialism*. We shall draw upon this article because it provides a way of introducing the general and shared tendencies of these writers; we shall then examine some of the more detailed and provocative arguments of each writer in turn – in particular the work of Fox and Flanders, and Goldthorpe.

Gilbert begins by indicating – as we did earlier in this chapter – the insufficiencies of the industrial relations emphasis on cohesion in the workplace, and concludes that this group of British writers 'show a more realistic appraisal of the problems of establishing order in economic life and industrial life than their predecessors – and a greater awareness of the subtleties of Durkheim's analysis'.[53] Three elements of Durkheim's conception of industrial anomie are abstracted: 1) excessive specialization, 2) the absence of legal and moral rules in industry and 3) the chaos of unrestrained appetites. The radical nature of Durkheim's analysis is here recognized: 'The measures, which Durkheim concludes are necessary to restore the anomic forms of economic life to a "normal" and healthy regulated form, however inadequate they may appear to us, taken together constitute a radical programme of social reform.'[54] In a thoughtful and even-handed summary Gilbert restores some of the balance in judgement of Durkheim, but perhaps he tilts *too* far in his estimation of Durkheim's radicalism. He correctly points out that Durkheim at least *acknowledged* some of the structural problems of achieving co-ordination and moral solidarity in an anarchic economy. He then applies Lockwood's distinction between social and system integration[55] to suggest that Durkheim had a greater awareness of systemic disorder in capitalism than did the neo-Durkheimians. This may place too great a weight on Durkheim's recognition, and frequent *mention* of market disturbances and economic crises, and too little weight on Durkheim's general failure to *explain* them or to incorporate his awareness of economic disorder in his analysis of social solidarity. In conclusion, however, Gilbert returns to the argument that 'anomie' analysis still founders upon its inadequate understanding of opposing interests and structured conflicts in a capitalist social system, suggesting indeed that the neo-Durkheimians may be seen as a latter-day variety of utopian socialists.

At one point at least Gilbert's enthusiasm for acknowledging the radical nature of Durkheim's analysis leads him to misrepresent his writings. In showing that Durkheim recognized that market anarchy required a solution that went beyond moral control of social relationships, he suggests that 'Durkheim proposes a socialist solution' quoting the passage in *Socialism*: 'To so regulate the productive operations, that they cooperate harmoniously – that is the formula of socialism'. Taking the quotation out of context neglects the fact that the sentence was part of a passage in which Durkheim was explaining his understanding of the distinction between socialism and communism, the former proposing the need for regulation of productive activity, and the latter the need for regulation and equalization of consumption. The passage culminates in his rejection of the socialist formula, for he argued that 'Socialism is essentially a process of economic concentration and centralization' and this he elsewhere roundly condemns. He concludes, 'Assuming a socialist state to be realized as completely as possible, there would still be wretched people and inequalities of every kind.'[56] It is clear that Durkheim equated socialism with the proposals current in contemporary France for the nationalization of industrial property, and this Durkheim saw as no solution, partly because he feared the consequences of creating an over-powerful state, and partly because he saw the programme as inspired by sectional (working class) material interests, and not by collective and moral interests and sentiments.

Gilbert concludes by arguing that Durkheim's analysis implied a programme of social and economic planning: 'In effect, Durkheim proposes some sort of rational economic planning by the state, with the professional associations performing a subsidiary rule by providing the state organs with detailed and relevant information about their particular industries'.[57] This is closer to the mark, since Durkheim's 'proposals' are implicit in his diagnosis of disorder rather than presenting an explicit programme. At every point, Durkheim's acknowledgement of the depth of the roots of economic disorder are balanced by his insufficient understanding or explanation of capitalist relations of production. Gilbert hints at this inadequacy at several points. He cites the fact that the socialization of production – the ever increasing interdependency of the division of labour – requires the planned co-ordination of tasks. But then Braverman's argument, that de-skilling and specialization in the division of labour originate from the desire (the need?) of 'capitalists to gain control of the productive process' is dismissed by Gilbert as 'not relevant here'.[58] Gilbert seems to be suggesting that, *irrespective of the determinate relations of production*, hierarchical control and overall planning are necessary if the advantages of specialization and standardization and predictability are to be realized. But we are entitled to ask 'advantages for whom'? Braverman is arguing that the capitalist's need to produce profits and control his labour force constitute the reasons for, or the logic of, the present exceptional degree of specialization and standardization. Durkheim's failure to understand *why*, in this sense, there was a progressive development of the division of labour beyond that necessary for 'rational production' constitutes a serious weakness in his theory.

As Gilbert himself points out, the interdependences of the division of labour may prove to be a damaging feature of economic organization where it increases the power of strikes or *increases* employees, control over productive processes. De-skilling and standardization are then seen as possible weapons in 'the employers' counter-offensive' and the whole process is increasingly portrayed as a power struggle. Once seen in such a light real difficulties arise for all the ameliorative attempts to modify the division of labour and cure the process of conflict – difficulties which the participants to the struggle in the shorter or longer run may perceive.

Fox and Flanders, Goldthorpe: anomie in the contemporary economy

Two essays in particular had been responsible for this new interest in anomie, one by Fox and Flanders and one by Goldthorpe.[59] The Fox and Flanders article, published in 1969, arose from reflections on the Donovan commission on trade unions and industrial relations, which had diagnosed a conflict between formal and informal systems of industrial relations, the former resting on industry-wide agreements, the latter on agreements in individual factories where managers exercise their autonomy by granting wage rises in solving local disputes, or particular work groups assert their sectional strength by achieving local agreements.[60] The two systems are in conflict as the effects of the informal system are to undermine the ability of the formal system to establish a broad area of predictability and control. The authors distinguish procedural norms from substantive norms, i.e. norms which govern the conduct of negotiations and the like, from norms which relate to actual wages and conditions of employment. They also argue that there are circumstances in which there is a *general* absence of regulation and a culminating condition of disorder where the specific forms of anomie result in a generalized and progressive breakdown of industrial order. Although the analysis centres upon the absence of moral and legal norms, they frequently refer to fundamental conflicts of interest and inequalities of power, suggesting that they have a realistic understanding of the force of collective interests and the balance (or imbalance) of power in industrial conflict. But it is also implied that these conflicts of interest and power struggles are 'bare', 'unbridled' and thus 'anarchic' *because* they are largely unchecked by any normative restraint, and not because such struggles are endemic. So the first two types of disorder, in procedural and substantive norms, occur when a group or groups are able to achieve changes in these norms *against the resistance of other groups*. The third type – the general absence of normative regulation – permits conflicts of interest and power to be worked out without any reference to rules. And the fourth condition of disorder entails the descent into a situation where industrial relations are thoroughly abandoned to competition, struggle and conflict in the absence of any regulative system.

Despite the predominance in their analysis of the sociological language of normative restraint, systems of norms, regulation of aspirations, and so on, there is, in their article a parallel language of 'brute' struggle in which compromises are one possible outcome, but in which the spoils frequently go to the strong and mighty.

Power is the crucial variable determining the outcome in such a situation. One group may have been able to impose its preferred normative system on another but a subjected group [may] . . . challenge the prevailing norms and force an agreed compromise.

Conversely a group may cherish normative aspirations which differ from the prevailing norms, but lack sufficient power to challenge them.[61]

We would be justified in wondering whether what is required is an analysis of power and collective interests, rather than an analysis of norms, and whether prescriptively what is needed is a reconstruction of power relationships rather than a reconstruction of 'normative systems'. They recognize that the problem is 'structural' in the sense that they acknowledge that particular agreements are not the basis of order, even when they are negotiated between wide representative groups. This is a kind of parallel of Durkheim's notion of 'corporate egoism', indicating that aspirations need not be individual to be disruptive. Even the *collective* agreement is not in itself a basis of order, but only, in Durkheim's terms, a truce in a continuing war. So Fox and Flanders are forced to recommend a yet greater extension of the 'institutionalization of conflict' with a heavy responsibility falling on the state in this process. Agreement is not consensus and only consensus can promote enduring order. In the end the authors are faced with no alternative but to fall back upon the need for some strong external authority:

A fire breaks out at sea and creates panic among the passengers, who proceed to fight for places in the lifeboat. Every man's hand is against his fellows until someone with *requisite authority* [my emphasis] restores order with the cry of 'Women and children first.' Uncontrollable though the scene at first appeared, a norm has been articulated to which all can respond.[62]

The writers draw from this analogy the argument that while representatives in particular industries may achieve agreements for that industry, 'for the promotion of order between industries we have to depend on vigorous initiative and stimulus from a *powerful external authority* [my emphasis] . . . We must therefore look to action by *the government* [my emphasis] and public agencies.'[63] The answer in the final analysis seems clear enough. Only the state can control the conflicts and struggles which create chaos in industrial life. How the state acquires and exercises this authority is not indicated, and Durkheim's admonition that authority, to be effective, must be grounded in moral legitimacy, is temporarily neglected.

Fox and Flanders go to some lengths in explaining the difference in the way in which industrial conflict is worked out, depending on whether the economy is deflated or inflated. Since they were writing in a generally inflationary period, they seem to suggest that unlimited aspirations (and the power to realize them) are the preserve of those demanding higher wages. Excessive individualism is a disease of the workers or their representatives, this image reflecting the widespread view that wage-led inflation and trade union monopoly power were the seat of industrial trouble. By contrast, in Durkheim's commentary employers and entrepreneurs are presented as equally afflicted by unlimited desires; the disease of infinite wants is general.

John Goldthorpe's article also responds to this 'wage-demand' definition of the problem, but he draws further upon Durkheim by adding that no system of moral restraint can promote solidarity as long as external conditions of inequality remain. Having begun by referring to the persistence of widespread inequality (of *rewards* rather than of structural conditions) he stakes out a position similar to that of Fox and Flanders:

the most far-reaching implications of inequality for the integration of British society occur not in the political sphere but rather in that of economic life; and . . . they are manifested, not in a situation of fundamental class struggle, but rather in a situation of anomie; that is, in a situation in which there is a lack of moral regulation over the wants and goals that individuals hold.

Fox and Flanders, he argues, by neglecting inequality, underestimated the degree of difficulty involved in achieving solidarity: 'in particular the difficulties of creating an area of relatively rational and orderly inequality in the present "wages jungle" when this jungle is simply part of a wider structure of inequality which has no rationale whatsoever'.[64] He suggests that this gross inequality is not only unprincipled (incapable of public moral legitimation) but also unexplained (that is it cannot be regarded as simply regrettable but 'explained' by some necessary economic logic). Rather the need to achieve a just distribution of resources and rewards should not be seen as an 'ideal', but as a practical necessity, as a precondition of achieving a minimum of friction in a successful economy:

It can be argued as a matter of sociology rather than ideology that, in a society that is both industrial and democratic, a *relatively* stable order in economic life can *only* be created through some minimum degree of consensus – as opposed to merely customary limitations on wants and goals. And such consensus in turn cannot be achieved without the distribution of economic resources and rewards becoming in some degree principled; that is more capable of rational and moral justification.

The article ends on a pessimistic note, concluding that such a reconstruction is less likely, and the perpetuation of existing disorder more likely, especially since 'the egalitarian restructuring of our society' does not appear 'to be on the agenda of any major political party'.[65]

If the interpretation of Durkheim's *Division of Labour* and related works presented in this book is more balanced and accurate than some previous interpretations, then Goldthorpe may be said to have presented an eminently Durkheimian analysis of 'the contemporary crisis in British society'. He defines the problem as one of social integration; he sees it in primarily moral terms; he diagnoses anomie in economic life as the root of the malaise, and he sees this malaise as diffuse and general. And, importantly, he recognizes Durkheim's insistence on the necessity of reducing external inequalities as a precondition of achieving solidarity. For inequality is 1) an important cause of the lack of solidarity, 2) external and arbitrary, i.e. 'unprincipled' and 3) capable of rational modification by a state possessed of the requisite foresight and will. What remains at issue in examining Goldthorpe or Durkheim is the blurring of the notion of inequality and the portrayal of inequality as external and arbitrary. If, in an international capitalist market economy, capital must expand and must accumulate, and must create the conditions for extracting the maximum surplus from labour as a commodity, in what sense can inequality be regarded as 'external' – or arbitrary (except in a purely moral sense)? The difficulty in both Durkheim and Goldthorpe lies in determining in what this inequality inheres. If it inheres in 'arbitrary' relative differences in rewards, or in particular conditions of employment, then these *are* capable of modification, within limits, by state or political action. If inequality inheres in the existence of capital, and in the relations between capital and labour, then it is difficult to see how this inequality is transcended without a transcendence of the social relations of production which they represent. We are then, once again, face to face with the opposition between revolutionary and non-revolutionary solutions to the 'contemporary malaise'. Unless Goldthorpe is setting aside the 'inequality' which inheres in the organization of social relations of production around capital and labour, and is concentrating on marginal inequalities in the distribution of incomes, it is difficult to know why he concludes that: 'It has not proved possible to give a satisfactory explanation of the degree and form of inequality, in Britain, or in any advanced society, otherwise than as a structure with important self-maintaining properties.'

The affluent worker: the working class community, instrumentalism and privatization

John Goldthorpe participated with David Lockwood and others in *The Affluent Worker* studies some time before he wrote his address on inequality and consensus which we have just examined. This series of studies has been influential and widely read but touches rather indirectly on Durkheimian themes, being mostly cast as a study of class attitudes along Weberian and Marxian lines.[66] Three related themes in the study do, however, point in Durkheim's direction.

Working class communities

The notion of the 'traditional working class community' – more specifically the evidence of its apparent decline in post-war Britain – was one of the main points of departure for Lockwood and Goldthorpe's work. Their main aim is to characterize and explain the political consciousness of the modern (affluent) worker and they begin by contrasting the 'traditional working class', rooted in local communal structures, with the modern worker, detached from traditional surroundings and thoroughly 'instrumental' in his pursuit of private rewards. They are suspicious of the idea that collective political consciousness of a 'moral' and radical kind depended on this traditional working class setting, pointing out that this may also be a source of social conservatism.[67] But, nonetheless, they appear to associate a kind of collective morality, transcending individual interests, with the traditional type, and a kind of privatized 'selfishness' with the new, mobile, affluent worker. This collective morality does not correspond with the 'occupational morality' of Durkheim's division of labour nor with his notion of the collective conscience of society, for it remains rooted in shared class experience. The Lockwood and Goldthorpe argument is concerned with the question of whether this shared class experience produces a collective political or an individualistic private response.

Privatization

In Durkheim's work there is little or no foreshadowing of this central theme of contemporary sociology – the theme of privatization, which plays an important part in Lockwood and Goldthorpe's analysis. When Durkheim emphasized the growing importance of the occupational milieu, he

nowhere appeared to envisage the possibility that modern men and women
– despite spending much of their time at work – may be capable of
consigning work activity and work-based social contacts to the social and
psychological periphery, concentrating their social and emotional energy
in the family and in private associations outside the work milieu. Lockwood
and Goldthorpe argue that the modern worker does precisely this, and so
largely cuts himself off from collective sources of class consciousness.

In Durkheim's work, the concept of 'egoism' may be said to correspond
roughly to privatization – a notion of social and moral dissociation from
collective life – but again, what is seen as a temporary pathology by
Durkheim has been seen as a central sociological tendency by later writers.

Herbert Marcuse's *One Dimensional Man* argued that private dreams of
material consumption had invaded and overwhelmed the cultural imagination of people in contemporary society.[68] American sociologists concluded that contemporary social consciousness was greatly confined within
the narrow structures of suburban life, or within the particular sensibilities
of immigrant and ethnic groups – groups defined by intimate ties of family
and neighbourhood.[69] Some sociological writing was more sympathetic
with Durkheim's theme – the thesis of the structural convergence of
industrial societies[70] rested squarely on a special form of the argument that
the division of labour has a broadly uniform effect in shaping modern social
structures. But at the middle range of sociological analysis it is more
common to find the argument that work experience is a source of alienation
and the work milieu a source of psychological indifference. Everett Hughes's
Men and their Work shows how non-work roles and non-work associations
penetrate and intersect with the work milieu. Peter Berger's *The Human
Shape of Work*[71] followed in much the same tradition, arguing for a three
fold division between (a) work roles which were socially and psychologi-
cally satisfying, (b) work experience which was 'alienative' and (c) work
roles and experience which were treated with routine indifference. (See
above on the sociology of occupation, pp. 65ff.)

Instrumentalism

Closely linked, in Lockwood and Goldthorpe's account, with privatization, is
the notion of *instrumentalism*: 'The meaning which workers gave to the
activities and relationships of work was a predominantly instrumental one;
work was defined and experienced essentially as a means to the pursuit of
ends outside of work and usually ones relating to standards of domestic
living.'[72]

Their analysis suggests the progressive dominance of instrumental
attitudes, unchecked by any moral force of a class character or otherwise.

More than this, Lockwood and Goldthorpe suggest that the instrumental attitude may be conceived as the basis of a largely 'rational' relationship between employer and employee. As long as relatively full employment persists (this was written in the late 1960s) and high wage industries prosper, demands are made and met, bargains are struck and the parties are satisfied. All this sounds uncommonly like Durkheim's description of a 'sociological monstrosity', in which agreements based solely on interests are mere truces in a protracted state of antagonism. Lockwood and Goldthorpe's notion of instrumental collectivism – where individual interests are projected on to a collective plane as long as the collective body, typically the trade union, appears likely to deliver the goods – bears a striking similarity to Durkheim's concept of corporate egoism, by which he intended to signify that the collective expression of individual wants did not relieve them of their egoistic character.[73] Unlike the later Goldthorpe article (see above) this study raised several relevant Durkheimian themes without ever treating them as the central issue.

Concluding comments

Durkheim's writings on the division of labour, professional groups, industrial conflict and social solidarity form, in his own hands, a consistent and generalized theory of advanced societies. Notwithstanding the emphasis on 'abnormal forms', his work envisages a progressive consolidation and co-ordination of economic, political and social life towards a planned and regulated industrial order, matched by political democracy and individual liberty, and by a balance of social freedom and restraint. In later writers influenced by his ideas, there has been a tendency for the component elements of his general theory to 'fly apart', and for particular arguments to be emphasized at the expense of others. This was seen to be especially true of Elton Mayo and the Human Relations school of industrial sociology, and of the post-war American industrial sociologists, who took the theme of group integration and made it the centrepiece of a sociology of 'belonging' or 'participation'.

The application of the concept of economic anomie to industrial and social discontents in Britain in the 1960s and 1970s involved a more rounded view of Durkheim's arguments but ran into difficulties which may be seen as being implicated in those arguments themselves. The more the question of solidarity in industrial societies is seen to draw in questions of inequality, property relations and class conflict, the more these sociologists have faced the difficulties of achieving successful reconstruction of the industrial social order, especially to the extent that this appears to necessitate a radical detachment of political power from private property. In any case, this later and broader application of Durkheim's theories illustrated, by its emphasis on 'anomie', that it was Durkheim's analysis of economic and social malaise which had caught the attention rather than his evolutionary view of the transition from ancient to modern societies.

Durkheim's emphasis on professional or occupational groups – more generally, as we shall see in other chapters, on *secondary groups* – has occasionally been taken up. But a compelling theme of modern sociology – the theme of privatization – is almost entirely absent from his work. If it appears that pathological individualism – the absence of regulation, i.e. anomie – has persisted in the modern economy, then it may appear that 'egoism' – pathological individualism and dissociation – has persisted in the privatized structures of modern social life. At least those social groupings which *have* been seen as providing a collective locus of social and symbolic attachment – the ethnic group, the traditional 'one-class' neighbourhood, the private networks of family and friends – do not correspond to the occupational groupings of Durkheim's expectations, nor do they meet the function, of linking the individual to the state, which Durkheim foresaw for the 'secondary group'.

3

✠✠

Political power, democracy and the modern state

Durkheim's politics were exemplified in his active public career; a certain political 'temper' or posture is evident in his total sociology and there are those of his writings which were directly addressed to the nature of political institutions. This chapter will be primarily concerned with the last, that is his political sociology, his commentary on the state and democracy. The first two chapters cover much of the other questions: chapter 1 deals with his public career,[1] and both chapters deal with the political implications of his writings on the division of labour. His stress on the importance of secondary associations is common to his analysis of the division of labour and of the political state. This requires some carrying forward of the materials of chapter 2, but in the present chapter citations of his views on secondary groups will be mostly confined to those directly relevant to his view of the state.

Chapter 1 dealt with the claim that his work should be regarded as the foundation of sociological conservatism.[2] One aspect of this debate is given further attention in the present chapter, and that is the question of his sociological posture towards religion. There are two reasons for this. One is that his emphasis on religion has been taken as a mark of a basically conservative attitude to authority, common belief and social control in the modern state; the second is that his attitude to religion leads directly into the question of morality in the realm of political power and authority. His views on the state, social control and discipline are further illustrated in chapter 5 on education, and in chapter 6 on the law and deviance; his sociology of religion *per se* is discussed in chapter 7. The present chapter will (a) provide a guide to his major writings on political questions, (b) discuss his view of the state and democracy, (c) illustrate his political sociology by reference to his writings on war, militarism and property (leading into a general discussion of 'morality' and 'coercion' in his work) and (d) discuss the ways in which Durkheimian themes have appeared in subsequent political sociology.

The beginnings of a sociological view of the state – and of such related issues as the collective conscience and secondary groups – are contained in his work on the division of labour. A clearer view of his political sociology, however, was not so readily reached because his most explicit and protracted work on the state, the essays and lectures collected as *Leçons de sociologie*, was not published until after his death; they became available in English as *Professional Ethics and Civic Morals* in 1957.[3] The important essay 'Individualism and the intellectuals' and some shorter pieces on war, militarism and anti-Semitism were also less well known until recently.[4] Because these pieces give support to the 'reformist' interpretation of his work, earlier essays on Durkheim's politics reflect the conservative views;[5] in 1960 an excellent article by Melvin Richter began to redress the balance.[6] In 1971 Anthony Giddens devoted a long article to 'Durkheim's political sociology' and has extended his argument in other works;[7] Edward Tiryakian has treated the subject with great skill and originality in his recent contribution,[8] and the topic has received due recognition in France, most notably in J. C. Filloux's commentary in *La Science sociale et l'action*.[9]

Giddens sees *The Division of Labour* as the foundational work which established the outlines of a political and economic sociology of a radical and reconstructionist kind; these outlines were carried through in all his later work. This is set against the interpretation which sees the progressive elements of his sociology as 'petering out' in his later work. Chapter 1 of the present book largely supports Giddens's view. Some small reconciliation of the two views might be found in the recognition that Durkheim understood the social order in all its aspects as a *moral order*;[10] he understood all facts, including political and economic facts, as moral facts in the sense that they all pointed to an explanation of solidarity, that is they pointed towards an understanding of the quality of social bonds as guided by moral ideas. We shall take up this issue in detail in the present chapter.

Durkheim's view of religion as it bears upon his politics

We have seen that an emphasis on Durkheim's fascination with religion has been taken to support a conservative view of his work. In particular we have encountered the claim that Durkheim concluded that some form of collective conscience as represented in mechanical solidarity was necessary in all societies. There is an alternative way of explaining why he was drawn to the study of religion, and of interpreting the conclusions he drew from his studies. He retained an interest in primitive societies (and hence in religion) because he never fully abandoned his evolutionary paradigm, nor the belief that the essential features of the modern world could be partially uncovered by understanding social facts in their simplest form. But this falls some way short of arguing that the essence of all modern facts is to be found in an understanding of their primitive forms, as if primitive forms revealed the outline of the 'same' modern forms. He does not argue for an utter discontinuity between primitive and modern; nor does he imply that by discovering the essential social fact in primitive settings we have determined its universal essence. This methodological subtlety is well illustrated by his argument with Lévy-Bruhl which we discuss in chapter 4. He accepts the existence of a profound difference between primitive and modern mentality, reflected in his portrayal of religion and science as different modes of apprehending the world; but he will not accept that these constitute two utterly different forms of thought. They are united by the fact they are 'two moments of a single evolution' and by the fact that both, however different, are founded in social organization at different stages of societal development; historically, scientific modes of thought develop *out of* religious modes of thought.

Primitive society was essentially religious, in a way which modern society could not reproduce. 'Precisely because religion is a primordial phenomenon', he wrote, 'it must yield more and more to the new social forms it has engendered.'[11] Giddens has concluded that Durkheim did not shift from one view to another, but rather that throughout his work Durkheim faced a dilemma:

The dilemma which Durkheim faced, and which was clarified – but never fully resolved – in *The Division of Labour*, stemmed, therefore, from his conviction that while 'defenders of the old economic theories are mistaken in thinking that regulation is not necessary today, the apologists of the institution of religion are wrong in believing that yesterday's religion can be useful today'.[12]

The notion that modern morality progressively acquires qualities which mark if off from previous forms is not disturbed. Indeed, '*The Elementary Forms of the Religious Life*, provides the foundation for an understanding of the processes which have led to the emergence of moral individualism.'[13] In any case the concern with morality (with moral–social facts) is the hallmark of *all* his work; he did not discover the need for morality at some later stage, rather all his work revolved around the question of *what kind* of moral order was appropriate to advanced societies. To call his search for the form, substance and institutional substrata of modern ethics a quest for a civil *religion* (by implication, an authoritative state ideology) is only to acknowledge that, on his broad understanding of religion, all moral–social facts had a 'religious' quality.

The continuing concern with the law, the state and with regulation of the intermediate institutions of society are all indications of his search for what may be called a 'a civic religion'. As Edward Tiryakian has pointed out, to derive from this quest a conversion to the Church or traditional religion would hardly square with the continuities in his views of religion and the Church in his contemporary France:

> The quest for a civil religion has to be kept in mind as one major factor if we are to make sense as to why Durkheim and so many of his ablest lieutenants devoted so much time and effort to the careful study of religious phenomena. Such an effort would otherwise appear incongruous with the Durkheimians' sympathies for laicisation, liberal republicanism, Jauressian socialism, and even anti-clericalism.[14]

The Republic's appetite for curtailing the influence of the Church had not been satisfied by the measures of 1882; the Dreyfusard victory (the release of Captain Dreyfus at the turn of the century) gave new impetus to this project. Tiryakian points out that, in the renewed debate, Durkheim's views were markedly anti-Church:

> In 1905, during the public debates over the controversial 'Loi Combes' which led to the separation of church and state, and the stripping of the Catholic Church of its own schools, Durkheim stated at a meeting of the progressive L'Union pour l'Action Morale, 'The Church from a sociological perspective is a monster.' He indicated by this he meant the Catholic Church, given its territorial vastness and multiple social constituencies, should have lost its intellectual and moral homogeneity long ago; the proposed legislation, he felt, would have the beneficial effect of stimulating the differentiation of the Church.[15]

Such evidence as this does not repudiate the importance he attached to religious phenomena but it gives no support of the thesis that he 'turned to religion' in recognition of the indispensability of religion as the foundation of social order. There are, of course, *several* senses in which a concern with religion may be tied to a conservative political perspective. We can specify three – and Durkheim can be disassociated from the first two, to be sure. First of all there is the reactionary view which finds in traditional religion images and guarantees of unquestioning respect for authority, and of a social order ordained by God. This is the view from which Durkheim most clearly departs. Secondly, we may see a modern revival of 'religion' in nationalist ideologies which demand unquestioning loyalty from citizens, and in which worship of the emblems of the state replaces traditional ritual obedience. Durkheim, as we shall see later in this chapter regarded such an elevation of the purposes and symbols of the state as a corruption of modern democracy, and as tyranny and absolutism. He tried to explain how and when democracy could be thus corrupted. Thirdly, a 'religious' view may be seen as conservative when it is linked with the idea of 'civic religion', more precisely with the view that, however vague and abstract it may be, a kind of consensus about central social and political principles *does* emerge in modern democracies, and is, to a degree, responsible for a necessary minimum of political stability.[16] This view is regarded as conservative, not because it echoes reactionary or absolutist principles, but because it is seen as overestimating the degree of consensus in modern societies *or* because it fails to recognize the precarious or ideological quality of this agreement. On this last view Durkheim may be viewed as a kind of conservative since he certainly suggested that there emerges in advanced societies a kind of collective conscience which holds dear such general principles as democracy and liberty. But he does not regard these ideas as fixed or as immune to challenge and revision. These abstract principles are only one of the forms which modern moral facts assume.

Political sociology: power authority and the moral order

The study of moral facts

In Durkheim social structures were always conceived as, in some sense, *moral* structures; social facts were conceived of as *moral* facts. Stated baldly thus, this principle is *the* principle of all Durkheim's sociology; without understanding this we cannot begin to understand any part of it. But it is not a principle whose significance can be grasped by, as it were, simply apprehending and comprehending the sentence. I have written 'were conceived in some sense'; grasping the *precise* sense in which this was so is the prerequisite to appreciating and evaluating his sociology. And if this 'intellectual grasping' of Durkheim is essential to a sympathetic appreciation of what he wrote, it is probably also necessary to an adequate construction of a critique of his sociology. For Durkheimian sociology, either as an analysis of 'what is' or as a projection of 'what must or should be', cannot be reconciled with a sociology which conceives society as an organization of interests, or as a balance or imbalance of power. This is not, as we have insisted, because he neglected to consider economic interests or political power; it is because he could, in the end, only proceed by subsuming his understanding of them in his general quest for a theory of society as a moral order.

Ordering or regulation is an inescapable fact of life; it is also a moral fact because regulation inevitably takes on a moral quality. Social life is always (morally) organized life; where forms of regulation have atrophied we are simply witnessing 'pathological forms of social life', we are emphatically not witnessing a new or different order of things, certainly not one which can be expected to endure. Social life without moral regulation is a monstrosity, it is a descent into anarchy, it is a denial of all that is elementally true of society. Moral regulation is simultaneously necessary to the health of the social order and the health of the individual. 'Individual' men and women never have lived 'free' of moral regulation; it is inconceivable that they ever will, or that social life can ever be understood *as if* they were; their freedom from regulation would indeed be no freedom at all. To imagine such a condition is to imagine anarchy in society, empty despair in the individual.

Durkheim's economic and political sociology proceeds from these presuppositions. To the extent that in so doing it neglects, or appears to leave unconsidered, *a whole terrain of sociological analysis* of power and interest, then the reason is to be found in the utter weight and consistency with which these presuppositions guide his thinking. Conversely it means that the reason for such 'neglects' are *not* to be found in *particular* analytic blindnesses, in the choice of emphasis and drift of analysis he brought to specific phases of his sociological work. It is true that specific elements of his sociology, (his analysis of say the division of labour, or of the state) can be examined separately and can be ranged against alternative analyses of the subjects. But in the end, for appreciation or critique, the reader is forced back to the guiding presuppositions of Durkheimian sociology.

'The Division of Labour'

The paramount exemplification of this principle in his economic sociology (as found in *The Division of Labour*) is contained in his critique of Spencer and utilitarian thought. Had *The Division of Labour* come later in his career we may have found that the 'negative paradigm' against which he developed his own analysis would have been Marxist rather than Spencerian. Suffice to say, at this point, that in *The Division of Labour* and related writings he tended to see them both as committing the same fundamental error, that of believing that social life organized around interests was a possible model of the actual or the 'virtual'. Economic activities had come to assume a dominating position in modern societies, and in their unprecedented growth they had acquired a certain (unhealthy) freedom from regulation. Pathological aspects of the contemporary state of affairs could not be taken as evidence that there was a class of behaviour which could escape the law of all organized social life, i.e. that it was morally regulated. To the extent that it had escaped regulation, institutional forms of regulation would be restored. Indeed the very centrality of economic institutions meant that the regulation of economic activities and the resocializing of the economy constituted the very core of the whole process of reconstruction.

This line of thought, especially that concerned with the importance of occupational groups to the moral ordering of society, therefore precedes his general outlining of a theory of the state and democracy. But it represents one of the central ideas reiterated throughout his writings on political structure – that is, it is the core of the belief in the necessity of fostering intermediate groups and institutions. As we turn from *The Division of Labour* to those writings in which his political sociology is more explicitly developed, we shall continue to find the recurring mention of the importance of secondary groups as constituting perhaps almost the defining and guiding idea; it is therefore as well to keep the origins of the idea in mind (see chapters 1 and 2).

Authority, the state and democracy

When Durkheim remarked 'tout dans le contrat n'est pas contractuel' he intended to indicate that a convergence or balancing of interests could never be the whole basis of economic relationships; from the point of view of analysis there was more to be said, from the point of view of social order (solidarity), more was necessary. An economic relationship was a social relationship which was bound to draw parties together in a way which also entailed some kind of moral bond. For example the contractual relationship also implied (over and above balancing of interest) the moral respect which the parties had for the contract, or it implied an awareness of those collective ideas which served to gauge whether a contract was just. Thus, as we suggested above, the analysis of economic relations is 'drawn into' the analysis of the moral bond and social solidarity. In the sphere of *political* sociology there is a certain parallel to be found in his understanding of power and authority, a parallelism in which 'economic interest' may be equated with 'naked power', and 'morally grounded interdependence' with 'authority'. There are three ways in which this parallel can be traced.
1 The power-interest dimensions are seen as indications of pathological (i.e. unhealthy) states of society, i.e. where power is 'naked'; where economic interest alone unites, we are seeing the symptoms of social pathology.
2 The concepts power-interest can never be sufficient to understand the full nature of the structures to which they refer.
3 The true analysis of power and interest must be drawn into the analysis of authority and moral bonds in order to make the analysis understandable in the context of Durkheim's view of the total social process.
It is interesting to note that Durkheim does speak of 'coercion' in both contexts; in the economic context he speaks of the forced division of labour where some parties to a contract have little real contractual choice because of the gross inequality of material circumstance; in the political context he means power without authority.

Coercion in economic relationships is a symptom of social pathology because, firstly it indicates a systematic inequality in the face of which socio-economic links can never be expected to fulfil their historical role of supplying the basis of solidarity; secondly because only the spontaneous division of labour can give rise to solidarity; thirdly because what should be one of the links in a solidary chain (just contracts) are merely truces in an underlying war. Coercion in political relationships constitutes a symptom of the failure or weakness of moral authority; similarly it can never be expected to endure as the basis of order. (In the field of education – see chapter 5 – he rejects forms of discipline which rely on coercion – punishment – rather than on appeals to the legitimacy of the constraint. Increasingly the person subject to discipline in an advanced society – be it discipline in the classroom, discipline in accepting moral and legal regulation in economic transactions, discipline in submitting to political authority – must accept the moral basis of his or her submission to this discipline.) Therefore, in Durkheim's work, forms of coercive power – military power, centralized state power, absolutist forms of government – are pathological and fragile, and do not accord with the main features of modern social development, all of which 'push' society towards the greater realization of democracy. This perspective on coercion in the economy and in the polity comes together in his rejection of proposals for state control of the economy; to place the economy in the hands of the state is not to cure the problem of solidarity in either the state or the economy; in both spheres the solution to the problem of solidarity lies in the generation of forms of moral regulation which are not imposed arbitrarily on people in society.[17]

The appearance of society as a mass of 'unorganized individuals' may make the solution of state control seem attractive; but where society itself does not, through the development of moral regulation in secondary groups, sufficiently provide the means of organization and moral order, the specialized organ of the state cannot be expected to provide this control. It can only impose its will on citizens in a way that is artificial, wholly 'external' and dangerous: 'A society composed of an infinite number of unorganized individuals, that a hypertrophied state is forced to oppress and contain, constitutes a veritable sociological monstrosity.'[18]

The thought is extended in *Professional Ethics* when he comments on the absence of moral regulation in 'the greater part of social functions', i.e. in the economic sphere: 'What is to become of public morality if there is so little trace of the principle of duty in this whole sphere that is so important in the social life?'[19]

It is precisely in these conditions that some may turn to the state as the necessary organ of control; but to do so is only to compound the problem, for the state cannot 'cure' a problem which in effect lies outside itself:

Let us imagine what would happen to the functions of the heart, lungs, stomach, and so on, if they were free like this of all discipline . . . Just such a spectacle is presented by nations where there are no regulative organs of economic life. To be sure, the social brain, that is, the State, tried hard to take their place and carry out their functions. But it is unfitted for it and its intervention, when not simply powerless, causes troubles of another kind.[20]

In both spheres then – bare interest in the economic sphere, naked power in the political sphere – there is the spectre of a sociological monstrosity.

This discussion not only explains why Durkheim did not, for the most part, discuss 'power' as the critical element in his political sociology, but also begins to reveal the meaning which he attached, diffusely throughout his writings, to the preferred term 'authority'. Things (laws, moral rules, regular patterns of action, institutions) carry authority when they are grounded in the true (healthy) nature of social life. On Durkheim's conception of society, which allowed for the distinction between healthy and pathological forms of social life, it was possible to determine those social facts which contributed to solidarity and could be seen as 'virtual' tendencies, i.e. tendencies which formed part of the progressive healthy development of society embodying all those values which modern social development had elevated to the highest point. When moral control emerged in this way (in economic or political life) men could accept constraint because they recognized the need for it. This moral self-consciousness is the true basis of the modern citizens' participation in the state, it is the essence of democracy. 'Democracy . . . is the political system which best conforms to our present day notion of the individual . . . The personality can only be itself to the degree in which it is a social entity that is autonomous in action.'[21] This autonomy itself is socially grounded for it is the *social* development of advanced societies – the process of differentiation – which has created the social basis of the value placed on individuality. Thus, in a sense, the individual receives everything from the social milieu, but whether he feels this as coercion or not depends on his consciousness of the *raison d'être* of constraint. And men cannot, of course, ever be expected to accept constraint which is unjust, arbitrary and not grounded in the healthy 'nature of things':

There are two ways in which a human being can receive help from exterior forces. Either he receives them passively, unconsciously, without knowing why – and in this case, he is only a thing. Or, he is aware of what they are, of his reasons for submitting and being receptive to them; in that case he is not passive, he acts consciously and of his own accord, knowing well what he is about.[22]

Freedom, as he repeats in different forms in his work, is not to be found in release from constraint; it is to be found in moral acceptance of the necessity for constraint; and this level of self-consciousness can only be expected to develop in a democracy, that relationship between state and society in which the state is responsive to the nature of things in society because of its lively connection with flourishing intermediate groups in the social order:

> To be autonomous means, for the human being, to understand the necessities he has to bow to and accept them with full knowledge of the facts. Nothing that we do can make the law of things other than they are, but we free ourselves of them in thinking of them, that is making them ours by thought. This is what gives democracy a moral superiority. Because it is a system based on reflection, it allows the citizen to accept the laws of the country with more intelligence and thus less passively. Because there is a constant flow of communication between selves and the state, the state is for individuals no longer like a force that imparts a wholly mechanical impetus to them. Owing to constant exchanges between them and the state, its life becomes linked with theirs just as their life does with that of the state.[23]

We can see that his conception of morality (of 'moral autonomy') was strongly implicated in his understanding of the state and democracy. We now turn to the way in which his prognosis of healthy social development was contained within his use and definition of these two terms.

Intermediate groups, the state and democracy

The idea of the importance of secondary or intermediate groups had been staked out in the first edition of *The Division of Labour*. This idea was elaborated in the preface to the second edition, and extended in *Suicide* and in the essays collected as *Professional Ethics and Civic Morals* (see chapters 1 and 2). It is not surprising therefore to find it at the heart of his discussion of political society, the state and democracy, both in *defining* them and in subjecting them to analysis. A political group is simply defined as one in which there has developed a distinction or opposition between governing and governed, between 'authority and those subject to it'; some simple societies may indeed have barely established this distinction and as such fall outside the definition. But we do not truly have 'political society' until, in the process of aggregation, societies with some form of unitary authority come to incorporate multiple secondary groups: 'We should then define the political society as one formed by the coming together of a rather larger number of secondary social groups, subject to the same one authority which is not itself subject to any other superior authority duly constituted'.[24]

He refines his definition in several ways. He points out that authority may be found in other institutions, such as the family, but the family is not, as such, 'political'. He accepts that in federal systems there are elements of cession of authority by political societies but argues that the *fundamental* process is a continuum of incorporation in which 'the major political societies are formed by gradual aggregation of the minor'.[25] The exercise of sovereign authority in a political society progressively gives rise to a functionally specific organ (the state) whose agents apply the rules of political morality determining the relation of individuals to the sovereign authority; the state is to be distinguished from the broader political society:

> We apply the term state more especially to the agents of the sovereign authority, and 'political society' to the complex group of which the state is the highest organ. This being granted, the principal duties under civic morals are obviously those which the citizen has towards the state, and, conversely those the state owes to the individual.[26]

The state then, in advanced societies, has become a highly specialized institution, whose directive functions are important, but it is not to be understood as 'above' society. It *is* dependent on society in the sense of being a development of society; society is prior to the state; it is *not* dependent on society in the sense of 'merely' reflecting the social will, for the state must retain its capacity to guide society and to direct it through the concentration of social intelligence in this organ of society. (We shall discuss this again in the context of democracy and the relation between the state and the more general 'collective conscience'.)

It is interesting to note that Durkheim insists upon this notion of 'specialized agents' engaged in thinking out social policy as the core of his definition of the state. By contrast with other definitions and usages it is a restrictive definition, signifying the balance between the importance he attached to state action and the apprehensions he felt about an over-powerful state. Some Marxist (or Marxisant) definitions, such as Miliband's in *The State in a Capitalist Society*, tend to draw a wide range of institutions into their scope.[27] Miliband speaks of state and 'quasi-state' institutions, thereby including not only the central organs of government but also the media, the education system, the Church, the police and the military. In Durkheim's definition at least (in which prescriptive and analytic elements were always fused) he insists on the error of drawing these kinds of institutions into the ambit of the state, even when he acknowledges the necessity for the state to relate itself to them. For much of his argument was concerned with the balance to be achieved in the state's relations with related institutions and secondary groups. It had a role to play (in directing and guiding) which required the state to be in contact with other institutions; but the state must not be permitted to overwhelm them or become remote from them (cf. his comments on the state and education). In emphasizing the 'intelligence' function of the state he even seeks to mark off (as the true core of the state) its reflective activities from the executive functions which are purely administrative. Administrative bodies may carry out changes but strictly speaking 'the state is the very organ of social thought . . . its principal function is to think'.[28]

The definition of democracy in Durkheim's work grows directly out of this discussion of the nature of the relationship between the state and an advanced polymorphous society. As ever, quite unafraid to disregard conventional definitions and conceptions of such terms he gives his own special force to 'democracy' by making it denote a healthy condition of the relationship between state and society. This is found, as we have seen, when well-developed secondary groups provide a moral and social centre for individual lives, when these groups are closely, but not too closely, articulated with the state, when the state can protect the individual from being a captive of the secondary groups to which he belongs, and is itself in contact with these groups without 'overpowering' them. This is democracy. One essential characteristic is the high level of awareness of political life – 'a democracy may then appear as the political system by which a society can achieve a consciousness of itself in its purest form'.[29] In Giddens's summation: 'A democratic system thus presupposes a balance between two opposed tendencies: on the one hand, that in which the state directly reflects the "general will", and the other in which the absolutist state, "closed in upon itself", is cut off from the people.'[30]

Threats to democracy; the state being too weak, too strong

At this point we encounter, in Durkheim's account, a web of argument of some considerable subtlety and complexity, and of no little contemporary relevance. My attention was drawn to it almost entirely by two excellent pieces of writing by Anthony Giddens, 'Durkheim's political sociology' and his introduction to *Emile Durkheim: Selected Writings*. In the latter he also translates a part of the 'Deux lois de l'évolution penale', an infrequently cited article, by Durkheim, which expands in such an interesting way on the materials of 'Leçons'.[31]

In *Professional Ethics and Civic Morals* he has made it clear that while secondary groups can shield the individual from the state, the state may also be required to protect the liberties and dignity of the individual; in fact the upholding of these socially founded values is one of its most sacred tasks. So there must be a distance between the state and society; this healthy balance is the essence of his conception of democracy. The argument is furthered when Durkheim writes of the relationship between the state and collective representations, and from there extends into a provocative thesis about the origins of despotic, absolutist rule and bureaucratic inertia. At the first mention, in elaborating his definitions, he warns against confusing the collective activity of the state with the collective representations of society.[32] The former refers to the collective aspect of the 'thinking' of the state, that is to the fact that when agents of the state reflect upon, say, the directions to be taken in a given reform, they are generating and discussing ideas which have a collective aspect because they refer to the common fate of the society. But these reflections are precise, scientific and highly self-conscious. By contrast the term 'collective representations of society' denotes the ideas commonly held in the nation, what we might call public opinion, expressions of the people's values and sentiments. These are more general, vague and diffuse; they may also be less well founded and more subject to change. There are obvious dangers in the state simply responding to and receiving these collective representations; in some cases it may even have to act against them – this last showing that Durkheim believed that the state may acquire a wisdom greater than that of the people. The state is sensitive to collective representations, it does not take them as its own thoughts: 'The state is not simply an instrument for canalizing and concentrating . . . It is in a certain sense, the organizing centre for the secondary groups themselves . . . It is not accurate to say that the state embodies the collective consciousness, for that goes beyond the state at every point.'[33] And so he comes seriously to question the idea of the state as 'mandated by the electorate', indeed in some passages questions the very idea of a 'mass' electorate in a conventional sense. It is wrong to view democracy as realized in the mandated state, for this only signifies the absorption of the state by society, a kind of inability of the directive agency to free itself from the dictates of the popular will as expressed in a moment.

If the state does no more than receive individual ideas and volitions to find out which are the most widespread and 'in the majority', as it is called, it can bring no contribution truly its own to the life of society . . . The role of the State in fact, is not to express and sum up the unreflective thought of the mass of the people but to superimpose on this unreflective thought a more considered thought.[34]

To argue otherwise would be to reduce the modern state to the condition of 'so-called primitive democracies' and the state 'would only allow those sentiments to prevail which seemed to have the most general currency'. Modern societies cannot recreate the conditions of primitive societies; traditionalism has lost its sway and traditional ideas are challenged at every turn; but new ideas have not readily taken shape to replace the old, at least not with the kind of depth and serious reflection that is required. Herein lies one great danger in modern democracies, when 'all becomes a matter of controversy and division':

There is no firm ground under the feet of society. Nothing any longer is steadfast. And since the critical spirit is well developed and everyone has his own way of thinking, the state of disorder is made even greater . . . Hence the chaos seen in certain democracies, their constant flux and instability. There we get an existence subject to sudden squalls, disjointed, halting and exhausting. *If only this state of affairs led to any real change* [my emphasis]. But those that do come about are often superficial. For great changes require time and reflection for sustained effort. It often happens that all these day-to-day modifications cancel each other out and that in the end the state remains utterly stationary. Those societies that are so stormy on the surface are often bound to routine.[35]

Giddens has suggested that here lies in Durkheim's writings a latent theory of bureaucracy:

A bureaucratic state, in which officialdom possesses the real power and, thereby, through adherence to bureaucratic routine promotes the maintenance of the *status quo*, is more likely to arise where the state is weak than where it is strong. In an absolutist state, although the officialdom may be used as an instrument of the domination of ruler or of an oligarchy, it is not the officials who dominate. But as in France, where the state tends 'to become absorbed' this situation of apparent democracy actually conceals a bureaucratic domination.[36]

The thought is extended in the 'Deux lois' where he draws out the implications of his earlier distinction between repressive and restitutive law, characteristic of simple and advanced societies. A crime in a primitive society is a transgression against the collectivity, and is therefore a religious transgression punished by violent repression. But democracy, as we have seen Durkheim argue, is not *assured* in advanced societies, especially when secondary groups are weak and the state is absorbed into society. In a phrase 'the nature of political power in a given form of society cannot simply be treated as a consequence of changes on the level of infrastructure'.[37] In pathological conditions the modern state may take on some of the characteristics of the primitive: 'This "religious" quality [of crime and punishment] is appropriated by the absolutist state, and that enables it to legitimate the use of coercive power: offences against the state are treated as "sacrilege" and hence to be violently repressed.'[38]

In his concluding comments Durkheim again argues that it is the strength of secondary groups (and not the state of advancement alone) which determines the character of political power.

So that our political malaise is due to the same cause as our social malaise; that is, to the lack of secondary cadres to interpose between the individual and the state. We have seen that these secondary groups are essential if the state is not to oppress the individual; they are also necessary if the state is to be sufficiently free from the individual.[39]

The growth of a wide range of state functions is not to be taken as the index of the over-powerful or absolutist state. Only in the advanced society, when this is combined with weak secondary groups, do we face the danger of absolutism. In primitive societies, secondary groups are typically less developed, but state functions are also narrow in range, and thus stability is enforced by the collective power of tradition. So, in primitive society we find a less developed state government and relentless traditionalism: in modern societies lacking in secondary associations we find weak government swayed by public opinion, controversy, vacillation, all the appearance of change but a reality of routine and rigidity. In modern societies only one form of secondary group can adequately fill the hiatus in the social structure – professional or occupational groups:

> The permanent groups, those to which the individual devotes his whole life, those for which he has the strongest attachment, are the professional groups. It therefore seems indeed that it will be they which may be called upon to become the basis of our political representation as well as of our social structure in the future.[40]

Durkheim's theory applied: his sociology of the state and the question of militarism and war

His essays on militarism and war present us with an opportunity to see his sociology of the state applied to a current issue. The role of the military in modern societies became an issue in the Dreyfus affair and Durkheim took up this theme in his *Enquête sur la militarisme* in 1899, a year after he had made his distinguished reply to Brunetiere's attack on the intellectuals. (He also wrote some notes on anti-Semitism, another strand of the Dreyfus controversy.)[41] When war did come in 1914 Durkheim wrote two political pamphlets directed at German militarism. Taken together these documents give us an interesting insight into his view of the ultimate resort to coercion in political affairs. They also further illustrate his evolutionary view of society – militarism was a characteristic of pre-modern societies:

> Concerning militarism, he held that it 'no longer has, should not have, a moral value', and that its present recrudescence was abnormal, due to temporary circumstances, and the exorbitant prestige of the army. Contemporary France needed 'qualities of another sort – those of the scientist, the engineer, the doctor, the industriel', and French men should pursue other goals: 'respect for the law, love of liberty, a proper concern for duties and responsibilities, whether they derive from individuals or society, and the desire for a more equitable distributive justice'.[42]

His brief comment in *Civic Morals* portrays war as a characteristic of pre-modern societies. War in the past has given the state a pretext to interfere where it should not. 'But, today, in war we have something of an anomalous survival and gradually the last traces of it are to be wiped out.' The complexities of modern industrial societies require that the state directs all its energies towards regulation of social life – it should have none left for the prosecution of war:

> Once, the action of the State was directed entirely outwards; now inevitably it tends more and more to turn inwards . . . The planning of the social milieu so that the

individual may realize himself more fully, and the management of the collective apparatus in a way that will fall less hard on the individual; an assured and amicable exchange of goods and services, and the cooperation of all men of goodwill towards an ideal they share without any conflict; in these surely we have enough to keep public activity fully employed . . . societies will have a growing need to concentrate their energies on themselves to husband their strength, instead of expending them outwards in violent demonstrations.[43]

This passage illustrates both his evolutionary view of progressive social change and his mental image or 'model' of the stable advanced society. The argument is not very convincing. The expectation that societies pre-occupied with internal development would have little energy for war seems rather forlorn, especially if we set it against the argument that militaristic gestures and war itself are often traceable to the internal political and economic strains of nation-states. But it was even enough for Durkheim to endorse Spencer's argument that 'military' societies were a thing of the past:

This is where Spencer's arguments have some plausibility. He saw clearly that the receding of war and of the social forms or methods bound up with it was certain to affect the life of all societies very deeply. But it does not follow that this recession of war leaves no other sustenance for social life than economic interests and that there must inevitably be a choice between militarism and commercialism.[44]

In other words the recession of war does not mean that the state becomes entirely concerned with production and consumption. The view of the state as the mere regulator of economic production and consumption (the socialist formula) was narrow and mistaken in its view of man's needs:

it is not simply that everyone should have access to rich supplies of food and drink. Rather that it is that each one should be treated as he deserves, each be freed from an unjust and humiliating tutelage, and that, in holding to his fellows and his group, a man should not sacrifice his individuality. And the agency on which this special responsibility lies is the state. So the State does not inevitably become either simply a spectator of social life (as the economists would have it) in which it intervenes only in a negative way, or (as the socialists would have it), simply a cog in the economic machine. It is above all, supremely the organ of moral discipline.[45]

One of the principal duties of the state, then, is to preserve individual rights, to foster the conditions in which individuality can flourish. It protects the individual, but does not have decisive power over the individual. War can and does give undue power to the state; war thus endangers human rights:

War of course leads to a disregard of individual rights. It demands severe discipline and this discipline in turn presupposes a strongly entrenched authority . . . The state, on the strength of this authority, has intervened in fields which by their nature should remain alien to it. It controls religious beliefs, industry, and so on, by regulation. But this unwarranted spread of its influence can only be justified wherever war plays an important part in the life of a people. The more it retreats, the less often it occurs, the more possible and imperative it becomes to disarm the state.[46]

Further indications of Durkheim's attitude to war, militarism and nationalism are given by two pamphlets *Qui a voulu la guerre?* and *L'Allemagne au-dessus de tout*, addressing themselves to the question of blame for the war, and to the work of German philosophers whom he believed to have led German culture along a path of destructive nationalism.[47] Both written during the First World War, they may be regarded as tracts rather than objective analyses; Lukes says the first 'stands up remarkably well to the historical record', giving a plausible interpretation of German and Austrian diplomatic manoeuvres as designed (by Germany) to provoke the war; the second he describes as 'altogether less coolly written'. Bottomore is less forgiving:

Durkheim's two pamphlets written during the First World War show a total disregard – astonishing for a sociologist – for the social causes of the war; the first provides a brief diplomatic history of the events leading up to the war, intended to demonstrate German guilt, while the second naively analyses the 'German mentality' as 'a system of ideas made for war' arising from Germany's 'will for power'.[48]

From the point of view of a political economy of war, Bottomore is right of course; Durkheim's analysis is confined almost exclusively to the ideas, rather than the material conditions, which inform the war-like 'mentality'. But his comments in *L'Allemagne au-dessus de tout* do demonstrate that it is impossible to reconcile his sociology with deification of the nation-state:

There is no state so great that it can govern eternally against the wishes of its subjects and force them, by purely external coercion, to submit to its will. There is no state so great that it is not merged within the vaster system of other states, and that does not, in other words, form part of the general human community, and that owes nothing to this. There is a universal conscience and a universal opinion, and it is no more possible to escape the empire of these than to escape that of physical laws, for they are forces which, when they are violated, react against those who offend them. A state cannot survive that has humanity arrayed against it.[49]

It may be thought that here Durkheim is responding to the pressing circumstances of 1916; but his thoughts on coercion, the limits of state power and the emergence of a universal morality are entirely in accord with similar themes written much earlier. Anxious as he was to promote the French war effort, he was disturbed by tendencies to allow the French war cause to justify blind nationalism.[50]

It is also interesting to note that Durkheim's comments here give no support to the argument that his understanding of the importance of the 'moral fabric of society' permitted a kind of social–moral relativism which would tolerate or justify unjust or barbaric social orders. It has been suggested that functionalist argument, stemming from Durkheim's influence in social anthropology, led anthropologists to insist on viewing any moral code as performing an integral function in the society in which it developed. This was then seen as a means of rescuing 'primitive' cultures from ethnocentric judgements. But, the argument goes, relativism faced a contradiction in apparently having to accept (on such relativist grounds) the inhumanity of the Third Reich (or any other barbaric society) – as against upholding universalist principles of civilization, justice and morality. Durkheim does not appear to be in any difficulty here, and it is clear that it is wrong to deduce this kind of relativism from his sociology. He sees German society as not only barbaric, not only an abnormality, but as contrary to universal principles of morality true for all advanced societies – a morality to which it will, in the long run, have to bow.

War, property, coercion; Durkheim's political sociology

These comments on war by Durkheim, do provide enormous insight into his sociological ideal of the state, and substantially refute some of the less temperate charges made against his work. But this is a far cry from claiming that they constitute an adequate sociology of war in the context of an adequate political sociology. Bottomore's blunt criticism surely has substantial justice on its side; Durkheim's analysis is almost entirely 'idealistic' or 'ideological'. This may seem odd for a sociologist who insisted on analysis of social facts *as they are* as against their reflections in the minds of men (i.e. as opposed to what he termed a 'purely ideological analysis'). But while Durkheim's sociology may be regarded as intensely idealistic in some of its phases, a better answer may be found in discarding the simple distinction between 'idealist' and 'materialist'. Durkheim did insist on the observation of 'social facts'; and he did see society in material terms, in terms of the division of labour. But, in Durkheim's understanding, there is no social fact, no actual arrangement of social relations between men, which does not simultaneously give rise to a moral fact. That is, the social relations between men necessarily give rise to customary beliefs about how men ought to relate to each other. Such beliefs are by definition 'moral' and these moral facts, attaching themselves to social facts, solidify and hence become a part of the natural order of things. Treating social facts as things means treating the moral language of social relations as things; it means treating moral facts as things. If for example the increasing organic interdependence of complex societies has 'freed' men and women from the social relations of homogeneous and traditional societies, has made 'individuals' of them, it has at the same moment given birth to a socially grounded faith in individuality; individualism is a moral and social fact. Therefore when Durkheim speaks of morals it is on this understanding. If Durkheim's sociology is in error, the error is to be found in the core of this critical argument about the nature of man, morals and society.

This methodological question is not one to be solved by a wave of the hand in a sentence or two. But the more we look at Durkheim's sociology, the more we see that his sociological arguments can only be understood by understanding this methodological point of view, and the more we see that criticism of his sociology is bound, if not always to start here, at least constantly to return to this point.

At the very least, in the context of his political sociology, we can see that it appears to have led him to a vast underestimation of the compelling coercive facts of social and political life. We can also see that the emphasis he places on the moral qualities of social life time and again leads him to replace analysis of the actual condition of social relations with an analysis of the moral forms which they produce, or are expected to produce. In other words, for all the insistence on the social infrastructure of moral facts, a gap enlarges between the analysis of the infrastructure and analysis of the moral beliefs. This is partly caused by his tendency to neglect the importance of what he knew to be true – the fact that moral forms had *not* developed, in response to social changes, in the way he believed to be necessary. It could well be argued, of course, that his understanding of *what kind of* moral forms were entailed in the sociological structures of advanced societies was an altogether faulty one, or that his very infrastructural analysis – his evolutionary model of social differentiation – was seriously flawed. What is certain is that he *did* believe that the evolution of moral conscience *was* tied to the evolution of social structure, that despite the agonies of transition from traditional to modern forms, the basis of a humanly 'satisfactory' or 'healthy' moral conscience was to be found in the emergent social structures of modernity. It is also undeniable that, once all these equations had been made in Durkheim's mind, the immensity of the distance between actual social structures and emergent moral structures receded almost tragically from his view. How else can we explain (what on a simpler view may be viewed as sheer blind optimism) his expectation that war was destined to 'recede as a social fact'? Optimism seems hardly the right word for such a sociological conclusion.

When we examine them closely we find that his views on war and property – two outstanding signifiers of coercion in political and economic life – alike betray what, for brevity, we may call his 'evolutionary optimism'. We have just seen that he sees the war-like state as a function of pre-modern social structures and that he endorsed Spencer's evolutionary thesis concerning the replacement of military societies by industrial societies. From here he proceeds to view the state prepared for war as abnormal in the modern context and the social and ideological configurations of a war-like state as abnormal; the abnormal is destined (and we may well ask why) to disappear. (In Durkheim the answer to my parenthetical 'why' seems to be that men and women will not long endure abnormal, unhealthy, repressive regimes; see the quotation below on economic anarchy.)

The same kind of thinking appears in his view of property. In so far as the inequality which property and inheritance represent is an unhealthy social fact, it is destined to recede. Property in any case has traditionally been held and passed on through the institution of the family and the family itself is waning as a social institution. To be sure, men must set their minds to correcting the pathologies of the disposition of property, to evolving new institutional and moral forms of property; at the same time the virtual evolutionary development can be expected to take its course. When he is stressing the actual and extensive insufficiency of the present state of affairs he appears to be under no illusion as to the nature of the real struggles entailed in economic conflict; at the same moment the assertive 'inevitability' of healthy development is re-stated (he is discussing the anarchy of economic relations):

There is a head-on clash when the moves of rivals conflict, as they attempt to encroach on another's field or to beat him down or drive him out. Certainly the *stronger succeed in crushing the not so strong* [my emphasis] or at any rate in reducing them to a state of subjection. But since this subjection is only a *de facto* condition sanctioned by no kind of morals, it is accepted only under duress *until the longed-for day of revenge* [my emphasis].[51]

The 'stronger' parties to contracts are indeed those with riches at their disposal, those who own property, and his comments on property in *Civic Morals* make it clear that he not only sees material inequality as a fundamental obstacle to solidarity, but also sees the disposition of property as a critical source of this inequality. It is true that he sees the main reason for this to be the fact that inherited wealth violates a fundamental emergent *moral principle* of advanced societies, that men should be rewarded according to the contribution they make: 'The property of individuals should be the counterpart of the services they have rendered in society.'[52] Nonetheless he has reached a position where he is bound to give active consideration to property. The discussion is far from clear, though he leaves little doubt about some of his conclusions. On the whole he appears to endorse the abolition of the inheritance of property, a simple matter, he implies, where there is no will (testament), a delicate matter when 'it is a question of testamentary inheritance in direct descent'.[53] We may expect some resistance to abolition, not, interestingly enough, because individuals can be expected to defend their material interest, but because 'a kind of conflict arises between our sense of justice and certain family customs that are very deeply rooted'. However, inheritance is destined to disappear because it is irreconcilable with the modern faith in justice expressed in the demand for just contracts. Historically, property is first distributed by inheritance, then exchanged through contractual arrangements. But:

it is by contracts which inevitably are in part unjust as a result of an inherent state of inequality in the contracting parties, because of the institution of inheritance. This fundamental injustice in the right of property can only be eliminated as and when the sole economic inequalities dividing men are those resulting from the inequality of their services. That is why the redevelopment of the contractual right entails a whole recasting of the morals of property.[54]

Here then the nettle is grasped, or appears to be. At precisely this point Durkheim's argument descends into the vague formulae of evolution. Inheritance of property is historically centred upon the institution of the family, and the family is progressively losing its place in advanced social structures; so too will inheritance. Even where it survives, its importance is bound to decline. It should at least be made insignificant in the distribution of things, so that the distribution of private property through inheritance assumes a small part in the total distribution of property and therefore does not create an unequal social order. The next step is equally vague and evolutionary in the same sense. We have seen that he has argued that as the family declines, occupational groups become progressively more important and take over many of the functions of the ancient family; so with property. He appears to envisage some system in which property will be vested in corporate occupational or industrial groups and as such will not constitute private property but a kind of corporate or communal resource.[55]

Let us now recall the remarks we made a little earlier about Durkheim's methodology – his definition of moral and social facts.[56] For, in these passages of *Civic Morals* we find, alongside the evolutionary perspective, further indications of his stress on the moral quality of social facts. We have seen, for example (in the passage immediately above), that he advocates a 'recasting of the *morals* of property'; that inheritance is to recede because it offends a vital *moral* principle; that resistance to abolition can be expected because of the deep-rooted attachment to family customs. At one point the methodological position becomes more strikingly and explicitly evident. He is discussing, in effect, the labour theory of value, and repeating his consistent theme that social facts cannot be reduced to 'material' facts.

It is not the amount of labour put into a thing which makes its value; it is the way in which the value of the thing is assessed by the society, and this valuation depends not so much on the amount of energy expended, as on the useful results it produces, such at least as they are felt to be by the collectivity, for there is a subjective factor which cannot be ruled out.[57]

Few, if any, quotations from Durkheim could better illustrate the fundamental presuppositions entailed in Durkheim's political and economic sociology, or better explain the limitations it was bound to suffer. Having assessed some of the strengths and weaknesses of his theories, let us now turn to the influence he has had on later political writers, and to the uses to which his ideas have been put.

Durkheim's influence and some strands of subsequent political sociology

We have noted the argument[58] that Durkheim's stress on solidarity and moral authority laid some of the foundations of the politics of irrationality and of uncurbed nationalism. This view can be set aside, as both his practical politics and his writings on democracy and absolutism demonstrate. He would have had no sympathy for the nationalistic and anti-Semitic politics of Charles Maurras and L'Action Française which subsequently drew France towards Vichy. These were an extenuation of the Rightist views to which he had been so strenuously opposed in his life, and an extenuation with an unpleasant flavouring of irrationalism and anti-Semitism. Durkheim does speak of duty and attachment to the group, but it is clear from his language that he had in mind a sturdy sense of social obligation based on a rational appreciation of the collective good, and not a blind emotion of 'belonging'.

Nationalism and despotism in mass society

His paper attaching war blame on the Germans took its stance from an attack on the cultural nationalism and heroic postures of German philosophers and, in the same period, his horror of militarism and absolutism is clearly exhibited. But there is more to be said than this. For the German political experience of the 1930s has become, for subsequent scholars, especially those writing immediately after the war, the very model *par excellence* of totalitarianism; understanding the conditions of its rise was anxiously pursued for the lessons it could teach. Some of the lessons that were drawn bear striking resemblance to Durkheim's own anxieties concerning the fragility of democracy and the danger of absolutism. In particular, scholars have diagnosed a weakness in societies, such as the German society of the late 1920s, which prepared the ground for absolutism. Germany they argued failed to support those secondary institutions which could have prevented the power of the state falling into the hands of a small group who were then able to penetrate and dominate most of the important posts of the social order. In reliving the tragedy, historians of the Third Reich traced the crucial points at which the courts, the constitution, the education system and the trade unions had been subverted and subordinated to the will of the nation-state. This is not of course, the only or even the dominant theme in the analysis of the German descent into totalitarianism, but it is an important one, and one which accords well with Durkheim's thoughts.[59]

Durkheim's work could not be counted a major influence in Western political science and political sociology in the period from 1918 to the present and this is partly explained by the relative obscurity of his publications on this theme, by contrast with his *Methods*, *Suicide* and *Elementary Forms*.

The relative obscurity of his political publications is not the only reason for his comparatively weak representation in political studies. We have mentioned that the Durkheimian school in France, where it might have been expected to flourish most, suffered considerable decline in the 1930s. But perhaps more important than any of these reasons was the competing influence of other great strands of Western social science, many of them stemming from German traditions, which gathered strength in the 1930s and in the aftermath of the Second World War. In short order, enter Marx and enter Freud; and enter Weber. Durkheim's ideas had taken shape before Marxist thought presented itself as a great competitor in France, although, as his career progresses, we find him making increasing mention of Marxist arguments:[60] we know of the mutual unawareness of Durkheim and Weber;[61] and there is no evidence that he knew of Freud's work. Whilst the ideas of Marx, Weber, and, to some extent, Freud, have passed into the corpus of social science, in that corpus they represent quite divergent models of the study of society, its method and purpose. The claims of the competing models is a continuing debate in the philosophy of social science, a debate which is relevant but not central to the purpose of this book.

Alternative models: Durkheim in the shadows

In contradiction to Durkheim's model of sociology as the science of social and moral facts projected toward the understanding of the conditions of solidarity in advanced society, Marxist thought contained at its core a view of society as founded upon an infrastructure of relations and forces of production and class struggle, and an ideological and institutional super-structure whose forms were, in the final analysis, shaped by the underlying historical 'economic' forces. Thus the state was to be seen as a 'product' of the dominant class forces in the unfolding of the career and eventual demise of capitalism. Since, in most instances, the state was seen to be 'subservient' to the interests of the bourgeois class, it could not be expected to play the role sketched out by Durkheim, i.e. crystallizing the wisdom of society and directing it in the collective interest. The 'collective interest' can have no part in Marxist analysis of capitalism; the state does not rise above the conflict between proletariat and bourgeoisie for it is a bourgeois state; it cannot mediate between class interests, because it is a class state; the transcendence of the present social order necessarily includes the transcendence of the state – it cannot be effected *by* the state. It is true that later Marxists have substantially modified this view of the relation between the state and class struggle, and a great debate has emerged concerning the 'relative autonomy' of the state. In the last decade especially, Marxism has become a broad church. But the fundamental methodological divergence from Durkheim cannot be bridged and it means that a whole terrain of political analysis is irreconcilable with Durkheimian precepts.

Weber's sociology is also the starting point of a highly distinctive mode of analysis but its strong German intellectual antecedents also mark it off sharply from Durkheim's sociology. Perhaps the key idea in Weber's sociology is the historical process of cultural change summarized in the term 'rationalization'. The dedication to the spirit of rationality, in Weber's view, spread through economic, religious and intellectual life, found institutional expression in the process of bureaucratization, and eventually penetrated into the personal life of the citizen of the modern secular world. His analysis of bureaucratization, the disenchantment of the modern world, the tragic failure of modern institutions to provide solutions to men's persistent anxieties and social dilemmas, has been characterized as a profoundly pessimistic social doctrine. As such it contrasts sharply with Durkheim's stern and serious optimism that men could and would transcend their current difficulties and create a more 'natural' (in accord with the nature of things) and satisfying world.

In Freud's work and influence too we find the establishment of a model of man and society, penetrating sociology, psychology, medicine, the arts and anthropology, which shares little with Durkheim's perspective. It is true that Durkheim paid considerable attention to psychology and looked for great advances in a field which could not avoid shaping sociology's development. But this did not include Freud's work, and, above all, contained little hint of the impact which the ideas of repression, sublimation and the role of the unconscious were to have. To the extent that Freud influenced social science, his work diverted study towards the analysis of personality and character as forged in the collision between libidinous urges and civilization's need for repression. Durkheim did have a conception of individual motives which imparted into this theory an element of 'natural, biological' urges, which stood in need of social restraint.[62] But this was not seen as the critical locus of society and culture as it was in Freud's analysis; the hand of social restraint, in Durkheim's view, sat quite easily on the shoulder of the individual, urging him to act readily in accord with transmitted social sentiments, and self-consciously recognizing and accepting the need for restraint. Thus Marx, Freud and Weber impelled social science's concerns in directions quite divergent from those of Durkheim; although Durkheim's contribution was immense, and continues to be recognized as such, there is no doubt that for some time after his death it remained in the shadows.

Explaining totalitarianism

Sociological and psychological models

Marxist and Freudian ideas had particular impact on the question with which this section began – the explanation of the rise of totalitarianism and the subversion of democracies in Europe. The Marxist analysis focussed on the crisis of capitalism, the displaced frustrations of the German petite bourgeoisie and the collapse of German socialism which allowed German capitalism to escape its demise, and be perpetuated under the dispensation of a fascist state.[63] At the same time a social psychological school influenced by Freud sought the roots of German totalitarianism in the personality dispositions of the German people as fostered by their culture and society. This found one celebrated expression in the work of T. Adorno and associates who elaborated the concept of 'the authoritarian personality', a character structure marked by submissive acceptance of authority and a simultaneous demand for compliance and a rigid need for order. This idea of the authoritarian personality was pressed into service in the explanation of political attitudes, interpersonal modes of relating and of racism and anti-Semitism, all of which were linked, bearing the same authoritarian mark, through their common source in the personality structure. In the writings of some of the Frankfurt school, and above all in the writing of Karn Horney, Erich Fromm and Herbert Marcuse, there is an attempt to merge the Marxist and Freudian influence by setting the analysis of culture and personality in a broader framework of social structural analysis.[64] So, for example, Fromm's analytic view is one in which the social, political and economic dislocations of capitalism are matched by private discontents, capitalism being seen as a system contrary to the realization of man's true nature. In Marcuse the dominance of corporate capitalist interests, and the increasing technological power of the means of physical and cultural production, combine to produce a one-dimensional culture which stifles the emergence of contrary modes of thought. It is a profoundly pessimistic view in which the looked-for source of transcendence of capitalism, the working class, is viewed as inextricably captured by the cultural imagination of capitalism, utterly seduced by the propaganda of a way of life.[65]

Weber's pessimism is allied to the pessimism of such as Michel's 'iron law of oligarchy' which popularized the view that organizations of all kinds, even those democratic in their ideology, succumbed to the sociological laws which fostered the crystallization of power in the hands of an established few.[66] Consider, too, Marxist analysis of the contradictions of capitalism, coupled with the failure of socialist revolution to arrive in developed capitalist nations; and Weber's pessimism and the disenchanted voices of the critical sociologists. These have arisen in the present century, and have been punctuated by the tragedy of war and cultural despair. They have conspired to set a mood of sociological pessimism which, perhaps more than anything else, contrasts with the implicit optimism of Durkheim's work.

It is significant that it is chiefly in the more hopeful years that followed the close of the Second World War that we see the emergence of a sociology of social reconstruction which bears some similarities to Durkheim's project of marrying secular social science with the task of social reform. I am thinking here of the work done in the 1940s by, and work later inspired by, Karl Mannheim in England. It bears few ostensible marks of Durkheim's influence, but much of the tone, the questions addressed and the nature of the vision of possible solutions can be seen to convey a similar spirit. The Marxist tradition, then, must be seen as standing quite apart from Durkheim's, and is properly called political economy rather than sociology. As such it contained at its core what Durkheim's sociology most notably lacked – a historical theory of economic process. The coercive facts of economic relations and political power structures, relegated to 'pathological forms' in Durkheim's analysis, were at the heart of Marxism. Nonetheless, a number of commentators have hesitantly suggested some point of convergence particularly in the sociology of knowledge in which both have a conception of a social infrastructure as the foundation of forms of thought: 'We regard as fruitful this idea that social life must be explained, not by the conception of it held by those who participate in it, but by profound causes which escape consciousness'[67] – this being Durkheim's comment in review of a Marxist work on historical materialism. It is also the case that Durkheim did not seek the perfection of democracy merely in the state's protection of, and elaboration of, constitutional rights and freedom. The full achievement of the ideals of the revolution required the extension of equality and liberty in the material base of the social structure. But his ideas concerning the 'forced division of labour' are not developed, and his hesitant comments on property, inequality and the abolition of private property are ambiguous and unsatisfactory. By contrast Marx not only sees democracy in European societies as imperfect, he sees it in a sense as a sham, as bourgeois democracy which can only be transcended, perfected, in the transcendence of the bourgeoise social order. These stark divergences, particularly, in the present context, with regard to the nature and role of the state, are more compelling than any suspicions of convergence.

Erich Fromm's well-known work *The Fear of Freedom*,[68] was an attempt to merge social psychological and Marxist ideas in a diagnosis of the maladies of capitalist society, and is not therefore notably Durkheimian in inspiration. But in some respects there are convergent themes. Fromm argued that capitalist society created an illusion of freedom rather than a society of people exercising rational choices. Men are seen to be linked together in rather fragile and fleeting associations, and the whole precariousness of social life engenders anxieties about acceptance and conformity. The emphasis on consumption of material commodities and the stress on confirmation of social status combine to produce men who, rather than asserting their individuality, dissolve their true selves in the anxious pursuit of recognition, and 'market' their personalities as acceptable packages. The soulless market society excludes social bonds of genuine depth among people; the experience of 'separation' is seen to be the essence of alienation – a world of men unable to realize their true selves. There are some similar themes in the writings of Marcuse and Papenheim.[69] In so far as these works attempt to link personality and social structure to the political economy of society, they give attention, as Durkheim does, to the *fabric of social life*, to the group contexts in which men live, as an indication of the moral and ultimately political quality of modern life. Conceived in this (some would say 'sociologistic') way, this concern with *social milieu* is largely absent from Marxist analysis, but critical to Durkheimian thinking.

Durkheim: some direct and some indirect influences

Although what I have indicated in the preceding passages is something of an eclipse of Durkheimian political sociology, there are three counter-indications which we must now consider:

1 The central concerns and the guiding components of analysis – the prospectus we might say – of Durkheim's political sociology as described in the first part of this chapter – have endured and recurred in many subsequent writings, although relatively infrequently with major reliance on Durkheim as a source. These are to be found in a broad band of literature concerned with the stability and fragility of democracy, with the conditions under which liberal democracy is subverted in the direction of totalitarian societies and in a literature which places the idea

of 'mass', as a quality of social structure, as the centre of analysis. As regards explicit citation, it is a literature which frequently derives from the writings of Alexis de Tocqueville and later exponents of the theme of 'mass society'. In it, the quality of social life and institutional arrangements are seen to be the keys to the understanding of political power and authority.

2 In certain instances, most notably William Kornhauser's *The Politics of Mass Society* and more diffusely Robert Nisbet's *Community and Power* and *The Sociological Tradition*,[70] key Durkheimian concepts, most strikingly 'individualism', 'anomie' and the role of secondary groups, *have* resurfaced with evident debt to Durkheim's own work.

3 The diffusion of Durkheimian analysis through sociology (via *Suicide* rather than via his explicit political sociology) has meant that his ideas have gained influence in general sociological analysis directly or tangentially concerned with the stability of democracy and the role of the state.

It is not easy to compare and contrast a series of political thinkers even when they are evidently writing about the same phenomenon, let us say, democracy, because the explicit definition, or emergent meaning of critical terms varies so much. Durkheim's definition of democracy was rather idiosyncratic, making the present task more difficult. What he regarded as the essential features of democracy, the growth of secondary associations in the political society and the evolutionary emergence of political self-consciousness in the population, have been treated by others not as defining characteristics but as variable characteristics, democracy being defined as a form of political institutions which maximized popular participation in government. Durkheim did not attach great importance to this last, even tending to see the 'mass electorate', based simply on residence, with direct access to governance, as a threat to democracy. Whilst we cannot find in Durkheim's writings *any* shadow of the idea of different 'qualities' of people, some more suited to leadership than others, or of contempt for the mass, the form of his argument converges with those, like de Tocqueville, who saw in popular democracy the seeds of a (benevolent?) state despotism. The more that social power was expressed through political institutions, the more the populace gained access to these political institutions, the more alert man had to be to the danger of concentrating power in the state, a state responsive to majoritarian wishes – such as the demand for equality. If democracy in this way meant the elevation of mediocrity – a persistent argument, this, in conservative and liberal thinking – then the solidification of state power, sought in the name of democracy and equality, could become a source of tyranny. 'I have always thought that servitude of the regular, quiet and gentle kind . . . might be combined more easily than is commonly believed with some of the outward forms of freedom, and that it might even establish itself under the wing of the sovereignty of the people.'[71] The theme of mediocrity, debate about the quality of popular culture, about the potential tyranny of the mass, were common currency in the mid- and late nineteenth century – consider for example the writings in England of Matthew Arnold, in Europe of Kierkegaard, and later in Spain of Ortega Y. Gasset.[72] The conservative reaction to the French revolution held similar views on quite different grounds believing, in one way or another, that acceding power to 'the people' was to fly in the fact of the necessity of hierarchy. In some nineteenth-century French thought (de Gobineau is the best example) this hierarchy was explicitly racial.[73]

The *liberal* fear of the mass was not based on any such belief about the differential qualities of classes or races of men, but in the possibility of social and political processes being permitted to subvert democracy and transform it into some form of tyranny or totalitarianism. De Tocqueville detected some of these dangers in his celebrated study of America, whilst he also singled out those characteristics which constituted a prophylactic against these dangers. Among these were the independence of the judiciary, the separation of Church and state, and other constitutional guards against the over-concentration of power in the state, but none was more important than the vitality of civil associations of all kinds and the strengths of regional and community ties. As long as these social institutions flourished, individual men were protected from the influences of massification, and the state protected from the mass pressure of an individualized electorate or populace. In the twentieth century, writers drawing on the nineteenth-century foundation, and on Durkheim, have applied the concept of 'mass' as a guiding idea in political sociology.[74]

The common theme in these writings is the contradistinction between 'group' and 'mass', the former composed of individuals with stable ties to each other, the latter being amorphous and composed of 'atomised' individuals. The emphasis varies. Some like Lederer stress that amorphous masses are peculiarly susceptible to a wilful leader who promises security and identity, and to irrational appeals. Ortega emphasizes what he sees as the unsuitability of mass men for government; people unaccustomed to power and unsuited for leadership have gained access to centres of power in a corruption of democracy, or 'hyperdemocracy'. Hannah Arendt's *The Origins of Totalitarianism* is more complex in that it includes the argument that the bourgeois class, through its greed and unrestrained impulse to expand, creates the amorphous masses whose existence is a precondition of fascism. The recurring theme, however, is the same: the absence of stable social bodies and the spiritual and social homelessness of the uprooted masses.[75]

Pluralism

In more recent political works, the concept of pluralism has covered some of the same ground. The main thrust of this idea – exemplified by Robert Dahl's *Who Governs?* – has been to question the thesis that modern bourgeois democracies exhibit a concentration of power in a relatively closed political elite recruited from a narrow social base, and to supplant this with the argument that power is diffused among competing interests, institutions, parties, representative groups and lobbies.[76] The argument has sometimes been a chiefly empirical one about how decisions are reached at national and local levels; it has also included the idea of countervailing power, the notion that competing blocs vie for position and influence in decision making, and that cross-cutting ties cancel each other out and prevent the crystallization of power in a few hands.[77] Although Durkheim did not use the term pluralism – he did speak of 'polymorphism' – a faint resemblance to his ideas can be seen; he certainly advocated preserving the independence and vitality of secondary institutions in political society. But the resemblance is slight since this group of modern pluralists concentrate almost exclusively on the exercise of power and decision making rather than on the broader sociological virtues of flourishing secondary associations. The concept of pluralism has also enjoyed a vogue in the analysis of 'multi-ethnic' or 'multi-racial' societies;[78] Durkheim's view of 'race' or 'ethnicity' as destined to be submerged in modern societies was hardly likely to provoke him to think along these lines.

William Kornhauser's *The Politics of Mass Society*[79] is most notable in the present context for its citation of Durkheim as a major influence. (In all the works mentioned above as echoing Durkheimian themes there are very few references to Durkheim as a source.) The central thesis is introduced early in the book: 'Mass society is a social system in which elites are readily accessible to influence by non-elites and non-elites are readily available for mobilization by elites.'[80]

Durkheim was not disposed to speak of 'elites', indeed there are, scattered through his writings, disparaging comments directed towards instances of concentration of influence and position in socially exclusive groups; his idea of the spontaneous division of labour corresponds closely to the meritocratic principle that individuals should be maximally free and able to fill the position suited to their talents and nature. But, if we substitute for elites 'agents of the state', the Kornhauser thesis is strikingly close to Durkheim's argument concerning the polar dangers of democracy. (That is, of the state absorbing society, or of society absorbing the state. See above pp. 92–5.) Kornhauser's chapter on the structure of mass society rests quite considerably on Durkheim, focussing above all on the ability of secondary groups to act as an antidote to massification. Non-elites available for mobilization are masses of individuals devoid of strong communal, associational and independent centres of belonging in social life. (It is interesting to note that Kornhauser's work incorporates the social psychological themes of culture and personality in the mass society, with references to such figures as Erich Fromm, Theodore Adorno and the more recent work of David Riesman (*The Lonely Crowd.*)[81]

Consensus in the political order

When we discussed Durkheim's posture towards religion we showed that his writings had nothing in common with the reactionary view of traditional religion as the foundation of political order, or with the replacing of traditional religion with the worship of emblems of the modern state. He did, however, embrace the notion of a civic religion, constituted by a collective accord with certain central principles like 'democracy' and 'liberty'. This theme has been repeated in some senses by a distinct, and quite large, group of modern political scientists and sociologists, who have claimed that there is evidence, in the USA and Great Britain, of a broad band of public agreement about the virtues of the central features of democracy, that this agreement takes on a certain 'sacred' quality, and that it is the main cause, or at least an important cause, of political stability.[82]

An early example of this school of thought was provided by two sociologists who used the occasion of the coronation of Queen Elizabeth of England (in 1953) to argue that such national ceremonials functioned to reaffirm the people's assent to some imprecise but shared 'moral' principles which served to unite the nation and strengthen the sense of collective destiny and identity.[83] The argument was consistent with the Durkheimian version in the sense that the authors stressed that these moral principles were highly abstract and vague – for example the notions of 'charity' and 'tolerance' and 'justice'. This leaves room for accommodating the criticism that the appearance of assent can *only* be achieved *because* the principles are vaguely expressed – people may mean rather different things by 'justice' but, under certain conditions, agreement on the value of justice can nonetheless serve to unify. The argument departed from Durkheim to the extent that the values stressed were perhaps vaguer than even Durkheim intended, for he most often stressed the broad principles of political democracy to illustrate what he meant. But in analysing the position of the Queen, the writers did point out that she symbolized the legitimacy of constitutional monarchy and parliamentary democracy in Britain. (Their main critic on the other hand, argued that the 'unity' was contrived and the occasion exploited to conceal a basic disunity.)[84] In one other respect the original analysis differed from Durkheim's emphasis. In focussing on the ceremonial, and on the common values which it ritually celebrated, the authors placed a greater stress on common culture as the basis of solidarity than Durkheim might have allowed.

This is only one example of the 'common culture' theme in post-war political analysis – the appearance of 'affluence' and relative stability in the 1950s and early 1960s stimulated an orthodoxy in political analysis which regarded class ideologies as having ended,[85] and general agreement on political and economic means and ends as being embraced by an ever broadening middle band of the populations of Western democracies. In the early 1960s Almond and Verba, two American commentators, coined the phrase 'civic culture' – strongly reminiscent of Durkheim's language – to denote this political consensus. And by this they *did* mean the kind of constitutional arrangements of liberal democracies to which people gave their assent. They wrote from American experience but they also ventured to suggest that Great Britain presented a classic case of an integrated and stable polity firmly grounded in constitutional legitimacy.

British writers took up the theme and while the general portrayal of a stable democracy was common ground among them, in other respects the arguments took some intriguing twists and turns. Whilst Durkheim argued that external and arbitrary inequality was a constant threat to solidarity – implying that an advanced sense of justice would not tolerate it – some argued that, in Britain, stability rested on resignation, acquiescence or apathy as much as on consensus, suggesting that disadvantaged classes may perceive inequality and regard it as 'unfair', but nonetheless 'live with it'. Others argued that a traditional sense of deference among sections of the working class muted any challenge to the prevailing order.[86] Indeed what underlies most of these analyses is the assumption that, if the stability of democracy is to be challenged, the challenge will come from the *working class*. If working class people give their assent to the procedures and outcomes of parliamentary democracy, the work of creating a civic culture has been completed.

Not all the British writers see the question in these 'ideal' terms, some suggesting a precarious balance between legitimacy and alienation, but the focus on the working class necessarily implies that an important place is to be given to the role of the British Labour Party. Following one line of argument, if oppositional tendencies are channelled into support for the Labour Party, and the Labour Party remains a moderate parliamentary party, then potential division is contained within the bounds of the constitutional process. Ralph Miliband's historical analysis of the Labour Party suggests that its central and overriding 'ideal' is parliamentary democracy rather than socialism.[87] The share of power which the Labour

Party enjoyed between 1964 and 1979 (in which they formed the government for eleven of the fifteen years) led to claims that the Labour Party was the establishment party, or the natural party of government. Since then the fortunes of the party have changed dramatically; the prolonged economic crisis and the civic disturbances of 1980–1 have at least severely dented what remained of the notion of the classic stable polity.

Durkheim and political sociology: summary and concluding comments

A review of some well-known, and some less well-known, parts of Durkheim's writings showed that he had developed a more systematic political sociology than was once thought. The two main components were his ideas about the *state* and about *democracy*. His definition and analysis of both were placed squarely within his theory of the structure of modern societies. Advanced societies were seen to be highly differentiated (composed of multiple interlocking groups and institutions), were characterized by rather diffuse and abstract moral cultures and were societies in which individuality, reverence for human dignity and a certain 'freedom of conscience' based on scientific understandings of the world had reached their highest pitch. So the state was understood in *moral* and *sociological* terms: sociologically, the modern state reflected the specialization and complexity of advanced society by itself becoming a more specialized organ of society, whose main function was a 'thinking' function – devoting itself to rational appreciation of the major trends and needs of society, and creating agencies capable of planning, co-ordination, guidance and ensuring justice; morally it gave support to those values which were shared by all – freedom, justice, peace and individuality – but in a complex world could not and should not see its task as imposing itself on all spheres of human action. Equally democracy was defined morally and sociologically; morally, democracy was characterized by a heightened awareness of social facts on the part of the people and, therefore, moral authority could no longer be arbitrary, taken for granted or accepted unquestioningly – it had to include an appeal to the rational appreciation of individuals. In other words people had to understand *why* a rule, a law or a conventional procedure was right, proper and necessary. Democracy necessarily involved a certain degree of questioning, controversy and fluidity. Sociologically, democracy was grounded in the vitality of multiple groups and institutions in society which provided the main foci of the lives of individuals; such strong social groups constituted the intermediate ground of social life – somewhere between 'the individual' and 'the state'. The absence of such stable groupings could lead to an over-powerful or to an unduly weak state, the first where the state attempted to impose order on a mass of unorganized individuals, the second where the state was over-responsive to the whims and changing fancies of popular opinion.

We also saw that Durkheim recognized that many writers had argued that the nature of *property relations* conditioned or greatly influenced the nature of the state. Freedom in the acquisition and disposition of property was seen by some as a necessary guarantee of political freedom; others regarded inequality in property relations as the cause of a general social and political inequality and argued that only when property became a collective resource could true freedom and democracy be achieved. Durkheim undoubtedly veered closer to the second view but he strenuously denied that the realization of political ideals was primarily a matter of property relations. Indeed he categorically argued that political morality and property ownership were in a sense independent of each other by suggesting that questions of justice and proper authority would remain even if property relations were transformed. On the other hand he believed that private property ownership was a declining institution, partly because it rested on the family, itself in decline, and partly because the arbitrary inequality of inherited wealth ran counter to modern ideas of justice.

Much of the early part of the chapter was devoted to showing how his view of political institutions was much coloured by his general methodology in which social facts were consistently represented as *moral* facts. To ignore this – to suggest that political sociology was simply the analysis of power – was, in his view, to neglect a central and inescapable facet of the science of society. But we suggested that, while this bears much truth in it, it also appears to lead him to underestimate the brute force of power and coercion in human society, both in the political and the economic sphere. So, for example, his view that property relations will change because present property relations run counter to growing moral precepts (about justice) seems singularly unconvincing. At the same time readers may well conclude that Durkheim's idea of the independence of the problem of 'justice' has been confirmed by the experience of societies in which common ownership of the means of production has been instituted. We may also conclude that the problem of the over-powerful state has not been overcome, either in capitalist or in communist societies – and that some of Durkheim's arguments as to *how* the state becomes too powerful retain substantial value and insight.

This view of the state and democracy was seen to constitute the core of Durkheim's positive contribution to political sociology. In reviewing and dissecting his writings it became clear that they could not be understood without appreciating the nature of the assumptions he made about the moral quality of social facts and of the social order. This was discussed in the passage concerning power, coercion and authority in the political order, and self-interest, contract and solidarity in the economic order. The peculiarity of his posture toward power and coercion – not properly termed a 'neglect' of power – makes for a curious political sociology, one which in specific phases of analysis (e.g. with respect to property) seems unduly 'optimistic', and one which does not readily engage with alternative views. At the same time some readers will concede that he both makes a case for the independent examination of sociological and moral aspects of power, and establishes a prospectus for such an examination.

That this is so is indicated by the use made of Durkheimian and quasi-Durkheimian ideas by subsequent scholars. This was in evidence in the works of subsequent writers dealing with themes such as the social bases of totalitarianism, with 'pluralism', secondary groups and the civic culture of advanced societies. For such efforts to be more fully rewarded, a much clearer specification of some of the central terms is required. There is considerable room for advance, theoretically and empirically, in the investigation of such concepts as the 'moral culture of advanced societies', or 'political culture' or what some would term 'the hegemony of bourgeois culture'. Equally the concept of pluralism – and its relationship to democracy – could yet yield more than it has delivered to date. But, above all, if we are to see a useful Durkheim-inspired contribution to the study of the social and moral aspects of power, more attention must be paid to the specification of the term 'secondary groups'. This is used in such a variety of ways, both by Durkheim and others, that the precise relationship of 'secondary groups' to the disposition of political power and the moral culture of sub-groups in society, and of all three to each other, cannot begin to be tapped.

4

꘏꘏꘏

Race and society: primitive and modern

This chapter differs from the others in this book in a rather striking and, perhaps, obvious way. In dealing with what Durkheim wrote on the subject of 'race and society' it is concerned with an area of sociology on which Durkheim has had little or no influence, and on which – at least by the standard of the present conceptual phrasings of the subject – he wrote little or nothing. One cannot, therefore, begin from the contemporary 'sociology of race relations' and ask 'what did Durkheim write about these things?', because the simple answer is 'very little'. Nor can one examine the contemporary sociology of race relations and ask 'what is Durkheim's influence here?', because the answer is, roughly, the same. The justification for this chapter is rather different. We set out to examine Durkheim's thought and to do this with a specific purpose in mind, that purpose being to trace his influence on contemporary sociological issues and, by examining his ideas in this contemporary context, throw new light on the issues themselves and on the value of the intellectual constructs applied to them. Thus the justification for the chapter is that the question of 'race and society' does occupy a critically important place in the range of present sociological issues. Looking at what Durkheim *has* written of relevance may turn up some interesting answers, even if among them is only the answer to the question of why he never treated it as a critical issue *sui generis*. Close examination of some critical intellectual aspects of the question of 'race and society' in fact reveal that there is more of relevance in Durkheim's work than many would have imagined and to reveal this is important and interesting. But, more than this, the general structure of his sociology in its relevance to 'race' can be construed, and, when we do this, we find the door opened to some interesting discussion of sociology and race. Finally, it will become evident that Durkheim's direct or indirect understanding of race and society is intricately bound up with his view of primitive and modern. The latter part of this chapter provides us with a context for discussing this aspect of his thinking in some detail. It will contain some overlap with the chapter on religion, this being the main part of his corpus of sociological

116

work in which he was very much concerned with the structure of primitive societies. This contrasts with the greater part of his work – and of this book – which is evidently concerned with the social structure of advanced societies. An approach to this subject is not made any easier by the fact that the contemporary sociology of 'race relations' is an amorphous field spreadeagled through a multitude of sociological inquiries differing in substance and theoretical style. Its loci are – variously – the study of immigrant or ethnic minorities in advanced capitalist societies, the study of post-slavery societies (the Caribbean, Brazil, the United States), the outstanding case of South Africa and the study of Third World societies; its approaches are variously framed as studies of social and cultural assimilation, studies of prejudice and discrimination, analysis of cultural minorities or the specific genesis of racism as a doctrine or ideology especially in the nexus between 'race' and class. Some of this variety may be seen through a reading of such works as Michael Banton's *Race Relations*, John Rex's *Race, Colonialism and the City* (in Britain), Van Den Berghe's *Race and Racism;* Robert Blauner's *Racial Oppression in America*, N. Glazer and D. P. Moynihan's *Ethnicity*, G. Bowker and J. Carrier's *Race and Ethnic Relations* and the recent Unesco publication *Sociological Theories: Race and Colonialism.*[1] The immense conflicts of argument cannot be reiterated here covering as they do a great divide between what may be broadly termed 'culturalogical' studies emphasizing the processes of cultural change among 'minority' populations, and 'class-context' studies covering a broad spectrum of work whose authors loosely agree on situating 'racially relevant' struggles within a class analysis, whilst they fiercely disagree on the appropriateness of one or another kind of class analysis in which the study of 'race or racism' is to be situated. But the Durkheimian tradition can be addressed to some critical points of this sociological discourse and it is to these points that we give our attention.

Durkheim's work relevant to the 'race' question

There are three aspects of Durkheim's work which disclose something of his views on race and society: 1) his involvement in the Dreyfus affair, 2) his methodological comments in *Methods* and *Suicide* on race and heredity as forms of scientific explanation and 3) his view of primitive man and primitive mentality contained in his sociology of religion and in his perspective on evolution. His connection with the Dreyfus affair was a practical and political one, but it was also the occasion for two intellectual contributions. Attacks on the Dreyfusard intellectuals provoked his celebrated article on intellectuals and individualism; Durkheim also contributed to a collection of discussion papers on anti-Semitism. In this context we glimpse Durkheim's views, not so much on 'race' as on 'racism' in the shape of anti-Semitism which he interprets as a product of displaced resentments and frustrations having their roots in economic discontents and social malaise. In *Methods* and *Suicide* his comments on 'race' form part of a general discourse on the part attributable to heredity in social explanation. He equates race with heredity and physical resemblances and he sees these as receding elements of modern civilization; the more the social world is elaborated the more these organic factors are effaced, the less significance they can possibly have in social explanation. But 'primitive' societies have not disappeared from the face of the earth; where they are found they are understood by Durkheim in terms of his conception of the simple society counterposed to the complexity of advanced societies. Thus in his views on primitive society we find some indication of his understanding of the distance between modern societies and primitive peoples. In all these phases of his work we find a common thread – the argument that racial and ethnic identity are disappearing as social facts and therefore are to be dispensed with as forms of social explanation. Sociologically 'race' is opposed to the 'individual' – and individualism progressively emerges as *the* social characteristic of advanced societies; methodologically 'race' is equated with the organic and this is discarded as a form of explanation in favour of explanation by reference to 'social forces'.

Durkheim and Dreyfus

The Dreyfus affair provides us with direct evidence of Durkheim's stance towards racism in his own country. It raised issues much wider than 'the question of the Jews' but it is certain that anti-Semitism was a significant element of the passions roused in the affair's protracted life: 'The Jewishness of Dreyfus was seen to be fundamental; the *sine qua non* of the affair. This is not to say that all the participants of the affair were either Jewish apologists or anti-semites.'[2]

The affair gave a focus to a powerful thread of anti-Semitism that had long run deep in French political life, a thread which was capable of affecting Left as well as Right in France's political spectrum.[3] But it succeeded in providing a specific focus for anti-Semitic sentiment and also in solidifying its identification with politics of the Right: 'The importance of the affair for racial tensions in France [was that] it crystallized anti-semitism and gave it a particular ideological and political character which had been latent but never explicit or organized'.[4] The Left, led by Durkheim's friend the socialist Jaurès, took a prominent part in the Dreyfusard movement and,

with the triumph of the Dreyfusards, the socialists, led by Jaurès, were no longer such an outsider group, whereas the anti-semitic nationalists of the affair continued, with the interval of the First World War, to oppose the values of the Third Republic . . . Thus . . . it can be seen that during the affair anti-semitism gained a specific right-wing political nuance.[5]

In all this Durkheim's sympathies are clearly diametrically opposed to those of the nationalist Right and equally clearly aligned with those of the Republican liberal-Left. He was indeed a prominent Dreyfusard, took a strong public stance in the debate, encouraged Jaurès to marshal the forces of the Left in support of the Dreyfusards and, finally, was active in the organization of La Ligue pour la Défense des Droits de l'Homme.[6]

Durkheim's statements with regard to Dreyfus provide an insight into his own view of racism and anti-Semitism in societies in general. It can be argued that the universalistic principles contained in the French revolution provided France with a certain immunity to racism and, although France has produced a notable collection of racist thinkers and politicians (some of whom – viz. Gobineau's acceptance in Germany – found a readier home in other countries), it has been hinted that the racist tradition was weaker in France than elsewhere.[7] Durkheim himself rejected the views of contemporaries who attributed anti-Semitism to the 'fundamental racism of the French people' and saw it rather as the 'consequence and the superficial symptom of a state of social malaise'. In Germany and Russia it may be seen as 'chronic and traditional' but in France it was due to 'passing circumstances'.[8] Lukes has provided an invaluable translation of a key passage of a brief note on anti-Semitism written by Durkheim; this is reproduced here since it provides such vital evidence of his view on the subject:

When society undergoes suffering, it feels the need to find someone whom it can hold responsible for its sickness, on whom it can avenge its misfortunes: and those against whom public opinion already discriminates are naturally designated for this role. These are the pariahs who serve as expiatory victims. What confirms me in this interpretation is the way in which the result of Dreyfus's trial was greeted in 1894. People celebrated as a triumph what should have been a cause for public mourning. At last they knew whom to blame for the economic troubles and moral distress in which they lived. The trouble came from the Jews. The charge had been officially proved. By this very fact alone, things already seemed to be getting better and people felt consoled.[9]

Two interesting conclusions may be immediately drawn. First Durkheim's view is a version of a scapegoat interpretation of racism; second we may note his insistence on looking for wider causes of this phenomenon, insisting that we look for its roots in a much broader social malaise. The latter point typifies Durkheim's response to the affair in that he showed his desire always to range beyond the narrow specificities of the case in hand. He saw it as part of a generalized moral problem rather than a narrow political problem and, furthermore, friends of Durkheim have confirmed that he never wished to see it as a specifically Jewish matter.[10] Although Durkheim was himself of a Jewish family he saw the affair as containing a threat to the human rights of all men and not just to those of Jewish people.

This general concern with the sacred rights of the individual constitutes the chief burden of the critically important article which he wrote in response to a public attack on the role of the intellectuals (such as himself) whose influence was seen by the Right as being wholly pernicious.[11] In reply to the charge that the academic's 'intellectualism' and 'individualism' amounted to nothing more than anarchy, Durkheim argued that the values of individualism properly understood were the very basis of morality in an advanced society. As we have seen he carefully distinguished individualism (moral respect for the individual, sympathy for all that is human, the desire for justice) from egoism, the unregulated pursuit of individual desires which Durkheim himself condemned. Individuality was a product of modern society and it was thus understandable that respect for the individual had reached its highest point.[12] These values had been partly realized in the achievement of political liberties; not only must these liberties be protected, they must also be the basis for the furtherance of economic and social justice.[13]

The defence of Dreyfus becomes, therefore, the defence of all men against the attack on the sacred values of individualism and human liberty. The Jewish aspect of the case was temporary: in any case 'the Jews are losing their ethnic character with an extreme rapidity. In two generations the process will be complete.'[14] Nonetheless, the government should take the responsibility, in the short term, to educate the public against race hatred and should treat incitement to hatred as a crime;[15] in the long term it must face the task of curing the underlying moral, economic and social malaise.

In conducting his argument in this way Durkheim repulsed the charge of disloyalty by showing that love of country was expressed through love of individual liberty. Patriotism should never be narrowly conceived because there were, in the final analysis, values which surpassed love of country in the narrow sense: 'Doubtless we have towards the country in its present form . . . obligations which we do not have the right to cast off. But beyond this country, there is another in the process of formation, enveloping our national country: that of Europe, or humanity.'[16]

Race: explanation and methodology

We turn now to a closer examination of Durkheim's sociological writings for evidence of how he understood 'race' both as an aspect of social structure and as a form of social explanation. Though we have seen that race played little part in his sociological understanding, several of his published works, and in particular *The Division of Labour in Society*, *Suicide* and *The Rules of Sociological Method* contain sufficiently frequent references to 'race' to enable us to construct a view of how he understood this concept.

In *The Division of Labour in Society* the items of greatest interest are his comments on the part played by race in social organization. We have already seen that he viewed racial and ethnic distinctiveness as declining and receding as bases of social organization. This was partly due to the fact that heredity itself 'has lost ground in the course of human evolution'.[17] If the distinctiveness of racial groups and peoples rests chiefly on the hereditary transmission of resemblances, then 'race' necessarily declines as heredity declines. Sociologically it is the progressive emergence of individuality, biologically the extent of interbreeding, which account for this decline, for 'race and individuality are two contradictory forces which vary inversely with each other',[18] and such is the extent of mobility and migration that we can scarcely talk of races, and, in any case, all 'physical varieties exist in Europe'.[19] Races and peoples lose their distinctiveness through interbreeding and the greater the mobility and migration the less possible it is that any division of labour, or any social structure based on 'race' can persist. In simple undifferentiated societies, resemblances (moral and physical) are at a maximum; in complex society resemblances are at a minimum – thus race as a fact recedes. Moreover, he reckons it a common mistake to attribute to 'race' resemblances which are properly understood as cultural or as the facets of a common civilization:

There are completely moral resemblances, which are established with the aid of linguistics, archaeology, comparative law, which become preponderant, but there is no reason for admitting that they are hereditary. They serve to distinguish civilizations rather than races. As we advance, the human varieties which are formed become, then, less hereditary. These varieties are less and less racial.[20]

There are, it is clear, questions which remain to be asked about his theory of advancement from simple to complex societies, but those we hold over for our discussion of his evolutionary views and his conception of primitive society. For the moment we may conclude that he saw heredity and race being effaced as principles of social life and therefore as modes of explanation of human social variation.

In *The Rules of Sociological Method* and *Suicide* we can find a more precise critique of race as a mode of explaining social phenomena. In his methodological pronouncements he almost always presents explanation by race and heredity (which mostly, but not always, and not wholly, seem to amount to the same thing) as instances of a general methodological category – explanation by organico-psychic factors – a reductionism which he firmly rejected. The disproof of race-heredity explanations was, for him, one aspect of his more general rejection of organic reductionism.[21] In these (i.e. methodological) contexts, race has for Durkheim a specific meaning – inbreeding groups who transmit resemblances, chiefly of a physical character, but also, by the hypothesis of some writers, other characteristics as well. Since he acknowledges that this definition of race contains much uncertainty, not least because of interbreeding ('croisements'), then he becomes uncertain in his own use and sometimes moves away from 'race' towards a broader connotation coming closer to the term 'people'. Symptomatic of this is the number of occasions on which he writes 'des races et des peuples', thus neatly obscuring the precise sense in which he is using 'race'.

So far we can identify three strands of argument:

1 an uncertainty about the concept of race, seen chiefly in biological terms but with the acknowledgement that, as such, it has little precise meaning;

2 a rejection of race as explaining anything as part of a general rejection of organico-psychic explanation;

3 a separate argument that if race (heredity) ever played an important part in social structure, its influence is steadily being effaced and replaced. Hence he wrote that

ethnic characteristics are organico-psychological in type. Social life must, therefore, vary when they vary, if psychological phenomena have on society the effects attributed to them. But no social phenomenon is known which can be placed in indisputable dependence on race . . . the most diverse forms of organization are found in societies of the same race, while striking similarities are observed between societies of different races.[22]

The confusion can be seen to stem from the fact that, at one and the same time, he continues to grant some form of 'reality' to the psycho-biological conception of race, whilst also developing the critical intellectual perspective that it is social organization and social milieu to which social variation can be attributed. Amid a general methodological renunciation of race he somehow treats it as real as, for example, in the sentence 'the patriarchal family is not found among the Slavs who are of the Aryan race'.[23] Nonetheless, the inability to use race as an explanation shows that 'the psychological factor is too general to predetermine the course of social phenomena' and any attempt to use race in this way can readily be seen to be unscientific: 'In short when [for example] the artistic character of Athenian civilization is related with such facility to inherited aesthetic faculties we show as little insight as did scholars in the Middle Ages when they explained fire by phlogiston and the effects of opium by its dormitive property'.[24]

The methodological position worked out in *Rules* is elaborated and put into practice in *Suicide* which work also contains references to the race scientists whom Durkheim read. Race, he asserts once more, is defined by organico-psychic characteristics (resemblance and filiation being the main components) and he cites De Quatrefages's definition of race as 'the transmission of characteristics of a primitive sort, by sexual propagation'.[25] Durkheim notes the difficulties with this definition: 'If this formula is accepted . . . the results are very uncertain' and races become almost impossible of definition. Interbreeding confuses the issue and makes it impossible to know 'where races begin and end'.[26] He adds that even the fundamental dispute between the polygenist and monogenist theorists remains unresolved (although De Quatrefages himself was a convinced monogenist). He goes on to observe that the difficulties with the 'biological' definition have led some to draw away from this as the conceptual base of 'race' but then quite naturally acknowledges that this makes its definition virtually indistinguishable from nations, groups or peoples. Later we find him asserting that 'the word race no longer corresponds to anything definite'.[27] After reaching this conclusion Durkheim yet again demonstrates his uncertainty (or the scientific uncertainty in the contemporary body of knowledge as he saw it) *by agreeing to use the concept* (as others since have done) in the very demonstration of its inability to explain (suicide). 'Let us agree', he writes, 'that there are certain great types in Europe the most general characteristics of which can be roughly distinguished, and among whom the peoples are distributed *and agree to give them the name of races*' (my emphasis).[28] Having done this he then proceeds to use very crude indicators of races (peoples?) which by his own standards or anyone else's would be recognized as most unsatisfactory; but remains content to conclude that (for example): 'facts thus concur in showing that Germans commit suicide more than other peoples, not because of their blood, but because of the civilization in which they are reared'.[29] Durkheim, in his own eyes, has succeeded in showing the explanatory uselessness of a set of categories, whose validity he seriously doubts, by applying the categories themselves. Finally he returns to the general methodological point saying that 'does not this show that the cause of the variations of suicide cannot be a congenital and invariable impulse, but the progressive action of social life?'.[30]

Race science and the sociological method

We can see that the burden of Durkheim's sociological methodology pointed to the rejection of the race thesis and in this sense his work can be taken to have played an important part in the demise of scientific racism with its foundation in psycho-biology. The several qualifications we may wish to make to this point merely reflect his closeness to a period in which race science still retained substantial eminence. That is to say, subsequent developments in sociology and social and cultural anthropology served to confirm the emancipation of social science thinking from race biology. It is in this sense that sociological and anthropological thought is non-racist by its very definition; in its nature it replaces non-social explanation of all kinds with explanations which rest on the inter-relations of social structure, milieu and culture. Within a decade of Durkheim's death an academic-consensus founded in this perspective was being confidently expressed:

If culture is the determining thing in ordinary human behaviour, and if culture is made up of acquired habits transmitted from individual to individual by a learning process, then it follows that the mechanism of organic evolution – variation heredity and natural selection – cannot have much to do with human society or social evolution.[31]

We alter the emphasis if we say the same thing in another way. What Durkheim, sociology and anthropology on this understanding achieved was the *intellectual dismantling of biological race science*. To recognize that racist thought need not be confined to biological racist thought and that neither of these are the same thing as race domination in political and economic practice is to recognize the limits of this intellectual advance.

Prominent among the race scientists to whom Durkheim referred were writers such as Gall, Broca, Topinard and De Quatrefages,[32] all of whom could be termed 'race scientists' and all of whom contributed to that body of research and argument which saw 'race' as the centre of social, historical and linguistic knowledge, both as *explanans* and as *explanandum*. Gall was an early nineteenth-century anatomist with a phrenological admixture,[33] Paul Broca was the mid-nineteenth-century doyen of cranial measurement, and De Quatrefages was a leading anthropologist and self-styled synthesizer of race theory.[34] Broca and De Quatrefages both held prominent official positions in the anthropological world and they are perhaps the two, of this type of thinker, to whom Durkheim refers most often.

The works of men such as these were undoubtedly taken seriously by the scientific public before, during and after Durkheim's working career, and social scientists who were not convinced, nonetheless probably felt obliged to meet these arguments. Although 'race science' was seized upon by political agitators, much of it cannot be dismissed as mere apologetics, rather it was the serious work of men who felt that the 'fact' of racial difference could not be escaped and had to be better understood. The gradual demise of this kind of thinking followed discoveries in the field of genetics, the growth of new perspectives in sociology and anthropology and the contradictory and confusing findings of the race scientists themselves; all these, in the long run, conspired to undermine a current of scientific thought which for a considerable period wielded great influence. Durkheim's writings can justly be regarded as significantly contributing to the stream of sociological and anthropological thought which, in the academic world, supplanted scientific racism. Much more directly involved in this intellectual struggle was the German-born anthropologist Franz Boas. As well as giving much of his energy to the practical and political struggle against racist thinking, he devoted much of his intellectual effort to demonstrating the weakness of the race hypothesis in the explanation of social differences. His work was published towards the latter part of Durkheim's life and Durkheim himself commented upon it in the pages of the *Années Sociologiques*. This provides an interesting insight into Durkheim's understanding of primitive man and the differences between peoples. It is one part of Durkheim's evolutionary perspective, the subject to which we now turn.

Evolutionary theory and colonial attitudes: social science and the primitive mind

Durkheim's writings on the nature of simple societies, his evolutionary perspective and his theory of primitive mentality contain little that is explicitly about 'race', or about scientific methodology and race in the manner of *Rules* and *Suicide*. Equally they contain little that is explicitly political. What they do contain is a view of peoples who lay outside European civilization but who were increasingly coming into its view through colonial relationships. As such these writings form part of a body of thought which has informed, and has itself been conditioned by, the practical and ideological relationships of European nation-states to what we now sometimes call the Third World.

Contemporary political thinking in the world by and large rejects (in theory if not in practice) racial and colonial domination, and the colonial relationship is seen to be in essence, regardless of its particular forms, an exploitative one. Few of our European predecessors thought in this way. In their inner intentions, beliefs, hopes and ambitions, from missionaries, merchants to mercenaries, they ranged from the most unscrupulous to the most philanthropic. To this extent colonial relations varied from the most brutal to the most peaceable. If colonial theory and practice varied, so too did the sociological and anthropological thinking by which Western intellectuals tried to relate to the 'undeveloped' world. Seen in this way, the relationship between colonial practice and social thought is an infinitely complex one – about which much has already been written.[35] In what follows we shall draw upon this literature to provide a mere sketch of this relationship and, thereafter, confine our analysis to Durkheim's own work.

The broad sketch will serve only as a rough 'map' upon which Durkheim's positions may be charted. Central to all this is the nature of evolutionary thinking.

Evolutionary thinking[36] took many forms and was open to a multitude of interpretations. In the simple sense that it helped to foster the idea that there were 'lower' peoples, inferior societies and lower orders of men, its justification of political and economic domination was transparent. Whether this was envisaged as a military conquest or as a civilizing mission must often have made little difference to the subordinated peoples themselves. Naturally there were differing shades of opinion as to how permanent or remediable this 'inferiority' was but many viewed the 'child races' as victims of an arrested development which rendered them fit only for serving white men. When evolutionary thought led in this direction its ideological functions are most clear.[37]

To say this is not the same thing as saying that racism or the justification of exploitation was inescapably bound into evolutionary social thought. In contrast to the versions of biologically based race science which stressed the permanent unequal heritage of distinct races, evolutionary theory was largely 'monogenist' and asserted the fundamental unity of mankind.[38] From this it was *possible* to argue that all men were equally capable of the highest human attainment – even if this was not the conclusion which was always the most readily drawn:

Thus preclassical anthropology, taking off from the homogeneity of history and the unity of man, ends up, because of its narrow and ethnocentric theory of knowledge, in establishing a break between indigenous culture and scientific culture, of which the new anthropology is an essential branch. [Thus] . . . primitive cultures abolish themselves theoretically in analysis. They must abolish themselves practically, really in real life. They must be suppressed because, says Tylor, 'of their connexion with the lower phases of the intellectual history of the world'.[39]

Equally, evolutionary thought could rank the peoples of the world without thus justifying the imposition of one society upon another. When colonialism was seen in this way, it was condemned, as interfering with the spontaneous evolutionary development of a society.

Spencer annoyed racists who favored imperialist domination of the primitive races. Laissez-faire meant to him, among other things, letting the native peoples alone. 'First men are sent to teach heathens Christianity, and then Christians are sent to mow them down with machine guns . . . the policy is simple and uniform – bibles first and bomb-shells after'.[40]

But while not all the evidence points in a single direction, it remains true that the period (1860–80) which saw the appearance of the great works of the evolutionary school – Bachofen, Maine, Tylor, Morgan – also saw the great expansion of colonialism. Leclerc concludes that: 'there can be scarcely any doubt that there existed at this time a certain accord between the colonialist ideology and the implicit ideology of the new anthropology'.[41] As a general point here we should remember that Durkheim wrote a generation and more after this period and his own writings reflect the growing dissatisfaction with the evolutionary scheme. Its place was taken by new strands of thinking such as cultural diffusionism, functionalism and cultural relativism which themselves display variable links with colonialist ideology. Durkheim stood at a watershed in this development of anthropology. We shall see that much of what he wrote *can* be looked at in the context of evolutionary thought but that his work also provides a glimpse ahead into a non-evolutionary social theory whose ideological implications are of a rather different order.

Evolutionary Perspectives in Durkheim's Work

The Division of Labour in Society contains the most explicit evolutionary schema and, although he weakened or abandoned some of its aspects, it remained a guiding part of his thinking. It was, it is true, a very rudimentary conception of evolutionary social development sometimes marked by little more than a distinction between simple and complex societies with the focus of development on the growing complexity of the division of labour. So unsystematic, at this stage of his work at least, was his knowledge of primitive societies, that references to 'older' societies in *The Division of Labour* are taken from a scatter of sources – Biblical sources, accounts of Ancient Greece and Rome, of feudal societies – which together form rather less than a coherent model of 'stages of development'. He was repeatedly to criticize 'the unilinear conception' of evolution,[42] but his own early conception was hardly precise enough to be called such.

The purpose of the account in *The Division of Labour* was to explain the nature of morality, as it existed in simple societies and as it developed in complex societies. Similarity in the pattern of life in simple societies promoted similarity in moral conceptions; mechanical solidarity meant moral homogeneity, the preponderance of repressive law and, above all, the absence of moral and social 'individuality'. Modern societies were characterized by complexity of social organization, a preponderance of restitutive law and the interdependence among increasingly differentiated groups and individuals.

Some tentative conclusions may be drawn straightaway. First, it can scarcely be argued that Durkheim included any idea of moral evaluation in his developmental theory. True he speaks of higher and lower societies but higher means, chiefly, more complex. The complex modern societies were in fact the industrialized societies of Western Europe with their massive growth of manufacturing industry and expanding markets, and Durkheim could never be accused of excessive enthusiasm for material advance, believing as he did that a healthy civilization could never be founded upon the unlimited seeking after material progress.[43] This at least distinguishes him from one type of Victorian enthusiasm for modernity. Secondly there is, consistent with his general methodology, nothing racial in his account of development, nothing which aligns civilizational progress with racial divisions of mankind, and nothing which attributes mental or moral inferiority to biological inheritance. His actual explanation of the change from simple to complex (hinging on population growth, the increasing dynamic density of peoples and the consequent elaboration of the division of labour)[44] need not detain us here, except to confirm that it contains no hint of the idea that certain races of peoples have any favoured position in a hierarchy of civilizational attainment. The race hypothesis, taken by many to be the indispensable key to unlocking the history of art, language, politics and society, had no place in Durkheim's scheme.

The overriding reason for his interest in 'primitive society' was what he believed to be their simplicity, for he believed that this meant that they offered the best chance of studying fundamental social phenomena in their simplest form. Science can here detect the elementary forms of social phenomena because they are found in their purity and simplicity – in societies as close as possible to the origins of evolution.[45] But despite the seriousness of his purpose, his work contains a largely erroneous, misleading and, perhaps, uncomplimentary image of primitive society. Not least among the reasons for this was his lack of anthropological experience. Durkheim was a classic example of the armchair theorist and though we may dispute as to where to lay the blame – on his own easy reliance on sources, on the weak development of field work, on his early lack of aquaintance with ethnographic data or on his obstinacy in face of the facts[46] – it resulted in a highly suspect view of primitive society.

In his early writings Durkheim 'had not yet come upon the growing body of ethnographic literature that was to transform his ideas and dominate his later work'. But the later *Elementary Forms of the Religious Life* was to attract some of the harshest criticism of his concepts and method:

This abundance of references to documents provided by sundry informants, police agents, unspecified colonists, obtuse missionaries etc, is not worth much, for there are pages of M. Durkheim's book in which the impartial ethnographer is bound to put question marks by each line . . . M. Durkheim has rushed into the Australian hornet's nest and . . . the idea he has derived of 'simple societies' is entirely erroneous. The more one knows of the Australians, and the less one identifies the stage of their material civilization with that of their social organization, one discovers that the Australian societies are very complex, very far from the simple and primitive but very far advanced along their own paths of development.[47]

This was not the only type of criticism that was made and later writers have undermined his analysis further, as with regard to, for example, the theory of the respective preponderance of repressive and restitutive law (see chapter 6). But are there any broader implications beyond a chapter of errors in the history of anthropology? We shall look at two; the first, more briefly, his analysis of morality, the second, in greater detail, his view of primitive mentality.

We have already said that he did not argue that modern man was morally superior and, in the sense of promoting a moral ranking of civilizations, this is true. Indeed some commentators have (wrongly) suggested that he saw greater virtue in the moral structure of pre-industrial society.[48] However, he did argue that the morality of modern man is of a type qualitatively different from the primitive in that it rests in part on rational appreciation, on intellectual recognition of the need for restraint.[49] By contrast the image of the moral responses of men in primitive society (the spontaneous repressive sanctioning of transgressors) derives directly from his view of (a) structural, and hence cultural and moral, simplicity in lower societies and (b) the absence of restitutive processes. Thus solidarity relies upon simple subscription to a homogeneous moral code. To many this may seem not very far removed from a rather unflattering view of primitive mentality, of the simple man lashing out blindly at the deviant, the stranger or the unlike, of a blind unthinking adherence to a repressive moral code. How much of this Durkheim intended is impossible to say, but it has much in common with vulgar prejudicial views of primitive man.

Primitive mentality

The nineteenth-century vision of material and technological progress was so firmly grounded in the faith in scientific reason that it is not surprising to find that the Victorian apostles of civilizational progress came to see the scientific mentality as the distinguishing mark *par excellence* of modern man. Because of this, and because of the contrasting image of the mentality of men in traditional and primitive society, the issue of the nature of primitive mentality has a critical part in the posture of Western society towards pre-industrial societies. As an element of race-science, the distinction between primitive and modern mentality would likely be grounded in a theory of inherited characteristics, or of immutable traits of the divisions of mankind. But conceptions of primitive mentality can exist quite independently of these foundations. To be sure the race-biological version of mental and intellectual variation frequently appears to be the most total and deterministic since inherited traits are presented as incapable of modification. By contrast we generally think that those theories, which stress the action on men of socio-cultural milieux, include a strong assumption of the malleability of human nature. But in practice non-biological deterministic theories may well imply a degree of fixity to the condition of peoples or races such that they are consistent with the consignment of a social group to a more or less permanent position of inferiority.[50] Leclerc has provided an example in his description of the place of the noble savage in Western thought.

As Western culture became more committed to the value of disciplined work, he argues, the Western romantic view of the noble savage was gradually replaced by the image of the savage as lazy. This laziness, we may note, was frequently attributed to the fertility of the soil and the ease of subsistence in Africa. As such it was a climatic–environmental explanation, but one which nonetheless promoted 'laziness' as a permanent characteristic of the African thus requiring him to be treated in a particular way.[51] The implications for '*malleability*' therefore assume considerable significance in the evaluation of theories of 'mentality'.

Durkheim's views on this subject have their deepest expression in *The Elementary Forms of the Religious Life*, and when he and Marcel Mauss came to review Lévy-Bruhl's 'Les Fonctions mentales dans les sociétés inférieures' they did so by way of comparison with the view expressed in Durkheim's own work.[52]

'The aim of Lévy-Bruhl's book', writes Durkheim (with Mauss), 'is to establish that the mentality of mankind does not have the invariability attributed to it by certain philosophers . . . Taking off from the postulate that the types of mentality must vary as the types of society vary, he undertakes to construct the mental type particular to that ill-defined group of societies ordinarily referred to as "lower".'[53] Lévy-Bruhl's discussion moves in the direction of seeing primitive mentality as clearly distinguished from the modern: 'In short, primitive thinking does not obey the principle of contradiction and this is why Lévy-Bruhl calls it prelogical.' Durkheim agrees with much of Lévy-Bruhl's analysis, in particular that primitive mentality is essentially religious; this must be so since both religion and mentality share the same source – society. But he goes on to say that Lévy-Bruhl, being preoccupied with primitive mentality as a type, tended to overstress the difference between primitive and modern as too much of an antithesis: 'These two forms of human mentality . . . far from deriving from different sources, are two moments of a single evolution.' Thus rejecting Lévy-Bruhl's accentuated antithesis of the prelogical and the rational, the primitive and modern, Durkheim saw clearly, writes Lukes, 'that there are criteria of truth and "objective" explanation, as well as principles of logic, which are non-relative and non-context dependent; and he further saw that these principles of logic are fundamental and universal to all cultures.'[54] Durkheim's position is, then, rather an 'intermediate' one, rejecting the idea of a fundamental split between two forms of mentality, but speaking nonetheless of 'higher and more recent forms' which evolved over the centuries from the primitive form.

Durkheim provided further evidence of his views on the subject in a review of a major work by Franz Boas and this could be seen as being doubly important in view of Boas's prominence in the criticism of racist thought:

In the United States some of the most significant events in the history of cultural anthropology were to take place and these were to have, in turn, a tremendous effect on race theories. The leader in this field was Franz Boas . . . The racists of the 1920s rightly recognised Boas as their chief antagonist. Although his opinion was then a minority one, he never wavered before the onslaughts of biological interpretations of history and civilization . . . It is possible that Boas did more to combat race prejudice than any other person in history.[55]

In 1911 Boas's *The Mind of the Primitive Man* was published and the *Année Sociologique* of the following year carried Durkheim's review – in the same issue, in fact, in which the review of Lévy-Bruhl appeared. He begins his review of Boas by setting out the author's main argument: 'Are there races which are intellectually poorly endowed? and others which are by contrast privileged? Are there races destined by their very makeup ("constitution") to a mental inferiority beyond which it is forever impossible to raise themselves?' From this explicit beginning, in which the question of 'modifiability' and unequal intellectual inheritance is directly raised, Durkheim proceeds to summarize the author's position. One could, according to Boas, make specific statements about 'primitive mentality' if:[56] 1) mentality were known to be linked to fixed physical characteristics; 2) the fixed physical characteristics could be identified exclusively in primitive peoples and that 3) these characteristics were known to be related to cultural inferiority.

None of these conditions, says Boas, is met. Even physical characteristics themselves are subject to modification by the effect of milieu. Durkheim appears to find such a radical reversal of the idea of 'racial' inheritance rather surprising and wonders if Boas has underestimated the effect of heredity. Heredity itself may be modified, argues Durkheim, but by interbreeding rather than by milieu.[57]

Durkheim proceeds to record Boas's view that the differences between civilized and primitive mentality are only matters of degree. 'The mental process which is at the basis of all judgement is the same among all men.' In the main Durkheim endorsed this view but he is not wholly convinced, he raises queries, insisting all the time on 'appealing to the facts'. Having summarized Boas's view he tries to clarify his own position in relation to it: 'We too believe that there is no difference in kind between primitive thought and the thought of cultivated man. All the essential mechanisms of judgement and reasoning are fundamental to civilization even of the most rudimentary kind'. There have been, he continues,

genuine advances in the course of history and such a complex evolution could not be retraced in a few works. Is this to say that there are races which are predestined not to surpass a certain level of intellectual development? Nothing could be less established; we think, on the contrary, that external causes, physical or social, have been the principal source of differentiation among peoples. But we should not conclude from this that, today, all men are equally suited for civilization. Long periods of development have been able to create pre-dispositions which did not exist in the first place. Without doubt it is very possible that some particular race is unjustly looked down upon: this is very obviously the case with the Blacks of America. But this is not a reason to state that all races and all peoples have an equal native aptitude for all possible forms of mentality.[58]

This seems to be a critical piece of writing for understanding Durkheim's views on race as well as illustrating the subtlety that is involved in shades of opinion on the potential and capacity of peoples and races.[59] He accepts that there is no difference in kind between primitive and civilized mentality and this is consistent with his critique of Lévy-Bruhl and that writer's over-emphasis of an antithesis between the two; consistent too with his clear view of the universality of principles of human reason. And yet again he stresses that 'race' cannot explain human social variation and differenti-ation. But the critical addition to this is his argument that all this does not necessarily mean that all peoples are 'equally suited for civilization ("aptes à la civilisation")'. Does not Durkheim mean here for *higher* civilization? Does not this suggest that, in this context at least, Durkheim is judging 'our' modern civilization to be *civilization* itself? If so, what are the defining elements of this higher civilization for which some peoples are not suited? Are they material developments, trade and industry, or political and moral forms for which they are not yet fit? There are no ready answers to these questions but even asking them is enough to show that, in this strand of Durkheim's thought (and any thought of a similar tendency) there is a conception of the native, the primitive, or the 'lower' peoples' mentality (or state of development) which leads to the conclusion that they are unsuited for advancement. When we take the short step from 'unsuited for civilization' to 'unready for self-government', the argument takes on an ominously modern ring. Systems of colonial domination have long been justified by the argument that the natives (the oppressed) are 'not ready' (for self-government).

There is no hint either, in his brief book review, of what might remedy this unreadiness (could it be education,[60] or amalgamation with other peoples?), or of how long it might take for this unreadiness to be overcome. An answer to both or either would be important for assessing his view of 'malleability'. But he does give a one-sentence view of what causes this unreadiness: 'Long periods of development have been able to create predispositions which did not exist in the first place'. By this he reasserts the fundamental and 'original' equality of all peoples but also argues that historical experience and circumstances have given rise to differences in outlook or temperament which, as we stand today, unequally suit different peoples for (whatever Durkheim means by) civilization. His view is ambiguous, almost seeming to take back with one hand what he has given with the other: 'Are there races which are predestined not to surpass a certain level of intellectual development? . . . Nothing could be less established', and some races 'have been looked down upon unjustly', but 'this is no reason to state that all races and all peoples have an equal native aptitude for all possible forms of mentality.'

There is ambiguity too in his shifting from 'les races' to 'les peuples', or simply, as above, using both. I am inclined to think that this is symptomatic of the fact that Durkheim was moving towards a position where the term 'race' was recognized to have no scientific validity, but fell short of such a recognition because of the pervasiveness of the race concept in con-temporary literature. The term 'peuple' might replace 'race'; and more than this, Durkheim increasingly regards 'sociétés' – socio-politically defined – as the proper unit of study. The contemporary sociologist would probably regard this as progress in the conceptual framework of the discipline. But we have also seen how some of the gains made in the move away from (biological) race determinism can be lost in their replacement by a cultural determinism whose practical implications may be little different. Finally it is difficult to determine what Durkheim meant by 'predispositions' created over 'des siècles de culture'. He may have wished to express some-thing like 'sentiments' or 'feelings' or he may have meant cognitive or moral assumptions or basic views of the world.[61] To be sure which he meant would be to get closer to knowing how he viewed the prospects for advancement of the 'lower peoples'.

In the section on Durkheim's understanding of the primitive and the concept of social evolution we have seen reflected in his work an ambiguity which is inherent in evolutionary sociology/anthropology. The meth-odological rejection of race-science remains clear and he is seen to be sceptical or at least hesitant about the very concept 'race'. We should remember too that in his concept of primitive society he in no way equated primitivity with 'actual' races nor did he equate stages of development with specified peoples. He accepts the universalistic premise of evolutionary thought in his caution concerning distinctive qualitatively different types of human mentality. Where this was the emphasis in evolutionary thought it less easily lent itself to the justification of domination of one people by another. But this idea – 'the history of the human race one in its source, one in its experience and one in its progress' – was not the sole emphasis as we have seen and as Leclerc has demonstrated.[62] When evolutionary thought connected primitive cultures with 'the lower phase of the intellectual history of the world' it was capable of justifying the forceful imposition of one people on another in such a way as to make highly improbable the spontaneous development of the subordinate people. Evolutionism for all its universalism could breed an arrogance towards 'lower peoples' which, in Durkheim's case, came closest to expression in his statements about primitive mentality. It was the *mind* of the primitive which, to Western observers of many kinds, was suspect above all.

Claude Lévi-Strauss: 'Man has always been thinking equally well'

Durkheim's consideration of primitive mentality can be seen to be part of a grand scheme of sociological reflection on civilizations of the world, human progress and social evolution. In the main, the divorce, inspired by sociologists and social anthropologists, between 'race' and 'civilization', has set aside this type of argument with respect to the 'race question' and has opened up the way for a sociology of 'race relations' in which such questions play little or no part. (We will turn shortly to the question of the relationship of Durkheimian analysis to modern sociology of 'race re-lations'.) But the question has not entirely disappeared, nor has the ambition of anthropology to deal with the grandest questions of human civilization been altogether submerged; this ambition has survived in the writings of Linton, Herskovits, Kroeber, White and, most recently, among others, Claude Lévi-Strauss. For our purposes the last mentioned deserves our attention, if only because it is clear that Lévi-Strauss, as the most eminent contemporary French anthropologist, in many respects takes as his starting point the thoughts of Lévy-Bruhl, Durkheim and the great French anthropological tradition.

Confining ourselves to two items of Lévi-Strauss's writings – one a brief passage on myth in his *Structural Anthropology* and the other his contribution 'Race and history' to the 1956 Unesco volume – we can see the clear continuation of the 'primitive mentality' debate.[63] His concern in the study of myth is to reveal the structure of myths in such a way as to reveal their inner logic, a logic which is not greatly different in form from the logic to be found in science. Science and myth, he concludes, are the products of the same universal structures of the human mind, and differ only in the materials upon which they work:

Prevalent attempts to explain alleged differences between the so-called primitive mind and scientific thought have resorted to qualitative differences between the working processes of the mind in both cases, while assuming that the entities which they were studying remained very much the same. [We hold] a completely different view – that the kind of logic in mythical thought is as rigorous as that of modern science, and that the difference lies, not in the quality of the intellectual process, but in the nature of things to which it is applied.[64]

He compares the field of technology and argues that the stone and the steel axe are 'equally well made' but that stone is quite different from steel.

In the same way we may be able to show that the same logical processes operate in myth as in science, and that man has always been thinking equally well; the improvement lies, not in an alleged progress of man's mind, but in the discovery of new areas to which it may apply its unchanged and unchanging powers.[65]

This formulation departs quite radically from Durkheim's, even though the tendency of argument is the same; for Durkheim dallied with the notion of 'aptitudes' in a way which Lévi-Strauss evidently does not. In the Unesco article he confronts the questions of race, culture, and civilization more directly, and, we might remember, having seen between Durkheim's death and his own writing, the evidence of the 1930s and the Second World War. He acknowledges that 'the biological foundations of racial prejudice have been destroyed' but concedes that the association of superiority and inferiority in the achievements of civilizations remains closely associated in the popular conception with 'racial' signs. 'We cannot claim to have formulated a convincing denial of the inequality of the human "races", so long as we fail to consider the problem of the inequality – or diversity – of human "cultures", which is in fact – however unjustifiably – closely associated with it in the public mind'.[66] He sets out to answer this question by challenging some conventional ideas about 'progress', about what we mean by 'different' cultures, and about social and biological evolution. He then proceeds to point out that the idea of a universal human kind is a relatively recent one – this clearly echoing Durkheimian themes about modern civilization – and that this is contrasted with the more common ethnocentric attitude:

This naive attitude [contains] a rather interesting paradox. This attitude of mind which excludes 'savages' (or any people whom one may choose to regard as 'savages') from human kind, is precisely the attitude most strikingly characteristic of these same savages. We know in fact that the concept of humanity as covering all forms of the human species, irrespective of race or civilization, came into being very late in history and is by no means widespread. Even where it seems strongest, there is no certainty – as recent history proves – that it is safe . . . from retrogression. So

far as great sections of the human species have been concerned, however, and for
tens of thousands of years, there seems to have been no hint of any such idea.
Humanity is confined to the borders of the tribe, the linguistic group, or even in some
instances to the village, so that many so-called primitive peoples describe themselves
as 'the men' (or sometimes, though hardly more discretely – as 'the good', the
'excellent', the 'well-achieved'), thus implying that the other tribes, groups or
villages have no part in the human virtues or even in human nature, but that their
members are, at best, 'bad', 'wicked', 'ground monkeys' or 'lousy eggs'. They often
go further and rob the outsider of even this modicum of actuality, by referring to him
as a ghost or apparition.[67]

This suggests that the tendency to make out-group classifications is a
strong one, but not a universal one, for the very fact of the emergence of
the conception of universal human kind, however precarious it may be,
shows that different conditions of social life are associated with new and
different definitions of people and peoples. If Lévi-Strauss's argument is
taken to indicate the strength of the tendency to see one's own people as
good, this is still clearly to be distinguished from racism which is much more
than an elaborated development of this tendency. The fact that racist ideas
flourish under some conditions and wither under other conditions tells us
that racism is no mere expression of a strong human tendency.

Lévi-Strauss devotes the rest of his article to the immensely complex
question of comparing and judging the civilizations and cultures that
human history has produced, and to disputing some of the most common
modes of argument by which hierarchies of evaluation are reached. He
faces squarely up to the most difficult question of all – how to explain the
present fact of the 'dominance' of Western civilization. He draws our
attention to a host of considerations – such as the small span of time in
which this dominance has existed, or, given its spread, *which* societies will
continue to lead *within* that culture, or the fact that much of its dominance
is attributable, simply, to force, or that the features of Western civilization
which most people welcome are accompanied by features which many in
the world would doubt, even reject – and leaves us in no doubt that there is
no place for the crude hypothesis of differential aptitudes. Furthermore, he
does all this without once resorting to a common relativism – the argument
that all civilizations are to be judged by their own lights, or, conversely,
that there can be no agreed standards by which all civilizations can be
ranked. In general it can be seen that, though starting from some of the
same beginnings, Lévi-Strauss takes the arguments about 'civilizations'
and 'primitive mentality' very much further than Durkheim did.

The sociology of race and society

The discussion of Durkheim's writings with reference to the question of race in society, race and its place in sociology, and the broader question of images of the primitive and modern, serves to demonstrate one of our opening arguments, that is that one can find in his work rather more that is relevant to these issues than may have been expected. Four specific points can be identified.

1 In Durkheim's commentary on the Dreyfus affair we find a tentative explanation of racism (anti-Semitism) which bears striking similarities to explanations which have since become established and gained general currency in the sociology of racism. His explanation emphasizes the way in which racist sentiments have their roots in general social and economic discontents and how the expression of these sentiments appears to give solace to people whose resentments are diffuse symptoms of a deeper social malaise.

2 His methodological arguments can be placed in an extended history of social thought with regard to race, particularly in the process wherein nineteenth-century conceptions of the reality of racial differences and of their explanatory power were progressively 'disproved' or displaced by sociological and anthropological thinking which stressed explaining social phenomena by reference to social and cultural facts.

3 His evolutionary modes of thought contained an ambiguous posture towards the 'lower' civilizations of the world which simultaneously stressed continuities and discontinuities between primitive and modern man.

4 His general approach, in the parts of his work which we have just discussed, and in the general body of his sociology, strongly suggests that 'race' progressively recedes as a factor in civilization, and what we today call *ethnic* modes of identity and social organization are also to be regarded as declining social forms.

It remains true, however, that Durkheimian thinking has had a negligible effect on the contemporary sociology of race relations and this makes it unwise to attempt to trace such influence as there is; much of it is so indirect and exclusively 'by implication' that any effort of this kind would not pay dividends. It remains therefore to mention those few instances where Durkheimian thinking has surfaced in this field and to add a few comments about the four specific areas which we have outlined above.

The notion of explaining racism by reference to displaced social resentments has indeed a kind of general currency. Its psychological forms can be found in arguments which suggest that the adoption of racist ideas and susceptibility to racial prejudice is likely to be found among individuals suffering from symptoms of personality inadequacy. Sometimes these symptoms are identified broadly in a population – as in mass psychology explanations of societies which have fallen at least temporarily under the general sway of racist ideologies. More commonly they are portrayed as the psychological inadequacies of a minority of individuals whose life experience has bestowed on them a sense of inferiority which appears to be assuaged by the embracing of racial ideas. In sociology racial sentiments have been identified in broader segments of the population, especially among dispossessed and disadvantaged members of 'majority' groups whose lives bring them in more or less direct status competition or economic competition with identifiable 'minority' groups. Racial beliefs are then explained as part of a pattern of status striving and status resentment. Durkheim's views are much less developed than these, but they constitute an early formulation of a pattern of argument which has since become familiar. This form of argument has also had repercussions for the advocacy of measures designed to eradicate or reduce 'racial' sentiments, measures which, like Durkheim's, imply a need to attack the deeper social causes of racism rather than its surface manifestations.

Durkheim's arguments with respect to the explanatory power of 'race' are really to be understood in the context of his general attack on biologistic and psychologistic explanations. His rejection of race as a mode of explanation is not as total as that of some of his contemporaries – Franz Boas being the primary case – but the general direction of his argument cannot be questioned. Since, then, not only has sociology and social anthropology progressively discarded the 'race' hypothesis but so too have those disciplines – biology and psychology – which have historically given it greatest support. The notion of explanation by 'racial difference' has not, however, been removed from the body of scientific thought, for it has occasionally resurfaced in socio-biology, and in the field of intelligence testing in psychology. When this does occur it is perhaps not surprising that academic ideas which appear to justify popular ideas of racial difference are seized upon and reproduced in less respectable quarters. There is little evidence to suggest that the demise of scientific racism is positively related to the undermining of popular racism. Thus whilst in some sociological quarters 'biological' notions of 'racial' difference have been replaced by 'culturalogical' notions of differences between peoples, these latter ideas have been used by advocates and apologists of systems of 'racial' domination. In South Africa a system of racial domination is 'justified' in part by reference to sociological conceptions of social and cultural pluralism which have acquired considerable importance and respectability in South African (white) sociology.

As some of our discussion has shown, Durkheim's ideas on the nature of primitive cultures were inserted into general anthropological postures to the 'non-white' peoples of the world. In the history of social anthropology this group of ideas has had some considerable importance but it is an importance which has receded as evolutionary conceptions of 'stages of civilization' have themselves declined. Sociological analysis of peoples and societies of the Third World have largely abandoned evolutionary ideas in favour of forms of analysis which stress the *relationship between* the so-called developed and undeveloped worlds. Thus the colonial and neo-colonial relationships which were commonly absent from the context of traditional social anthropological analysis have taken their place at the centre of contemporary analysis. This constitutes such a transformation of social scientific perspective that Durkheim's thoughts on this subject genuinely appear to belong to a 'pre-history' of social science.

Turning to his general view that racial or ethnic identities were destined to disappear in advanced societies we find that contemporary sociology presents a rather ambiguous picture; in some respects modern sociology endorses this view, in other respects it contradicts it. Durkheim's view is expressed, in part, in his comments on the Jewish people of France when he suggests that Jewish ethnic identity is weakening. He may have been reflecting on his own experience, having been brought up in a traditional Jewish family and community setting, and then seeing his own life and career draw him steadily away from this background. He could no doubt have looked around him and seen others for whom the same was true. But his view on 'ethnicity' is also expressed indirectly in his general sociology of advanced societies, for he understood these as societies in which men and women were progressively drawn away from traditional settings of domestic and kinship circles, of village town and region, and of the Church. At the same time these traditional collectivities loosened their grip over the moral and social life of modern peoples. Since ethno-religious identities depended for their sustenance on these traditional solidarities, their weakening simultaneously effaced these sources of identity. He wrote of the modern cities as largely populated by immigrants and, rather than concluding that these immigrants carried with them forms of identity and association which would serve as social and psychological reinforcements in an individualized society, assumed that the life of the city would act to dissolve them. Family life and religious attachments were ever weakening and their social and psychological functions were taken up by the associations that developed in the occupational milieux.

That modern sociology has endorsed this view is evidenced by the currency of a wide range of characterizations of modernity which reflect the influence of such as Toennies's distinction between *Gemeinschaft* and *Gesellschaft* societies, societies based on primordial ties as against societies based on secular contractual relationships, and of distinctions between 'folk' and 'urban' societies. Chapter 3 and chapter 2 have discussed some of these questions in relation to industrial sociology, the nexus between work and non-work life, and in relation to the conception of modern society as 'mass society'. With regard to the study of immigrants and ethnic identity – especially in American sociology – the earlier studies, such as those of Park and the Chicago school, recognized the initial importance of ethnic associations among first generation immigrants but tended to assume that the longer run would see the assimilation and disappearance of ethnic distinctiveness.

But some more recent sociological writings have challenged this orthodoxy about modern societies, deriving their support from what has been taken to be evidence of the continued flourishing of ethnic and religious forms of association and identity. The idea of American civilization as a melting pot, as a powerful solvent of traditional solidarities has been questioned by evidence of ethnic structures persisting 'beyond the melting pot' and particularly by evidence of the undiminished power of 'Black' identifications, revived and reclaimed by a cohort of Black nationalist and Black Power advocates in the 1960s.[68] Similarly in Britain recent trends in the study of 'race and ethnicity' indicate a questioning of the assumptions of earlier observers of immigrants, particularly in respect of the concepts of integration and assimilation.[69] There has been something of a bandwagon effect in the 'revival of ethnicity' school but enough has been written to raise serious doubts about the assumption that ethnic solidarity inevitably recedes in advanced societies.

There are, as we have said, only a few instances where contemporary specialists in race relations have discussed the work of Durkheim; we will briefly mention two here. The first really constituted an extension of the use of the idea of anomie, as it was applied to industrial relations (see chapter 3), into the field of race and society. In the early seventies the journal *Race* provided a forum for discussing approaches to the study of race in Britain and in the January, April, and July issues of 1973, Halsey, Rex and others disputed about the proper approach to the field.[70] Halsey had written a summary article which contained the controversial phrase 'will the coloureds revolt?' but the main drift of which took off from the argument that, despite symptoms of industrial discontents in Britain, British social and political life exhibited a curious kind of stability which could be attributed to a range of traditional attitudes, of accommodations to relative deprivation, and of postures to authority. Halsey was, in effect, asking whether 'racial' sentiments could disturb this. Rex and others were, understandably, perturbed by this limited phrasing of the 'question to be asked' in race relations research. Tracing Halsey's approach to the influence of the 'neo-Durkheimians', Rex suggested that the focus on 'the problem of order' was consistent with the broad-based conservatism inherent in Durkheim's sociology. On inspection it appears to be an intellectually shallow controversy which was not taken any further; the application of the concept of 'anomie' to British race relations was not advanced subsequently. The episode does however give us an instance of the loose and casual identification of Durkheimian ideas with a 'conservative' stance in sociology.[71]

A more extensive and valuable application of Durkheim's ideas can be found in Geoffrey Dench's book *Maltese in London*.[72] His account shows that Maltese immigrants to Britain in the 1950s were often anxious to dissociate themselves from ethnic associations and identifications because of the ill-repute of a minority of Maltese people who were involved in the world of crime. This dissociation was reinforced by assimilationist attitudes in society at large and thus the associational and psychological benefits of ethnic community were lost. Dench then raises the question as to whether this is a healthy process, conceding that it accords with the assumptions of liberal individualism, but also speculating as to the potential of group solidarity for providing a basis of collective integration. He argues that in societies where ethnic identities have persisted, representatives of ethnic groups have been able to act as 'ethnic brokers' representing specific ethnic group interests in a pluralistic distribution of elite power and influence. Drawing on Durkheim's analysis of egoism and anomie, Dench's constitutes a rare challenge to the liberal consensus which regards any form of persistance of 'ascriptive' characteristics as inappropriate. He argues that Rex has tended to elide 'racialism' with *any* form of ascription, thus neglecting the important role which forms of ascription may continue to play in societies despite their modernity and their stress on individualism.

Summary remarks

We can see that there are but few traces of Durkheim's direct influence on the contemporary sociology of race relations. There are the occasional references to the group of ideas associated with the concept 'anomie'; and, with respect to his remarks on anti-Semitism and the Dreyfus affair, we see that his ideas correspond to hypotheses about the origins of racism which are still current today. However, the indirect links between Durkheim's writings and subsequent arguments about 'race and society' are perhaps much more important, even where they are very much open to question. His comments on anti-Semitism indicate that (in some respects, like Marx) he believed it was wrong to concentrate on the specific elements of the so-called 'Jewish question', and he projected the debate as one about human rights in general. This question has not disappeared – contemporary struggles for minority group rights reflect the same debate as to whether the emphasis should be on the position and rights of particular groups or on the general rights and needs under which minority claims can be – or can be thought to be – subsumed.

Equally, *some form* of the question of 'race and civilization' is still with us, as Lévi-Strauss's writings illustrate. There are many sociologists and anthropologists who would contend that the emancipation of social science from racist ideas about 'underdeveloped societies' is by no means complete, and that the problems associated with the concept of 'primitive mentality' have not been resolved. As Lévi-Strauss remarked there is a sense in which social science has destroyed the biological foundations of racism, but, as he implied, there is another sense in which the question has not 'gone away'. Since Durkheim believed that the question of race and society was primarily a question of biology and sociology, his dismissal of biological reductionism tended to lead him to a corresponding dismissal of questions of race and racism. This blinded him – and others – to the necessity for continuing to consider the question under a new theoretical dispensation. His understanding that ethnic particularities were destined to disappear also led him to neglect forms of group association which remained important but did not correspond with the outlines of his theory of the division of labour and social structure. Both these failings may be seen to spring from his underestimation of such 'irrational' phenomena as racism, and his overestimation of the spread of the liberal values of advanced cosmopolitan societies. (Lévi-Strauss was well aware of the possibility of 'retrogression' from these values.) It was a failure to recognize that '*race*' – as a complex of socially constructed meanings (including the doctrines of racism), and '*ethnicity*' – as a complex of secondary group affiliations and forms of cultural identity (and each overlapping with the other) – retain social significance in modern society, both with respect to cultural differences within 'cosmopolitan societies', and in their intersection with class structures.

5

���������������������������

The sociology of education: discipline and moral autonomy

It was in the last few years of the nineteenth century and the first few of the twentieth, when Durkheim had established himself at the Sorbonne, that he gave a great deal of attention to education and prepared lectures on the topic which have subsequently been collected as *Education and Sociology* and *Moral Education*.[1] He lectured about a number of facets of the topic, the most important of which were the relevance of sociological science for the theory and practice of education, the nature of education as a social institution, the nature of knowledge, the elements of morality and the role of the school in inculcating moral precepts in children, and the history of education. This area of his work yet again illustrates his enormous energy, originality and influence; many of these lines of inquiry have become established within sociology and in faculties of education.

In the next few pages we shall: 1) introduce the reader to the main ideas of Durkheim on education, 2) show how certain critical elements of his sociology of education help us to understand his total sociology and 3) examine his ideas on education as they bear upon our judgement of his sociological reformism. The latter part of the chapter will trace some of his ideas through subsequent work in the sociology of education.

As in other areas into which he ventured, he found it necessary to devote himself, at the outset, to establishing the claims of sociology. So, he insists that educational institutions, ideals and practices are rooted in society; they reflect the state of development of a society, and they reflect the central tendencies, features and forms of that development. At best they should be an instrument through which societies achieve their ends, in particular their moral ends, that is they should express, inculcate and further the moral virtues of the society which they serve. Even more fundamentally, educational institutions are essential to the survival of a society since, to the extent that they have taken over the duties of the family and other organs of social life, they are concerned with the socialization of children, and the preparation of them for adult life. Since sociology concerns itself with the study of the development of societies, with the study of the relationship between different elements of social organization and, above all, with the relationship between society and morality, then it was evident to Durkheim that sociology had much to offer to the study of the theory and practice of education.

It may seem at the outset that Durkheim had a 'conservative' view of education, since he viewed it as being bound to subordinate itself to the ends and 'morality' established in society at large. Is this not a prescription for a school system dedicated to preserving things as they are, and for inculcating acceptance of things as they are? It is certainly true that he saw it as self-evident that education should express the moral and practical virtues of a society. But this is a general, and, in a sense, an ideal, view, for it presupposed that the society which education served was itself 'normal', 'healthy' and aware of its own condition. By examining Durkheim's work on the division of labour in advanced societies where economic activities are highly developed but poorly organized and pathologically lacking in regulation, we know that he was aware that this condition was *not* met.

When a society finds itself in a state of relative stability, of temporary equilibrium, as, for example, French society in the seventeenth century; when consequently a system of education is established which, while it lasts, is not contested by anyone, the only pressing questions which are put are questions of application. No serious doubt arises over the end . . . only controversy over the best way to put them into practice. I do not have to tell you that this intellectual and moral security is not of our century; this is at the same time its trouble and greatness. The profound transformations which contemporary societies have undergone or which they are in the process of undergoing, necessitate corresponding transformations in the national education. But although we may well be aware that changes are necessary, we do not know what they should be . . . Public opinion remains undecided and anxious . . . It is no longer a matter of putting verified ideas into practice, but of finding ideas to guide us. How to discover them if we do not go back to the very source of educational life, that is to say, to society? It is society that must be examined; it is society's needs that must be satisfied. To be content with looking inside ourselves would be to turn away from the very reality that we must attain; this would make it impossible for us to understand anything about the forces which influence the world around us and ourselves with it.[2]

Sociology as a study of education is essential to the furtherance of educational theory, and practice; it is also essential to the process of education itself since we live in a world which demands a reflective ability, a comprehension of the forces underlying social facts, especially when social development is encumbered by pathological forms, and when moral certainty is so deeply undermined. His sociology of education, then, contains a recognition of the deficiencies of modern societies, and sees the sociology of education and the school system as bound to partake of these uncertainties, whilst doing what they can to cure them.

We should also be careful to note that Durkheim did not reduce his view (that education was rooted in society) to a purely relativistic notion i.e. that education, subordinated to society, merely reflected the morals of the society it served. For, although he rejected the idea that there could be any universal principles of education, knowledge or moral instruction good for all time (entirely compatible with his general historical sociology) he quite clearly avoided a relativist position by asserting that certain fundamental moral principles were expressed in and founded in the social organization of modern civilizations, and it was these that educationalists had to understand, appreciate and teach. These were the principles that he spoke of in *The Division of Labour* and other works as we have discussed: the fact, for example, that moral diversity was expressive of the social diversity of modern life, that individual consciences were more fully developed and more emancipated from the collective conscience, that the collective conscience indeed came to express above all a faith in individual dignity, in the need for justice and liberty. It was not *any* moral principles that a school system in modern society could express, but these – respect for the individual, an understanding of civic duty and morality, an appreciation of the individual – that a school system must teach its students in order to prepare them for adult life.

There are other elements of his argument which should be balanced against his stress on discipline,[3] moral education and preparation for civic duty. For in teaching the importance of moral education he stressed above all that moral education could no longer be a process of imparting moral certainties founded upon religious faith. As we have seen in examining his general sociological analysis of modern society, he was quite sure that modern morality could no longer be founded upon religion; science and knowledge and morality were founded in or originated from religion in the sense that secular science, knowledge and morality have in religion their precursor, but they have also superseded it. Moral knowledge can no longer be based on blind acceptance and therefore religion in the traditional sense can no longer be the basis of education. This too was entirely consonant with his understanding of morals in modern societies as set out in his explication of the transition from simple to complex society (from mechanical to organic solidarity).

Durkheim's work also advanced an elaborate theory of the social origins of modes of thought – a sociology of knowledge – in which the principal claim was that our categories of thought arise from our experience of organized society. In *Primitive Classification*[4] and *The Elementary Forms of the Religious Life* he advanced the argument that categories of thought – cause, space, time, class and so on – were modelled on social organizational forms and derived from them through collective representations which carried a certain moral authority. In pre-modern society these collective ideas were typically represented in a religious form: 'It is science that elaborates the cardinal notions that govern our thought . . . before the sciences were constituted religion filled the same office; for every mythology consists of a conception, already well elaborated, of man and the universe'.[5] While scientific ideas grow out of religious conceptions, they also come to replace them; thus, in modern education, science is expected to take an increasingly important place. It is not just the 'superiority' of scientific knowledge which demands this but the fact that, in moral and practical terms, science accords with the spirit and needs of the age. For each age, or stage in the development of civilization, requires and forms a type of total approach to knowledge and learning which is appropriate to it. In this way too, then, Durkheim in his own era, was clearly a 'radical' in the sense of participating in an anti-clerical spirit which undermined the claims of the Catholic Church in education and argued for a secular scientific attitude and practice.

His approach to education was thoroughly sociological in a further sense – in his stress upon the fact that schools were not only dispensing knowledge but were also participating in the socialization of children. For this reason, his studies in education provided yet another base for the examination of the nature of morality, perhaps the subject area in fact in which his precise notions of moral character and development are most explicitly advanced. The first nine chapters of *Moral Education* are essential reading for any student who wishes to grasp not only Durkheim's conception of morality, but ideas about morality which have become widely influential in the social sciences. We have already been introduced to his conceptions 'anomie' and 'egoism' representing on the one hand a state of deregulation, the absence of weakness of coherent moral restraints, and on the other hand, social isolation, the lack of attachment of individuals to social groups which are capable of giving purpose and collective meaning to individual existence. In *The Division of Labour* and *Suicide* he stressed that his lack of regulation (through law, moral precepts, and collective agencies) and this absence of collective life were chronically, most seriously and most evidently revealed in economic life. Therefore economic life was most in need of reorganization and control, and occupational groups most in need of encouragement, both to be achieved in part by the spontaneous action of industrial groups themselves and in part through the intervention of the state. In *Moral Education* he examines the very nature of morality itself and the problem of transmitting collective ideals and ideas to young people. He begins by proposing three essential elements of moral facts: discipline, attachment to social groups and autonomy. As to *discipline* he argued that life in society without some regularity was not possible, that the absence of regularity was a pathological symptom. Normal healthy social life inevitably developed a certain predictability and routine assurance without which, at an extreme point, it disintegrated. This alone may appear to be a thoroughly conservative notion, and the emphasis on discipline and conformity gives understandable grounds for such an interpretation. But it should be seen as being coupled with his argument that 'freedom' from moral restraint was no freedom at all, but the curse of insatiable desires.[6]

The second feature, the collective source of ideals, is an extension of this assumption contained in the first – the essentially social nature of man and morals. 'Moral goals are those the object of which is a society. To act morally is to act in the light of a collective interest'.[7] In this regard we can see a further extension of the ideas about solidarity which are developed elsewhere. Whilst in pre-modern societies, collective ideals are relatively simple and all-embracing, the multiplicity of group life in modern society inevitably promotes a diversity of moral cultures. At the same time modern society promotes a universal respect for these broader and more abstract moral ideas – individualism, justice and peace – which we have mentioned before. As a consequence he argues that the system of education must cater for both these moral facts. It must inculcate ideas of a broad and abstract kind as well as satisfying the differential needs of students preparing for different social functions. Again this may appear to endorse an education system designed to prepare students at different levels, for different and unequal roles; but his endorsement of diversity in the education system presupposes his argument that the division of labour need not and should not entail unjust inequalities. We are led back to his highly contentious but important argument that the division of labour is not inherently unequal. At least, those inequalities, of property, wealth and inheritance, which Durkheim calls 'external' are not intrinsic to the division of labour, and their perpetuation prevents the division of labour from fostering moral solidarity. Certainly children are not to be seen as destined by heredity for a specific role in society: 'In most cases we are not predestined by our intellectual or moral temperament for a given function. The average man is eminently plastic.'[8] So the child must be prepared in a specialized way: 'Each occupation . . . constitutes a milieu *sui generis* which requires specialized knowledge and particular aptitudes';[9] and in a general way, 'for whatever may be the importance of these special educations, it is indisputable that they are not all of education'. And thus Durkheim proceeds to outline that even in a modern society there are certain fundamental ideals developed which the education of the child must embrace.

Discipline and the collective ideal are the first two characteristics of moral facts. Discipline confers freedom from infinite insatiable desires 'For to be free is not to do what one pleases; it is to be master of oneself.'[10] Collective life is the source of all moral life, the application and understanding of which is vastly complicated in modern society by the requirement to understand the balance between those specific moral ideals associated with different milieux, and the abstract ideals expressed in collective life as a whole.

The third characteristic is autonomy. His conception of this is eloquently expressed in this passage from *Moral Education*:

> To act morally, it is not enough – above all it is no longer enough – to respect discipline and be committed to a group. Beyond this, and whether out of deference to a rule or devotion to a collective ideal, we must have knowledge, as clear and complete an awareness as possible of the reasons for our conduct. This conscious-ness confers on our behaviour the autonomy that the public conscience from now on requires of every genuinely and completely moral being. Hence we can say that the third element of morality is the understanding of it. Morality no longer consists merely in behaving, even intentionally behaving, in certain required ways. Beyond this, the rule prescribing such behaviour must be freely desired, that is to say, freely accepted; and this willing acceptance is nothing less than an enlightened assent. Here it is that perhaps the moral conscience of contemporary peoples is confronted with the greatest change; intelligence has become and is becoming increasingly an element of morality.[11]

This awareness of morality extends beyond the moral act merely being intentional, and therefore requires a new attitude in teaching.

> Beyond this first level of awareness, we require another, which goes deeper into the nature of things – the symbolic explanation of the rule itself, its causes and reasons for being. This explains the place we accord to the teaching of morality in our schools. For it is not to preach nor to indoctrinate; it is to explain.[12]

Durkheim's argument here – about the nature of morality and the teaching of it – should be seen as a very significant indication of the atmosphere which he encourages French teachers to impart to their classroom. He has already acknowledged that the moral culture of modern society is in a state of rapid change and upheaval; his stress on explanation suggests that he viewed discussion and scientific intellectual consideration of the rationale of moral principles as an inescapable element of modern education. There is no suggestion of 'layered' education in which intellectual consideration is appropriate for some but not for others. This element of Durkheim's analysis should be placed alongside the emphasis on discipline and the sturdy authority of the teacher. He did not argue for the teachers' authority simply because he believed in authority and discipline but because he thought it to be inevitable that in an advanced society the essential elements of moral and practical culture were so vast and complicated (and so the socialization of children was a burdensome and vital task) that teachers were necessary agents of this transmission whose appreciation of society was bound to surpass that of their charges. From this, and from the collective nature of life and morality itself, stemmed their authority.

Since the desire to demonstrate how sociology could contribute to education, and the wish to understand morality and its place in the educational process, were Durkheim's main aims, the arguments which we have outlined above cover the central themes of his work. There are, however, some further points which appear in his work which are particularly useful for understanding his sociology, and some which have a special interest in relation to recent concerns in education. His argument about the role which the state should play in education reflects his general view of state action (explained in the Introduction and chapter 3). On the one hand the state should not be accorded too much power, on the other hand its increasing importance in modern societies meant that it could not and should not refrain from some intervention:

Since education is an essentially social function, the state cannot be indifferent to it. On the contrary, everything that pertains to education must in some degree be submitted to its influence. This is not to say that it must necessarily monopolize instruction . . . One can believe that scholastic progress is easier and quicker where a certain margin is left for individual initiative; for the individual makes innovations more readily than the state. But from the fact that the state, in the public interest, must allow other schools to be opened than those for which it has a more direct responsibility, it does not follow that it must remain aloof from what is going on in them. On the contrary, the education given in them must remain under its control.[13]

This suggests that he envisaged an education system in which perhaps the majority of institutions were directly administered by the state, but that it should also allow other schools to flourish because of their capacity to innovate. It also suggests that where schools are not under direct state control they ought nonetheless to submit to a kind of state inspectorate which would license these schools as long as they met certain standards – an arrangement of things which is remarkably similar to what has actually happened in several countries. There is little justification for the view that his work on education provides evidence of his increasing attachment to the role of the state and its function of creating and sustaining a powerful collective conscience. As in his earlier recognition of the uncertain state of public opinion (see above) he acknowledges that where opinion is divided the state itself cannot simply create and impose a 'collective conscience':

It is nevertheless necessary to recognize that the state of division in which we now find ourselves, in our country, makes this duty of the state particularly delicate and at the same time more important. It is not indeed up to the state to create this community of ideas and sentiments without which there is no society; it must be established by itself, and the state can only consecrate it, maintain it, make individuals more aware of it.

But in France today:

We are divided by divergent and even sometimes contradictory opinions . . . It is not a question of recognizing the right of the majority to impose its ideas on the children of the minority. The school should not be the thing of one party . . . But, in spite of all the differences of opinion, there are at present, at the basis of our civilization, a certain number of principles which implicitly or explicitly, are common to all, that few indeed, in any case, dare to deny overtly and openly: respect for reason, for science, for ideas and sentiments which are at the base of democratic morality. The role of the state is to outline these principles.[14]

This is perhaps the kind of passage which has led some commentators to argue that after *The Division of Labour* he increasingly argued for the necessity of a strong collective conscience in modern society (what Nisbet has called his recognition of the continuing need for elements of mechanical solidarity). But if we look closely we see that the argument here differs little from that in *The Division of Labour*, since it illustrates the much greater abstraction of the collective principles of an advanced society. Respect for reason, for science, individual dignity and democratic morality are not 'guides to action' or precise norms of conduct in the sense that the mores of simple societies were; they represent the much more general and abstract values which constitute the collective conscience of a typical modern society.

His *Moral Education* is also a conclusive refutation of the argument that in advancing the claims of sociology he wholly neglected psychology, for in it he deals with and refers to psychological questions in a most detailed fashion. He recognized that psychology was a weakly developed science, but combined what he considered to be the best of it with his own judgements to try and outline a psychology of education. He was led to this because, in considering the method by which children could receive a moral education, he felt obliged to consider theories of the personality and moral structure of children. Although haphazard and conjectural, or based on questionable studies, his comments are nonetheless frequently striking and illustrate his concern with questions whose relevance has persisted. He speculates as to how fully a moral conscience has developed in the young child, and as to how much the teacher may rely, in building a moral foundation, on the force of habits inculcated by regular practice. He considers the attention span of young children, what he considered to be the inconstant and erratic nature of their behaviour. In general he concluded that the psychology of children meant that they could not be wholly treated as adults, rather as proto-adults for whom allowances had to be made, all the while keeping their attention turned towards the adult ideals. He even argued that children in a sense resembled 'primitive men', that is they had a moral and intellectual structure resembling 'primitive mentality'. The question of Durkheim's view of primitive men is discussed at length in the chapter on race – it was by no means a flattering view, and it was certainly fed by some very unreliable sources, such as travellers, tales and missionary accounts. The comparing of children and primitives is not so much unflattering to children, as unflattering to and ignorant of primitive society and personality. However, his general argument – that the moral psychology of the child is different from that of the adult – is not necessarily undermined by his attachment to this error. (For full discussion see chapter 4.)

It is true that his work conveys (in Giddens's words) a dour image of the school and the classroom, stressing the importance of discipline and regularity; but he nowhere advocates a stern punishment regime for its own sake. Consistent with his total approach he argues that the vital function of punishment is to reinforce attachment to a moral rule; if it fails to do this it achieves nothing. Indeed over-reliance on punitive sanctions may itself be a symptom of the failure of moral authority in a school (an argument again with many echoes today). On corporal punishment his argument was quite unequivocal:

Such punishments today constitute quite a serious moral handicap. They affront a feeling which is at the bottom of all our morality, the religious respect in which the human person is held. By virtue of this respect, all violence exercised on a person seems to us, in principle, like sacrilege. In beating, in brutality of all kinds, there is something we find repugnant, something that revolts our conscience – in a word, something immoral . . . One of the chief aims of moral education is to inspire in the child a feeling for the dignity of man. Corporal punishment is a continual offence to this sentiment.[15]

His work on education is important in a great variety of ways, not least because of the amount of time and energy which he devoted to it in the middle period of his career. It shows him grappling with problems of vital practical relevance, and struggling to establish the nature of the contribution which social science can make to social practice. It provides perhaps the clearest expression of his view of moral character and individual psychology, and further elucidation of his understanding of the state, the division of labour, group life in modern societies, inequality and the elements of collective morality. It is indeed a dour, stern moralistic view of education and society (with scant mention or regard for sport and leisure), but it is emphatically not 'reactionary', or even conservative in the

sense that many commentators have contended.[16] Rather, it constitutes
further evidence of the great consistency of all his sociological work,
evidence of almost unbroken continuity with the themes outlined in *The
Division of Labour* and further elucidation of these ideas through their
application to a fresh special field of inquiry.

The history of educational ideas in France*

Many English language commentaries on Durkheim's sociology of education and its subsequent influence have only covered the works mentioned
thus far. But in 1904 Durkheim delivered a series of twenty-seven lectures
on the history of French educational thought, lectures of astonishing
breadth and depth. These were published posthumously in Paris in 1938
and 1969 but were not translated into English until 1977.[17] We shall now
examine this work in some detail both for its substantive insights on the
subject and as a model of a historical sociology of education.

Over a thousand years of educational history are covered in this
remarkable work of scholarship and yet the reader never gains an
impression of superficiality. This is partly because of Durkheim's great
erudition and partly because he was so masterly in defining and circum-
scribing the areas of attention. The main object of inquiry is the 'evolution
of pedagogy', the tracing out of the major ideas which have guided
education throughout the period of study. These, he demonstrates, are
conditioned by the much wider range of ideas about man and God and
Nature, by the changing social priorities and sensibilities, and by the
purposes for which educational institutions are founded. Furthermore, all
recognizable educational practices and purposes have, before long, taken
on some institutional form – such as monastery school or university – and
these institutions take on, within limits, a 'life of their own' such that aims,
beliefs and structures of the past become embedded in the present in
organizational forms (like the colleges and faculties of universities) and in
the transmission of central cultural ideas. These institutions may be slow to
change and this inertia may be either detrimental or beneficial. It is
detrimental when institutions whose characteristics are wholly grounded
in a past age fail to respond to new sociological conditions. It may be
beneficial when proposed changes are ill-considered, merely dismissive of
the past and insufficiently 'reflective'. Thus although this work covers a
large tract of history the focus is clear. It is on the major ideas which have
guided teaching and learning, the major shifts in social structure and social

---

* Since in the whole of this section all references are to Durkheim's *Evolution of Educational
Thought*, page references appear in brackets after each citation. For full reference see n. 17.

consciousness which have influenced changes in pedagogy, and on the institutions which have formed the channels through which education has flowed.

He begins by providing a rationale for the study of education in general and its historical study in particular. As in other areas Durkheim feels himself to be fighting against academic prejudice, and modern readers might be comforted to find that Durkheim senses that, in the matter of 'educational theory', he was pursuing a subject held in low regard: 'there is an old French prejudice which looks with a kind of contempt on the whole business of educational theory. It seems to be a very inferior form of study' (p. 4). He dismisses this contempt with some speed. 'Educational theory is nothing more than reflection applied as methodically as possible to educational matters' and no modern activity can afford to neglect reflection on itself.

If we are to learn from this reflection, our study must be historical and sociological for if educational ideas have changed it is because society has changed. Historical study provides us with an understanding of the reasons for things, and with a catalogue of errors; at best it protects against 'neophobia and neophilia', the unconsidered fear of the new and the rash embracing of innovation.

> For while on the one hand one acquires immunity from that superstitious respect which traditional educational practices so easily inspire, one comes to feel at the same time that the necessary innovations cannot be worked out *a priori* simply by our imagination which longs for things to get better, but rather that they must be . . . rigorously related to a totality of conditions which can be objectively specified.
>
> (pp. 9–10)

The study of the past is necessary to the understanding of the present because the past lives on in our present lives:

> for in each one of us, in differing degrees, is contained the person we were yesterday and indeed in the nature of things it is even true that our past personae predominate, since the present is necessarily insignificant when compared with the long period of the past because of which we have emerged in the form we have today.
>
> (p. 11)

At critical periods of social change, the traditions of past ages are challenged, but in the struggle between old and new there is no 'Darwinian' guarantee that the fittest survives. The 'champions of new ideas will willingly believe that there is nothing worth preserving in the old ideas' and 'thus it is that aspects of the past disappear which could have and should have become standard features of the present and future' (p. 13). Few passages could better illustrate Durkheim's temperamental and intellectual disposition towards social change, especially as planned and projected by human intention. Change is necessary and healthy. But if unnecessary damage is to be avoided it must be based on mature reflection. Nor is this just a temperamental disposition; it is an intellectual position which is elaborated throughout this work, especially in relation to its central feature – the challenge of the Renaissance to Scholastic traditions.

Durkheim's story really begins with the early Church influence on education. The zone that is now France had absorbed Roman, Christian and 'pagan' influences but it was the Christian Church above all which provided the reasons and the institutions for organized education in the medieval period. An understanding of language was essential to reading of the Holy Scripture, of history for a chronology of the world, and of rhetoric for a defence of the faith. Thus the earliest schools were opened in the environs of the Cathedrals. 'Cathedral schools and cloister schools, very humble and very modest as they were, were the kind from which our whole system of education emerged. Elementary schools, universities, colleges; all these derived from there; and that is why it is here that we have had to make our starting point' (p. 24).

It would be too easy to conclude that the Church monopolized education simply to indoctrinate; 'One might think that the Church seized the schools in order to be able to block any culture which tended by its nature to embarrass the faith' (p. 25). But the Church was the only institution which could have performed an educational role. 'It alone could serve as the tutor of the barbarian peoples and initiate them into the only culture which then existed, namely classical culture'. In any case, education in the hands of the Church always contained the contradiction that it incorporated the specifically religious and Christian and the secular. 'There was on the one hand the religious element, the Christian doctrine; on the other, there was classical civilization and all the borrowings which the Church was obliged to make from it, that is to say the profane element' (p. 25). Institutions which are primarily religious were bound to take on an increasingly secular character.

The creation of the Carolingian Empire gave new impetus to education inspired by the Church. Although Christendom and the Papacy had great influence, the emergence of an Empire gave European Christendom an organizational form and a material power which made more possible and more urgent the spread of Christian ideas among a diverse grouping of peoples. To attribute the growth of interest in education and the founding of institutions to the Emperor Charles alone would be to grant too much to the genius of a single man: 'this involves reducing an event which exercised so vast an influence on the whole of subsequent history to the fortuitous appearance of a single individual' (p. 38). The true causes were 'certain sociological facts' – the bringing of disparate peoples under a single institutional form which required a new and higher level of unity of thought and belief (p. 40). Schools and colleges were founded so that the Church could achieve its purpose, in educating a clergy able to understand the mysteries of the Scriptures, their minds 'sharpened and exercised by a scholarly training' and accorded prestige and authority as learned men among the people (p. 43). Thus the importance of language and grammar was established to which the Scholastics would add logic and dialectic (p. 59).

From this point Durkheim traces the founding of the universities, the nature of whose earliest beginnings is surrounded by historical disputes, but which, by the twelfth century had begun to take on a distinct institutional shape (p. 90). He draws upon this history to show that certain contemporary ideas of the essential nature of the university are without secure historical foundation. For example, the word 'university' does not relate to the 'universality' of the knowledge taught and sought there but to the fact of some form of incorporation (see chapter 8); indeed several of the earliest universities in Europe (such as that at Bologna) taught few subjects, even only a single subject. Only gradually did separate Faculties begin to emerge. Nor were universities exclusively either religious or vocational, nor solely concerned with the education of the young. The University of Paris from the earliest period had an ambiguous relation with the Church. When it once found itself in conflict with Papal authority it used its strongest weapon – 'the strike'. Rather than submit itself to a Papal decree it declared itself dissolved (p. 89). For a long time universities were bereft of patrimony (p. 89) and had no roots in the ground (p. 89); as scholars and students who could group and regroup where and as they wished they were able to preserve their independence. But for all their peculiarities the universities, in their long period of development, acquired characteristics which have endured. 'A medieval student returning among us and hearing talk of universities, faculties, colleges, the baccalaureate, the licence, the doctorate, the course of studies, essential lectures and special lectures might well think nothing had changed except that the French words have replaced the Latin words formerly used' (p. 162). On hearing the lectures he would see how academic life has been transformed but 'it continues to flow in the same channels'.

By this mid-point in his work Durkheim has established the central features of medieval education and the central elements of his argument. The role of the Church was crucial and educational needs were largely defined in terms of the Church's needs; hence the importance of language, grammar, logic and dialectical argument. Hence also the ambiguous relationship between the sacred and secular elements of the content of education. But the Church also responded to profound sociological and political changes and it is to these that he devotes the major part of the rest of the book, specifically to the social changes implicated in the emergence of Europe from the Middle Ages into the period of the Renaissance.

The closing of the medieval period: the Renaissance, education and the Jesuit order

Apart from some brief closing comments on the French revolution and the nineteenth century, discussion of the Renaissance and the Jesuits' role in education occupies the whole of Part Two of *The Evolution of Educational Thought*. In it Durkheim embarks on a major exercise in the macro-sociology of education, focussing primarily on a process of social and cultural change when theories of education were strongly contested, and illustrating the relationships between social structural change, educational theory and practice, and the innovations introduced by the Jesuits. With regard to the last he examines both what they taught (their definition of appropriate subjects) and how they taught it (their organization of classes and methods of discipline) in considerable detail, providing us with an elegant model of how to study 'curriculum' and 'regulation' in the context of a social and cultural transformation.

Educational ideas and forms of organization changed at the end of the Middle Ages, through the Renaissance, he argues, not only in response to the efflorescence of culture which the Renaissance represented, but also in consonance with profound changes in the fundamental structures of social life, chief among which was the movement towards 'individualism' (see chapters 1 and 3) perceived by Durkheim as simultaneously a social structural, cultural and moral change. He begins by remarking that the rediscovery of classical Greco-Roman culture is seen to be the outward sign of the Renaissance, and indeed that the chance uncovering of hidden cultural treasures may be thought to be the cause of this striking transformation in social consciousness. But this will not stand as an explanation. For one thing it is an exaggeration to speak of classical culture as having lain buried; more important was the lack of will or social impetus to draw upon it except in a narrow and selective manner. 'The Middle Ages' he writes, 'knew all about the main aspects of classical civilization but it only retained what it regarded as important, what answered to its own needs' (p. 168). The stirring of new cultural interests cannot be attributed to chance occurrences. For 'we can be certain in advance that the Renaissance derives not . . . from the fortuitous fact that certain classical works were exhumed at this time, but rather from the profound changes in the organization of European societies' (p. 169). From here he expounds the general principle that 'educational transformations are always the result and symptom of the social transformations in terms of which they are to be explained' (p. 166). Sociologists are always on their guard against accepting the interpretations of historical actors as sufficient in themselves – 'People involved in action are the least well placed to see the causes that underlay their actions, and the way in which they represent to themselves the social movement of which they are a part should always be regarded as suspect and should by no means be thought as having any special claim to credibility' (pp. 167–8). A new and expanded taste for classical education was a response to a new need, 'an urgent need . . . for a kind of culture that would be more refined, more elegant or literary' (pp. 167–8).

The principal social changes, in terms of which the educational and aesthetic changes must be explained, were in the economic realm, in the relations between classes, and in the new social – and more specifically 'status' – sensibilities which were emerging. In the economic sphere 'general welfare had been increased: vast fortunes had been amassed and the acquisition of wealth stimulated and developed a taste for the easy elegant life of luxury' (p. 169). Class horizons and aspirations changed, for, up till then, 'the bourgeoisie had not even dared to raise its eyes to look at the aristocracy across what it felt to be a great fixed gulf' (p. 170). But the bourgeoisie had seen their economic power grow and were no longer prepared to accept a ritualized social inferiority vis-à-vis the aristocracy. Men and women of lowly origin too were swept up in the fashions of status striving and were less and less prepared to endure a philosophy which resigned them to a harsh and mean existence. Manners of the aristocracy were affected by the bourgeoisie, and plebeians adopted the styles of bourgeois gentlemen and women.

Along with this social change went a cultural search for experiences in imaginative literature and expansive thinking. In pedagogy it meant that the stern disciplines of medieval groups of pupils could barely be sustained in face of the demands of individual sensibilities and the thirst for elegance: 'the aesthetic ideal of the Middle Ages was quite unsuited for pupils who had acquired a taste for luxury and the life of leisure' (p. 172). This was then not simply an intellectual revolt against the rigours of Scholasticism. 'The sixteenth century did not accuse Scholasticism simply of having engaged in certain debatable or regrettable academic practices but rather of having constituted a school of barbarousness and coarseness' (p. 204). The new intellectual appetites stemmed from a sociological phenomenon, 'the establishment of polite society' (p. 205).

Having said this much, Durkheim turns his attention primarily to the Jesuits, who, while being in the Catholic Church and tradition, clearly perceived the need to capture and implement the new spirit if all its attractions were not to be lost to the Church; thus they represented, in part, a response to the increasingly threatening progress of Protestantism. Hence the Jesuits reshaped the *curricula* of study, to include the refound admiration for classical literature, art and philosophy, and also created new forms of *organization* of study, both signalling a change in the basic ethos of pedagogy. This was essential if Jesuit teachers were to capture the imagination and loyalty of their pupils in an age when individual personalities 'were emerging from the mass'. 'Now that particular personalities were beginning to stand out from the homogeneous moral and intellectual mass that had been the rule in preceding centuries, it was essential for the Church to be close to individuals, to accommodate its influence over them to intellectual and temperamental diversities' (p. 232). The Jesuits, Durkheim, suggests, were 'the light troops of the Catholic Church' (p. 232).

Durkheim is quick to point out that we should not overestimate the numbers of those who had real access to either the new opportunities for prosperity or the benefits of a culture of elegance that might accompany it. The essential character and at the same time the flaw of this educational theory was that it was essentially aristocratic in nature. 'Neither Erasmus nor Vives had any awareness that, beyond this small world, which for all its brilliance was very limited, there were vast masses who should not have been neglected and for whom education could have brought about higher intellectual and moral standards and an improved material condition' (p. 206). Subtlety and elegance have little relevance for simple survival.

For the majority the supreme need is survival and what is needed in order to survive is not the art of subtle speech, it is the art of sound thinking so that one knows how to act. In order to struggle effectively in the world of persons and the world of things, more substantial weapons are needed than those glittering decorations with which the humanist educationalists were concerned to adorn the mind to the exclusion of anything else.

(p. 206)

The fact that the Jesuits looked back to the traditions of the Catholic Church and forward to the new cultural adventures meant that they were in a peculiar position – and this provides Durkheim with the opportunity to show how a historical group was compelled to manipulate educational materials in order to turn them to good account, whilst retaining control over their charges. They had a 'dual identity as conservatives, even reactionaries, on the one hand, and as liberals on the other' (p. 234), they had to be careful in what they taught and how they taught it. The fact that the materials of classical culture were legendary or remote history facilitated their selectivity. Proper lessons could be derived from skilful use of myths and legends, and historical figures of Greece and Rome could be moulded to suit instructive moral models. The study of the present does not allow this.

The present, because it is before our very eyes, forces itself upon our attention and does not lend itself to this kind of reworking; it is virtually impossible for us to see it other than as it is with all its ugliness, its mediocrity, its vices, and its failings – and this is why it seems to us ill adapted to serve our educational ends.

(p. 251)

(One is bound to wonder if Durkheim is making an oblique comment here on the place of sociology in moral instruction!)

If the Jesuits, in propounding new pedagogical theories, were responding to changes in class relations, status sensibilities and social aspirations, for Durkheim one master process summarizes this social transformation, and that is the moral and social process of individualization.

With the Renaissance the individual began to acquire self-consciousness; he was no longer, at least in enlightened circles, an undifferentiated fraction of the whole . . . he was a person with his own physiognomy who had and who experienced at least the need to fashion for himself his own way of thinking and feeling. We know that at this period there occurred, as it were, a blossoming of great personalities. Now it is clear that in proportion as peoples' consciousness becomes individualized, education itself must become individualized.

(p. 263)

It was in the face of *this* challenge that the Jesuits had to introduce new *contents* into education and new modes of social control in the organization of learning. In respect of *content* their response, as we have seen, was to adapt classical materials to their own ends. In respect of *social control*, and organization, Durkheim stresses two features – the close relationship between master and pupil, and the use of competition as a spur in the organization of teaching and the act of learning. In order to cater for individual feelings the Jesuit teacher had to know each pupil intimately and become familiar with his personal needs. The individual pupil received great attention, but he was never left free to his own devices. Supervision enabled the Jesuit to 'study at his ease character and habits so that he might manage to discover the most suitable method of directing each individual child' (p. 239). In this way the teacher could appeal to the self-esteem of the pupil and to his personal dignity. Hence close, even lifelong relationships were formed between master and charge.

Nonetheless Durkheim reckons there was a clear need for a more general and powerful and organized stimulus to learning. That stimulus was to be competition. Classes were subdivided into groups with 'prefects' responsible for the minute organization of activities and discipline, and groups pitted against each other. Works of individuals of outstanding merit were read out publicly, and less able students were set to evaluate the work of their superiors. Two pupils would even be matched with each other, the one spurred to emulate the work of the other. In clear anticipation of more recent sociology of education, Durkheim is quite explicit in regarding the close relationships of master and pupil, and the reliance on competition as an incentive, above all as mechanisms of social control. Indeed he sees the Jesuits as, in considerable measure, having relied excessively on these principles. Perhaps because of their contradictory role as simultaneously 'reactionary and liberal' they were led, in their search for closeness with the pupil, to overwhelm and smother him; their reliance on competition was carried to painful extremes. His final comment on this gives us a broader insight into his view of competitiveness: 'How can we fail to consider immoral an academic organization that appealed only to egotistical sentiments? Was there no other means of keeping the pupils active than by tempting them with such paltry bait?' (p. 264).

In the last part of the book Durkheim deals with some aspects of the educational innovations made by the revolution, and with nineteenth-century disputes which persisted as issues in his own lifetime. Prior to the revolution, the expansion of commerce and trade had already inspired greater interest in scientific and practical education. But in face of the weight of prestige of the tradition of literary studies, the study of nature had as yet gained little recognition. Leaders of the revolutionary period, inspired by the encyclopaedic view of knowledge, sought to introduce new scientific subjects into the school curriculum and to modify the organization of schools and classes to accommodate them. In so doing they faced new problems; the teaching of more different subjects led towards a 'courses' structure rather than a 'classes' structure and while Durkheim can see the logic of permitting choices in a specialized course structure, he regrets the loss of the unity of the class in which pupils are in continuous contact with each other. Out of the history of centuries he begins to see forming all the dilemmas of modern educational systems: specialization as against general knowledge, 'course-based' as against 'class-based' structures, practical as against aesthetic, and compulsory as against optional. The revolution gave dynamic expression to new ideas, but did not always know how to implement them whilst at the same time retaining the essentially moral character of educational experience.

In sum the achievement of the revolution in the realm of education was more or less what it was in the social and political realms. Revolutionary effervescence was immensely productive to brand-new ideas; but the revolution did not know how to create organs which could give these ideas life . . . It might have been because the revolutionary views were excessive . . . It might have been because institutions cannot be improvised or plucked out of nothing and (since those of the *ancien regime* had been demolished) the essential materials for reconstruction were lacking. It might have been for both reasons simultaneously that the revolution proclaimed theoretical principles far more than it created realities. Even the attempts which it made to translate the theories into realities often redounded to their discredit; for since these enterprises generally ended in failure, the failures were taken as a condemnation of the ideas which had inspired them.

(p. 305)

In the final section he comments upon the issues facing educational policy makers in the France of his day, among whom he himself ranked very highly. The conflicting priorities stressed by past movements in pedagogy represent themselves as the dilemmas of the present, and in many instances Durkheim seems to seek a middle road, extracting what is valuable from past experience and rejecting its excesses. Clearly education must respond to the need to prepare pupils for many different types of occupation; but education which is purely practical or vocational is excessively narrow and cannot fail to deny to the student essential elements of the educational experience. So too must a place be made for the study of language but we must be open to the possibility that the riches which the study of language provides can be reached through translations and by the study of the civilizations which languages expressed. Aesthetic appreciation cannot be ignored but it must avoid a descent into triviality and frivolity. Natural science must be accorded its proper place in the curriculum but if this is only to provide students with the means of understanding and mastering 'things' then it is deficient in that essential quality of education – its moral function:

No-one seriously doubts that teaching is educational only in so far as, by its very nature, it has the capacity of exerting a moral influence on the way we are and the way we think; in other words, in as far as it effects a transformation in our ideas, our beliefs, and our feelings.

(p. 336)

The greatest lesson which historical study can teach us is that human nature is much more flexible than men typically believe. The very notion of a fixed human nature is a false one which has been used in all ages to justify opposition to change.

While it is obvious that human nature cannot become just anything at all, it is equally certain that the limits of what it can become are set very much farther back than is suggested by the crude examination on which popular opinion is based. It is only because we have got so used to it that the moral order under which we live appears to us to be the only one possible; history demonstrates that it is essentially transitory in character. For by showing that this moral order came into being at a particular time under particular circumstances, history justifies us in believing that the day may eventually come when it will give way to a different moral order based on different ethical principles.

(p. 329)

Durkheim's influence on the sociology of education

Traditions in the study of education, perhaps more than in other fields, vary considerably from one country to another and a comparative international survey of Durkheim's influence on these traditions would occupy much more space than is warranted here. We shall look at some general aspects of his influence on the sociological study of education, and then examine some specific instances of Durkheimian inspiration in recent British sociology.

His impact on the sociology of education and on the education system itself in his native France has already been commented on. As the incumbent of a Chair in Education and Sociology at the Sorbonne, he could hardly have been in a more strategic position to shape the discipline and the practice. To the extent that sociology in France was the creation of the Durkheimians, his influence was naturally pervasive in guiding teachers, administrators, and policy makers at all levels of the education system.[18] The distinctiveness of his influence here – by contrast with his influence on other areas of sociology – is marked by the immediacy and practicality of the problems he directly addressed. Therefore the outlines of his sociology of education could be readily translated into the actual curriculum presented to the students who passed through his hands and the hands of his colleagues; the outlines of his prescription for the practical system of education are reflected in the gradual ascendancy of the spirit of educational policies which he advocated. That is, he had always urged the placing of educational studies and education itself in the context of society and the study of society. As to the ascendancy of the *spirit* which his work represented, this is evidenced by the passing of educational reforms freeing public instruction from the grip of the Church, and the replacing of the moral influence of traditional religion with the secular scientific spirit. In the field of education, more than in any other, Durkheim can be seen to have been a man of his time, actively participating in the setting-up of an agenda of public discussion, but also responding to movements in French society which, as it were, set the agenda for him; he was simultaneously the spearhead of a new direction in educational circles, and borne along by external processes of education and institutional change.

National interests and education

The development of systems of education in particular countries bears the marks of the particular agendas set by each nation and for this reason the direct influence of Durkheim's sociology of education is less marked than one might have expected. It is true that, in different countries, some of the same dilemmas are faced – for example, the conflict of religion and science, of the practical as against the aesthetic, of shaping national education to changing national needs, of access to educational opportunity, and the question of the virtues of public intervention in the control of the content and organization of schools; but each country has tended to produce its own heroes of education and educational theory who have set the framework of the study of education in that country.

In the United States, John Dewey's writings confronted the problems of the relationship of school and society, particularly as the change from a basically agricultural–rural nation to an urban industrial one demanded changes in the services which education provided. The educational practices of schools in small towns could become divorced from the needs of a population drifting steadily to the expanding metropolitan areas; his pragmatic proposals for education reform were designed to narrow this gap.[19] A more striking peculiarity of American social history is its dependence on successive waves of immigrant arrivals to labour in its industries and services and to populate its cities. This has entailed a recurring concern with fostering national identity, with assimilating newcomers into the American way of life, and has thus inspired the introduction of a strong theme of *citizenship* in American schools, stressing American political history and the virtues of its constitution. These same immigrant groups brought with them 'national' and religious loyalties which many were anxious to preserve; corporate groups and individual benefactors were anxious to sustain the traditions of the peoples with whom they identified. In the case of American Blacks, educational segregation was not only sought, as it was by some, but also forced upon them. The great majority of private colleges especially in the American South were religious foundations; others were the legacy of the 'racial' uplift doctrines of the Black ex-slave leader Booker T. Washington in his wish to create a 'place in the sun' for the Black man in American society.

More recent educational preoccupations also reflect the particularity of American history. In the late 1950s American educators were spurred by the shock of the Soviet launching of the first Sputnik to search for the reasons for the nation's 'falling behind' in scientific advance. In the sixties and seventies women's movements and the Afro-American and cultural nationalist movements have succeeded in forcing new items on to the national agenda of educational politics; more recently we have seen a widespread concern about standards of educational provision, about the privacy of educational records and about the accountability of educational institutions to public and citizen scrutiny. Some of these concerns reflect the strength of the American civil liberties tradition, others reflect the recurring anxiety to tailor education to national economic needs, and yet others constitute a surfacing of the problems of racism or racial disadvantage. It is not that these issues have no parallel in other countries, rather that the strong particularity of American society gives a high degree of specificity to the phrasing of educational studies. The sheer practicality and urgency of specific educational reforms means that 'the issues' in one country are much more a reflection of national concern than they are of a common concern with 'education and society'. Durkheim's writings have had considerable influence in the United States – especially through the work of Talcott Parsons; but his has been one voice among many.

Sociology and education in Great Britain

In Victorian England, when the question of adapting educational institutions to a greatly changed social order was addressed, it was not only a question of how should people be educated but of who should be educated. The debates were about the appropriateness of education for the masses, and when it was conceded that this was necessary, considerable emphasis was placed on the moral mission aspects of this education. The idea of a divide between minority and majority culture has persisted, but in the twentieth century educational reformers have broadly endorsed universal education as the means of creating a stable, democratic and more just society, as well as one tuned to the needs of a changing industrial base. Lloyd George, the Fabian writers, Beveridge and, after the war, Butler (in the 1944 Act) and Robbins (in Higher Education) are the figures whose careers have punctuated the politics of education. But the sociology of education as an academic field of study and as a direct participant in educational reform, did not make any great impact in Britain or England until the 1940s.

Centred around London University and the London Institute of Education, the greatest intellectual impetus came, not from Durkheim-inspired sociologists, but from the refugee from Nazi Germany, Karl Mannheim.[20] Like Durkheim, Mannheim held an influential if less exalted post, close to the political centre of the country. For much of the 1940s, though attached to the London School of Economics, he gave regular lectures at the London Institute of Education to young teachers, researchers, sociologists and others, people likely to be in a position to influence the new directions in educational provision. In 1946 he was appointed to a Chair at the Institute but his death cut short his tenure to a mere one year. This period of activity was long enough for him to influence men and women who outlived him and he played a major part in shaping education and sociology in England.

Although the direct influence of Durkheim on Mannheim is slight – Marx, Weber, Freud and Mead all receive more references than Durkheim in his group of essays on education – the prospectus of the work is, in some respects, similar. Mannheim, the refugee from Germany, deplored totalitarian forms of political society; as an intellectual liberal he rejected unfree government of 'Left' or 'Right' and dedicated himself to establishing the intellectual foundations of the middle way; if Hitler could plan the enslavement of men and women, people of goodwill could plan for freedom. Planned reconstruction was necessary to preserve the sacred values of freedom and democracy, and this could be guided by a secular social science dedicated to objective study, yet aware of its values. Since educational provision was critical to the achievement of mobility, justice and self-realization, and was the foundation of the moral conscience of the people, few areas could command the attention of the sociologist more urgently. These are all marks of the work of Mannheim and his colleagues which are highly reminiscent of Durkheim and his school. As among the Durkheimians, so with Mannheim sociology was expected to play a major part in explaining the place of education in society, and in understanding the school as a social institution. This was to be supplemented by the discipline of psychology addressed to many of the issues which Durkheim stressed – i.e. discipline, the social and moral development of the young pupil and the question of variable talent and potential. Sociology slowly became established in the 1950s, more rapidly in the 1960s as new universities were built, but it remained for some time excluded from Oxford and Cambridge, getting its main impetus from London and the provincial universities.[21] The impact on Colleges of Education and Faculties of Education was not immediate; sociology slowly took a place alongside psychology which dominated in the teacher training curricula. One of the central themes of British sociology of education – a theme not seen so much in Durkheim's writings – has been the question of educational provision, achievement and the relationships between social class, schooling and social mobility. Durkheim's influence on this was not very great, although some textbooks gave him honourable mention as a founding father of the discipline – as late as 1968 a British sociologist reviewed the field of education and suggested that Durkheim's mark was negligible.[22]

The judgement, if ever at all accurate, would probably have to be modified today. Durkheim's work is better known and understood now than previously, and, with the publication of a translation of his work on pedagogy, it can be seen to have a broader prospectus and relevance. Though several competing models remain in evidence, in the work of Bernstein, Hargreaves and others, the direct influence of Durkheim can be seen in their studies of curriculum, social control and the ethos of education; the interest in macro-sociological questions relating to education shows clear continuities with the Durkheimian tradition.

In a recent article reviewing trends in the sociology of education in the decade of the 1970s, Olive Banks refers to three main approaches. The 'old' sociology of education was primarily concerned with social stratification, educability and social mobility, and this dominated the 1950s and 1960s. The 'new' sociology of education was inspired by ethnomethodological ideas and concerned itself more directly with activities in the classroom and with the influence of teachers' expectations on the educational process. The third strand she refers to as the 'neo-Marxist' contribution and is directed towards the ways in which structural and ideological features of capitalist society are reproduced in the education system.[23] Although Banks makes no mention of Durkheim, the influence of the neo-Durkheimian Bernstein on classroom and curriculum studies, and on studies of the structure and culture of the school, indicates that Durkheim has a significant place in this recent work.

The continuing interest in the ideology or cultural context and cultural message of education bears considerable similarity to Durkheim's whole project in his history of pedagogy – though today the influence of Marxist thought is much more clearly marked. In part, the choice of perspective would seem to turn on whether the culture, or cultures, influencing educational ideas and ideals are principally *class* cultures, and on whether these class cultures are representations of struggle and manifestations of domination. Of course Durkheim's analysis of theories of education in the Middle Ages and the Renaissance attributes considerable importance to social configurations of class and status (see above); the fact that he does not translate this into a general 'class theory of education' simply reflects those understandings of class and the division of labour which we outlined in the earlier chapters. Bourdieu's work represents something of a bridge between the two views, since he clearly relates educational cultures to class sources, but also speaks of institutional sources of shared culture which are not immediately traceable to class interests, and of the sense in which culture and the process of cultural transmission may detach themselves from a readily apparent alignment with society's dominant class. This, of course, strengthens the legitimating role of shared culture.[24]

Bernstein too is mindful of class influences on social consciousness and forms of expression; but he also represents the structure and culture of the school in a distinctly Durkheimian manner. Perhaps the most striking difference between Durkheim and recent writers on the culture of the school is the fact that Durkheim paid relatively little attention to the nature and origins of the beliefs, attitudes and forms of consciousness which *pupils* bring to the school situation, particularly with regard to the possibility that a single institution may contain within it, among teachers and among pupils, sharply divergent cultures or sub-cultures. Bernstein and Hargreaves have considered this question and it is to their work that we now turn.

Class, codes and control

As indicated by the title of his collected essays,[25] Bernstein has been concerned with forms of social control in education, with the 'languages' in which teaching and learning are expressed, and in the class cultures which differentially structure pupils' experience of education. The location of a family in a class position and a class culture tends to endow children within the family with forms of expression, called codes by Bernstein, which shape their receptivity to educational materials. Typically, working class children learn what he calls 'restricted codes' which are less abstract and more immediate in their expression than the typical middle class elaborated code which is more in consonance with the language forms used and rewarded in schools: 'The class assumptions of elaborated codes are to be found in the classification and framing of educational knowledge, and in the ideology which they express.'[26] Thus at the very outset Bernstein is acknowledging one of the ways in which class structures reproduce themselves in educational experience. But he always makes it clear that he does not see class position or class culture as the simple keys which open up the problems of educational experience. For one thing, there are variations within classes in their dispositions towards learning, and for another the culture of the school is not simply an expression of a class code but is also shaped by the varying forms of discipline it imposes or attempts to impose, and by the ways in which curricula and the relations of pupils to teachers are organized. Through variations in these factors, different degrees of congruence are produced in the relationship between family, pupil and school.

He extends his analysis by suggesting that the culture of the school may be understood as containing both expressive and instrumental elements, the expressive represented by the school's attempts to transmit images of proper character, conduct and style, the instrumental represented by the school's efforts to equip the student with skills, facts and the means of making judgements. Families (or their children as pupils) may accept much of the instrumental order of the school but have a strong sense of distance from the expressive order; some may accept the expressive order but have little understanding of the instrumental ends of the school, whether they might accept these or not. A whole range of more and less congruent relationships in conceptually and actually possible. If modifying, adapting to – or accommodating – the different attitudes and 'understandings' of parents and children is considered difficult enough, the difficulties of congruence are compounded by the fact that school cultures are themselves almost constantly changing, pulled by the conflicting demands made upon education, and by the fact that in many schools the culture of the school may be uncertain, ambiguous or in transition. The traditional rituals of school life, under the right circumstances, may function to create or reinforce a relatively homogeneous moral order in the school, expressed in assemblies, corporate activities, the school emblems and uniform, and in the sustaining of a code of punishment and reward. School rituals may be 'consensual', incorporating the whole body of the school's members, or 'differentiating', marking off groups within the school in terms of age, sex, or 'house' membership. The difficulties of ordering relationships in schools by means of these differentiating statuses are amplified when the corresponding marks of status in the wider society are changed or greatly reduced in significance:

The net effect of changes in the significance of age, sex, age relation, and family status for the ordering of social relations is to increase the possibility of innovation within a society and to widen the area of individual choice. At the same time this creates problems of assuring cultural continuity for those transmitting the society's culture, and creates problems of boundary, order ambivalence and thus the identity of the young.[27]

This kind of argument is clearly in accord with Durkheim's analysis of the increasing importance of individualism and individuality, and of the way in which certainties of social status may be undermined. Both Durkheim and Bernstein appear to agree that order founded upon moral and cultural homogeneity and certainty can scarcely be sustained in a modern social order, and that modern social structures necessarily involve a degree of flexibility and ambivalence which they must accommodate. The problem they both faced is the nature of the basis of order which may replace the 'mechanical' forms of the past. In pursuing this question further Bernstein relies quite explicitly on Durkheim's distinction between mechanical and organic solidarity.

Although some schools persist, more or less successfully, in appealing to a sense of common loyalty among their pupils and other schools remain in an ambivalent state in respect of their bases of order, many schools, as moral and social structures, come to approximate to Durkheim's model of the society characterized by organic solidarity. Two typical directions of change may be cited: one is the trend towards greater subject specialism among teachers as branches of knowledge come to be more and more differentiated, the second is that the need or demand for problem-based or area-based studies undermines traditional discipline boundaries (e.g. environmental studies as against 'geography', Caribbean studies as against history). The specialization of teachers' duties leads to a high degree of structural differentiation, but at the same time new emphases in curricula compel teachers to co-operate with each other in new ways:

Under these conditions of cooperative shared teaching roles the loss of a teacher can be most damaging to the staff because of the interdependency of roles. Here we begin to see the essence of organic solidarity as it affects the crucial role of the teacher. The act of teaching itself expresses the organic articulation between subjects, teachers and taught. The form of social integration in the central area of the school's function is organic rather than mechanical.[28]

More important than this primary application of Durkheimian concepts to school organization, are the conclusions he begins to draw out. For he has gradually developed the argument that new forms of teaching – subjects as issues treated in breadth, rather than as disciplines treated in 'narrow' depth – not only affect the social structure of the school but also relate to the total conception of authority in society:

Education in breadth, with its implications of mixture of categories, arouses in educational guardians an abhorrence and disgust like the sentiments aroused by incest. This is understandable because education in breadth arouses fears of the dissolution of the principles of social order. Education in depth, the palpable expression of purity of categories, creates monolithic authority systems serving elitist functions; education in breadth weakens authority systems or renders them pluralistic, and it is apparently consensual in function. One origin of the purity and mixing of categories may be in the general social principles regulating the mixing of diverse groups in society. But monolithic societies are unlikely to develop education in breadth, in school systems with pronounced principles of organic solidarity. Such forms of social integration are inadequate to transmit collective beliefs and values.[29]

Here Durkheim's linking of organic solidarity, or 'plural' social structures, with freedom, individualism and democracy are strongly echoed. But Bernstein's tone is more foreboding, seeing the integrity of the organic system – what he then comes to call the open school or open society – as precarious, and susceptible to threat from elite representatives demanding order and loyalty to uniform values. In the open school 'staff and students are likely to experience a loss of structure and, with this, problems of boundary, continuity, order and ambivalence are likely to arise'.[30] The open school presupposes the open society, and the conditions favouring 'openness' or 'closedness' exist side by side in the social milieu of education. Bernstein insists that his anxiety about the precariousness of 'open' structures is not to be taken as 'a long sigh over the weakening of authority',[31] for, like Durkheim, he is too conscious of those aspects of social change which make traditional forms of authority inappropriate. The weakening of traditional authorities poses problems for modern society, but these are not soluble by efforts to reimpose old certainties, rather they represent a challenge to reconcile the need for moral regulation with the differentiated social structures of advanced societies, the seedbeds of individualism and liberty. But, again, like Durkheim, he is afraid that the anxieties of living in a less certain world, when the new social structures of organic solidarity have incompletely replaced the old, will from time to time strengthen the wish for a 'false' certainty. Here Bernstein is hinting at something like a 'fear of freedom' or a low tolerance for ambiguity. Pupils, for example, may react to the open school with its 'personalized forms of social control, the indeterminacy of its beliefs and moral order', by seeking solace and identity in peer group solidarity.[32]

The strengths of Bernstein's analysis are parallel to those in Durkheim's, that is in the theoretical sociological phrasing of the study of the specifically educational – the relation of pupil to teacher, the rationale of the subjects studied, the direct and indirect effects of different forms of curriculum, and all these particularly in their symbolic and 'moral' aspects – and in the relating of the specifically educational to wider movements of social structural and cultural change. Bernstein has been criticized for an insufficiently sharp specification of class structure and class struggle, or conversely – in tandem with Durkheim – for harbouring an over-consensual view of society.[33] (Indeed the Open University reader on the Durkheimian tradition in the sociology of education, dealing with both writers, provides a classic example of the kind of unbalanced and uninformed view of Durkheim which we discussed in the opening chapter, the blind reliance on Nisbet being a sure symptom of this old orthodoxy.)[34] It is undoubtedly true to say that Durkheim's understanding of class structure and power, as we showed in chapters 2 and 3, is inadequate to say the least. But to say that Bernstein, or Durkheim, was 'not enough of a Marxist' is to say little or nothing at all. But if one accepts, as I do, that there are considerable riches of insight in the Durkheimian tradition, then a more pertinent set of questions is whether these insights can be accommodated within a sharper analysis of class formation and class relations (which may within limits be possible), whether they are only reconcilable with a radical but non-Marxist conception of inequality and social classes, or whether we should simply regard the social institutional, cultural, symbolic and moral framework of Durkheim's analysis as directed towards a different, but nonetheless important, order of sociological question. (Some of these issues are discussed in our concluding chapter.)

While Marxist inspiration has undoubtedly predominated in recent writings, it is nonetheless clear that both Durkheimian and Marxist traditions contrast sharply with narrower, purely prescriptive, and 'micro'-interests in the sociology of education. They stand together against psychologistic, interactionist and 'practical' definitions of the subject, in both laying the foundations of (admittedly different) types of analysis which insist on locating the school and educational system in the broadest moral and material structures of society. As Hargreaves has elegantly pointed out,[35] these (the moral and the material) may be seen as conceptually separate enterprises, united in their 'totalizing' methodologies, and neither of which can be seen as escaping the necessity of the other. Durkheim, as we have seen, fully acknowledged the existence of material inequalities in the social system of capitalism but barely explored their full effects, or the conditions necessary for their eradication or amelioration (see chapter 2). Marx, it could be argued, devoted his energy to the study of the material structures of capitalism, never fully resolved the question of the 'dependence' or 'partial autonomy' of ideal or moral structures, and only dipped his fingers in the analysis of a sociological realm which, for Durkheim, was the essence of society.

It is not therefore surprising that the recent revival of macro- and historical concerns in the sociology of education has drawn, if unevenly, on both traditions. The Marxist influence can be seen in the studies of the cultural and material linkages between the way schools 'process' young people, and the lives and futures they may expect, in the study of the ideological content of school curricula and disciplines, and in some of the studies of deviance. But in the field of the sociology of knowledge (how knowledge is produced and reproduced) Marxist influence has been accompanied by Durkheimian influence and in the case of Bourdieu a fusing of both influences can be found.[36]

Durkheim, deviance and education

A further illustration of the new interest in Durkheim that is both recent and innovative can be found in David Hargreaves's essay on Durkheim, deviance and education. As we indicated earlier, Hargreaves begins by showing that the Durkheimian inspiration has been neglected by scholars with a similar set of interests because of a misapprehension of the import of his work. Hargreaves acknowledged that after Durkheim explored the inequalities 'external' to the division of labour, he left this theme without greatly developing it. Neo-Marxist writing, he suggests, has partially begun to fill that gap. But, if we can, for the moment, sustain this distinction between 'moral' and 'material' aspects of the social order, and conclude that Durkheim at least concentrated upon the former, the choice of emphasis should not be taken to invalidate the work that he did do: 'If sociologists of education are right to develop those aspects of Durkheim's work which he neglected so badly, they are wrong to act as though the aspects which Durkheim himself furthered are themselves unimportant, for they are not.'[37] One part of the proper resolution of this question is the recognition that in dealing with the moral and institutional structures of education Durkheim was dealing with something 'real', something partially 'autonomous' and something important; the other part lies in recognizing that the categories he used (primarily 'egoism' and 'anomie') to analyse moral and social structures in particular (i.e. educational) spheres are continuous with the categories of analysis of society as a whole, so that it is wrong to regard his moralistic analysis as stranded and separated from any understanding of macro-sociological movement, an understanding which was by no means wholly 'cultural', 'symbolic' or idealistic.

Hargreaves illustrates his case by applying Durkheimian ideas to the analysis of deviance in schools. He begins by suggesting a sensible typology of pupils: the committed ('conformist'), the instrumentalist, the indifferent and the opposition. The first share the ideals of the school and its teachers, the second do not, on the whole, but are prepared to play the game for what they may gain from it, the third are bored, only occasionally and with difficulty roused to interest, but lack any systematic critical position towards the 'system' and the last show overt opposition to school and teachers. And it is the last group who are most readily designated (by teachers, administrators, researchers) as deviants. But this group do not readily fit with the analysis of deviance and sociologically rooted pathology as seen by Durkheim, that is in terms of egoism (the individual's moral and social detachment from the community) and anomie (the absence of moral regulation). The opposition do not suffer markedly from these social pathologies (i.e. social disengagement and untempered appetites) and furthermore Durkheim points the way to understanding some types of deviance as indications of necessary social change (i.e. as innovators whose inclinations are at first received with hostility). There is, however, says Hargreaves, 'a much better match between egoism and anomie and the indifferent and instrumental pupil', the indifferent often being the 'loner' with weak ties to friend and family, the instrumental being prepared to 'sacrifice group affiliations for private interests'.[38] These may be close to Durkheim's notion of egoism as excessive individualism, characteristics of the society reflected in the school. Seeing 'unchecked striving' – both in the school and society at large – as potentially pathological rather than normal causes us to rethink our views of meritocratic and progressive principles in schools. This rethinking forces on us reconsideration of topics which modern liberal theories of educational practice have made thoroughly unfashionable:

Here is a vocabulary – discipline, authority, duty, will – which a sociologist of education hardly dare whisper; he will be tempted to close the covers of the book with impatient haste. It soon becomes apparent, however, that discipline is understood as a condition of, not a barrier to, freedom; it is unrestrained egoism which is the true tyranny.[39]

Some of the force and clarity of Hargreaves's argument is lost when he appears to do what others have done – elide egoism and individualism as precisely used by Durkheim (see chapter 1). For he suggests, in summation, that 'Durkheim saw the profound dangers of an individualistic morality'. This is inaccurate if we recall what Durkheim meant by individualism as a healthy development in modern societies (see for example his comments in *L'Évolution pedagogique* reviewed above); it is only 'accurate' if he meant that Durkheim did not see a privatized 'morality' and egoistic striving as the basis of a healthy society.

Concluding comments

Durkheim's sociology of education was an ambitious theoretical and practical project which created a prospectus for the discipline and set it squarely in the context of the discipline of sociology as a whole. The implications of his work are far less 'conservative' than has frequently been judged; in his own time his ideas were counterposed to traditional and reactionary views. This is evidenced in his views on specific questions – on the relation of education to society (i.e. it was not simply to legitimate the social order), his view of religion, science and innovation, his stress on autonomy and his views on human potential, in his views of deviance and punishment – and this particular judgement on his sociology of education parallels our judgement in other fields.

His influence on later work has been rather less than might have been expected. This may have been due to the obscurity of some of his works (at least in English translation), the pull of national agendas of debate, the multi-disciplinary nature of educational studies, the narrowness of empirical and practical interests and, to some degree, the continuing, though slackening, effects of identifying Durkheim with an irrelevant and reactionary posture.

But recent work and recently developed perspectives have given rise to a partial revival of interest in Durkheim's theories. Some of these interests have been Marxist-inspired, but have opened doors to Durkheim as well. The sociology of knowledge, the study of the conditions under which knowledge is produced, shaped and transmitted, is one such instance. Marx and Durkheim shared the view that the understanding of knowledge and ideas could not be abstracted from the study of the social bases upon which they were founded. The great difference was that Marx related cultural production to the class basis of society, whereas Durkheim looked at the relationship between ideas and social structure differently conceived. The Marxist approach has its difficulties – for example the question of the relative autonomy of cultural movement – but does Durkheim offer anything better or at least complementary?

The strongest indications came from *L'Évolution pedagogique en France*. Changes in teaching organization and content were related to an understanding of institutional and cultural and moral change conceptualized in a way which is almost entirely absent from Marx. Although Marx and Durkheim often approach convergence in their interpretation of 'individualism' (i.e. as bourgeois individualism or as egoism), Durkheim's effort to distinguish individualism as the doctrine of the dignity of the individual and civil liberty from 'excessive individualism' – the separation of men and women from any solidary social and moral context of being – takes his sociological imagination into an area unexplored by Marxist thought.

Applied to education, Durkheim's analysis raises the prospect of a critique of liberalism which goes beyond a critique of bourgeois ideas. It raises the spectre of the de-structuration of social life and of authority, and of the absence of *any* form of moral regulation. There is not enough justification for saying that the transcendence of capitalist society results in the problems of 'authority' and 'cultural meaning' solving themselves. True, Durkheim's project does not envisage the 'transcendence of capitalism' – but it does envisage its radical *re*-formation, ideologically and structurally. In the reforming of society, the problems of authority, social integration and cultural meaning are central. Durkheim does not advocate revolutionary struggle; nor, it should be clear, does he accept 'liberalism' as an acceptable formula for a healthy society.

6

꘡꘡

Crime, law and deviance: the Durkheim legacy

ROBERT REINER

Introduction

The work of Emile Durkheim has exerted considerable influence on the subsequent sociological study of crime, law and deviance – more so, perhaps, than on any other major branch of the discipline. A shadowy reflection of his ideas is also discernible in the folk-criminologies of current practitioners in the criminal justice field, specifically in the nostrums of some fashionable tendencies amongst social workers and police officers. The much discussed 'community policing' philosophy of John Alderson (the ex-chief constable of Devon and Cornwall), and his acolytes explicitly draws on Durkheim to argue that a measure of crime is inevitable and ineradicable in any social order, but that a (rather sketchily defined) pathological condition of 'anomie' in society exerts an avoidable crimino-genic pressure.[1] In the introduction to a collection of papers by Alderson and others heavily influenced by his approach, Graham Howes described the contributors as 'Durkheimians to a man – they pledged themselves implicitly, and sometimes explicitly, to the restoration of yesterday's moral community'.[2] This illustrates clearly that the social theory which under-pins the community policing approach is what I have elsewhere called 'bowdlerized Durkheim'.[3] The crux of this is to attribute present problems of policing to a supposed decline in the hold of informal, community-based social controls, and a collapse of authority and discipline within family, education system and industry. The police cannot suppress the resulting crime and disorder by strong-arm, repressive tactics, nor remain a narrow, crime-fighting force. They must adopt a broader service role, co-operating with other social agencies, and (in Alderson's pet words) 'activating the good' that lies within the community. They must research the social sources of crime and monitor the results of their activities, thus building up a police science on which claims to professional status can rest, and more broadly participate in the reconstruction of a social ethic to provide the moral cement for a modern complex, differentiated society, resting on a philosophy of individual liberty.

This conception is *bowdlerized* Durkheim because it neglects the radical side of his concern for the social solidarity of modern industrial societies.[4] Durkheim is clear that solidarity cannot be based on '*yesterday's* moral community', but requires new forms of morality. Furthermore, structural social reform is a necessary though not sufficient condition of the attainment of organic solidarity, for this cannot be based on a social order riven by objective sources of conflict derived from pathological, unjust, forced forms of division of labour.

This version of Durkheim's writings, picturing him as the apostle of a conservative and functionalist approach concerned with the protection of a consensually based morality enshrined in the law, has not only inspired criminal justice practitioners, but also served as a convenient stalking-horse for radical criminologists.[5] As the other chapters of this volume argue, Durkheim's position is too complex to be neatly pigeon-holed as a straightforward conservative or consensus theory.

Durkheim has also been rather ill-served by numerous research papers of a narrowly empiricist kind which attach isolated propositions of his to bodies of data as a way of importing a cachet of theoretical significance to narrowly empirical studies. The purpose of this chapter will be to survey not only what Durkheim said about the related issues of crime, law and deviance, but to review some of the impact of this on later research, and assess the contemporary significance of his perspective.

Durkheim on law, crime and deviance

Law was a fundamental concept in the thesis developed in Durkheim's first book, *The Division of Labour in Society*. Durkheim's main concern here, as elsewhere in his work, was with understanding the problems and preconditions of social solidarity in complex, differentiated, industrial societies. Central to his account was the distinction he developed between two contrasting forms of solidarity – 'mechanical' and 'organic'. 'Mechanical' solidarity is said to be characteristic of simple societies with only a rudimentary division of labour. The individual members of society are uniformly enveloped within a common 'conscience collective', sharing the same values, beliefs and roles. Notions of individual difference, rights and responsibilities are only weakly developed, if at all. Solidarity of such societies is mechanical in that it arises from the similarity of the different atoms constituting the whole.

'Organic' solidarity, by contrast, is that which develops on the basis of an advanced and complex division of labour. Such societies are characterized by the interdependence of units differentiated by economic and social function. Although organically solidary societies do not have a pervasive collective conscience like that associated with mechanical solidarity, the practical interdependence arising out of the division of labour, if combined with an appropriate social ethic recognizing and based upon respect for the individual differences produced by specialized functions, could bind such societies into tightly knit, albeit differentiated, social organisms.

Durkheim's concern with the solidarity of societies in itself logically indicates an indirect interest in deviation and crime, but he brings law explicitly and centrally into his discussion of solidarity for methodological reasons. He observes that 'social solidarity is a completely moral phenomenon which, taken by itself, does not lend itself to exact observation nor indeed to measurement'.[6] Empirical research requires an externally observable and measurable indicator of solidarity, which cannot be directly apprehended in itself. 'We must substitute for this internal fact which escapes us an external index which symbolises it and study the former in the light of the latter. This visible symbol is law.'[7]

This usage of law as the index of social solidarity is based upon a highly tendentious conception of the law–society relation, which Durkheim explicitly elaborates and defends.

Social life, especially where it exists durably, tends inevitably to assume a definite form and to organise itself, and law is nothing else than this very organisation in so far as it has greater stability and precision. The general life of society cannot extend its sway without juridical life extending its sway at the same time and in direct relation. We can thus be certain of finding reflected in law all the essential varieties of social solidarity.[8]

Durkheim recognizes that there may be rules and relations in society which 'fix themselves without assuming a juridical form' and are based on custom. But he sees these as 'assuredly secondary; law produces those which are essential and they are the only ones we need to know'.[9] Custom and law are in conflict only in 'rare and pathological cases which cannot endure without danger.'[10]

Law itself is not explicitly defined by Durkheim. But the implication is that law is the set of rules which are more or less formally promulgated and enforced in a society. It is a kind of legal positivism in that rules need not have any particular substantive content nor any specific formal character to count as law. What is tendentious is the direct linking of law to the moral consensus of a society. This rules out by definitional fiat the exploration of such issues as the conflicting social interests which law might serve, or an adequate account of the process of legislation which may reflect struggles between competing interests and conceptions of morality. The methodological strategy of assuming law to be an index of solidarity seems to presuppose a consensus view of law, even though later in the same book, when discussing the forced division of labour, Durkheim acknowledges that legal rules may reflect and even exacerbate class conflict.[11]

Having established to his satisfaction that 'law reproduces the principal forms of social solidarity', the next task for Durkheim is 'to classify the different types of law to find therefrom the different types of solidarity which correspond to it'.[12] In line with his general conception of sociological method, Durkheim argues that we cannot simply take on board the distinctions already drawn by jurists, such as that between private and public law. 'To proceed scientifically, we must find some characteristic which, while being essential to juridical phenomena, varies as they vary.'[13] He finds this in the essential character of law as 'sanctioned conduct', and develops a distinction between two forms of legal sanction which correspond to the two types of social solidarity.

'Repressive' law is enforced by penal sanctions which 'consist essentially in suffering, or at least a loss, inflicted on the agent'.[14] It is associated with mechanical solidarity in that it expresses strong, shared social sentiments. Violations of these result in sanctions harming the offender and extracting vengeance for the assault on the conscience collective. Repressive law does not necessarily require any specialized judicial machinery for its enforcement – it may be exercised by the collective as a whole, although this must be an organized act.

'Restitutive' law, by contrast, 'consists only of *the return of things as they were*, in the reestablishment of troubled relations to their normal state'.[15] It is concerned with the regulation and co-ordination of relations arising from the division of labour. Restitutive sanctions do not result from violations of the conscience collective, and do not reflect the same strong sentiments as those producing a penal reaction. Restitution is 'not expiatory, but consists of a simple *return in state*'.[16] Restitutive law may be negative, involving 'pure abstention', i.e. rules delimiting areas of personal rights such as property, or positive, constituting the co-operative relations of the division of labour, e.g. contract or administrative law.[17] Restitutive law corresponds to a highly developed division of labour. It is more specialized and complex in both substantive content and organizational machinery and personnel for its administration. It is a reflection of a movement towards organic solidarity based upon positive co-operation.

Durkheim's theses about law stimulated a debate about their empirical validity which still flourishes today.[18] Although presented as if it were a readily testable empirical hypothesis, Durkheim's claims about legal evolution are extraordinarily difficult to assess. Durkheim himself states blithely that 'it will suffice, in order to measure the part of the division of labour, to compare the number of juridical rules which express it with the total volume of law'.[19] This, however, is no simple job for a pocket calculator. Given that there is a distinction between 'the law in the books' and 'the law in action', it is not clear that it is satisfactory to take all written codes, statutes and case-law (even if this Herculean task could be accomplished) as corresponding to 'the total volume of law' which is active in a society. This problem applies *a fortiori* to non-literate societies without any 'law in the books'. Nor is there any simple metric for counting the number of rules of different kinds. Is a statute with eight sub-sections detailing special applications one law or nine? Furthermore, the nature of sanctions is postulated as the index of the character of law. But how are these to be assessed precisely? Is a sanction of capital punishment for a particular offence which is seldom applied in practice more or less 'repressive' than a sanction of imprisonment which is regularly applied? As the criminologists and penal reformers of the classical school argued at the turn of the eighteenth century, there is a payoff between the nominal severity of sanctions and the likelihood of their effective application. Which for Durkheim is the most important? As the classicists also argued prevention of crime by professionally organized policing may control society more tightly than the threat of severe sanctions seldom enforced. But is a penal code safeguarded by intensive police patrol and surveillance more or less repressive than one nominally buttressed by severer sanctions which are very uncertainly applied? Does the contention that restitutive law advances in relation to repressive mean that restitutive sanctions displace repressive ones for the same offence, or that new offences with restitutive sanctions are added on in disproportionate volume to the existing penal code? The impression created by Durkheim that the path of legal evolution may be readily charted by a quantification of sanctions is clearly misleading.

Durkheim's interest in social solidarity and the character of legal sanctions as the index of this led him to more specific analyses of crime, deviance and punishment, in *The Division of Labour*, and in some of his later works, particularly *The Rules of Sociological Method, Suicide*, and 'Two laws of penal evolution'. The starting point for Durkheim's treatment of crime and deviance is the formulation of a definition of crime which has been highly influential in subsequent criminology, particularly since the development of the 'labelling theory' perspective in the early 1960s. Durkheim rejects the definition of crime which would constitute the commonsense of any society – that crimes are acts which are harmful to society or contrary to natural justice. He points to the enormous variation between societies in the acts which have been regarded as criminal in order to rebut the claim that conceptions of crime are rooted in the social evil represented by particular actions. 'There are many acts which have been and still are regarded as criminal without in themselves being harmful to society.'[20] The only attribute applicable to crimes in general is that they are socially proscribed and punished. 'The only common characteristic of all crimes is that they consist . . . in acts universally disapproved of by members of each society . . . Crime shocks sentiments which, for a given social system, are found in all healthy consciences.'[21] It is social reaction and labelling, not the intrinsic character of an act, which constitutes it as a crime. 'We must not say that an action shocks the common conscience because it is criminal, but rather that it is criminal because it shocks the common conscience.'[22] To this primary definition Durkheim adds two riders. Crimes are distinguishable from more minor moral peccadilloes by the *strength* of social disapproval. 'The collective sentiments to which crime corresponds must, therefore, singularise themselves from others by some distinctive property; they must have a certain average intensity. Not only are they engraven in all consciences, but they are strongly engraven.'[23] Furthermore, only specific acts can be criminalized, not diffusely defined patterns of conduct, no matter how intense the moral condemnation they attract. 'The wayward son, however, and even the most hardened egotist are not treated as criminals. It is not sufficient, then, that the sentiments be strong, they must be precise.'[24] In sum, 'an act is criminal when it offends strong and defined states of the collective conscience'.[25]

Crime thus defined is a universal feature of all societies argues Durkheim. This is because crime performs a vital social function in any society. Through the punishment of offenders not only are the moral boundaries of the community clearly demarcated, but the strength of attachment to them is reinforced. The purpose of punishment is neither deterrence, rehabilitation of the offender, nor the administration of his just deserts. Punishment strengthens social solidarity through the reaffirmation of moral commitment among the conforming population who witness the suffering and expiation of the offender.

Its true function is to maintain social cohesion intact, while maintaining all its vitality in the common conscience . . . We can thus say without paradox that punishment is above all designed to act upon upright people, for, since it serves to heal the wounds made upon collective sentiments, it can fill this role only where these sentiments exist . . . In short, in order to form an exact idea of punishment, we must reconcile the two contradictory theories which deal with it: that which sees it as expiation, and that which makes it a weapon for social defence. It is certain that it functions for the protection of society, but that is because it is expiatory.[26]

To this functionalist argument for the universality of crime and punishment, Durkheim adds another line of reasoning in his later treatment of crime as a 'normal' rather than 'pathological' feature of societies in *The Rules of Sociological Method.* This rests upon the statistical assumption of inevitable variation in individual character. 'It is impossible for all to be alike, if only because each one has his own organism and that these organisms occupy different areas in space.'[27] Although specific offences may become inconceivable due to progressive refinement of the moral sentiments of society, this will make people more sensitive to the marginal failures to conform which inevitably still remain, rather than eliminating crime.

Imagine a society of saints, a perfect cloister of exemplary individuals. Crimes, properly so called, will there be unknown; but faults which appear venial to the layman will create there the same scandal that the ordinary offense does in ordinary consciousnesses. If, then, this society has the power to judge and punish, it will define these acts as criminal and will treat them as such.[28]

As the final strand of his demonstration of the normality of crime, Durkheim unites the functionalist and statistical arguments in the claim that crime can have a positively beneficial, progressive role in social evolution. Individuals who anticipate necessary adjustments of social morality to changing conditions may be stigmatized as criminal at first. Crime is the precondition and the proof of a society's capacity for flexibility in the face of essential change.

How many times, indeed, it is only an anticipation of future morality – a step toward what will be! According to Athenian law, Socrates was a criminal, and his condemnation was no more than just. However, his crime, namely, the independence of his thought, rendered a service not only to humanity but to his country.[29]

The conclusion of Durkheim's argument is that contrary to the conventional view that crime is a social pathology that must be eradicated, it is a normal and inescapable phenomenon which can play a useful part in facilitating social progress. So much for the familiar image of Durkheim as the apostle of social control.

Contrary to current ideas, the criminal no longer seems a totally unsociable being, a sort of parasitic element, a strange and unassimilable body, introduced into the midst of society. On the contrary, he plays a definite role in social life. Crime, for its part, must no longer be conceived as an evil that cannot be too much suppressed. There is no occasion for self-congratulation when the crime rate drops noticeably below the average level, for we may be certain that this apparent progress is associated with some social disorder.[30]

Durkheim stresses that it does not follow from the normality of crime that it is not to be abhorred. His argument is not an apologia for the criminal. Firstly, there is nothing contradictory about abhorring something which is inevitable or even functional, as we do with physical pain in illness. But more fundamentally, it is largely through the process of *punishment* that crime becomes functional, apart from the Socrates-type case of the progressive deviant.[31]

Furthermore, although Durkheim does not bring this out in his general consideration of crime, even if *some* level of crime is necessary in any society, the *actual* rate may well be pathological and a reflection of social disorganization. Durkheim gives us no ready recipe for calculating the 'normal' rate for particular social types, but his treatment elsewhere of specific forms of deviance both illustrates the possibility of pathological levels of crime, and provides a model for its analysis. The best-known and most fully articulated study of a specific kind of deviance is his celebrated *Suicide*, but Durkheim also offers a rather more cursory account of homicide in *Professional Ethics and Civic Morals*, chapter 10.

Durkheim's basic concern is to demonstrate that the rate of suicide (and by extension other kinds of deviation) is a function of the general state of social integration and regulation. His two basic types of suicide, egoistic and anomic, are results of the breakdown of social integration and regulation respectively. The egoistic type of suicide (induced from the greater suicide-propensity of Protestants rather than Catholics, the unmarried and childless rather than the married or those with families, and the drop of suicide rates at times of war or national crisis) is the result of a weakening of bonds integrating individuals into the collectivity. The anomic type of suicide (induced mainly from the relationship between suicide and sudden dislocations of economic life) is the product of moral deregulation, a lack of definition of legitimate aspirations through a restraining social ethic which could impose meaning and order on the individual conscience. Both are symptomatic of a failure of economic development and the division of labour to produce that organic solidarity which Durkheim anticipated as the normal condition of industrial societies. The remedy lies in social re-construction to provide the material and moral preconditions of solidarity. This account of the way that the roots of deviation lay in pathological states of the social order, in particular anomie, has been one of the most influential aspects of Durkheim's work on subsequent criminology.[32]

A decade after his initial treatment of legal evolution in *The Division of Labour*, Durkheim returned to the subject in his essay on 'Two laws of penal evolution', which contains his most developed statement on law, crime and punishment. Paradoxically, he makes no reference to his earlier treatments, even though he clearly takes account of some of the contemporary criticisms of his work.

In this essay Durkheim seeks to establish and explain two laws which he claims have governed the evolution of the apparatus of punishment. The first, which he calls 'the law of quantitative change', he formulates thus: 'The intensity of punishment is the greater the more closely societies approximate to a less developed type – and the more the central power assumes an absolute character.' [33] This is clearly a reformulation of his legal evolution hypothesis from *The Division of Labour*, with the concepts of mechanical and organic solidarity being displaced by a rather looser notion of degrees of development. Most importantly, however, a subsidiary hypothesis relating the penal system to the character of the state has been added, evidently to explain exceptions to the postulated primary 'law'. The second law, 'of qualitative changes', is formulated as: 'Deprivations of liberty, and of liberty alone, varying in time according to the seriousness of the crime, tend to become more and more the normal means of social control.' [34]

To substantiate his first law, Durkheim adduces the augmented forms of the death penalty (discussed in stomach-turning detail) found in some ancient societies. [35] For non-capital offences, physical punishments symbolic of the crime (such as tearing out the tongue of a spy) were used. With the development of 'city states' the augmented forms of capital and corporal punishment decline, a process accelerated in 'Christian societies'. This process of progressive decline in penal harshness is reversed after the fourteenth century as 'the king's power became more and more firmly established', reaching a climacteric in the increasingly severe penal codes of most European countries during the eighteenth century. 'The apogee of the absolute monarchy coincides with the period of the greatest repression.' [36] This interlude is an illustration of the subsidiary hypothesis in Durkheim's first law, relating punishment to state power. The late eighteenth century and nineteenth century witnessed a renewal of the major trajectory towards less severe punishment, as the arguments of the penal reformers such as Beccaria, Bentham and many others began to prevail. The reforms associated with the liberal utilitarians involved not only quantitative declines in harshness of punishment, but the qualitative change to imprisonment as the dominant penal techniques which Durkheim enshrines as his second law.

In explaining the laws Durkheim argues that changing forms of punishment are due to changes in the character of crime, which in turn is related to the form of social solidarity and conscience. 'Since punishment results from crime and expresses the manner in which it affects the public conscience, it is in the evolution of crime that one must seek the cause determining the evolution of punishment.' [37]

Durkheim distinguishes between two kinds of crime. The criminality characteristic of primitive societies offends against sentiments which have *collective* things as their object, as well as being sentiments which are collectively shared. The offended sentiments and objects are imbued with a strong religious element, which gives crime an exceptionally odious character calling down violent repression on the perpetrator. By contrast the crime associated with modern societies offends collective sentiments which have the *individual* as their object, it is a human rather than religious criminality. This lessens the intensity of repression for the 'offence of man against man cannot arouse the same indignation as an offence of man against God'.[38] Moreover, the punishment of the offender evokes sentiments of qualitatively the same kind of horror for individual suffering as that for the victim, thus mitigating the force of the collective sentiment for reprisal. The result is that 'Seeing as, in the course of time, crime is reduced more and more to offences against persons alone, while religious forms of criminality decline, it is inevitable that punishment on the average should become weaker.'[39]

While focussing on the changing character of repressive law (from religious to human) as societies develop, thereby implicitly recognizing the strength of survival of penal law in modern societies, Durkheim does not pursue further *The Division of Labour*'s insights into the proliferation of non-penal, restitutive forms of law. The argument that harshness of sanctions is related to absolutist state power allows him to modify his claim that punishment is completely determined by social structure. But the theoretical advance of introducing a political dimension into the explanation of punishment is weakened by his insistence that state forms vary quite independently of the changing social structure (a claim which contradicts Durkheim's other writings on the state, as chapter 3 shows). This closes off the possibility of developing a political sociology of punishment which would have to relate state, law, and social structure in a way that explores their interdependence. In effect in the 'Two laws' essay, Durkheim introduces the state as a residual category to explain away apparent deviations from his primary thesis.

The second law postulating the emergence of imprisonment as the dominant penal technique in modern times, is explained largely by the coincidence of the development of a notion of individual rather than collective criminal responsibility, requiring pre-trial detention of offenders, with the practical availability of secure buildings due to social centralization and urbanization. The move towards imprisonment as a pure form of punishment is explained as a corollary of the first law, declining penal harshness, once the means and practice of incarceration had become established. Durkheim's account of the second law is altogether sketchier and subordinate to the first, and he fails to develop in any serious or sustained way the obvious inter-connections between imprisonment and utilitarian penal philosophy which would be consonant with his general conception of modern society, notably its suitability for precisely graded variations of severity. Nor does Durkheim consider the varying penal philosophies which developed in the nineteenth century to justify imprisonment and explain its purpose. He ends rather limply with the vague call for new forms of penal institution to be 'born which correspond better to the new aspirations of the moral conscience'.[40]

The influence of Durkheim on criminology and sociology of law

The Durkheimian legacy is manifest primarily in three strands of contemporary work on crime and the law: (a) the influence of his conception of crime on 'labelling' theory; (b) theories of crime causation within the 'anomie' framework; (c) debates about legal and penal evolution.

(a) Durkheim and 'labelling' theory

Durkheim's conception of crime had a considerable influence on that paradigm shift in criminology in the 1960s which can loosely be called 'labelling theory', primarily through the work of Kai T. Erikson, one of its leading progenitors.[41] What was influential was Durkheim's basic conception of the dependence of crime on social reaction, and his arguments about the normality of deviance. In so far as any model of crime *causation* can be induced from Durkheim it would be at odds with the basic thrust of labelling perspectives. The core idea underlying all the diverse strands of 'labelling theory' and the various other 'new criminologies' was that the understanding of crime had to be related to that of social control. Contrary to the correctionalist stance of criminology hitherto, which had concerned itself only with the causation of criminal behaviour, 'labelling theory' directed sociological attention to the emergence and application of criminal law itself. Labelling theorists rejected the taken-for-granted notion of crime as an unequivocal social problem which had dominated criminology hitherto. This all echoes Durkheim's remarks to the effect that crime is not necessarily pathological or harmful and that 'the only common characteristic of all crimes is that they consist . . . in acts universally disapproved of by members of each society'. But the dominant theoretical tendency in recent explanations of the labelling process has been a symbolic interactionist one, stressing the face-to-face encounters of potential deviants and control agents. This is sharply at odds with Durkheim's view that particular societies exert special pressure for higher rates of deviation.

The explicit importation of Durkheim's conception of crime into labelling theory was through the work of Kai T. Erikson, who wrote *Wayward Puritans*, a study of deviance in seventeenth-century Massachusetts, as well as a theoretical paper 'Notes on the sociology of deviance' which has been reprinted in all the standard 'labelling theory' anthologies.[42] Both works draw heavily on Durkheim.

Erikson begins his book by citing Durkheim's observations on the normality of crime, and its 'integral part in all healthy societies'. He develops Durkheim's arguments about the functionality of crime in reinforcing social cohesion, and regards his work as an empirical historical study 'addressed to the question he [Durkheim] originally posed: does it make any sense to assert that deviant forms of behaviour are a natural and even beneficial part of social life?'.[43] In his study Erikson examines closely what he calls three 'crime waves' (i.e. episodes of heresy and witch-hunting) in the seventeenth-century Bay colony, to demonstrate the boundary-maintaining role of deviance, and also claims to show that the court records for the period imply long-term stability in the offender rate. This is used to bolster the argument that 'societies somehow "need" their quotas of deviation and function in such a way as to keep them intact'.[44]

Erikson's work is evidently congruent with Durkheim's arguments about the normality of crime. However, there are crucial differences between Erikson (and other labelling theorists) and Durkheim's overall perspective. Firstly, whilst Durkheim argues that the definition of crime is socially relative and not necessarily explained by social harmfulness or injustice, he does recognize some constancies in what are seen as crimes, notably homicide. It seems that he does recognize a 'minimum content of natural law' (in H.L.A. Hart's phrase) even if he is aware of the rich variety of behaviour that has been defined as crime in different societies. Second, although Durkheim stresses the social relativity of what counts as crime between societies, he does not see as problematic the attachment of deviant labels to individual offenders and instances of offending within a society, which is the prime concern of labelling theorists. 'Crime shocks sentiments which, for a given social system, are found in all healthy consciences.' Durkheim ignores the ambiguities and conflicts about morality within a society which are the stock-in-trade of the work of labelling theorists. Thirdly, while Durkheim regards a certain rate of crime as a normal, inescapable feature of society, he is also aware that particular societies may be in a pathological condition which generates excessive deviance. His accounts of this are far more congruent with traditional sociological criminology than labelling theory, and it is to his impact on theories of the aetiology of crime that we turn next.

(b) 'Anomie' and theories of crime causation
Durkheim has been a major influence on American criminological theory through Robert Merton's adoption of the concept of anomie as the basis of his explanation of crime in a classic paper first published in 1938.[45] Merton sets out to develop an 'analysis of social and cultural sources of deviant behaviour', explicitly intended as a sociological critique of biological or

psychological conceptions of the deviant as individually abnormal. 'Our primary aim is to discover how some *social structures exert a definite pressure upon certain persons in the society to engage in non-conforming rather than conforming conduct.'* [46]

Merton's account rests upon a distinction between two central elements of social structure and culture: (a) the goals which are culturally defined as desirable; (b) the institutionalized means which are defined as legitimate and available for the pursuit of the culturally sanctioned goals. In a well-regulated society these goals and means are harmoniously integrated. The population as a whole both accepts the cultural goals and has available legitimate means for their fulfilment. But malintegration can occur if there is disproportionate emphasis on either goals or means. In some societies the goals might be overemphasized without corresponding emphasis on the availability and legitimacy of means, while in other societies the goals may be lost sight of and the means become exclusively emphasized as meaningless rituals.

Merton points to contemporary American society as an example of the first type of malintegration, where there is undue emphasis on goals to the exclusion of concern about the availability of legitimate means. Specifically, he argues, money has come to be elevated as a value in itself, the main purpose of life. The desire to make money is extolled by the culture without corresponding attention to the way in which it is made. Money becomes an end at the cost of the satisfactions it might bring, for success in monetary terms is 'indefinite and relative'.[47] The limit of aspiration can never be clearly defined. Overemphasis on material goals measured exclusively by money implies a breakdown in the capacity of the regulatory structure of society to set limits to individual aspirations, i.e. anomie results (enter Durkheim).

In the United States an anomic strain arises not only from the cultural emphasis on monetary success, but also from the disjuncture between some central ideological tenets and structural reality. A core part of American ideology depicts America as a basically meritocratic society where opportunities for success are evenly distributed and careers are open to the talents. Behind the facade of rags-to-riches mythology, however, opportunities are unequally structured. Thus on the one hand American culture bombards people with messages about the importance of continuous striving for material, specifically monetary, success, and stresses the equal possibility of its attainment for everyone, thus rendering failure the fault of the individual, whilst in reality an unequal social structure sets differential barriers to success. The result is anomie, a strain in the regulatory structure, deriving from the disjuncture between culturally prescribed goals and the means available for their realization.

Mode of adaptation	Culture goals	Institutionalized means
I. Conformity	+	+
II. Innovation	+	−
III. Ritualism	−	+
IV. Retreatism	−	−
V. Rebellion	±	±

The effects of strain are experienced differently by individuals at various points in the social structure, and the different pressures typically produce various sorts of outcome. Merton develops a famous typology of these adaptations.[48]

The last four of these are seen as 'deviant' adaptations. 'Innovation' is the response that involves most of what is labelled as crime in America. A climate which stresses the importance of material success as a goal for everyone, but fails to provide the legitimate opportunities for its achievement, puts pressure on people to engage in the pursuit of the goal by illegitimate means, i.e. resort to crime. 'Ritualism' is the adaptation of the person who cannot achieve the prescribed goals, but has been so strongly socialized into following only legitimate methods that he clings to these in a ritualistic way, losing sight of the original ends. Merton sees this as a typically lower middle class adaptation, based on the coincidence of strict socialization and limited opportunities. 'It is the perspective of the frightened employee, the zealously conformist bureaucrat in the teller's cage of the private banking enterprise or in the front office of the public works enterprise.'[49] 'Retreatism' involves rejection of both goals and means – withdrawal from the social race altogether. The retreatist is '*in* the society, but not *of* it'. He has so strictly internalized notions of the legitimacy of certain means that he cannot innovate, but lacking the opportunity to use legitimate means he escapes from moral conflict by renouncing both means and goals. Into this category Merton places 'psychotics, autists, pariahs, outcasts, vagrants, vagabonds, tramps, chronic drunkards and drug addicts'.[50] 'Rebellion' involves not merely the negative rejection of social goals and means of the retreatist, but a positive attempt to replace them with another set seen as morally superior. Rebels endeavour 'to introduce a social structure in which the cultural standards of success would be sharply modified and provision would be made for a closer correspondence between merit, effort and reward'.[51] If they succeed they become the 'culture heroes' of the future society. As Merton argues in a later paper, 'the rebel, revolutionary, non-conformist, heretic or renegade of an earlier day is often the cultural hero of today'.[52]

The major thrust of Merton's argument is to explain how the structure and culture of a society can produce pressure towards deviation, deriving from an anomic disjuncture between goals and means. A society which places great emphasis on the goal of monetary success for all, but offers differential chances for achievement (like contemporary America) will be an especially criminogenic one, pressurizing people to achieve by illegitimate means. However, modes of coping with this strain will vary according to position in the social structure. The pressure will be greatest on those at the bottom to whom the success goal is held out, but who are ill-equipped to succeed in legitimate ways, and are not as strongly socialized as the lower middle class into the conventional morality which precludes illegitimate means. Thus Merton not only claims to explain the overall criminogenic pressure of modern society (especially the US) with its ethos of universal material success, but also its patterning as represented by official criminal statistics, i.e. that crime appears to be a lower class phenomenon. While emphasizing the especial weight of anomic strain on the relatively deprived, Mertin is acutely aware of the extensive deviance (largely hidden from discovery by law-enforcement agencies) of the more privileged. Indeed, he begins his section on 'innovation' with a lengthy discussion of 'white-collar' crime before turning his attention to working class offences.[53] Merton is certainly not an uncritical interpreter of official crime statistics, but he nonetheless argues that it is plausible that criminality is inversely related to class position, whatever the deficiencies of the data indicating this.

> But whatever the differential rates of deviant behaviour in the several social strata, and we know from many sources that the official crime statistics uniformly showing higher rates in the lower strata are far from complete and reliable, it appears from our analysis that the greatest pressures towards deviation are exerted upon the lower strata.[54]

Numerous criticisms have been levelled against Merton's theory since its original appearance, and Merton himself responded to some of these when his original article was re-published in book form.[55] Later discussions of Merton can be divided into two groups: extensions and *empirical* criticisms which develop the detail of his account but do not challenge his overall framework, and *theoretical* criticisms.

(1) Extensions and empirical criticisms (i) There are many aspects of the theory which are undeveloped. Indeed, Merton stresses this in the concluding paragraph of his original paper. 'This essay on the structural sources of deviant behaviour remains but a prelude.'[56]

Since Merton's original formulation numerous attempts have been made to spell out the structural and social-psychological processes which explain the varying deviant responses to anomic strain. This constitutes a significant tradition in the theory of deviant sub-cultures.[57] The work of Cloward and Ohlin in particular offers an account of the formation of different delinquent sub-cultures as a function not only of the inequality of opportunities to succeed by legitimate means, but as a result of inequality in the distribution of the means of *illegitimate* success.[58] Their notion of an *illegitimate* opportunity structure co-existing alongside the legitimate one described by Merton is an important addition to his basic theoretical framework. It explains the development of retreatist sub-cultures, for example, as a product of double disadvantage in both the legitimate and illegitimate opportunity structures.

Albert Cohen's account of the violently expressive, rather than utilitarian and calculative, character of much delinquency as a 'reaction formation' in the face of failure is another important extension of Merton's analysis. Cohen himself denies that his theory derives from Merton's, which he sees as satisfactory only for explaining 'adult professional crime' and 'property delinquency'[59]. But as Merton himself argued in a reply to Cohen, there is nothing in his original formulation which implies that deviance will be calculative or rational.[60] His typology says nothing about the emotional quality of the deviance which results from anomic strain, and this requires the specification of intervening variables (such as Cohen's concept of 'reaction-formation'). In this sense it seems clear that Cohen's theory of delinquent gangs is an extension rather than rebuttal of Merton's framework. The same argument applies to Cohen's later critique of anomie theory as concentrating on individual rather than group deviant responses, and neglecting the tentative and contradictory nature of the process of development of delinquency, as well as the interaction between the delinquent and the labelling responses of social control agents.[61] All these points are ones which (while valid) can be seen as compatible with Merton's basic analysis of the social structural sources of strain towards deviance.

(ii) Merton's assumption that American culture holds out the same success goals to all social strata has been challenged. An example of this criticism is a paper by Hyman which demonstrates on the basis of opinion-poll data that higher proportions of those in more advantaged positions affirm the success goal than among the relatively deprived.[62] Merton replies to this at length, arguing that it is only essential to his theory that there be greater strain at the bottom of the hierarchy.[63] The lower proportions of the deprived who affirm the success goal still represents higher absolute numbers. Furthermore, the *degree* of strain may be greater upon those among the less advantaged who have internalised the success goal.

(iii) Many critics influenced by the phenomenological critique of official statistics have argued that Merton's analysis takes at face value the disproportionate working class criminality which appears in counts of people processed by social control agencies. Studies of the criminal justice system have demonstrated the bias against the socially powerless which operates at each stage of the processing of suspects, while studies of self-reported deviance and white-collar crime testify to the prevalence of offending at the top levels of the social scale. '"Deviance" is far more widespread than Merton would allow . . . Anomie theory stands accused of predicting too little bourgeois criminality and too much proletarian criminality.'[64]

It has already been pointed out that, *pace* his critics, Merton was well aware both of the extensiveness of white-collar crime in the suites, and of the way that official statistics disproportionately record crime in the streets. However, the assumption of his critics that the apparent prevalence of lower class criminality is solely a product of the system's biases is implausible. In a society where most crime is property crime, and where material success is generally valued but resource distribution is skewed, it is plausible to suppose that the pressure to deviate is greater lower down the social scale, exactly as Merton argues. Moreover, the more powerful sections of society are able to shape the legal definitions of licit as opposed to illicit property accumulation (as well as the pursuit of other gratifications) to their advantage. On *a priori* grounds, therefore, it is reasonable to suppose that law-breaking (as defined by the state) is more prevalent among the less successful, even if the biases of the criminal justice system exaggerate this and tend to ignore the often far more significant crimes of the powerful. But precisely because the 'dark figure' of unrecorded and unsolved crime cannot be penetrated the issue can never be fully resolved.

(II) Theoretical criticisms (i) Merton has been much criticized by recent radical criminologists, influenced by interactionism, for depicting deviants as passively responding to pressure, rather than as creative social actors whose definition of the situation is relevant to understanding their action, and are not merely determined functions of structural strain. 'In classical anomie theory, the typical actor is in a box, in a social position, and he is not to get out until social reformers have opened the opportunity chest . . . The individual actor – boxed into a fixed social position – is rarely seen to evolve a solution to his problem in his own terms.'[65]

It seems to me, however, that there is nothing in Merton's account that precludes an examination of the deviant's interpretative framework or the process of development of deviation. Merton's analysis of the structural strains conducive to crime is compatible with a dialectical view of the interdependence of social system and individual response. He stresses that pole of the dialectic involving the limitation of the conditions under which people act, but this does not foreclose analysis of consciousness, volition or interaction processes.

(ii) Merton is also accused of failing to recognize the possibility of deviants espousing alternative moral codes or notions of social reality, other than as a response to failure to succeed in conventional terms. This rules out the existence of varying ethnic, religious or other sub-cultures which may have less materialistic traditions, or of the explicit rejection of non-materialistic ways of life by people who could succeed conventionally. Merton does not distinguish between 'retreatism' and bohemianism as a deliberate and conscious moral choice. This argument is not altogether convincing. Firstly, to say that some 'deviants' may have chosen to deviate in a genuine rather than constrained way is not to invalidate the postulate that anomic strain may also be a source of deviation in others. Secondly, Merton's conception of 'rebellion' could be extended to cover those whose moral rejection of conventional materialism leads to the creation of underground or alternative sub-cultures rather than more explicitly political strategies of social change.

(iii) A third theoretical criticism of Merton's account has pointed to the absence of a historical dimension in his work. Merton does not raise as problematic the questions of where do the social structure and cultural goals he describes come from, but simply takes them for granted. This argument has been best summed up by Laurie Taylor in an analogy which it has become *de rigueur* to cite in discussions of Merton:

It is as though individuals in society are playing a gigantic fruit machine, but the machine is rigged and only some players are consistently rewarded. The deprived ones then either resort to using foreign coins or magnets to increase their chance of winning (innovation) or play on mindlessly (ritualism), give up the game (retreatism) or propose a new game altogether (rebellion). But in this analysis nobody appears to ask who put the machine there in the first place and who takes the profits. Criticism of the game is confined to changing the pay-out sequences so that the deprived can get a better deal (increasing educational opportunities, poverty programmes). What at first sight looks like a major critique of society ends up by taking the existing society for granted.[66]

It is certainly true that Merton does not explain the origins and development of the structural patterns that concern him. But Taylor himself implies a misleadingly simple conspiratorial notion of historical origins ('who put the machine there in the first place'). Although Merton himself does not do so, it is entirely compatible with his elaboration of the consequences of anomic strain to ask the further question of how the particular combination of rags-to-riches mythology and unequal social structure developed historically.

(iv) A final criticism of Merton's position has been directed at his basic conceptualization of anomie. This claim has been most forcefully posed by John Horton, who in an influential paper argued that contemporary American social scientists had 'dehumanized' the essentially critical concepts of alienation and anomie as developed originally by Marx and Durkheim respectively.[67] His arguments about the weakening of the critical edge of the concept of 'alienation' as it has been operationalized into a psychological index of malaise are very convincing. But his critique of Merton's treatment of anomie is sketchy in the extreme, and his allegations unsupported by any citations from Merton. The essence of his argument is that Merton's concept of anomie

differs from Durkheim's in one crucial respect – in its identification with the very groups and values which Durkheim saw as the prime source of anomie in industrial societies. For Durkheim, anomie was endemic in such societies not only because of inequality in the conditions of competition, but, more importantly, because self-interested striving (the status and success goals) had been raised to social ends . . . Durkheim questioned the very values which Merton held constant . . . Classical concepts are radical and utopian; their values refer to ideal social conditions. Contemporary concepts are ideological in their identification with existing social conditions.[68]

There is nothing in Merton that can sustain Horton's reading of him. Merton certainly does not restrict his criticism to the opportunity structure of American society. He discusses at length the anomic consequences of the goal of monetary success in itself. On the other hand, Durkheim did not ignore the issue of structural inequality of opportunity, or support Horton's claim that 'to maximise opportunities for achieving success would in no way end anomie'. Durkheim's discussion of the 'forced' division of labour implies that a fair opportunity structure is a necessary, though not sufficient, condition of organic solidarity. 'Labour is divided spontaneously only if society is constituted in such a way that social inequalities exactly express natural inequalities.'[69] The claim advanced by Horton (and the radical criminologists influenced by him) that Merton domesticated Durkheim by substituting a conception of anomie as the product of an unequal opportunity structure rather than the materialistic ethos of capitalism itself is quite false. Merton's conception of anomie is broader, not narrower, than Durkheim's. It encapsulates not only the inadequate normative regulatory structure that Durkheim called anomie, but also the unjust opportunity structure which Durkheim called a forced division of labour. To Durkheim and Merton alike social justice and harmony requires the reform of both social ethos and structure.

The nub of the radical criminologists' dislike of Merton is summed up by Taylor, Young and Walton's characterization of him as a 'cautious rebel'. But what is wrong with cautious rebellion? The vaunted radicalism of

Horton's position, though avowedly Marxist, seems to be precisely what Marx would have castigated as 'utopian socialism', indeed Horton explicitly celebrates 'classical concepts' as 'radical and utopian'. With the hindsight of the 1980s it seems utopian in the worst sense to dismiss 'increasing educational opportunities' and 'poverty programmes' rather sneeringly as sops to the status quo. The Merton–Durkheim approach is to argue for both structural equalization and moral reconstruction as the basis of a just social order. Merton's explicitly 'middle-range' theory has been much criticized for its 'caution', but at least it raises what Trotsky might have called 'transitional demands' that point to a realistic strategy of change, rather than utopian postulations of an ideal society.

Horton's strictures are more validly levelled against a more recent genre of American criminology – studies which attempt to provide a quantitative explanation of rates of crime and deviance nominally drawing on Durkheim's concepts, but drastically simplifying them in the interests of operationalization. A recent example is Marvin Krohn's 'A Durkheimian analysis of international crime rates'.[70] Krohn first operationalizes Durkheim's model of crime causation into a path diagram linking population in turn to urbanity, industrialization and division of labour, and anomie. He then suggests a set of empirical indicators for these theoretical concepts, and proceeds to test the model using a data set comprising the crime rates for a sample of thirty-three countries produced by Interpol. (The problems of interpreting official crime statistics, and *a fortiori* of international comparisons, are acknowledged although hardly resolved.) The results supported the relationship postulated between all the variables and crime rates, with the crucial exception of 'anomie'. Krohn is in fact suitably modest about the extent to which his results can be taken as a refutation of Durkheim. In particular, anomie was hard to operationalize, and Krohn's solution is not very satisfactory, to say the least. 'The measure is computed by comparing satisfaction of social want (measured by four variables representing the availability of commodities in a society) to social want desire, as measured by the literacy rate.'[71] The adequacy of this measure as an index of Durkheim's concept of anomie is most dubious. It seems clear that as a test of Durkheim's, or indeed any, theoretical account of crime this kind of study is vitiated by the tailoring of concepts to available data rather than the reverse. The data may have a limited interest in their own right, but are hardly adequate to the theoretical burdens they are made to carry.

(c) The legal evolution debate

Durkheim's account of the evolution of law has provoked considerable criticism ever since the initial publication of *The Division of Labour*; indeed 'Two laws of penal evolution' partly represents Durkheim's response to some early critiques. Since the mid-1960s there has been a revival of interest in Durkheim's model of legal evolution, and a steady stream of papers debating it.

The nub of the criticism of Durkheim's thesis has been that he simply got his facts wrong, in particular in characterizing primitive societies as dominated by repressive law which becomes progressively less punitive as societies develop. As Faris forcefully put it in a review of the first English translation of *The Division of Labour*:

> Published when the author was thirty-five years old, the work accepts as accurate the crude misconceptions of the 1880s concerning the life of primitive man as set forth in the books of those who were no more competent to describe them than a botanist would be to write a treatise in his field without ever having seen a plant . . . Not to be severe with a writer who, forty-one years ago, accepted what is now known to be untenable, it would at least seem that extended discussion of an argument based on abandoned premises might be considered an unnecessary expenditure of energy.[72]

Despite this warning, many writers have ventured to expend considerable energy in this area. But the conclusion that Durkheim's account was factually wrong has been confirmed by later work. Reviewing *The Division of Labour* and its significance in 1966, Barnes wrote: 'the main weakness . . . is that the ethnographic evidence shows that, in general, primitive societies are not characterised by repressive laws'.[73]

In a seminal article which sparked off much of the revived interest in the legal evolution debate Schwartz and Miller provided some quantitative evidence to confirm this rejection of Durkheim's thesis.[74] They arranged a sample of fifty-one societies for which data was available in the Human Relations Area Files on a scale of social complexity, following the methodology of an earlier study by Freeman and Winch.[75] They then developed a scale of the evolution of legal systems based on three elements: counsel ('the regular use of specialised non-kin advocates in the settlement of disputes'), mediation ('regular use of non-kin third party intervention in dispute settlement') and police ('specialised armed force used partially or wholly for norm enforcement'). The data for the fifty-one societies showed that these items constituted 'a near-perfect Guttman scale' of legal evolution. Schwartz and Miller found that the scales of legal evolution and social complexity were closely related – the more complex societies were characterized by more highly developed legal systems. Although this was not a central concern of theirs, Schwartz and Miller observe that:

> Superficially at least, these findings seem directly contradictory to Durkheim's major thesis in *The Division of Labour in Society*. He hypothesised that penal law – the effort of the organised society to punish offences against itself – occurs in societies with the simplest division of labour. As indicated, however, our data show that police are

found only in association with a substantial degree of division of labour . . . By contrast restitutive sanctions – damages and mediation – which Durkheim believed to be associated with an increasing division of labour, are found in many societies that lack even rudimentary specialisation. Thus Durkheim's hypothesis seems the reverse of the empirical situation in the range of societies studied here.

Schwartz and Miller's study has provoked extensive debate about whether there is any value, or validity in Durkheim's account of legal evolution. What is uncontentious is that Durkheim's work is significant in opening up the issue of the relationship between law and social development, and more broadly emphasizing the social context of law in general. As Sheleff put it: 'Durkheim was probably right in his theoretical premise that the law is the visible outer symbol of the nature of a society. He was almost certainly wrong in his empirical assessment of the direction of the law from repressive to restitutive.'[76]

As Jones has pointed out, until recently contemporary criminology has been marked by 'a failure to consider the relationships between crime, punishment and social change'.[77] Although in the last few years histories of crime and law have proliferated, recent studies have either been ethnographic rather than theoretical, or subject to 'a discernible trend . . . to overcompensate for Durkheim's failure by giving too much attention to the role of economic and political interests, at the expense of more sociological concerns'.[78]

On the substantive question of the direction and explanation of legal evolution recent work has continued to refute Durkheim. Several writers have accepted Schwartz and Miller's data as an effective rebuttal of Durkheim's arguments. Clarke, for instance, cites them as showing that Durkheim's depiction of the direction of legal evolution was mistaken, even though their evidence confirms the more general proposition of a link between societal and legal development.[79] Moreover, Clarke adduces another study by Schwartz, on social control in two types of Israeli kibbutz (which was not related to Durkheim by Schwartz himself) as evidence that repressive sanctions and formal legal procedures develop in more differentiated social systems, casting doubt on the postulated link between repression and mechanical solidarity.[80] Other writers have attempted to refine the Schwartz and Miller study, while accepting its framework and conclusion. Wimberley showed, for example, that another stage of legal evolution could be added to Schwartz and Miller's scale, courts and judges, which occurs after the development of mediation but before police.[81]

The adequacy of Schwartz and Miller's work as a test of Durkheim is questionable. Baxi pointed to three ways in which their operational definitions failed to do justice to Durkheim's concepts.[82] First, by restricting the concept of penal law essentially to the police, Schwartz and Miller restrict its meaning to a specific organizational form. But penal law may exist without any particular type of specialized enforcement agency. Second, Baxi points out that Durkheim's contention was about the relative weights of repressive and restitutive law at different stages of development, so that merely showing the existence of restitutive law in primitive society or repressive law in advanced society does not amount to a refutation of his claims. Third, Baxi contends that Durkheim's concern was less with the details of the organization of social control than with the determinants and explanation of types of control. Cotterrell has effectively summarized the limitations of Schwartz and Miller's data as refutation of Durkheim by pointing out that Durkheim's concern was with *law* not enforcement. 'For Durkheim the *substantive* content of legal rules (and the moral ideas they reflect) is far more important, given the purposes of his inquiry, than *procedures* of dispute resolution or enforcement of norms.'[83]

The only study actually to provide some empirical support for Durkheim is an analysis of support for capital punishment in different areas of Canada carried out by Chandler. His findings indicate that more mechanically solidary areas (more culturally homogeneous, religious, less developed) will 'support retribution and induce their MPs to vote for the death penalty'.[84] As Chandler himself recognizes, however, such a cross-sectional analysis cannot in itself be taken as indicating anything about evolution (the same point can be made, of course, about the numerous attempts to refute Durkheim by cross-sectional data). More crucially, support for the death penalty specifically does not tell us anything about the relative preponderance of repressive or restitutive law in general.

The most important deficiency in Durkheim's account of legal evolution is one that he partially acknowledged in the later formulation in 'Two laws' but which remains only sketchy and undeveloped: the relation between the state and law. It is clear that Durkheim himself quickly became aware of the errors in his conception of primitive law as repressive, and the distortions involved in his initial thesis about a unilinear path of evolution towards less punitive law. Some writers have even claimed that Durkheim completely abandoned his views on legal evolution after the first publication of *The Division of Labour* in 1893, as evidenced by the fact that he never again uses the distinctions mechanical versus organic solidarity or repressive versus restitutive law in his later work.[85] But the primary thesis advanced in his first 'law of penal evolution' in the 1900 essay is essentially the same as that proposed in *The Division of Labour*, linking social development to declining punitiveness. The crucial difference is that he introduces the subsidiary clause relating punitiveness to the growth of centralized state power. It seems clear that this is to provide an explanation of an obvious and damaging exception to the first law: the increasing harshness of penalties in seventeenth and eighteenth century Europe that followed in the wake of royal absolutism. Furthermore it is even clearer in the 'Two laws' essay that all Durkheim's evidence about the harshness of primitive law is drawn from fairly advanced and complex ancient societies rather than small, simple tribal societies. Putting together the two aspects of Durkheim's first law the overall pattern of development of punishment predicted is a curvilinear one, with an increase in punitiveness as centralized state powers emerge, followed by declining harshness (or possibly even more complex sequences if the evolutionary starting point is pushed back to tribal societies). Jones cites a later book review by Durkheim which actually claims the 'role of discipline grows with civilisation', though whether this amounts to a repudiation of the idea of an inverse relationship between social complexity and punitiveness, or merely recognition of the fact that the growth of centralized state power had outweighed the effects of social development to produce a net increase in repressiveness is not clear.[86]

What is evident is that Durkheim did come to see the evolution of law and punishment as related not only to social structure and morality, but also to state power, conceived of by him as an independent variable. Although this is an advance on his earlier formulation, the thesis of the 'Two laws of penal evolution' remains unsatisfactory. Sheleff maintains that Durkheim's conception of the path of legal development is still the wrong way round. He demonstrates that Durkheim considerably overstates the role of repressive law in ancient societies, as well as primitive ones.[87] Above all, Sheleff shows that Durkheim misinterprets the work of Maine, his main source for the attribution of predominantly penal law to ancient societies. Maine demonstrates that the main mode of protection of individuals against harm in the ancient legal codes he studied was the law of torts, not the criminal law. As Sheleff sums up Maine's depiction of ancient law: 'The chief task of the laws and customs was to ensure that the person harmed would be adequately compensated. It was only in exceptional cases that repressive, vengeful action was taken on behalf of the community against the offender.'[88] More dubiously, Sheleff also argues that modern societies have evolved from a basically restitutive model of law to a repressive one. To support this contention Sheleff adduces a rather haphazard collection of trends: the lack of concern of modern criminal justice systems with the victim, the growth of stage agencies with an interest in extending the scope and power of criminal law, the 'over-reach' of criminal law to control 'victimless' or sumptuary offences, political uses of criminal law not only in 'totalitarian' but also in nominally democratic societies, and the burgeoning legislation controlling health, safety, economic and family life and the environment, all buttressed by penal sanctions.[89] Although Sheleff does not explicitly spell this out, it seems to me that the thread connecting his rather disparate collection of instances of increasing repression in modern society is that, *pace* Durkheim's view of organic solidarity, the more complex and divided a society, the greater the potential for conflict and disorder, which produces an expansion of state intervention and regulation with the criminal law as its weapon.

A similar argument is adduced by Spitzer in an empirical test of Durkheim's 'Two laws of penal evolution', using the same techniques and data source (the Human Relations Areas Files) as Schwartz and Miller.[90] Spitzer's evidence shows that:

(1) The severity of punishment does not decrease as societies grow more concentrated and complex. On the contrary, greater punitiveness is associated with higher levels of structural differentiation. (2) While variations in political structure are related to punitive intensity, these variations are neither historically contingent, nor idiosyncratic. (3) Although the 'religiosity' of deviance is correlated with punitiveness, collective crimes are more common in complex than simple societies. (4) Controls involving social and geographical segregation are not represented by incarceration alone and are not peculiar to advanced societies.[91]

Spitzer argues that Durkheim was fundamentally wrong not only at the factual level but in seeing punishment as primarily a function of the collective conscience. Instead both punishment and the moral beliefs legitimating it can be explained by the changing requirements of the maintenance of hegemonic control and domination. As societies become more complexly differentiated and divided so the problems of control intensify, as does the repressiveness of punishment, at least until a particular form of domination is stabilized and established, at which point the ordering mechanisms of social routine and ideological legitimation may become effective enough to permit a relaxation of punitiveness. If any broad pattern is applicable to the evolution of punishment it is a curvilinear one: 'Sanctions are lenient in simple egalitarian (reciprocal) societies, severe in non-market (redistributive) complex societies, and lenient in established market societies.'[92]

Even if Durkheim's account of the evolution of law and punishment is largely discredited at the empirical level, it nonetheless remains of enduring significance in a more substantial sense than merely to have sparked off an important debate. This is because Durkheim's work on legal development has another face than its evolutionary one, as Turkel and Cotterrell in particular have emphasized.[93] Durkheim's overriding theoretical and moral/political concern and project was to identify and understand the problems and prospects of achieving social solidarity in complex and differentiated societies. Giving a substantive account of the path of legal evolution was subordinate to and instrumental for this primary goal. In this perspective Durkheim's contrast between mechanical solidarity with repressive law and organic solidarity with restitutive law can be seen not so much as two concrete poles of an evolutionary progression which had actually occurred in history but rather as ideal-types for elucidating the requirements of solidarity in modern societies. Durkheim's contention is that organic solidarity is possible in complex societies, given both structural change and moral reconstruction. (Durkheim's programme for social reform is elaborated in chapter 1.) The form of law appropriate to such a society would be restitutive rather than repressive. It would be concerned with the adjustment and co-ordination of differentiated functions and individuals, and rooted in their diverse conditions of life as expressed by a framework of semi-autonomous corporations, rather than the imposition of a uniform, monolithic morality. The evolutionary flavour of Durkheim's account arises in part because he was anxious to depict organic solidarity not as a remote utopian ideal but as the culmination of virtual tendencies which could already be discerned (although Durkheim undoubtedly exaggerated these and neglected the extent and systematic nature of the conflicts engendered by the forced and anomic forms of division of labour actually prevalent). Durkheim's perspective continues to be of value because he points to problems which conservatives, liberals and Marxists alike tend to ignore. Against conservatives he levels cogent demonstrations that solidarity in modern societies cannot be based on resuscitation of obsolete moral forms. But he also points to the problems of moral cohesion and meaning, and the sociological (as opposed to economic or political) preconditions of this, in terms of the importance of intermediate levels of social organization and grouping between state and citizen, issues which liberals and Marxists are inclined to overlook. However, while his problematic is of continuing relevance, Durkheim's proposals for its achievement are sketchy and unconvincing. In particular, the experience of nearly a century of reform attempts to realize a fairer distribution of rewards and opportunities in industrial societies suggests that both the structural impediments to this and the resistance of the privileged classes pose a more considerable obstacle than he realized to 'the work of justice' which Durkheim saw as 'the task of the most advanced societies'.[94]

Conclusion: Durkheim's legacy for criminology

Durkheim's work on crime, law and punishment continues to be an important reference point and inspiration for contemporary arguments, as we have seen. His conception of crime has been one of the sources of growth of the 'labelling-theory' perspective. The concept of anomie has stimulated a major tradition of work on the causes of crime, which has moved from dominant orthodoxy to unjust neglect. The relationship of crime, law and punishment to social and political development is being increasingly studied, even if current work suggests that Durkheim's substantive account is at best grossly oversimplified, at worst the obverse of the historical record. Above all, the moral and political concerns which animated Durkheim's whole enterprise remain relevant, even if he provides little satisfactory guidance to their resolution. But an increasingly significant tendency among criminal justice practitioners and penal reformers argues along Durkheimian lines (even if not explicitly citing him) that restitution rather than punishment ought to be the target of modern penology.[95] Durkheim's prophecy of restitution rather than repression as the basis of modern law may yet be fulfilled, although the issue is uncertain and dependent on the outcome of both intellectual debate and political conflict.

7

⚜⚜⚜

Durkheim and the study of religion

IAN HAMNETT

Durkheim and 'Elementary Forms'

Durkheim lived until 1917, but his last major publication in any field was *The Elementary Forms of the Religious Life*, which appeared in 1912.[1] He had grown increasingly interested in religious phenomena from the period of *Suicide*[2] (1897) on, an interest most explicitly evidenced by the articles and reviews published largely under his own direction in the serial volumes of *L'Année Sociologique*, and most particularly in the long essay 'De la Définition des phénomènes religieux' in volume 2 (1899).[3] This study adumbrates many of the central themes of *Elementary Forms*, especially the concept of the 'sacred' and the social character of religion. Durkheim referred to this early essay in two footnotes in the later work, which trace both the continuities and the developments of his thought over the intervening years.[4] *L'Année Sociologique* carried many papers and reviews by colleagues and associates of Durkheim on religious topics, of which one of the most notable was the joint essay on sacrifice by H. Hubert and M. Mauss.[5] This concern with religion reflected the contemporary interest among anthropologists and ethnologists in primitive religion, especially in the English-speaking world. Durkheim read and criticized such celebrated British ethnologists as Sir E. B. Tylor, author of *Primitive Culture* (1871),[6] and Sir James Frazer, whose *Totemism and Exogamy* (1887) and *The Golden Bough* (1890) were reviewed in the pages of *L'Année Sociologique*.[7] The twelfth volume of the *Année* also contained a careful review of Lucien Lévy-Bruhl's *Les Fonctions mentales dans les sociétés inférieures* (1910),[8] which appeared almost contemporaneously with *Elementary Forms*. This review is an important statement of Durkheim's views on the relation between science and religion, and on the sociology of knowledge generally.

Interest in primitive religion had been especially stimulated by the researches of Spencer and Gillen whose studies of Australian totemism were (or were held out as being) the empirical basis for *Elementary Forms*. Later work has not only resulted in very considerable revision of Spencer and

Gillen's work but has also eroded the very concept of totemism itself.[9] But, as with so much of Durkheim's writing,[10] this hardly matters. The importance of *Elementary Forms* does not lie in the account it gives of a particular set of facts or supposed facts about aboriginal Australia but in the general theory erected upon an almost arbitrary empirical base. Here we encounter a very real problem in any study of Durkheim's view of religion and his subsequent influence. *Elementary Forms* is a work of almost unlimited sociological ambition. In a real sense, the religious aspects of Durkheim's inquiry, while at a superficial level the most obvious and dominant theme, are secondary to his fundamental concerns. These were nothing less than to offer an account of the source of social solidarity itself, and (beyond that) to propose an entire epistemology calculated to supersede the doctrines of Kantianism and empiricism alike.[11] Insistently though 'religious' instances and data are paraded before the reader as 'evidence', they are often little more than stalking-horses for Durkheim's much wider intellectual ambitions. A balanced study of *Elementary Forms* would have to achieve a comparable sweep. The present discussion will be limited to those aspects of the work that are concerned with 'religion' in a more or less exact sense,[12] more general sociological and philosophical ideas being attended to only in so far as they further the 'religious' argument.

Religion defined

It saves time to anticipate Durkheim's well-known definition of religion, towards which (in his familiar cat-and-mouse way)[13] he obliquely works in the first forty or fifty pages.

'A religion', he writes, 'is a unified system of beliefs and practices relative to sacred things, that is to say, things set apart and forbidden . . ., which unite into one single moral community, called a church, all those who adhere to them' (p. 47).

One or two features of this definition call for immediate commentary. First of all, religion is defined not merely as belief but as 'beliefs and practices',[14] which moreover are integrated (unified) into a system. It is possible to see, in Durkheim's use of the word 'system' in this particular place, one of the growing points of the kind of sociological preoccupation with functional interdependence which dominated the minds of anthropologists particularly (Radcliffe-Brown, the principal exponent and apostle of Durkheim in the English-speaking world, being an early and powerful instance[15]). Secondly, this definition refers to 'sacred things . . . set apart and forbidden', and with these words, and especially with the notorious term 'sacred', it sets the scene for a great amount of later discussion and controversy.[16] Thirdly, the definition closes with a stress on 'one single moral community'. There is, Durkheim insisted, 'no church of magic'; but it should be understood that this emerges as little more than a tautology, since he is here defining the terms of his inquiry rather than offering a description of religious behaviour.

Durkheim makes much play, especially in the earlier chapters but intermittently throughout *Elementary Forms*, with the notion that there is a substratum of truth in religion: it cannot 'rest upon an error or a lie' (p. 2); 'the unanimous sentiment of the believers of all time cannot be purely illusory' (p. 417). Such assertions, while provocative, are little more than double-talk. Durkheim was not a believer and his sociology of religion is too reductionist to leave much room for belief. These disingenuous courtesies to belief stand for the much less 'interesting' recognition that a widespread and deeply rooted social institution must be explained *by reference to* something more substantial and intellectually authentic than either a simple and awe-struck misunderstanding of natural forces or else the 'nightmares of savage minds' (p. 69).[17] The first, naturalist, kind of explanation, represented by Max Müller and others, suggested that violent natural events (lightning, thunder, earthquakes, etc.) were the original source of supernatural belief; personified by language ('the dark shadow on thought'), they are reified and become the objects of religious cults.[18] For Durkheim, however, 'natural forces are only natural forces however great their intensity' (p. 87) and are not adequate explanations for the peculiar characteristics of sacred things. The other fallacy is associated with the speculations of Herbert Spencer and (with some differences) E. B. Tylor, whose 'animist' account sought to explain religious beliefs by tracing them back to the bewildered puzzlement of 'savage minds' in their contemplation of the phenomena of death and dreaming.[19] The natural (or cosmic) and the psychological having been thus eliminated, Durkheim moved confidently on to a sociological aetiology of religious belief and practice.[20]

Sacred and profane

First, the sacred is equated with the 'collective' (or the social). The sentiment it provokes is not one of servile fear but of moral respect. This is because a human being is *homo duplex*, leading a double and conjoint life: at the 'individual' or 'profane' level, and at the 'collective' (social) or 'sacred' one. What he reveres in the sacred is not simply outside him; it is also lodged in the intimate depths of his selfhood – indeed, it represents 'the best' in us. It is still, today, crucial to stress this *internalization* of the collective force in Durkheim's religious sociology. It is not that the self is coercively acted upon by society, so much as that it is – at least in its most characteristically human and 'moral' features – *constituted* by it. 'The collective force penetrates us and becomes an integral part of us' (p. 209). It is 'a moral power which is immanent in us though it represents something not our-selves' (p. 211). 'Outside of us there exists something greater than us, with which we enter into communion' (p. 228). Religion is thus a system of ideas by which individuals represent society to themselves (p. 225); religious interests are the symbolic form of social interests (p. 316); religious forces are social forces hypostatized (p. 322). They are made up entirely of the impressions aroused in individuals by the group (p. 223). God and society are one (p. 206).

Evans-Pritchard has criticized Durkheim's strong dichotomy between sacred and profane on empirical grounds. He had seen a spear used in sacrifice at one moment and employed for quite profane purposes at the next, all within one ritual event (*Theories of Primitive Religion*, p. 65). E. R. Leach has incorporated this kind of criticism within a more general theoretical re-casting of Durkheim's distinction. He argues that 'sacred' and 'profane' should not be regarded as descriptive of whole items or events, but rather as analytical *aspects* of almost all items or events. Anything, or any process or relationship, will have its sacred and profane aspects, the relative primacy of the one or the other varying from case to case (*Pul Eliya: A Village in Ceylon*, Cambridge University Press, 1961, pp. 299f). This preserves the opposition of the two categories, on which Durkheim laid such emphasis, while avoiding the empirical and ethnogra-phic difficulties which the distinction involves when it is applied as a descriptive classification.

An obvious question, though one seldom posed, is: why should the way in which 'individuals represent society to themselves' take a *religious* form? One answer would, of course, assume the tautology of defining religion as being precisely such a representation: we give the name of 'religion' to whatever set of ideas we use for the representation of society to ourselves. Durkheim, however, looked for an answer with substantive content, and proposed that since the abstractions of collective and social life could not easily be conceptualized in human cultures, they must in the normal course be symbolically figured and mediated to the common or general under-standing in religious guise. There is in Durkheim's argument here an unacknowledged movement towards precisely that antithesis between 'primitive' and 'scientific' which Lévy-Bruhl urged in at least his earlier studies,[21] and which Durkheim was perhaps too quick to assail.[22] Durkheim asserts, and appears at certain points actually to believe, that science and religion share the same cognitive and experiential source. Both take their origin, directly or at a remove, from the 'collective representations' ('conventional understandings'[23]) in society that at once distance them from the vulgar perceptions of crude commonsense[24] and also bestow on them that universality and impersonality (p. 436) which mark what we regard as the 'objectively' true. From one point of view, Durkheim's uncompromising sociologism[25] left him no alternative but to relativize all purported knowledge by subjecting it to this reductionist analysis. Yet from another, his own commitment to a 'scientific' view of the world, and his repudiation of religious belief, made it in the end impossible for him to maintain any consistency in this debate. Towards the end of *Elementary Forms*, he delivers himself of a particularly astonishing piece of intellectual legerdemain, when he purports to find a sort of congruity and even identity between two radically contrasting kinds of thinking at the very moment of putting his finger on their differences: 'The concept', he writes (p. 437), 'which was first[26] held as true because it was collective tends to be no longer collective except on condition of being held as true: we demand its credentials before according it our confidence.' 'Quite', a rationalist or a Weber might reply. The most subversive consequence of Durkheim's view of cognition is in fact that he solves the problems of religious 'error' only at the expense of creating a new problem of scientific 'truth'. If religion is no worse than science, then science is no better than religion. Yet Durkheim was too firmly committed to a 'modern' and scientific world-view ever to have been able to accept the implications of his thinking. It is only with the latter-day erosion of positivism within science itself[27] that anything of Durkheim's arguments can (in spite of their author) be saved from the wreck.[28]

Totemic emblems

Durkheim also concerned himself with the narrower issue of 'totemic' religious emblems. These were, for him, a special case – and, since he took this supposed totemism to contain the essence of all religion, a specially revealing case – of all symbolic representations of the social group. They were acceptably concrete representations of that intangible and invisible 'society' which could never be directly available to sense perception. As Lévi-Strauss notes, totemic emblems for Durkheim were good to *depict* with.[29] Radcliffe-Brown took over much of Durkheim's argument, though in stressing the 'totemic' function of incorporating nature within society and in pointing to the salience of culturally valued items (especially animals and comestibles generally) among totemic species, he can be said to have regarded them more as good to *eat* (*bons à manger*). Lévi-Strauss seems to effect something of a return to Durkheim's more intellectualist approach, though in a radically new manner, when he suggests that the natural species, etc., that were thought of as constituting the now annihilated 'totemism' should be seen rather as good to think with (*bons à penser*): the controlling logical operators of a system of classification that orders not only nature and culture both, but also the relationship that at once connects and distinguishes them.[30] Durkheim's 'sociocentrism' is directed towards a view of society not simply as a pre-given constraint but as itself the creature and construct of the practice it expresses.

It is notorious that Durkheim's argument accounting for the totemic cult by referring it to the cohesion and solidarity of the group ran into difficulties with the disclosure, rather embarrassedly conceded in chapter one of Book Two in *Elementary Forms*, that the cult was regularly associated not with those groups that seem to take first place in the critical life-experiences of the community – the co-residential, co-operative and largely commensal horde – but with the dispersed matrilineal marriage classes. He accounts for this partly[31] on the grounds that without the cult the matrilineal moieties would risk the loss of their identity, whereas the groups in which day-to-day social life is conducted do not need this ritual and emblematic support. Such an argument, however, is a dangerous one for a theorist whose general thesis depends on a direct and intimate link between cultic belief and practice on the one hand and the solidarity of the social group on the other. Nevertheless, the quandary has given rise to some interesting discussion, prompting the hypothesis that a religious cult may serve to underpin a set of values that are at one and the same time critical for the persistence and maintenance of a social order *and at risk.*[32]

Cause and effect

These questions raise an enduring doubt in any first reading of Durkheim's account of religion and its relation to the social group, namely the sequence of supposed cause and effect. Does religion *express* the pre-given solidarity of the group, or *bring it about*? Some commentators take Durkheim to task for failing to explain what he promised, viz., religion, and instead treating religion as the *explanans* of a quite different *explanandum*, viz., social solidarity.[33] This (it is argued) is the typical fallacy of functionalism – the reversal of the proper order of explanation. Religion must be accounted for by showing, not what it causes, but what causes it. The methodological debate is familiar and can be protracted indefinitely.[34] An alternative response to this Durkheimian crux which sidesteps the general logical issue is well exemplified by Roy Rappaport in a masterly essay on ritual acts and utterances.[35] Relying on Austin's discussion of performatives,[36] Rappaport shows how the opposition between expressing a state of affairs and bringing it about can misrepresent the role of both words and deeds. To give verbal or ritual expression to sentiments of solidarity can both reflect what already exists and also constitute and confirm it.[37]

All the same, Durkheim's functionalist account raises questions about the definition and status of 'religion' as an element in a theory of society that create difficulties when it comes to the sociological study of religion in 'modern' secular societies. It would be grotesque to suggest that either liberal democracies or Marxist states derived whatever social cohesion they possess from anything that could colourably be labelled 'religious', unless of course 'religion' were tautologously defined as whatever does in fact help to generate such cohesion. This latter course would involve us in treating the Communist Party of the Soviet Union, or the Football League, or the market, as religious institutions – an obvious affront to good sense and semantic convention.[38] Students of religion in modern societies have thus found little guidance in Durkheim's professedly religious writings. The work of Max Weber has proved much more helpful in this respect. The lines of thought generated in *Elementary Forms* have, however, exercised a continuing spell over the study of religion in non-literate societies and especially within social anthropology – though, ironically, perhaps the most unrepentant Durkheimian of all is the sociologist and political scientist, Guy Swanson. The rest of this chapter will accordingly be largely concerned with Durkheim's contemporary influence in these areas, particularly as it can be seen in the work of Swanson, Mary Douglas and Lévi-Strauss.

Guy Swanson

No reputable anthropologist or sociologist has followed Durkheim's footsteps in the study of religion more faithfully than Guy Swanson, whose short book *The Birth of the Gods*[39] is the most ambitious attempt so far to give operational effect to Durkheim's ideas about the relationship between religious belief and social structure. Swanson proposes a sociological explanation not only for 'supernatural'[40] belief in general, but also for observed variations in such belief. Methodologically, this represents an important turn in the argument. If 'religion' is treated as a unitary phenomenon, and if it is as nearly universal as Durkheim held it to be,[41] it is difficult for sociology to find a toe-hold from which to press towards an explanation that is in any way open to testing. Swanson therefore looked for major and significant variations in religious belief and sought to relate them to analogous (in terms of his theory) variations in social structure, in this way hoping to set up a genuinely comparative and testable set of hypotheses.[42]

Substantively, Swanson asserts that supernatural forces take two forms. One is that of *mana* (a term of art for Swanson) – an impersonal and amorphous substance or essence imbued with supernatural power. The other is that of spirits, which are supernatural beings differing from the diffuse and generalized power of *mana* by being personified and possessing purposes and intentions. These forces are 'supernatural' in the sense that behind 'natural' events there lies a realm of 'potentialities and purposes' of which the natural realm is merely the concrete expression. *Mana* stands for the potentialities which underlie nature. Spirits are organized clusters of unseen purposes. Supernatural forces of either kind are free from natural limitations, possess superhuman powers and are usually immortal.

Why do people believe in the supernatural? Swanson accepts that ideas arise from experience,[43] and sets out to determine from what particular experience ideas of the supernatural arise. It was, he writes, Durkheim's 'exceptional merit' to have suggested that 'men develop a concept of supernatural beings directly from the model which their society provides[44] . . . [His] position is plausible just because it begins to explain why men come to know intangible forces which can enter human lives . . . and why these are forces with which people must come to terms' (pp. 16f). The principal question which Swanson directs to Durkheim is to ask, 'What is the society that is venerated? Is it the composite of all the effects which contacts with one another have on people's conduct? . . . Is it but one special kind of social relationship? . . . Is it all of society . . . or just some of its aspects?' (p. 17). Swanson's own response is to assert that people experience supernatural properties in social life because *social relationships inherently possess supernatural characteristics* (p. 22). By this he means that the implicit structures[45] underlying these relationships have the dual characteristics of being at once *immanent* in their guidance of particular experiences and *transcendent* in the continuity of their influence over experience in general. The similarity of this conception to Durkheim's view of the sacred as reflecting the presence of society both outside us and within us could not be more marked. These underlying structures or forces possess powers not given to men as individuals, which operate continuously and determine people's relationships and activities in a hidden, invisible and unconscious way. They also embody a deeper and wider 'knowledge' than any individual or even any group possesses, in that they contain more potentialities than those of which actors are aware at any one time.[46] They are in fact entities which are not directly perceived, with powers that transcend the means-end processes of nature, that can affect nature without being part of it, and that can be experienced as having enduring identities. Moreover, the structures in which Swanson claims to detect the hidden cause of the supernatural are found pre-eminently in what he calls 'sovereign groups'; these are groups or institutions enjoying 'ordinary', i.e. original and non-delegated, jurisdiction over some sphere of life, together with the ability to make effective decisions within that sphere.[47] This echoes an important feature of Durkheim's own sociologistic theory of knowledge, namely that the categories of thought are derived from the structure and organization of society itself, and not merely from 'social interaction' or 'culture' in a general or diffuse sense.[48] Indeed, Swanson takes Durkheim further. He locates the origin of supernatural belief in the specifically political realm, finding the distribution of power in society to be the key variable that shapes – even perhaps determines – the religious beliefs of its typical members.[49] He then seeks to relate variations in political structure to variations in the content of supernatural belief. If his success in this is very limited,[50] that does nothing to erode the validity of the underlying principle. So he sets out to test a variety of concrete hypotheses, deductively derived from his general theory, postulating correlations between particular types of political order and particular types of belief (monotheism, polytheism, ancestor worship, reincarnation and several more).[51]

His overall conclusion is that

participants in a society experience and formulate significant aspects of that society's total structure, and are not limited to those aspects of their society with which they personally are in intimate touch. If there is any value in the idea of a group mind, it lies in its stress on the notion that the overarching structure of social organisation acts upon the participants in those groups.

(p. 191)

Swanson at this point dares to take seriously precisely that notion of Durkheim – *l'âme collective*[52] – which has been most contemptuously derided. His general view of why the structures of society are perceived in supernatural terms corresponds closely to Durkheim's argument that society as a 'moral being' can be only symbolically represented in individual or collective perception. Moreover, just as Durkheim (for all his protestations) saw the advancement of knowledge and self-knowledge – not least that self-knowledge which expresses itself in an ever clearer understanding of society and of our relationship to it – as leading inexorably to the radical transformation, indeed erosion, of conventional religion, so Swanson too sees secularization as the consequence of a changed relationship between individuals and the political order. Swanson, in fact, like Durkheim but more openly, is committed to a 'sociology of error' approach to religious belief.[53] Supernatural beings do not exist, and the problem is to explain how it is that people come to believe that they do. His answer is that such belief is primarily the response of social actors caught up in a political structure which involves them intimately but which they do not fully understand and cannot fully control.[54] Once they are detached from that structure, or alternatively arrive at a position of understanding and control, belief is attenuated and eventually withers away.

The disabling weakness of Swanson's study lies in its methodology and in the consequent implausibility of many of his empirical 'findings'.[55] This discussion is not concerned with those aspects of the book, but rather with its theoretical formulations. These represent not merely the patient following of a 'Durkheimian tradition' but the bold and exciting carrying forward of many of the basic ideas of *Elementary Forms*. The most serious theoretical weakness probably lies in the fallacy of composition in Swanson's move from 'social relationships' to political structures. There is some uncomfortable faltering in the argument that leads him from immediate social experience (social relationships in the concrete sense) up to the less closely experienced macro-structures, whose emergent properties cannot be deduced by simple extrapolation. Swanson's achievement, nevertheless, remains. He has been willing to take the 'grand questions' of sociology and anthropology seriously and to attack a huge intellectual problem at an uncompromisingly theoretical level. *The Birth of the Gods* is, at worst, a heroic failure in the contemporary study of religion.

Mary Douglas

Mary Douglas[56] also explicitly professes her allegiance to the Durkheimian tradition, even more circumstantially than Swanson. In what is her most influential book to date, she proclaims her intellectual ancestry in the opening paragraphs. The introduction to *Natural Symbols* begins by acknowledging the apparently contradictory nature of the book's very title: symbols are essentially cultural products, and moreover any symbol derives its meaning from its place in a system or pattern of symbols.[57] Nature is precisely *not* culture, and its elements have no strictly inherent 'meanings' if they can be said to have meanings at all. Yet, Douglas writes, there is an 'intuition' going the other way, and she continues:

This book attempts to reinstate the intuition by following the line of argument of the French sociologists of *L'Année Sociologique*. For if it is true, as they asserted, that the social relations of men provide the prototype for the logical relations between things, then . . . where regularities . . . are found, we should expect to find recurring . . . the same natural systems of symbols. Society was not simply a model which classificatory thought followed; it was its divisions which served as divisions for the system of classification. The first logical categories were social categories; the first classes of things were classes of men . . . It was because men were grouped and thought of themselves in the form of groups that in their ideas they grasped other things. The centre of the first scheme of nature is not the individual; it is society . . . The quest for natural symbols becomes by the force of this argument the quest for natural systems of symbolising. We will look for tendencies and correlations between the character of the symbolic system and that of the social system.

(pp. 11–12)

The direction taken by the argument in the rest of the book, as in much else of Mary Douglas's work, falls somewhat outside the special area of the sociology of religion and belongs – like Durkheim's own monograph – largely within the sociology of knowledge and of the general relationship of ideology to social structure.[58] Douglas has made extensive use of the 'grid' and 'group' concepts – her own coining – and although these are difficult and indeed rather ambiguous ideas a little must be said about them since they are important for what she has to say about ritual.[59] 'Group', as she uses the term, is a dimension or aspect of social structure which defines common membership. It is marked by boundaries, the most significant question in relation to it being whether a person or collection of persons is inside or outside. The ranking of those within the group may be of little importance, though the element of social control through a rigorous *conscience collective* may be strong. 'Grid' is a dimension or aspect of structure which is primarily concerned with rules and roles controlling interpersonal relationships, typically associated with an ego-focussed network with no, or with only loosely defined, boundaries. Grid and group vary both continuously and independently, yielding at their extremes four limiting types: high grid/high group, low grid/high group, high grid/low group, and low grid/low group. To these kinds of structure correspond various types of cosmology, reflected in (among other things) their ritual attitudes and practices. Thus, for example, low grid/low group societies have little or no ritual. 'When public classification and pressures are withdrawn or cast aside, the individual left alone with himself develops a distinctive cosmology, benign and unritualistic. As Durkheim suggested, this experience is the beginning of consciousness . . . the sense of escape from others and of self-discovery' (pp. 91–2).[60] High grid/high group, on the other hand, yields 'sacralized institutions, strong boundaries between purity and impurity; this is the prototype original Durkheimian system in which God is Society and Society is God' (p. 91). Such societies are the most ritualist of all. Douglas offers as one instance of the first the Mbuti pygmies of the Ituri forest. Their ethnographer writes of them that 'the pygmies seem bound by few set rules. There was a general pattern of behaviour to which everyone more or less conformed, but with great latitude given and taken.'[61] 'In such a society', Douglas observes, 'a man can hardly need to be preoccupied with the formalities of social intercourse . . . Pygmies move freely in an uncharted, unsystematized, unbounded social world' (p. 34). She uses this observation to press the point that secularism and even irreligion are not peculiar to modern urban society. 'The contrast of secular with religious has nothing whatever to do with the contrast of modern with traditional or primitive' (p. 36),[62] and she gives a pointed illustration from the work of Fredrik Barth, who at first was so under the sway of the

Durkheimian thesis according to which tribal society always finds a direct religious expression that he was inclined to think it was a defect in his field work that he failed to find this to be so among the people he studied.[63]

Among instances of societies or cultures displaying a strong commitment to symbolic forms and ritual action she cites the Bantu neighbours of the pygmies (pp. 34f), the Mandari (pp. 128ff) and (especially in chapter 3) the 'Bog Irish' and 'traditional' Roman Catholicism.[64] Of these, the first is in some ways the most striking since she uses it to found a startling assertion:

> I am not merely saying that the people's behaviour to their god corresponds to their behaviour to each other, though the truism could well be underlined. I am saying that religious forms as well as social forms are generated by experiences in the same dimension. Pygmies move freely in an uncharted, unsystematized, unbounded world. I maintain that it would be impossible for them to develop a sacramental religion, as it would be impossible for the neighbouring Bantu farmers, living in their confined villages in forest clearings, to give up magic.
>
> (pp. 34–5)[65]

Though Mary Douglas has been heard to deny it, these sentences have an uncompromisingly deterministic ring, and little of the substantive argument of the book tends to contradict this.[66] However, it is as well to be clear that what is being implied in this passage differs from the simple sociological determinism involved in Durkheim's usual approach.[67] Douglas is not saying that social forms determine (or 'generate') religious forms, but that *both* owe their origin to 'experiences in the same dimension'. It is far from clear, however, why the 'impossibilities' asserted a few lines later should therefore follow. Nevertheless, her reluctance to be committed to a determinist view enables her to handle the relations between symbolic forms on the one hand and 'nature' – the given world – on the other with a suppleness unrivalled by any other contemporary thinker. *Purity and Danger* is a good instance of this, in particular her discussion of the clean/unclean dichotomy in Jewish law.[68] We find here an example of the 'natural systems of symbolizing' referred to in the introductory passage quoted above, whereby a classificatory system is not read directly from the social world, in the stricter Durkheimian sense, but is a systematic component of it, and develops an autonomy going well beyond the necessities of the case. When she applies her methods to religion in modern societies, however, she largely limits herself to a contrast between traditional Tridentine Catholicism and the de-ritualizing tendencies to be found in the post-Vatican II reforms. As Walsh observes (p. 20), this means that she omits both low grid/high group and high grid/low group manifestations. These are represented respectively by charismatic congregations, and by the individualistic and anonymous 'service station' churches of the busy urban type, both of which are perhaps more important developments in actual contemporary religion than are the two cases on which Douglas concentrates.

Claude Lévi-Strauss[69]

In the view of many, Lévi-Strauss is the greatest anthropologist of our day. In the view of all, he is a dense and complex as well as immensely productive writer, whose many-faceted work defies summary and presents a formidable challenge to all discussion. There is no question, in what follows, either of presenting an introduction to structuralism – the method and philosophy of which he is the effective creator – or of picking out for inspection those parts of his work which bear upon 'religion' (of these there are rather few); it will not even be possible to offer a rounded account of the relation which his output so far bears to the general tradition of Durkheim. There is, however, one major theme or strategy in Lévi-Strauss which can be traced back to ideas put forward in Durkheim's specifically religious studies, and which is significant enough to form a point of entry into the thought of this great contemporary.[70]

It was seen above that Durkheim accounted for the prevalence of items of the natural world in the totemic system of sacred objects, by arguing that people selected objects that 'can be designed', or (as Lévi-Strauss put it) were 'good to depict' (see nn. 29 and 30 above). But when Durkheim confronted the more general question of the 'sacred' and inquired what kinds of object or action fell into this category in religious systems as a whole, he argued that 'anything can be sacred' (*Elementary Forms*, p. 27). He writes that anything has been, or could be, reckoned as belonging to the sacred category, and that, in the last analysis, it is not a quality of the item itself that renders it apt for sacred status, but simply the fact that it has – for reasons internal to the society and culture involved – been so classified. 'There is nothing left with which to characterise the sacred in relation to the profane except their heterogeneity' (p. 38). In other words, nothing is inherently or 'naturally' sacred; anything can be so. The two categories of sacred and profane depend upon each other: neither could exist except in contrast to the complementary set.[71] It is the act of constituting something as 'set apart and forbidden' (p. 47) that makes it sacred, not the other way round.

At first sight this claim, though certainly interesting and to many people perhaps provocative, does not seem so significant as to mark a point of departure for a major line of thinking in the social sciences. On its own, indeed, it might not have done. It was the confluence of this part of Durkheim's analysis with other currents of theorizing that opened up those new perspectives which Lévi-Strauss has displayed and explored. *Elemen-*

tary Forms itself provides one further element in this coming together, in the passage referred to earlier in this chapter where, in his definition of religion, Durkheim refers to religion as 'a unified system' (p. 47). Putting this stress on system together with the autonomy of the sacred emblems ('anything can be sacred') we find ourselves at the threshold of the modern approach to symbols, seen as essentially 'arbitrary' – in the sense of not answering to any 'natural' necessity outside themselves – and systematic – in the sense that they have no intrinsic meaning apart from their place in a whole system of symbols, in which the 'value' of one symbol arises only from its distinction from ('opposition to', as some would have it) other symbols in the system.

Language is, of course, the type-case of such a unified system of 'arbitrary' signs,[72] and the modern science of linguistics was in fact being developed along these lines by Ferdinand de Saussure at Geneva in the first decade of this century. A group of Saussure's students collaborated in the production of his *Course in General Linguistics*[73] in 1915. Here, the distinctive approach to symbolism adumbrated in Durkheim's work was given explicit and detailed treatment. It was not, however, until the 1940s that the two converging theorizations were integrated into a systematic philosophical anthropology. This integration was the signal achievement of Lévi-Strauss.[74]

To appreciate both his debt to the original Durkheimian impetus and his developing independence from it, it may be helpful to recall Mary Douglas's reference, quoted above,[75] to 'the quest for natural systems of symbolising'. Durkheim's obsession with sociology as a *sui generis* discipline, and society as a *sui generis* entity, led him to repudiate with misplaced vigour any suggestion that the 'social' could be explained by, or reduced to, other levels of reality, whether 'psychic' or natural. The methodological point is one that most sociologists and anthropologists would support, but not at the cost of eliminating the 'natural' as irrelevant to human culture and society: for, to put it at its lowest, man is himself a 'natural' being, and his potentiality for culture is a 'natural' fact (just as the *distinction* between culture and nature is *cultural*). Lévi-Strauss views man as perhaps above all a classifying animal, whose types and symbols are indeed 'cultural' in as much as they are not copies of an external reality imposing itself on the human mind,[76] yet whose very cultural propensity and classifying activity are themselves imperatives of that mind which is itself a 'natural' fact.

The 'intellectualist' view of man which this implies can be illustrated in a fairly simple form by taking the example of 'totemic' species in their relationship to human groups.[77] This example, moreover, allows us to take leave of Lévi-Strauss in a still 'religious' context.

A typical 'totemic' correspondence identifies sub-groups (clans, moieties, etc.) within a society with natural species (such as foxes, crows or kangaroos), often setting up a one-to-one correspondence between the items. The social groups, however, are strictly exogamous, and have this as one of their principal structural characteristics. In this respect they are precisely the opposite of animal species. Members of Clan A must marry into (say) Clan B. The very thing that foxes do not do is mate with crows or fish. For Lévi-Strauss, so-called totemic institutions evoke a homology 'not between social groups and natural species but between the differences which manifest themselves on the level of groups on the one hand and on that of species on the other. They are thus based on the postulate of a homology between *two systems of differences*, one of which occurs in nature and the other in culture' (p. 115, original italics).[78] It is, in other words, the differences and not the items that resemble each other. He illustrates his argument as follows.

Nature	species 1	≠	species 2	≠	species 3	≠	. . . species n
Culture	group 1	≠	group 2	≠	group 3	≠	. . . group n

The vertical lines indicate correspondences *between differences* and not between items.[79]

It can perhaps be objected that an analysis of this kind is so far-fetched as to strain credulity. Is it seriously being maintained that non-literate peoples are postulating homologies not between groups and species but between 'two systems of differences'? A sophistication that is not easily grasped even by those educated in a tradition of discursive philosophy is being attributed to persons who, in Lévi-Strauss's own view, replace abstract thought with 'the science of the concrete'. But this is to mistake the nature of the argument. The model that Lévi-Strauss constructs here, like the incomparably more complex ones to be found (for instance) in the *Mythologiques* (see n. 69), is an analytical or observer's model. It can be compared to a physiologist's or neurologist's highly complex account of a simple operation like raising an arm, which we perform without thinking about it, in happy ignorance of the processes that make it possible. In a famous phrase, Lévi-Strauss has written that 'myths think themselves in men, and without their knowledge'.[80] With this displacement of the individual from the centre of the stage, we return, though with a difference, to Durkheim.[81]

Conclusion: Durkheim and religion

In view of much of what has been said in this chapter, it is no surprise that those with a personal or professional religious commitment tend on the whole to regard Durkheim's sociology of religion with suspicion or even hostility, though it is fair to add that an element of fascination is often present too.[82] Precisely because Durkheim offers so plausible an account of religion as a human activity reflecting the collective experience of man and underpinning the solidarity of society, those whose primary concern with religion is to proclaim it as in some real sense *true* are likely to find Durkheim's apparent endorsement of the validity of religious experience alarmingly ambiguous. Where society, state and religion seem to chime together in harmony, the resulting order may seem (at least to those who are happy with it) to bear a Durkheimian interpretation. Some of the more roseate accounts of pre-industrial England, now rather out of date, fit into this picture,[83] and it is probably true that a strongly Erastian view of the relations between Church and state is implicitly shared by many in Britain today.[84] Committed believers, however, are more likely to stress the transcendent values of religious belief and practice, and react against attempts to represent religion as a purely human activity, explicable in sociological, psychological or even philosophical terms.

One particular variant of this response derives from the radical neo-orthodox theology of Karl Barth,[85] whose general approach has been given eloquent expression by Helmut Gollwitzer[86] and was at one time shared by the American Protestant sociologist Peter Berger.[87] According to Barth and Gollwitzer, pagan religions are indeed forms of human cultural activity, often rich in aesthetic power and psychological and social value, and may well be open to reductive analysis of a Durkheimian (or other) kind. This is especially the case where, as in many tribal societies, political, religious, legal, economic and kinship relations or activities are not empirically or institutionally distinguished, and where in consequence everything can be seen as functionally interdependent with everything else, in a mutually reinforcing harmony. Christianity, on the other hand, runs counter to the cultural expectations and products of human nature, which is seen as totally corrupted and saved only by the gratuitous intervention of a God who is 'wholly other'. It is precisely idolatrous to confuse the service of this transcendent God with any human activity, though it is acknowledged that such confusion has marked most religious systems, in the Christian world as much as in any other, and has often been used as a means of legitimating the *status quo* in the interest of particular groups or strata. The true prophet, however, always acts against the stream of human injustice and pride, and his proclamation can never be contained within the cosy 'solidarity' of a Durkheimian universe. Weber for all his professions of being 'religiously tone-deaf' has proved a more congenial analyst here.[88]

Mary Douglas is unusual in apparently settling down into an admittedly modified Durkheimianism. Other Roman Catholic anthropologists such as Evans-Pritchard[89] and Victor Turner[90] have been much more cautious, though like all within the British tradition they acknowledge a debt to Durkheim, particularly to what he bequeathed to his readers and followers in the fields of ritual and symbol. It can reasonably be claimed that Durkheim's contribution here has been permanent and irreversible: his successors – like Lévi-Strauss, Turner, Douglas and others – have moved on from the point to which Durkheim had brought them. If they see so much further than he did, it is because they are standing on the shoulders of a giant.

8

꠹꠹

Assessing Durkheim: classical sociology and modern society

A classical tradition

It need not be taken as self-evident that contemporary students of society, sociologists in particular, should ground their thinking in the work of Marx, Durkheim and Weber. Other disciplines move away from their classical foundations, although some – like philosophy – hold to traditions of thought which are considerably more remote in time. Equally there is no self-evident reason for abandoning such works. It is a question of considering the kind of arguments which might persuade us that one or another balance of attention to past and present writings is right.

The most obvious first consideration would require a judgement of whether a way of thinking has been superseded, either because central assumptions have been seriously questioned, or because evidence has falsified the main argument of a thesis of theory. We would want to add to this an assessment of whether older theories have been substantially augmented, whilst the central elements of the old have been incorporated in the new. Thirdly, one might conclude that the whole world-view and world circumstances which surrounded earlier work have been superseded in quite radical ways, rendering this work out-moded or 'dated' in its whole conception and execution.

It does not seem to me that, with regard to Marx, Durkheim or Weber, we can speak of the clear overthrow of the very central, admittedly conflicting, assumptions of their work, nor can we point to an unqualified falsification of expectations by evidence. It is true, of course, that Marx's expectations of revolutionary struggle in mature capitalist societies could be said to have been falsified by events. But, without having to accuse more recent Marxists of sleight of hand or avoidance of 'the facts', one can readily concede that the whole problematic of class struggle and social change, much as Marx conceived it, remains highly relevant. Similarly one might suggest that central Marxist assumptions have come under serious question – I am thinking of the methodological questions of materialism, idealism and determinism. But these have been challenged, or counterposed to alternatives, rather than overthrown. In the same way, Weberian assumptions about the interpretation of cultural meaning in social history, or Durkheimian assumptions about the moral quality of the social order, have been challenged; but no one could say that there has been an even 'relatively final' judgement about any or all of these.

Looking to the second point, any argument that a subsequent consolidation of founding theories had occurred would not, on its own, force the conclusion that the time had come to relegate these founding theories to a minor place in the discipline. One would also have to be assured that the newer consolidations contained all of the virtues and few of the vices of the old, represented undeniable advances on the earlier work, and that they made the arguments of founding fathers as clear and as inspiring as in the hands of their original authors. Whatever one may think of subsequent grand theorists in the sociological tradition – Parsons springs most readily to mind – few, if any, would argue that their works fulfil each of these criteria. *The Structure of Social Action*[1] was, principally, a secondary discussion of Durkheim, Weber and some others, with extensions of their thoughts in some particular directions, rather than a work of consolidation. The attempt to consolidate came in the *Social System*[2] which pushed sociological thought rather more narrowly down the 'functionalist' path, with an increasing tendency to see norms and values, and the process of institutionalization, as the central terrain of sociological inquiry.

There have been some major works of secondary interpretation which, by the very weight and intensity of evaluation, have extended sociological thought beyond the horizons of the classical founders. Among these we would include, for example, Gouldner's *The Coming Crisis of Western Sociology* and Anthony Giddens's *Capitalism and Modern Social Theory*;[3] the continued intellectual production of writers such as these stretches the sociological imagination into new territory. But I would still think that, for the most part, their work would have to be read in the context of a sound prior understanding of Marx, Durkheim and Weber. It may be that, increasingly, students will come to rely on these sources for their understanding of the classical tradition, and the quality of many of these works – for example Lukes's work on Durkheim – would not entail serious risk of misrepresentation. But the work of sociologists as teachers, writers and researchers – including the most innovative work in the discipline – continues to rely on not only an acquaintance with early writings, but also on an immediate concern with the substance of past work as a source of inspiration for renewed applications.

The third possibility – that the nature of the original context of writing may have made the work of early scholars seriously 'dated' in a number of senses – is most likely to be the one with force and conviction as a reason for moving on. As regards the non-human sciences, we may assume on the whole that, while paradigms may change and methods of study are revolutionized, the object of observation – the natural world – remains constant. The revolutions in thought may then be traced to paradigm shifts or to dramatic advances in techniques of observation, experimentation or measurement. Of course there are also significant shifts in the priorities of study which do reflect changes of a sociological kind. But in the social and human sciences, the more *historically* one conceives the disciplines, the more the objects of observation are themselves changing in such ways as to make the paradigms of the past inadequate because they were founded on views of human society which have been undermined by subsequent events, unforeseen and unforeseeable.

At this point we must consider two important factors. One is that sociological theories and approaches vary, even when they *are* historically conceived, in the breadth or *span* of historical imagination. Secondly, there are sociological questions which, rightly or wrongly, may be asked in a way that is not principally historical, rather they are based on some universalized conception of fundamental problems or fundamental features of human association. With regard to the question of historical span, it is clear that the theories of Marx, Durkheim and Weber are all developmental in a grand sense. In Marx's evolutionary schema there is something approaching a grand pattern of human history with reference to speculation about the earliest forms of human association, 'ascending' to the most advanced stages of capitalism. But the enduring element has been the analysis of – principally – Western capitalist societies, and the transition to socialism. In Durkheim, as earlier chapters have shown, there is a fading evolutionary scheme, with a quite explicit interest in the character of primitive society. But as this book has also shown (with some exception to be made for chapters 4 and 7) there is a primary concern with the nature of *modern* societies, and with their 'pathological' and 'healthy' tendencies, which stands quite independently of the model of 'the primitive'. In Weber the interest in the nature of modern Western social organization is even more marked. In all three cases we can see an interest in some grand aspects of modern societies and the underlying movements of change. The net is cast wide enough – far enough 'back' and far enough 'forward' – to provide us with schema which are not wholly rooted in quite temporary social configurations, or to passing definitions of the intellectual issues emerging in different periods of history. Marx is concerned with the development and future of Western capitalist societies; Durkheim with the social and moral structure of advanced societies; and Weber with the major cultural and organizational features of Western civilization. The question that remains is to assess the precise features of – for our purposes – Durkheim's theoretical constructs, in so far as they continue to provide an adequate and inspirational starting point for sociological inquiry.

One point may be made in passing before turning to this last question. There are certain ways in which any social theory with a basically nineteenth-century social foundation cannot be expected to cope with the twentieth century. In the broadest terms no one could have expected nineteenth-century writers to anticipate twentieth-century technological advances. That advance would take place could be readily anticipated; what forms it would take, and with what consequences, could not. Advances in communications are probably the most immediately striking. But as Giddens, for one, has argued, the whole range of technological change, and of related social and political change – especially in the field of weaponry and the accompanying centrality of military institutions – has contributed to a radical discontinuity in social change of an unprecedented kind. This discontinuity in social change means that evolutionary models of any kind, purely endogenous models of social change, and an exclusive attention to the 'economic engine rooms' of history have to be seriously questioned.[4] Allowance for those arguments certainly has to be made in ensuing claims for the continuing value of Durkheimian inspiration in sociology.

We should also observe here that Durkheim by contrast with Marx or Weber – has a 'universalistic' element in his sociological theorizing which, if such a thing is possible, lifts his questions (about social solidarity, ritual and social cohesion) out of a historical context altogether. There is something to be said for this view of parts of Durkheim's work, but, on the whole this volume has argued against this view of his major thrust. Certainly he was concerned about, let us say, 'solidarity' as a fundamental problem of human societies, but his analysis was very much applied to the question of how particular modern societies achieved solidarity.

The claims of Durkheimian sociology

There are three main elements of Durkheim's theories which we shall consider in this concluding section – the evolutionary or developmental schema, the analysis of the political and social structure of advanced societies, and the view of society as a moral order. I suggest that the first was unsatisfactory and can safely be discarded except as an explanation of how Durkheim's thinking was founded. The strengths and weaknesses of the last two are bound up with each other. The weaknesses of the analysis of political and social structure stem from the fact that the concern with the moral qualities of the social order became, at crucial points, a view of the social order as primarily, even wholly a moral phenomenon. While the analysis of the division of labour and the state raises some very interesting questions, it fails at the point where the raw exercise of power and interest are squeezed out of the analysis in favour of an analysis of the moral conceptions which circulate in political and economic institutions. The corresponding strength lies in the fact that, to the extent that social orders, from the point of view of observer and participant, *are* moral phenomena, Durkheim creates a sociological language for comprehending this fact, and points to the ways in which social and institutional changes, and changes in the ways we conceive of our duties and obligations to one another, are bound together.

Durkheim's sociology insists that social relationships 'give rise to' or 'necessarily involve' moral conceptions of these relationships. The moral qualities of human life reside in the inescapably social character of human life. We live in association with others, we derive our essentially human qualities from our association, and in truth the life of the 'individual' is inconceivable outside the context of participation in a social world which is not simply an aggregation of individuals. This thought is expressed in several ways in Durkheim's work. It is expressed through the argument that all the major tools of human transactions – language, symbols, systems of exchange – have a supra-individual quality to be found, at the simplest level, in the fact that they precede and outlive specific individuals. At a more psychological level the same idea is expressed throughout his study of suicide in the contention that individual life can barely be sustained without a supportive social milieu. Since it is our associations which give us all that we have that is essentially human – ideas of worth and dignity, a sense of attachment without which we feel ourselves to be nothing, ideas of obligation and proper restraint of desires – the collapse or fragmentation of these associations destroys or threatens to destroy the existential sentiments which sustain us from day to day. It is undoubtedly true that this form of argument has been put to some loose and unsatisfactory use – in the simple-minded interpretation of social phenomena as responses to a 'need for a sense of belonging' – but this, on its own, does not invalidate the Durkheimian argument.

It seems to me that history is replete with evidence of the importance to people of a sense of dignity and worth, and of evidence of the way in which ideas of worth and human meaning are socially constituted. The historical study of modern slavery is in part a political economy of slavery: but it is also a record of how people respond to the most severe threats to their associated sense of worth. Orlando Patterson's account of the early days of plantation slavery in Jamaica provides us with a picture of society which in many respects scarcely met the elementary conditions of a constituted social order.[5] Few white 'colonists' had any sense of permanent attachment to the social order, and African slaves had been detached from all the familiar supports of a way of life. No doubt the pathologies of such a society are partly understandable in terms of the brutalities of economic exploitation. But there are moral and social psychological elements of this social configuration – the despair, detachment, human alienation, the abandonment of 'decency' – which must be linked to the absence of a constituted moral and social order. The other revealing aspect of the same story is the struggle to create forms of identity, orderliness and human meaning throughout Jamaican history in the most unpropitious of circumstances.

The same sort of question reappears in consideration of modern racism. There is, again, a political economy of racism which ties the emergence of political ideologies to the contours of class struggles which come to be defined in a language of race. But there remains a core element of racist ideology which cannot be ignored and must, in good measure, be examined in its own terms. Racist ideas, whether in systematic political forms or in the unco-ordinated expressions of day-to-day interaction, contain at their centre the assertion or implication of the unequal worth of human beings. As Lévi-Strauss has argued, this idea has, historically, been very common in the sense that most pre-modern and many modern societies support a conception of 'the people' which is exclusive and ascribes true moral qualities only to the included. Such a notion is relatively 'harmless' when contact is infrequent or insignificant. However, Lévi-Strauss suggests that the very idea of mankind in a universal sense is both recent in origin and fragile in its hold.[6] The forces which sustain this idea and those which erode it may be crucial in determining the fate of the world in the modern era. In his discussion of nationalism, patriotism and citizenship, and of the institutions which protect the idea of the dignity of the individual, Durkheim had begun to fix his ideas on this question. At the very least he had provided a sociological language in which we might begin to think about it.

While students may tire of the exegesis of classical thinkers, the exploration of examples with potential for new inquiries can bring ideas to life. The concept of 'citizenship' is a good example because it is an idea which Durkheim investigated, it has been relatively neglected in sociology, and yet has clear legal, social structural and moral aspects.[7] One of the difficulties of continued reliance on classical sources is that these works – including the translations of them – have a style of expression which inhibits imaginative reading. The reader should be able to see what is meant by a reference to the 'moral and social order'. In the case of Durkheim, students need to understand that what is being examined is, for example, the ideas which people hold of the obligations which they have towards each other. If, let us say, there is a marked change in the social regard which people have of unmarried mates, extending to a view that the couple have the same sort of moral, and legal, obligations towards each other as do married couples, then here we have a profound change in human relationships, expressed partly through the moral ideas which develop in and around those relationships. Moral ideas are ideas about what people ought to do, what they owe to each other, what constraints they ought to put on their behaviour, what significance they attach to collective symbols, and about what kind of 'appeals' are legitimate when people are asked to recognize a duty or obligation. Such facts of life are not life itself, but they are an integral part of it; they are part of the texture of everyday life and of the symbolic life of nations or societies. This exemplification of the sense of Durkheim's moral sociology is a necessary preface to a concluding assessment of the evolutionary, social structural, and moral aspects of his theories. For, although the last may be seen as an 'aspect' of his theorizing, it must also, as we argued in chapter 3, be seen as permeating all his thinking.

Evolution

Whilst his rudimentary evolutionary theory may be regarded as an explanation of the central features of social change, its purpose is to explain the changing bases of moral cultures in societies differently structured. But, for the moment, taking the developmental model *per se* I think that one is bound to conclude that, on the whole, continued exploration along the lines of Durkheim's analysis would not be rewarding. For one thing, the idea of the primitive (or pre-modern, or simple) social orders from which advanced societies spring, as expressed in Durkheim's work, is far from satisfactory. Durkheim illustrated his arguments by reference to whatever materials came to hand, and this is especially so in *The Division of Labour*. Examples are lifted out of history with scant regard for any understanding of context, or of continuities and discontinuities. Equally serious in consequence are the great doubts cast over the reliability of much of the material upon which Durkheim drew, particularly the Australian accounts which he used in illustrating 'primitive religion' (see chapter 7). Similarly, as was demonstrated in chapter 6, the evolution of types of legal system in accordance with changes in social structure, has been investigated by later scholars and conclusions quite contrary to Durkheim's own have been reached. If we add to this record the abandonment of Durkheim's sketch of population growth as a propelling factor in social change, we are left with very little.

There are only a few cautions that one may wish to add to this general conclusion. One is that the discarding of the model of evolution need not inflict serious damage on the major corpus of Durkheim's work. The fundamental conceptions elaborated within a rough evolutionary framework retain their value when extricated from it. In the case of the study of law and society, the most critical scholars are inclined to agree that the distinction between systems relying on punishment and sanctions flowing from a collective moral sensibility, and those relying on concilation and the restoration of injuries suffered, remains a distinction of value, even if the correlation with types of society is unsound. Similarly, chapter 5 shows that Bernstein was able to make imaginative use of the distinction between 'mechanical' and 'organic' solidarity (in school systems) quite independently of evolutionary ideas. Seizing upon the core of Durkheim's concepts Bernstein was able to explore the different possible bases of order, discipline and integration. Schools do face the problem of the indirect moral effects of what they teach and how they teach it, as well as problems of order and discipline within the school. Some schools have strenuously appealed to a sense of moral identification with the institution, loyalty to the school and respect for its emblems and traditions; under some conditions this appears impossible of achievement, and in some minds it represents an undesirable and outmoded form of obeisance. Hargreaves has suggested that the modes of relationship between pupil and school can vary from an enthusiastic embracing of its ends and a sense of corporate loyalty, to instrumental compliance, simmering hostility or dull indifference. These are all examples of Durkheimian categories being put to use in the absence of a developmental scheme.

We might also add that there is something to be said for a developmental model when it actually amounts to a grounded historical account, where the claims are less ambitious and the historical referent clearly defined. This is certainly the case with Durkheim's interpretation of changes in the pedagogic ethic of French education. In this case the institutional arrangements of education, the moral ideas which pervaded teaching and learning, and the wider social sensibilities of the period are drawn together in a relatively detailed account of an identifiable period of history in such a way that subsequent changes in each of these things could be traced through to the modern period (see chapter 5). In this phase of his work Durkheim is at his historical best.

Social and political structure

As regards Durkheim's analysis of social and political structure, chapters 2 and 3 provide us with a basis for assessment and the reader is particularly directed to the discussion of 'coercion and interest' in chapter 3. It became clear that Durkheim's inclination to define inequalities of material condition as 'external' to the division of labour separated things which cannot or should not be wholly set apart. Of course 'class structure' and the 'division of labour' are properly analytically distinguished but this does not mean that they can be understood independently of each other. In particular Durkheim is unable to convince his reader of his argument that social differentiation in the division of labour is the master process in the historical development of modern societies.

However, even if we concede that the division of labour cannot be understood in isolation from the configuration of interests and conflicts of interest with which it is bound up, we can still recognize that a primary focus on the division of labour itself, and its institutional and 'ideological' concomitants, raises important sociological questions. It keeps in view, for example, the question of assessing the extent to which the elaboration of the division of labour is either desirable or inevitable, and leaves open the question of whether progressive differentiation – including what Durkheim called 'excessive specialization' – is a feature of modernity rather than 'simply' of the necessity to extract the maximum value from the working day.

Durkheim could see that the progressive elaboration of the division of labour, and more generally social differentiation, could further the growth of spheres (or milieux) of society which might become increasingly separate from each other both in structure and in spirit. This in itself posed problems of co-ordination, for what a sphere of activity – let us say education and its administration – gained in expertise and close familiarity with its own activities, it might lose in consciousness of a broader interdependent view of its function. And the growth of institutional separation was, he expected, likely to be accompanied by an increasing divergence of expertise (the knowledge base of an activity) and of ethos (the moral sentiments peculiar to a milieu).

It seems to me that none of these questions have disappeared from the agenda of societies or of observers of societies. Countries which have undergone socialist transformations – China might be a good example here – face a number of questions with regard to the division of labour in a society in which the class basis of economic organization is supposed to have been removed. There is the matter of rewards – how does one allocate rewards to different functions in the absence of 'market mechanisms'? There is the matter of social mobility – how does one guard against occupational inheritance or the passing on of enhanced opportunities? And there is the matter of authority – how does one prevent power gravitating towards those with technical expertise in an area of decision making? The same sorts of problems were faced on a smaller scale in some of the socialistic Israeli Kibbutz where communities attempted to prevent a division of labour becoming permanent, and from becoming a source of unequal reward and prestige.[8] In capitalist societies we see something of the same order of problem in the inaccessibility of an institutional sphere to inspection because of the highly specialist nature of its functions and the knowledge which informs those functions. The authority of the 'professionals' has been challenged by 'consumers' (for example of medical services) who are essentially reacting to the authority claimed by those whose authority appears to rest principally on their monopolization of a body of knowledge. It is also argued that specialization, necessary for a high degree of professional competence, at the same time provokes a narrowing of the perspectives of practitioners, making them blind or unreceptive to the demands of others. If the weakness of the Durkheimian commentary on the division of labour lies in the neglect of what he regarded as external to it, the strengths lie in a form of sociological imagination which continues to alert us to the more specifically 'sociological' institutional and ideological consequences of specialization and differentiation.

Some of the same arguments can be brought to bear in assessing Durkheim's analysis of the state and politics in advanced societies. If Marxism has, for some time, suffered from an inadequately developed theory of the state, or a theory which rested too heavily on the conjunction of class power and political power, then Durkheim's work can be seen to have suffered from never having located political power and institutions in an understanding of power exogenous to the political system itself, or of the nexus between the two. Furthermore, by defining simple coercion or unlegitimated power as pathological he tends to exclude it from analysis altogether (see chapter 3). But, as we argued in that same chapter, Durkheim's writings do provide a source of inspiration for the consideration of institutional and ideological aspects of modern political systems, and it is a source which has not lost all its vigour.

To illustrate this, three themes may be extracted. One is the question of the relationship between sociological qualities of life in society and forms of political consciousness; the second is in the balance of power between a centralized state and secondary institutions; and the third relates to an analysis of the conditions favourable or unfavourable to the preservation of the values which we summarize in the term 'democracy'. By the first I mean that, whilst no one need claim that the *quality* of social experience in the family, neighbourhood, school or workplace is the *principal* determinant of political consciousness, it is reasonable to suppose that their influence is more than negligible. For example, the very existence of forms of social separation – whereby sections of the population are never or rarely in any significant contact with each other, divided along lines of age, ethnic origin, social class or stage in the life cycle – creates the conditions for a massified conceptions of others. People who have no real contact with another group in a population are particularly likely to be susceptible to the appeal of stereotypical images, especially as projected by mass means of communication against whose message they have no ready means of check or test by experience. It is likely that there are many people in Britain or the United States who have 'strong views' on race or immigration without having any relevant experience of either. The lonely, disaffiliated, disappointed individuals, whose lives have given cause for a sense of detachment and resentment, may find solace in political ideologies which seem to relieve the sense of distress and frustration. In brief, there is something to be said for the argument that 'mass' societies give rise to 'mass' forms of political consciousness. In chapter 3 we tried to show how Durkheim's analysis of disaffiliation and social detachment, especially in their relationship to volatile political sentiments, pre-figured many of the themes of subsequent political sociology. The danger of course lies in a descent into behaviouristic or psychologistic explanations of politics in which political movements and moods are reduced to psychological factors, or in which those factors are exaggerated in their importance.

The second theme – the relationship between the state and 'secondary' institutions – has been adequately illustrated in chapter 3, in which we showed that a number of interpretations of state power and totalitarianism followed Durkheimian lines of analysis. This issue unquestionably remains a vital one in all modern societies having a claim to being democratic. Trade unions, the legal professions, and the judicial system, educational institutions, and medical and social services are some of the principal spheres of activity in which this question is relevant. They are all areas in which elected and appointed officers can lay claim to some form of control (over people and procedures) and they are areas in which conceptions of proper practice and of the collective good are promulgated. Their ideas of the collective interest and of ethical standards may be at variance with one another and with a 'central' political view. There are both legal and customary supports of the autonomy of workers or practitioners in these institutions; for example medical practitioners derive some of their authority from the customary prestige which they enjoy, but they are at the same time both protected and restrained by the law. Their autonomy is also subject to challenge, on the one hand by patients who may demand more information about or control over their treatment, and on the other hand by governments who decide that certain decisions cannot be safely left to professional discretion.

The way in which these relationships take shape varies considerably from one democratic society to another. The use of litigation in respect of medical treatment – a form of patient control – is much more common in the United States than in Great Britain; the same two countries also differ in respect of ownership and control of national media, the United States having nothing really comparable to the British Broadcasting Corporation (whose freedom from political interference was sharply tested in the South Atlantic conflict of 1982). Although the kinds of example we can think of – where the boundaries between the state and autonomous or semi-autonomous secondary institutions are at issue – take many different forms, there are core elements relevant to Durkheim's discussions of common ideas and the proper role of state power. Not surprisingly these issues can become highly politically charged – other examples would be the independence of trade unions, the rights of teachers to control what they teach, the responsibilities of doctors on such issues as abortion, and of social workers in their interventions in family life. It is as well to remember that Durkheim not only feared that a modern state may be led to wield too much power over secondary institutions, but also recognized that it was possible that these very institutions could exercise a kind of tyranny over those they claimed to control and guide, in which case the duty of the state was to protect the individual against the undue power of the secondary group.

Most of the issues we have mentioned directly or indirectly raise the more general Durkheimian question about the moral basis of democracies. Complex societies, he argued, cannot be expected to sustain uniform moral cultures, at least not in the sense of widely shared moral ideas which can provide a guide to daily actions. In the regular performance of duties, people develop moral ideas which are peculiar to their sphere – the moral precepts of the doctor cannot be wholly assumed by the lawyer. But Durkheim pointed to a number of moral ideas which, he argued, tended to gain acceptance throughout democratic society, which were more abstract than everyday rules but nonetheless important, and which the state had a sacred duty to uphold. These were the values which were most dramatically put to the test in the Dreyfus affair – the values of justice, individual freedom and dignity, and the recourse to due process which could rescue the individual from the curtailment of his or her rights and liberties.

Durkheim's sociology does not provide ready answers to these questions, either at the sociological level of explaining the conditions under which democratic values are threatened, or at the political level of preference for one arrangement or another. But it does have the virtue of placing them on the agenda of sociology, of opening the lines of inquiry, and of framing an analysis. It is clear that Durkheim rejected, on sociological grounds, a solution in terms of maximization of the freedom of the individual; there is, as we have seen, a conception of liberty and individualism in Durkheim's work which is quite at variance with common understandings. It is also evident that he was not prepared to entrust the state with all major functions of control in industrial or advanced societies. And although Durkheim was principally concerned with France, or societies structurally and ideologically similar to it, one could fairly raise the same questions about socialist societies. Whilst radical critics of Western democracies would argue that the 'freedoms' of capitalist societies are more apparent than real – that democracies are bourgeois democracies – few would argue that the outstanding examples of socialist societies have solved the problems of reconciling social justice, or the search for it, with the demands of individual freedom. For Western socialists this remains a major intellectual and practical problem. Whilst Durkheim himself rejected the concentration of economic power (ownership and control) in the hands of the state, there is no very strong evidence that he regarded the protection of individual property rights as a guarantee of democratic freedoms in general.

Of course there is a simpler way for the author, at the end of a book like this, to seek to justify – or, more generally, assess – the study of Durkheimian themes, and that is to appeal to the evidence of the preceding chapters. I have tried to demonstrate that Durkheim creates a sociological language for analysis of questions of social reconstruction in what he called advanced societies. This book will have shown the weaknesses as well as the persistent vitality of Durkheim's ideas at this broadest level of sociological inquiry. At the same time it would be fair to conclude from the foregoing chapters that Durkheim's inspiration has been found more productive in some areas than in others. The law, deviance, religion, education and, to a lesser degree, the study of the state and the ethics of democracy are all areas which have built on Durkheimian foundations, both by promoting the stronger and rejecting the weaker elements of his thought. It may be that the reason for this is that in all these areas there are vital elements of a moral and symbolic kind. The question of morality and individualism, of the social basis of moral obligations, and of the relation of the individual to society, are the questions with which Durkheim began his inquiries, and they may well be the very ones which are the foundation of his enduring claim to *some* of our attention.

Notes

Introduction

1 Cf. Talcott Parsons, *The Structure of Social Action*, McGraw-Hill, New York, 1937; and R. C. Hinkle and G. J. Hinkle, *The Development of Modern Sociology*, Random House, New York, 1954, p. 51.

2 A special issue of this journal, devoted to Durkheimian interests appeared in February 1979: *La Revue Française de Sociologie*, 20 (1) 1979. There has also been the formation of Le Groupe d'études Durkheimiennes, led by Phillippe Besnard at the Fondation Maison des Sciences de L'Homme, which publishes regular bulletins concerning current work. *Social Forces*, 59 (4), June 1981, is also dedicated to Durkheimian themes, coming out under the title 'Durkheim Lives!' The major special 'Durkheim' issue of the French review was *À Propos de Durkheim RFS 17 avril juin 1976*.

3 One of the best, early and influential expressions of this view can be found in John Rex, *Key Problems in Sociological Theory*, Routledge and Kegan Paul, London, 1961.

4 See n2 above, but also Steven Lukes, *Emile Durkheim, His Life and Work*, Allen Lane, London, 1973; E. Wallwork, *Durkheim, Morality and Milieu*, Harvard University Press, Cambridge, Mass., 1972; D. La Capra, *Emile Durkheim, Sociologist and Philosopher*, Cornell University Press, Ithaca and London, 1972; Y. Nandan, *The Durkheimian School*, Greenwood Press, Westport, Conn., 1977 (a bibliographical work); J. C. Filloux, *La Science sociale et l'action*, a collection of Durkheim's articles with notes and introduction, Presses Universitaires de France, Paris, 1970; forthcoming P. Besnard (ed.), *The Durkheimians: Constructing the Sociological Domain*, Cambridge University Press, Cambridge, 1983; and A. Giddens, *Studies in Social and Political Theory*, Hutchinson, London, 1977, chs. 6, 7, 8 and 9. In the last ten years most of Durkheim's major works have been translated into and published in Japanese.

5 J. Horton, 'The dehumanisation of anomie and alienation', *British Journal of Sociology*, 15, 1964, pp. 283–300.

6 Joseph Neyer, 'Individualism and socialism in Durkheim', and Melvin Richter, 'Durkheim's politics and political theory', both in K. Wolff (ed.), *Emile Durkheim: Essays on Sociology and Philosophy*, Ohio State University Press, Columbus, 1960.

7 Lukes, *Durkheim, Life and Work*; A. Giddens, *Capitalism and Modern Social Theory*, Cambridge University Press, Cambridge, 1971, and his introduction to *Emile Durkheim: Selected Writings*, Cambridge University Press, Cambridge, 1972. Compare, however, I. Zeitlin, *Ideology and the Development of Sociological Theory*, Prentice-Hall, New Jersey, 1968.

8 Robert Nisbet, *The Sociological Tradition*, Basic Books, New York, 1966, and 'Conservatism and sociology', *American Journal of Sociology*, 58, 1952, pp. 165–75; Lewis Coser, 'Durkheim's conservatism and its implications for his sociological theory', in Wolff, *Emile Durkheim*, pp. 211–32.

9 Robert K. Merton, 'Social structure and anomie', *Social Theory and Social Structure*, Free Press, Glencoe, 1957, ch. 4.

10 Emile Durkheim, *Professional Ethics and Civic Morals*, Routledge and Kegan Paul, London, 1957, p. 30.

1. Durkheim's life, public career and sociological thought

1 For example in the discussions recorded in *Libres Entretiens*, 'Sur l'internationalisme', Durkheim readily accepts the existence of class conflict in industrial societies, but only questions whether it always takes the same shape in different countries. 'We must not leave aside the question of finding out what class conflict is in different societies . . . [but] we can take it as agreed that there exists an antagonism between the working class and other classes' (*Libres Entretiens*, 2nd Series, 1905, p. 412). See also Harry Hoefnagels, 'La "Question sociale" dans la sociologie de Durkheim', *Bulletin de l'Institut de Recherches Économiques de l'Université de Louvain*, 24 (8), 1958, pp. 673–703.

2 Henri Peyre, 'Durkheim: the man, his time, and his intellectual background', in Wolff, *Emile Durkheim*, pp. 3–32. For commentary on Durkheim's life and public career, see Lukes, *Durkheim, Life and Work*; Edward A. Tiryakian, 'Emile Durkheim', in Tom Bottomore and Robert Nisbet (eds.), *A History of Sociological Analysis*, Basic Books, New York, 1978; Robert Nisbet, *Emile Durkheim*, Prentice Hall Englewood Cliffs, New Jersey, 1965; H. Alpert, *Emile Durkheim and His Sociology*, Columbia University Press, New York, 1939, repr. 1961. I have drawn on all these but especially on the chapter on Durkheim in Lewis Coser, *Masters of Sociological Thought*, Harcourt Brace Jovanovich, New York, 1971.

3 Peyre, 'Durkheim', p. 4.

4 Coser, *Masters of Sociological Thought*, p. 156 (main source for this section).

5 *Ibid.*, pp. 156–7.

6 *Ibid.*, p. 143.

7 *Ibid.*, p. 144.

8 Terry Clark, 'Emile Durkheim and the institutionalization of sociology in the French university system', *European Journal of Sociology*, 9, 1968, p. 43.

9 See Coser, *Masters of Sociological Thought*.

10 Clark, 'Emile Durkheim', p. 44.

11 Coser, *Masters of Sociological Thought*, p. 157.

12 *Ibid.*, p. 159.

13 See my comments earlier in this chapter, and in chapters 2 and 3. He tended to view the socialist Left as mainly committed to national ownership of the means of production, a solution he referred to as 'magical', i.e. promising something it could not deliver.

14 Written in 1898, it was translated as 'Individualism and the intellectuals' (by S. and J. Lukes), *Political Studies*, 17, 1969, pp. 14–30.

15 Lukes, *Emile Durkheim*, p. 333, footnote 49.

16 *Ibid.*, Chapters 2 and 3.

17 Durkheim's *Le Socialisme* was published posthumously in 1928; it was primarily a discussion of the work of Saint-Simon. This was translated and published as

Socialism and Saint-Simon, Routledge and Kegan Paul, London, 1959, with an introduction by Alvin Gouldner. In the introduction Gouldner discusses Durkheim's debt to Saint-Simon, and doubts the common portrayal of Durkheim as a disciple of Comte (pp. 10ff).

18 *Socialism and Saint-Simon*, Gouldner's introduction, pp. 16ff.

19 *Ibid.*, p. 14.

20 Tiryakian, 'Durkheim', p. 190. See also 'The principles of 1789 and sociology', in Edward Tiryakian (ed.), *The Phenomenon of Sociology*, Appleton Century Crofts, New York, 1971, a translation of Durkheim's review article, *Revue Internationale de l'Enseignement*, 19, 1890.

21 'We have already seen that among European peoples there is a tendency to form . . . a European society which has, at present, some idea of itself, and the beginning of organization.' Emile Durkheim, *The Division of Labour in Society*, Macmillan, New York, 1933, p. 404.

22 Perhaps even more explicitly he wrote, 'To determine the part played by France in the development of sociology during the nineteenth century is, in large measure, to write the history of that science: for it is among us that it was born, and it has remained an essentially French science.' 'La Sociologie en France au 19e siècle' *Revue Bleue*, 4 (12), 1900, pp. 609–13.

23 See Lukes, *Emile Durkheim*, pp. 338 ff.

24 He distinguished patriotism from nationalism and was disturbed by the unthinking nationalistic militarism which war engendered. 'Doubtless, we have towards the country in its present form . . . obligations that we do not have the right to cast off. But beyond this country, there is another in the process of formation, enveloping our national country: that of Europe or humanity.' Cited in Lukes, *Emile Durkheim*, p. 350.

25 *De la Division du travail social: études sur l'organization des sociétés supérieures*, Alcan, Paris, 1893. In translation *The Division of Labour in Society*, Free Press, New York, 1964.

26 A. Giddens, 'Durkheim's political sociology', *Sociological Review*, NS, 19, 1971, p. 478.

27 In translation these are now: *The Rules of Sociological Method*, Free Press, Glencoe, 1950 (hereafter cited as *Rules*); *Suicide: A Study in Sociology*, Routledge and Kegan Paul, London 1951 (hereafter cited as *Suicide*); *The Elementary Forms of the Religious Life*, Allen and Unwin, London, 1976 (hereafter cited as *Elementary Forms*); *Moral Education*, Free Press, Glencoe, 1961 (hereafter cited as *Moral Education*); *Socialism*, Collier Books, New York, 1962; *Professional Ethics and Civic Morals*, Routledge and Kegan Paul, London, 1957 (hereafter cited as *Professional Ethics*).

28 Edward A. Tiryakian, 'L'École Durkheimienne à la recherche de la société perdue: la sociologie naissante et son milieu culturel', *Cashiers Internationaux de Sociologie*, 66, 1979, p. 100.

29 *Rules*, p. 1–13.

30 *Ibid.*, p. 86.

31 *Ibid.*, p. 64.

32 *Ibid.*, p. 64.

33 Lukes has provided an excellent discussion of this, and readers should note his comments on Lévi-Strauss and Durkheim at p. 235, n41. See in general, Lukes, *Emile Durkheim*, pp. 226–36. For another discussion of objectivism and subjectivism in Durkheim see Charles Stephen Fenton, 'The myth of subjectiv-

ism as a special method in sociology', *Sociological Review*, NS, 16 (3), November 1968.

34 *Suicide*, p. 213.
35 *Ibid.*, pp. 254–55.
36 *Elementary Forms*, p. 10.
37 *Ibid.*, p. 23.
38 *Rules*, p. 14.
39 At page 648 in a review of A. Labriola, 'Essais sur la conception matérialiste de l'histoire', *Revue Philosophique*, 44, 1897, pp. 645–51. 1897.
40 *Elementary Forms*, p. 232.
41 *Ibid.*, p. 233.
42 Van Gennep's criticisms, cited in Lukes, *Emile Durkheim*, p. 525.
43 See chapter 4 of this book for a further discussion of 'race' and 'primitive mentality' and chapter 6 (R. Reiner) for a further discussion of the relationship between social evolution and legal forms (repressive and restitutive law).
44 Giddens, 'Durkheim's political sociology', p. 493.
45 Contribution to discussion: 'Sur l'internationalisme', p. 424.
46 Nisbet, *The Sociological Tradition*.
47 *Ibid.*, p. 86.
48 *Ibid.*, p. 86. citing Durkheim, *Division of Labour*, at p. 277.
49 *Division of Labour*, p. 113.
50 *Ibid.*, p. 129. Note that these indications of the way in which Durkheim qualifies his definition of organic solidarity, cited here and immediately above, occur before Nisbet's 'mid-point' of Durkheim's thesis.
51 *Division of Labour*, p. 228.
52 See *ibid.*, at p. 203 and p. 204, and cf. Lukes, *Emile Durkheim*, at p. 143.
53 Giddens, 'Durkheim's political sociology', p. 478.
54 *Suicide*, p. 376.
55 *Ibid.*, p. 378.
56 Cf. Lukes, *Emile Durkheim*, p. 341.
57 *Division of Labour*, p. 37.
58 'Individualism and the intellectuals' (1898) in translation (S. and J. Lukes) in *Political Studies*, 17, 1969, pp. 14–30. See also chapters 3 and 4 below.
59 All these quotations come from Nisbet, *The Sociological Tradition*, pp. 301–4.
60 *Ibid.*, at p. 301, citing *Suicide* at p. 213.
61 Nisbet, *The Sociological Tradition*, p. 301.
62 Now *Pragmatisme et Sociologie*, Vrin, Paris, 1955.
63 *Ibid.*, p. 184. See Lukes's bibliography, p. 588.
64 Lukes, *Emile Durkheim*, p. 339.
65 Cited in Lukes, *Emile Durkheim*, p. 350.
66 There is no textual or other evidence that de Maistre constituted a significant influence on Durkheim. Nisbet has spoken of Durkheim as the heir of de Maistre and others have happily repeated the claim (*The Sociological Tradition*, pp. 12, 13, 59 and *passim*). But Lewis Coser has written that Nisbet acknowledges that 'there exists no evidence that Durkheim ever read any of these thinkers' (i.e. the anti-enlightenment French traditionalists). See Coser, *Masters of Sociological Thought*, p. 151.
67 Rex, *Key Problems in Sociological Theory*.
68 Kingsley Davis, 'The myth of functionalism as a special method in sociology and anthropology', *American Sociological Review*, 24, December 1959.

69 Percy Cohen, *Modern Social Theory*, Heinemann, London, 1968. p. 59.
70 Robert Bellah, 'Durkheim and history', *American Sociological Review*, 24, December, 1959. Compare Giddens, *Capitalism and Modern Social Theory*, p. 106.
71 Alan Dawe, 'The two sociologies', in Kenneth Thompson and Jeremy Tunstall (eds.), *Sociological Perspectives*, Penguin Books, Middlesex, 1971, pp. 542ff.
72 Dennis Wrong, 'The over-socialized conception of man in modern society', *American Sociological Review*, 26 (2), April 1961, pp. 183–93.
73 See Karl Marx, 'Critique of Hegel's philosophy of right' (1843), in David McLellan (ed.), *Karl Marx: Early Texts*, Blackwell, Oxford, 1971.
74 Durkheim did come to be seen by some French Marxists as a bourgeois reformer whose work had contributed to the shoring up of the capitalist regime. Seen from this perspective, the very breadth of his analysis was viewed as being more 'dangerous' than that of the less imaginative dealers in conciliation. Paul Nizan saw Durkheim as the main ideologue of the Third Republic; the effects of Durkheim's general and educational sociology was that 'teachers taught children to respect the French nation, to justify class collaboration, to join in the cult of the Flag and bourgeois democracy'. See Lukes, *Emile Durkheim*, p. 356.

2. The division of labour, class conflict and social solidarity

1 Both these passages occur at pp. 15–16 of *Professional Ethics*.
2 For a review of this literature, see Milton Gordon, *Assimilation in American Life*, Oxford University Press, New York, 1964.
3 Durkheim, 'Sur l'internationalisme', p. 412.
4 *Professional Ethics*, p. 7.
5 *Division of Labour*, p. 2.
6 *Ibid.*, p. 367.
7 *Professional Ethics*, pp. 36ff.
8 See Lukes, *Emile Durkheim*, pp. 268–75.
9 Some of the best indications of his attitude can be found in the preface to the second French edition of *The Division of Labour* (1902) and in the first sixteen pages of *Professional Ethics*; but he also outlined his views in discussions reported in 'Sur l'internationalisme' (see the following note, 10). The general argument is that 'insatiable demands' are a product of the unregulated state of economic affairs. They can be 'cured' neither by satisfying them (by definition this is not possible with insatiable demands!) nor by suppressing them, but by correcting the unregulated state which gives rise to them. This implies, as we shall show again later, a planned economy. 'There should not be alternating periods of over and under production. No regulated planning means no regularity.' *Professional Ethics*, p. 16.
10 Some of Durkheim's most relevant remarks on this issue can be found in his contributions to *Libres Entretiens*, second series, 1905, translated and discussed in Lukes, *Emile Durkheim*, at pp. 543 and ff.
11 *Professional Ethics*, p. 39.
12 *Ibid.*, p. 40.
13 *Ibid.*
14 Compare chapters 1 and 3 of this book.
15 *Professional Ethics*, p. 41; and compare Lukes, *Emile Durkheim*, p. 541.
16 *Division of Labour*, p. 30.
17 *Ibid.*, p. 371.

18 Georges Friedmann, *The Anatomy of Work*, Heinneman, London, 1961, p. 75.
19 *Division of Labour*, p. 374.
20 *Ibid.*, p. 375.
21 *Ibid.*, p. 384.
22 *Ibid.*, p. 387.
23 See, for example, Claude Lévi-Strauss, *Structural Anthropology*, Basic Books, New York, 1963, pp. 356–7.
24 Friedmann, *The Anatomy of Work*, ch. 5.
25 *Division of Labour*, pp. 389ff.
26 See chapters 1 and 7 for further discussions of anomie.
27 Elton Mayo, *The Social Problems of an Industrial Civilization*, Routledge and Kegan Paul, London, 1949, p. 39.
28 Dunham's foreword to Mayo, *Social Problems*.
29 Mayo, *Social Problems*, p. 120.
30 *Ibid.*, p. 104.
31 Tom Burns, 'The sociology of industry', in A. P. Welford, M. Argyle, D. V. Glass and J.N. Morris (eds.), *Society: Problems and Methods of Study*, Routledge and Kegan Paul, London, 1962, pp. 200–1.
32 *Suicide*, p. 139.
33 *Ibid.*, p. 209.
34 Harold Wilensky, 'Orderly careers and social participation', *American Sociological Review*, 26 (4), August 1961, pp. 521–2.
35 *Ibid.*, p. 522.
36 *Ibid.*, p. 529.
37 *Ibid.*
38 Peter Blau, *Bureaucracy in Modern Society*, Random House, New York, 1956, p. 59.
39 Everett Hughes, *Men and their Work*, Free Press, Glencoe, 1958; and for an overview see Ronald Pavalko, *Sociology of Occupations and Professions*, Peacock Publishers, Itasca, Illinois, 1971.
40 Durkheim, *Suicide*, p. 378, *Division of Labour*, p. 56 and p. 26.
41 *Division of Labour*, pp. 3–4.
42 'At first I thought of these studies as merely interesting and informative for what they would tell about people who do these humbler jobs, i.e. and American ethnology. I have now come to the belief that . . . their deeper value lies in the insights they yield about work and behaviour in any and all occupations.' Hughes, *Men and their Work*, p. 49.
43 See Richard Hall, 'Professionalization and bureaucratization', *American Sociological Review*, 33 (1), February 1968.
44 Alvin Gouldner, 'Cosmopolitans and locals: towards an analysis of latent social roles', *Administrative Science Quarterly*, 2 December 1957, pp. 281–306.
45 Hughes, *Men and their Work*, pp. 7, 12, 25.
46 Cf. Graeme Salaman, *Community and Occupation*, Cambridge University Press, Cambridge, 1974; and S. Wallman (ed.), *Ethnicity at Work*, Macmillan, London, 1979.
47 Hughes, *Men and their Work*, p. 40.
48 W. J. Goode, 'Community within a community: the professions', *American Sociological Review*, 22, 1957, pp. 194–200; Joel Gerstl, 'Determinants of occupational community in high status occupations', *Sociological Quarterly*, 1961, 2, pp. 37–48.

49 Leonard Pearlin, 'Alienation from work: a study of nursing personnel', *American Sociological Review*, 27, June 1962, pp. 304–26.
50 Harold Wilensky, 'From religious community to occupational groups: structural assimilation among professors, lawyers and engineers' *American Sociological Review*, 32 (4), August 1967, pp. 541–61.
51 See Gordon, *Assimilation in American Life.*
52 Nathan Glazer and Daniel Patrick Moynihan, *Beyond the Melting Pot*, MIT Press, Cambridge, Mass., 1963.
53 Michael Gilbert, 'Neo-Durkheimian analyses of economic life and strife: from Durkheim to the Social Contract', *Sociological Review*, NS, 26 (4), November 1978, p. 730.
54 *Ibid.*, p. 734.
55 David Lockwood, 'Social integration and system integration', in G. Zollschan and W. Hirsch (eds.), *Explorations in Social Change*, Routledge and Kegan Paul, London, 1964, pp. 244–57.
56 *Socialism*, pp. 88–90.
57 Gilbert, 'Neo-Durkheimian analyses', p. 732.
58 *Ibid.*, p. 736; Harry Braverman, *Labour and Monopoly Capital*, Monthly Review Press, New York, 1974.
59 A. Fox and A. Flanders, 'The reform of collective bargaining', *British Journal of Industrial Relations*, 8 (2), July 1969, pp. 151–80, reprinted in A. Flanders, *Management and the Unions*, Faber and Faber, London, 1970 (page references to the book); John H. Goldthorpe, 'Social inequality and social integration in modern Britain', *Advancement of Science*, 26 (128), December 1969; and later John H. Goldthorpe, 'Inequality and the consensus', *New Society*, 10 January 1974. See also J. E. T. Eldridge, *Sociology and Industrial Life*, Nelson, London, 1971, pp. 73–138.
60 Cf. Eldridge, *Sociology and Industrial Life.*
61 Flanders, *Management and the Unions*, p. 250.
62 *Ibid.*, p. 274.
63 *Ibid.*, p. 275.
64 Each quotation from Goldthorpe, 'Inequality and the consensus'.
65 We noted, on p. 70, that the neo-Durkheimian ideas found some echoes in Labour Party policy and in the Social Contract of the Labour government. The concern with economic appetites (wage demands) was central; but inequality and integration was also discussed in the same context. The Social Contract (between government and unions in effect, though occasionally defined as a grander compact of all the people) was based on an exchange in which the labour unions were to guarantee voluntary pay restraint within government guidelines, and the government was to: (1) institute economic planning designed to overcome market anarchy; (2) make a broad based attack on social and economic inequality; and (3) draw workers into the direction and planning of industrial enterprises through schemes or participation (Gilbert, 'Neo-Durkheimian analyses', pp. 748–51). The elevation of Pay Policy to the national political agenda illustrated a flaw in the argument that a national policy could create a consensus about the justice of rewards. National debate had the opposite effect, heightening public awareness of 'differentials' and exposing to argument the moral basis of different claims. However I suspect that if Durkheim had been British in this period he would have voted Labour; but he would have been unenthusiastic about Clause Four and pro-Common Market!

66 The studies titled *The Affluent Worker* were published in three volumes: we shall refer mostly to the last, *The Affluent Worker in the Class Structure*, Cambridge University Press, Cambridge, 1971.

67 *Ibid.*, Vol. 3, p. 19.

68 Herbert Marcuse, *One Dimensional Man*, Routledge and Kegan Paul, London, 1964.

69 *Cf.* Bennet Berger, *Working Class Suburb*, University of California Press, Berkeley, 1960; Herbert Gans, *The Urban Villagers*, Free Press, Glencoe, 1962.

70 For a review of these arguments see John H. Goldthorpe 'Social stratification in industrial society', in *The Development of Industrial Societies*, *Sociological Review*, Monograph No. 8, Paul Halmos (ed.), Keele, 1964.

71 Hughes, *Men and their Work*; Peter Berger (ed.) *The Human Shape of Work*, Macmillan, New York, 1964.

72 Goldthorpe *et al.*, *The Affluent Worker*, Vol. 3, p. 164.

73 *Ibid.*, pp. 186–7.

3. *Political power, democracy and the modern state*

1 His involvement in the Dreyfus affair is given more detailed coverage in chapter 4 because of its relevance to his views on 'race'.

2 See chapter 1 and the discussion of Nisbet's thesis. We also mentioned later Marxist attacks on his sociology (see chapter 1, p. 46 and fn 74). Marxists have rejected the 'conservative' interpretation *and* the radical interpretation, locating him as a classic bourgeois reformer. I accept some of this critique, but it is over-simplified. It is insufficiently attuned to the subtlety of Durkheim's thought and confuses a plausible view of the Third Republic (with which Durkheim was unquestionably identified) with a closer appreciation of his own intentions. It also stresses the ideological components of Durkheim's thought. This is, falsely, to portray him as a kind of moral re-armer, neglecting the degree to which his view of the need for a new morality was coupled with his diagnosis of the need for social institutional change.

3 Durkheim, *Professional Ethics*.

4 S. and J. Lukes, 'Individualism and the intellectuals'; Durkheim's contribution to 'Enquête sur la guerre et le militarisme', *L'Humanite Nouvelle*, May 1899; contribution to H. Dagan, *Enquête sur l'antisemitisme*, Stock, Paris, 1899; contribution to discussion 'Sur l'internationalisme'.

5 See chapter 1.

6 Richter, in Wolff, *Emile Durkheim*.

7 See Giddens, *Studies in Social and Political Theory*.

8 Tiryakian in Bottomore and Nisbet, *A History of Sociological Analysis*.

9 *La Science sociale et l'action* a collection of articles by Durkheim from 1888 to 1914, with an introduction by J. C. Filloux, Paris, Presses Universitaires de France, Paris, 1970; see also Bernard Lacroix, *Durkheim et le politique*, Fondation National de Science et Politique, Paris 1981.

10 For a similar interpretation see Alvin Gouldner in his introduction to Durkheim's *Socialism*, pp. 20–1.

11 Durkheim, preface to the *Année Sociologique*, 2, 1897–8, in Wolff, *Emile Durkheim*, pp. 352–3.

12 Giddens, 'Durkheim's political sociology', pp. 492–3.

13 *Ibid.*, p. 493.

14 In Bottomore and Nisbet, *A History of Sociological Analysis*, p. 191.
15 In *ibid.*, pp. 227–8fn; Tiryakian is referring to *Libres Entretiens*, 13, May 1905, pp. 368–70.
16 C. W. Chamberlain and H. F. Moorhouse, 'Lower class attitudes towards the British political system', *Sociological Review*, NS, 22 (4), November 1974; E. A. Nordlinger, *The Working class Tories*, MacGibbon and Kee, London, 1967; G. Almond and S. Verba, *The Civic Culture*, Princeton University Press, New Jersey, 1963; Goldthorpe, 'Social inequality'.
17 *Professional Ethics*, p. 10.
18 *Division of Labour*, p. 28.
19 *Professional Ethics*, p. 29.
20 *Ibid.*, p. 30.
21 *Ibid.*, p. 90.
22 *Ibid.*, pp. 90–1.
23 *Ibid.*, p. 91.
24 *Ibid.*, p. 45.
25 *Ibid.*, p. 47.
26 *Ibid.*, p. 48.
27 Ralph Miliband, *The State in a Capitalist Society*, Weidenfeld and Nicolson, London, 1969.
28 *Professional Ethics*, p. 51.
29 *Ibid.*, p. 89.
30 Giddens, 'Durkheim's political sociology', p. 500.
31 Giddens, 'Durkheim's political sociology'; Giddens, *Emile Durkheim*; and Durkheim 'Deux lois de l'évolution penale', *Année Sociologique*, 4, 1899–1900, pp. 65–95.
32 Compare discussion towards the end of chapter 1.
33 *Professional Ethics*, pp. 49–50.
34 *Ibid.*, p. 92.
35 *Ibid.*, p. 94.
36 Giddens, 'Durkheim's political sociology', p. 501.
37 *Ibid.*, p. 498.
38 *Ibid.*, p. 499.
39 *Professional Ethics*, p. 96.
40 *Ibid.*, p. 97.
41 Cited in n4 of this chapter.
42 Lukes, *Emile Durkheim*, p. 344.
43 *Professional Ethics*, p. 60.
44 *Ibid.*, p. 71.
45 *Ibid.*, p. 72.
46 *Ibid.*, p. 53.
47 Published (Paris) in 1915; cf. Lukes, *Emile Durkheim*, pp. 549–50.
48 Tom Bottomore, *Political Sociology*, Hutchinson, London, 1979, p. 111.
49 Translation from Lukes, *Emile Durkheim*, p. 552.
50 *Ibid.*
51 *Professional Ethics*, p. 11.
52 *Ibid.*, p. 214.
53 *Ibid.*, p. 216.
54 *Ibid.*, p. 215. Most of Durkheim's comments on inheritance can be found in *Professional Ethics*, pp. 213–20. At p. 213 he writes 'Therefore as long as such

sharp class differences exist in society fairly effective palliatives may lessen the injustice of contracts; but, in principle, the system operates in conditions which do not allow of justice.'

55 *Ibid.*, p. 218.
56 See above in this chapter.
57 *Professional Ethics*, p. 216.
58 See M. M. Mitchell, 'Emile Durkheim and the philosophy of nationalism', *Political Science Quarterly*, 46, 1931, pp. 87–106.
59 Cf. Hannah Arendt, *The Origins of Totalitarianism*, Harcourt Brace, New York, 1951; Eric Hoffer, *The True Believer: Thoughts on the Nature of Mass Movements*, Harper and Row, New York, 1951; A. James Gregor, *Interpretations of Fascism*, General Learning Press, New Jersey, 1974.
60 See G. Kagan, 'Durkheim et Marx', *Revue de l'Histoire Economique et Sociale*, 24 (3), 1938, pp. 233–45; A. Giddens 'Durkheim as a review critic', *Sociological Review*, 18, 1970, pp. 171–96; B. Lacroix, 'Àpropos des rapports entre Durkheim et Marx: de l'analyse de texte à l'analyse sociologique', in *Études Offertes au Professeur Emerentienne de Lagrange*, Libraire générale de droit et de jurisprudence, Paris, 1978.
61 Edward A. Tiryakian, 'A problem for the sociology of knowledge: the mutual unawareness of Emile Durkheim and Max Weber', *European Journal of Sociology*, 7 (2), 1965.
62 See Lukes, *Emile Durkheim*, pp. 17–18.
63 See Gregor, *Interpretations of Fascism*, ch. 5: 'Fascism as the consequence of class struggle', and ch. 6: 'Fascism as a function of a particular stage of economic development'.
64 See Martin Jay, *The Dialectical Imagination: A History of the Frankfurt School and the Institute of Social Research 1923–50*, Heinnemann, London, 1973.
65 Marcuse, *One Dimensional Man*. The same thinking led Marcuse to look to other sources of 'counter-cultural' expression, especially among students. Hence the influence of Marcuse on the student discontents of the 1960s, particularly in France and the USA.
66 Robert Michels, *Political Parties*, Free Press, Glencoe, 1949.
67 Durkheim's review of Labriola. 'Essais sur la conception matérialiste de l'histoire'.
68 Erich Fromm, *The Fear of Freedom*, Routledge and Kegan Paul, London, 1942.
69 Fritz Papenheim, *The Alienation of Modern Man*, Monthly Review Press, New York, 1959; Marcuse, *One Dimensional Man*.
70 W. Kornhauser, *The Politics of Mass Society*, Routledge and Kegan Paul, London, 1960; Nisbet, *The Sociological Tradition*; and Robert Nisbet, *Community and Power*, Oxford University Press, New York, 1962.
71 Alexis de Tocqueville, *Democracy in America*, Knopf, New York, 1945, p. 319.
72 Matthew Arnold, *Culture and Anarchy*, Cambridge University Press, Cambridge, 1963 (first published 1869); Soren Kierkegaard, *The Present Age*, Harper Torchbooks, New York, 1961; J. Ortega Y. Gasset, *The Revolt of the Masses*, Pelican, New York, 1950.
73 Le Comte Henri de Gobineau, *Essais sur l'inegalité des races humaines*, Firmin-Didcot, Paris, 1853–5, and Belfont, Paris, 1967.
74 The two best discussions can be found in Raymond Williams, *Culture and Society*, Penguin Books, Middlesex, 1968; and Leon Bramson, *The Political Context of Sociology*, Princeton University Press, Princeton, New Jersey, 1961. See

Bramson's ch. 2: 'European theories of the mass and mass society' for discussions of the work of Hannah Arendt, Erich Fromm, Ortega Y. Gasset (see above) and Karl Mannheim, *Man and Society in an Age of Reconstruction,* Harcourt Brace, New York, 1950; and Emil Lederer, *The State of the Masses,* Norton, New York, 1940.

75 Cf. also Gregor, *Interpretations of Fascism,* ch. 4: 'Fascism as the consequence of the rise of the amorphous masses'.

76 Robert Dahl, *Who Governs? Democracy and Power in an American City,* Yale University Press, Yale, 1961. The debate has ranged over both national and local centres of power.

77 J. K. Galbraith, *The New Industrial State,* New America Library, New York, 1968, and *American Capitalism, the Concept of Countervailing Power,* Hamish Hamilton, London, 1952.

78 See John Rex, *Race, Colonialism and the City,* Routledge and Kegan Paul, London, 1973, for a discussion of the concept of pluralism in sociological theory applied to 'race relations'. Cf. M. G. Smith *The Plural Society in the British West Indies,* Sangster's Books, and University of California Press, Berkeley, 1965.

79 Kornhauser, *The Politics of Mass Society,* 1959.

80 *Ibid.,* ch. 1.

81 Fromm, *The Fear of Freedom*; Theodore Adorno, *The Authoritarian Personality,* Harper, New York, 1950; David Riesman, *The Lonely Crowd,* Doubleday Anchor, New York, 1953.

82 See Chamberlain and Moorhouse, 'Lower class attitudes'; and Goldthorpe, 'Social inequality'.

83 E. Shils and M. Young, 'The meaning of the coronation', *Sociological Review,* 1, 1953, pp. 63–81.

84 Norman Birnbaum, 'Monarchs and sociologists', *Sociological Review,* 3, 1955, pp. 5–23.

85 Daniel Bell, *The End of Ideology,* Free Press, New York, 1961; and for a discussion of 'end of ideology' and 'class homogenization' theories, see Goldthorpe *et al.,* *The Affluent Worker,* Vol. 3, in the first and last chapters.

86 Almond and Verba, *The Civic Culture*; Chamberlain and Moorhouse, 'Lower class attitudes'.

87 Ralph Miliband, *Parliamentary Socialism,* Merlin Press, London, 1961.

4. Race and society: primitive and modern

1 M. Banton, *Race Relations,* Tavistock, London, 1967; John Rex, *Race, Colonialism and the City,* Routledge and Kegan Paul, London, 1973; P. Van Den Berghe, *Race and Racism,* Wiley, New York, 1967; Robert Blauner, *Racial Oppression in America,* Harper Row, New York, 1972; N. Glazer and D. P. Moynihan, *Ethnicity,* Harvard University Press, Cambridge, Mass., 1975; G. Bowker and J. Carrier, *Race and Ethnic Relations,* Hutchinson, London, 1976; Unesco, *Sociological Theories: Race and Colonialism,* Unesco Press, Paris, 1980.

2 Kedward, R., The Dreyfus Affair, Longman, London, 1965, p. 50. I have relied mainly on two sources: Lukes, *Emile Durkheim,* pp. 330–54 and Kedward, *The Dreyfus Affair.*

3 Kedward, *The Dreyfus Affair,* p. 55.

4 *Ibid.*

5 *Ibid.,* p. 57.

6 Lukes, *Emile Durkheim*, p. 347.
7 J. Barzun, *Race: A Study in Superstition*, rev. edn, Harper Torchbooks, New York, 1965, pp. 19–20 and throughout.
8 Lukes, *Emile Durkheim*, p. 345.
9 *Ibid.* (translation of Durkheim, 'Notes sur l'anti-semitisme', in Dagan, *Enquête sur l'antisemitisme*).
10 Filloux, *La Science sociale et l'action*, p. 257: 'Il est intéressant de noter ici qu'il était engagé au nom d'exigences morales, et non pas en fonction de considérations étroitement politiques, ou encore moins en tant que Juif, ainsi que G. Davy et Henri Durkheim en ont porté témoignage.' Translation: 'It is interesting to note here that he was involved in the name of moral demands, and not for the sake of narrowly political considerations, still less as a Jew; and of this G. Davy and Henri Durkheim have provided evidence.'
11 Emile Durkheim, 'L'Individualisme et les intellectuels, *Revue Bleue*, 4th Series, 10, 1898, pp. 7–13; see also Lukes, *Emile Durkheim*, pp. 337ff.
12 Lukes, *Emile Durkheim*, pp. 338–9, comments: 'Durkheim's article is of considerable interest. It offers a conclusive refutation of a certain interpretation of him as fundamentally anti-liberal and anti-individualistic, as a right wing nationalist, a spiritual ally of Charles Maurras and forerunner of twentieth century nationalism, even fascism – an interpretation that relied on a selective misreading of certain of his writings and, in some cases, a mistaken importation into his centralised guild socialism of the connotations of fascist corporatism.'
13 Durkheim argued consistently for the extension of political liberties and for carrying justice into the social and economic spheres: 'It was vital that political liberties be put to use by working towards economic and social justice.' See Lukes, *Emile Durkheim*, pp. 343–4.
14 Translation by Lukes, *Emile Durkheim*, p. 346, from Durkheim, 'Notes sur l'anti-semitisme'.
15 Summarized by Lukes, *Emile Durkheim*, p. 346, from Durkheim, 'Notes sur l'anti-semitisme'.
16 Durkheim's contribution to discussion on 'Pacifisme et patriotisme', meeting of 30 December 1907, pp. 44–9, 51–2, 66–7. Contained in *Société Française de Philosophie Bulletin*, Paris, 8 1908, translation by Lukes, *Emile Durkheim*, p. 350.
17 *Division of Labour in Society*, p. 323.
18 *Ibid.*, p. 304.
19 *Ibid.*, p. 324.
20 *Ibid.*, p. 309.
21 This at least is the preponderant view in his work. Lukes however speaks of his equivocal attitude to the category of 'organic' (Lukes, *Emile Durkheim*, p. 17). His ambivalence about the identification of race and heredity is discussed later on in this chapter in an account of Durkheim's review of Franz Boas. In this review he seems to speak of heredity as 'the greater part of race' – greater than milieu – thus implying that race includes both in some measure. The uncertainty in his use of the term reflects the general ambiguity surrounding the biological and cultural components of the concepts race and people (*race et peuple*).
22 Durkheim, E., *The Rules of Sociological Method*, Free Press, New York, 1966, p. 108.
23 *Ibid.*
24 *Ibid.*, p. 109.

25 Durkheim, E., *Suicide*, Free Press, New York, 1966, p. 83.
26 *Ibid.*
27 *Ibid.*, p. 85.
28 *Ibid.*
29 *Ibid.*, p. 89.
30 *Ibid.*, p. 102.
31 C. Ellwood, 'The development of sociology in the United States since 1910', *Sociological Review*, Keele, 19, 1927, p. 31.
32 There were others who could be mentioned in the same kind of context such as Morselli, Lombroso and Lebon.
33 The most extraordinary instance of Durkheim being seduced by the craniologists can be found in *The Division of Labour in Society*, pp. 55ff. He is arguing that, as society becomes more complex, male and female become more differentiated. This is supported by evidence that the average difference in cranium size is becoming greater – in 'favour' of males!
34 Accounts of these men and their contemporaries can be found in Barzun, *Race: A Study in Superstition*; T. F. Gossett, *Race: The History of an Idea in America*, Schocken Books, New York, 1965; Ruth Benedict, *Race and Racism*, Routledge and Kegan Paul, London, 1942.
35 See T. Asad (ed.), *Anthropology and the Colonial Encounter*, Ithaca Press, London, 1973; and G. Leclerc, *Anthropologie et colonialisme*, Librairie Fayard, Paris, 1972.
36 I am mostly concerned with the doctrine of evolution in *social* thought and in anthropology in particular. See J. W. Burrow, *Evolution and Society: A Study in Victorian Social Theory*, Cambridge University Press, Cambridge, 1970.
37 V. C. Kiernan, *The Lords of Human Kind*, Pelican Books, Harmondsworth, 1972. See p. 242 for a discussion of the 'child races'.
38 Leclerc, *Anthropologie*, pp. 24–6: 'In all cases [in evolutionary thought] the concept of history assumes the unity of man.'
39 *Ibid.*, p. 32.
40 Gossett, *Race*, p. 152.
41 Leclerc, *Anthropologie*, p. 24.
42 For a discussion of Durkheim's evolutionism and his use of the term 'primitive' see Lukes, *Emile Durkheim*, p. 456.
43 *Professional Ethics*, p. 16: 'What is the purpose of heaping up riches if they do not serve to abate the desires of the greatest number, but, on the contrary, only rouse their impatience for gain? That would be to lose sight of the fact that economic functions are not an end in themselves but only a means to an end . . . Society has no justification if it does not bring a little peace to men – peace in their hearts and peace in their mutual intercourse.'
44 *Division of Labour*, pp. 245ff.
45 Lukes, *Emile Durkheim*, p. 456: 'He [Durkheim] took it as axiomatic that there is an identity between (cultural and structural) simplicity and evolutionary priority.'
46 Bergson recalls of Durkheim: 'When we told him that the facts were in contradiction with his theory, he would reply "the facts are wrong".' Lukes, *Emile Durkheim*, p. 52.
47 These were Van Gennep's criticisms cited in Lukes, *Emile Durkheim*, p. 525.
48 See Nisbet, *The Sociological Tradition*, pp. 85–6.
49 Emile Durkheim, *L'Éducation morale*, Alcan, Paris, 1925, pp. 136–7. 'Morality no longer consists simply in performing, even intentionally, certain given actions;

beyond this, the rule preventing such behaviour must be freely willed, that is freely accepted, and this acceptance is nothing else but an enlightened acceptance.'

50 I am only suggesting a general tendency of 'biological' as against 'culturalist' ideas. The actual historical materials (the history of ideas) do not fit at all into any classification. For example some of the biological racists envisioned very rapid change because they believed that interbreeding was fast increasing. Writers who stressed cultural and environmental forces may have expected civilizational change to take centuries. It should also be recalled that Lamarckian writers produced various versions of inheritance being affected by practices and learned traits.

51 See Leclerc, *Anthropologie*, p. 17. One could argue that the theory of change, the view of the possible manner and speed of change, was more critical for the ideological import of a social theory – more important than whether the theory was based on biological race.

52 The following references are two book reviews written by Durkheim and both appearing in *L'Année Sociologique*, 12, Paris, 1913. The first is a review of Lévy-Bruhl's *Les Fonctions mentales dans les sociétés inférieures*, pp. 33–7; the second is of Franz Boas's *The Mind of Primitive Man*, pp. 31–3.

53 Giddens, *Emile Durkheim*, pp. 246–9, contains a translation of this review; the one in the text is my own translation but it differs little from Giddens.

54 Lukes, *Emile Durkheim*, p. 440.

55 Gossett, *Race*, p. 418.

56 The force of the French is: 'One could accept that primitive mentality was something specific, was a specific thing, if . . .'. The conclusion is, since Boas does not see the conditions being met, that primitive mentality is *not* a specific thing.

57 The relevant passage reads: 'Setting aside milieu, a much more important factor concerning race is heredity, which tends to make permanent the characteristics which it transmits.'

58 All references here are to *L'Année Sociologique*, 13, Paris, 1913; note that Durkheim refers to *les noirs* and not *les Nègres*.

59 It is worth noting again that Durkheim uses both 'peuples' and 'races'. A discussion of the use of terms such as these (but excluding 'race') can be found in Durkheim's contributions to the debate on 'Sur l'internationalisme', pp. 17 and 27. At p. 27 he says: 'There is a group which we call political society. This is the group which, whilst containing secondary groups, does not itself belong to any larger group. It is the highest and most individualized form.' At p. 40: '*Le peuple* – we need this word to designate those who, in a state, do not have a part in the government.'

60 He had no great enthusiasm for workers' education since he believed that as long as the lives of workers were incompatible with cultural growth, then the effect of extra education would be minimal.

61 'Predispositions' is ambiguous in English and in French; 'inclinations' is a possible translation.

62 Leclerc, *Anthropologie*, p. 27.

63 Lévi-Strauss, *Structural Anthropology*; Claude Lévi-Strauss, 'Race and history', in Leo Kuper (ed.), *Race, Science and Society*, Unesco Press and Allen and Unwin, Paris and London, 1975.

64 Lévi-Strauss, *Structural Anthropology*, p. 230.

65 *Ibid.*, p. 230.
66 Lévi-Strauss, in Kuper, *Race, Science and Society*, pp. 96–7.
67 *Ibid.*, p. 100.
68 Glazer and Moynihan, *Beyond the Melting Pot*; T. N. Draper, *The Rediscovery of Black Nationalism*, Viking Press, New York, 1969.
69 Wallman, *Ethnicity at Work*; J. L. Watson (ed.), *Between Two Cultures*, Blackwell, Oxford, 1977.
70 A. H. Halsey, 'Race relations: the lines to think on', *New Society*, 19 March 1970. John Rex, 'The future of race relations research in Britain sociological research and the politics of racial justice', *Race*, 14 (4), April 1973, pp. 481–8. And then subsequent exchange of letters from both Halsey and Rex in *Race*, 15 (1), July 1973. See also Lee Bridges, 'Race relations research: from colonialism to neo-colonialism? Some random thoughts', *Race*, 14 (3), January 1973, pp. 331–41.
71 See Charles Stephen Fenton, 'Race, class and politics in the work of Emile Durkheim', in Unesco, *Sociological Theories: Race and Colonialism*, pp. 180–1, n128.
72 Geoffrey Dench, *Maltese in London*, Routledge and Kegan Paul, London, 1975, esp. ch. 7.

5. The sociology of education: discipline and moral autonomy

1 Published posthumously in French in 1924, translated as *Education and Sociology*, Free Press, Glencoe, 1956; published in French in 1925, translated as *Moral Education*, Free Press, Glencoe, 1961.
2 *Education and Sociology*, p. 134.
3 Of course, in referring to discipline, Durkheim meant something like personal self-discipline or self-control, rather than classroom control. But then he did also believe that authoritarian forms of control were no longer appropriate, and persons in positions of authority had to appeal to the internalised morality of their charges.
4 First appearing as an article with Marcel Mauss in *Année Sociologique*, 6, 1903, translated as *Primitive Classification*, Cohen and West, London, 1963.
5 *Education and Sociology*, pp. 76–7.
6 His notions of egoism and anomie are ambiguous here, modelled on the one hand on a conception of man as an organism driven by primitive wishes (and thus animal-like) but on the other hand – more importantly – seen as fundamentally different from animals in that men's desires are essentially socially defined, and hence in theory potentially infinite. They are therefore only capable of being *socially* restrained. Men's desires are not to be restrained because restraint is *per se* virtuous, but because restraint is necessary to individual and social health. Society is the only possible source of this restraint. Cf. Lukes, *Emile Durkheim*, p. 17.
7 *Moral Education*, p. 59. For an analysis of Durkheim's sociology and philosophy of morals, see Wallwork, *Durkheim, Morality and Milieu*.
8 *Education and Sociology*, p. 118.
9 *Ibid.*, p. 117.
10 *Ibid.*, p. 89.
11 *Moral Education*, p. 120.
12 *Ibid.*, p. 120.
13 *Education and Sociology*, p. 80.

14 *Ibid.*, pp. 80–1.
15 *Moral Education*, p. 183.
16 For an example of the 'conservative' interpretation, see R. Dale *et al.*, the Open University Course E 202, *Schooling and Society*, Unit 18, Curriculum and cultural reproduction, the Durkheimian tradition, 1977, p. 13.
17 *L'Évolution pedagogique en France*, Presses Universitaires de France, 1938, republished 1969; Emile Durkheim, *The Evolution of Educational Thought*, Routledge and Kegan Paul, London, 1977, translated by Peter Collins.
18 See chapter 1 of this book, and Clark, 'Emile Durkheim'.
19 See Martin Trow, 'The second transformation of American secondary education', in J. Karabel and A. H. Halsey (eds.), *Power and Ideology in Education*, Oxford University Press, New York, 1977.
20 Karl Mannheim, *Ideology and Utopia*, Harcourt Brace and World, New York, 1936, *Essays on the Sociology of Knowledge*, Routledge and Kegan Paul, London, 1952, *Man and Society*, Routledge and Kegan Paul, London, 1941, republished 1980, and especially Karl Mannheim and W. A. C. Stewart, *An Introduction to the Sociology of Education*, Routledge and Kegan Paul, London, 1962.
21 See Basil Bernstein, 'Sociology and the sociology of education, a brief account', in John Rex (ed.), *Approaches to Sociology*, Routledge and Kegan Paul, London, 1974.
22 See A. K. C. Ottaway, 'The educational sociology of Emile Durkheim', *British Journal of Sociology*, 3, 1955, and *Education and Society*, Routledge and Kegan Paul, London, 1953 and 1962.
23 Olive Banks, 'Sociology of education', ch. 4 in Louis Cohen (ed.), *Educational Research and Development in Britain 1970–80*, NFER-Nelson, Windsor, 1982.
24 See Dale *et al.*, Open University Course E202, Unit 18, pp. 34ff.
25 See principally, Basil Bernstein, *Class, Codes and Control*, Vol. 1, Routledge and Kegan Paul, London, 1971; Vol. 2, Routledge and Kegan Paul, London, 1973; Vol. 3, Routledge and Kegan Paul, London, 1975. The last of these contains the essay 'Open schools – open society?' which best illustrates his debt to Durkheim. In Vol. 3, at p. 17, we find Bernstein writing 'I have yet to find any social theorist whose ideas are such a source (at least to me) of understanding of what the term social entails.'
26 *Ibid.*, Vol. 3, p. 22.
27 *Ibid.*, p. 59.
28 *Ibid.*, p. 71.
29 *Ibid.*, p. 74.
30 *Ibid.*, p. 74. Cf. Brian Davies, *Social Control and Education*, Methuen, London, 1976.
31 Bernstein, *Class, Codes and Controls*, Vol. 3, p. 75.
32 *Ibid.*, p. 75.
33 Dale *et al.*, Open University Course E202, Unit 18, pp. 13, 31–20.
34 *Ibid.*, p. 32.
35 David Hargreaves, 'Durkheim, deviance and education', in L. Barton and R. Meighan (eds.), *Schools, Pupils and Deviance*, Nafferton, Driffield, 1979.
36 See Dale *et al.*, Open University Course E202, Unit 18, at p. 44. Some of the works discussed are P. Bourdieu, *Cultural Reproduction*, Sage, London, 1977, (translation of Paris, 1970), and 'Intellectual field and creative project', in M. F. D. Young (ed.), *Knowledge and Control*, Collier-Macmillan, London, 1971; Davies, *Social Control and Education*, ch. 7. Well-known neo-Marxist works include S.

Bowles and H. Gintis, *Schooling in Capitalist America, Educational Reforms and the Contradictions of Economic Life*, Basic Books, New York, 1976; P. Willis, *Learning to Labour*, Saxon House, London, 1978.

37 Hargreaves, 'Durkheim, deviance and education', p. 20.

38 *Ibid.*, p. 23.

39 *Ibid.*, p. 26.

6. Crime, law and deviance: the Durkheim legacy

1 J. Alderson: *Policing Freedom*, Macdonald and Evans, Plymouth, 1979, pp. 111–12.

2 J. Brown and G. Howes (eds.), *The Police and the Community*, Saxon House, Farnborough, 1975, p. 2. A similar comment about the elective affinity between the community policing perspective and Durkheim's was made by Keith M. Macdonald in 'A police state in Britain?', *New Society*, 8 Jan. 1976, pp. 50–1, and 'The forces of social control: "community liaison" by the police', unpublished paper delivered at the British Sociological Association Conference, 1977.

3 Review of D. W. Pope and N. L. Weiner (eds.), *Modern Policing*, Croom Helm, London, 1981 (a recent collection of essays by lecturers at the Police Staff College, Bramshill) in *New Society*, 24 September 1981, pp. 531–2.

4 In addition to the problems of the community policing approach which derive from mis-(or non-?) reading of Durkheim, it shares with him a lack of concern for the concrete institutional structures and channels which might assure the democratic accountability of state agencies.

5 Examples are: W. J. Chambliss: 'Functional and conflict theories of crime: the heritage of Emile Durkheim and Karl Marx', in W. J. Chambliss and M. Mankoff (eds.), *Whose Law, What Order?*, Wiley, New York, 1976, pp. 1–28; and L. McDonald, *The Sociology of Law and Order*, Faber, London, 1976.

6 Emile Durkheim, *The Division of Labour in Society*, Free Press, Glencoe, 1973, p. 64.

7 *Ibid.*

8 *Ibid.*, p. 65.

9 *Ibid.*, p. 66.

10 *Ibid.*, p. 65.

11 'It is not sufficient that there be rules, however, for sometimes the rules themselves are the cause of evil. This is what occurs in class-wars.' *Ibid.*, p. 374.

12 *Ibid.*, p. 68.

13 *Ibid.*

14 *Ibid.*, p. 69.

15 *Ibid.*

16 *Ibid.*, p. 111.

17 *Ibid.*, pp. 115–29.

18 Durkheim himself accepted some of the initial criticisms, as his later 'Two laws of penal evolution' shows. Originally published in *Année Sociologique* in 1899–1900, this important essay was only translated into English relatively recently by T. A. Jones and A. Scull in *Economy and Society*, 2 (3), 1973, pp. 278–308. Many earlier English critiques of Durkheim fail to take account of the reformulations of his arguments in the later work.

19 *Division of Labour*, p. 68.

20 *Ibid.*, p. 72. Later Durkheim comments that the acts defined as criminal need 'relate neither to vital interests of society nor to a minimum of justice' (p. 81).

21 *Ibid.*, p. 73.
22 *Ibid.*, p. 81.
23 *Ibid.*, p. 77.
24 *Ibid.*, p. 79.
25 *Ibid.*, p. 80.
26 *Ibid.*, pp. 108–9.
27 E. Durkheim: *The Rules of Sociological Method*, Free Press, New York, pb. edn, 1964 (of 1938 translation), p. 69.
28 *Ibid.*, pp. 68–9.
29 *Ibid.*, p. 71.
30 *Ibid.*, p. 72.
31 A difficulty in this position is that the distinction between progressive and ordinary crime cannot readily be made without moral judgement as opposed to the objective science which Durkheim advocates.
32 Durkheim's less well-known analysis of homicide in *Professional Ethics* also relates levels of murder to states of the social order, in this case arguing that a strong collectivist orientation is positively related to the murder rate, which is higher in times of war and social crisis, and in Catholic rather than Protestant communities. Homicide is regarded as the supreme offence in both primitive and modern societies, however, because while in the former it is regarded as an attack on the social order, in the latter it is an assault on the 'individual', the highest value of advanced moral codes. The strong individualist ethic of modern societies is associated, according to Durkheim, with a decline in the frequency of homicide.
33 Durkheim: 'Two laws of penal evolution', trans. by Jones and Scull, in *Economy and Society*, p. 285.
34 *Ibid.*, p. 294.
35 *Ibid.*, pp. 289–300. For example, he cites a study of the effect that the Assyrians spurned strangulation and beheading as too mild, and threw criminals to ferocious animals or into furnaces, or put their eyes out.
36 *Ibid.*, pp. 292–3.
37 *Ibid.*, p. 300.
38 *Ibid.*, p. 303.
39 *Ibid.*, p. 303.
40 *Ibid.*, p. 307.
41 For a recent overview see K. Plummer: 'Misunderstanding labelling perspectives', in D. Downes and P. Rock (eds.), *Deviant Interpretations*, Martin Robertson, Oxford, 1979; Jeffrey Reiman, in a brilliantly provocative study of the American criminal justice system, integrates the Durkheim–Erikson account of the inevitability of deviance with a Marxist analysis of its functionality, specifically for the dominant class, *The Rich Get Rich and the Poor Get Prison*, Wiley, New York, 1979, pp. 35–8.
42 Kai T. Erikson, *Wayward Puritans: A Study in the Sociology of Deviance*, Wiley, New York, 1966; 'Notes on the sociology of deviance', *Social Problems*, 9, 1962, pp. 307–14, reprinted for example in H. S. Becker (ed.), *The Other Side*, Free Press, Glencoe, 1964; and E. Ribington and M. S. Weinberg (eds.), *Deviance: The Interactionist Perspective*, 4th edn, Macmillan, New York, 1981.
43 Erikson, *Wayward Puritans*, p. 5.
44 *Ibid.*, p. 181.
45 Merton, 'Social structure and anomie', pp. 131–60.
46 *Ibid.*, p. 132.

47 *Ibid.*, p. 136.
48 *Ibid.*, p. 140.
49 *Ibid.*, pp. 150–1.
50 *Ibid.*, p. 153.
51 *Ibid.*, p. 155.
52 Merton, 'Social problems and sociological theory', in R. K. Merton and R. Nisbet (eds.), *Contemporary Social Problems*, Harcourt Brace and World, New York, 1966, pp. 822–3.
53 Merton, 'Social structure and anomie', pp. 141–4.
54 *Ibid.*, p. 144.
55 Merton, 'Continuities in the theory of social structure and anomie', in *Social Theory and Social Structure*, pp. 161–94.
56 Merton, 'Social structure and anomie', p. 160.
57 For a more extensive review and critique than offered here see I. Taylor, P. Walton and J. Young, *The New Criminology*, Routledge and Kegan Paul, London, 1973, pp. 133–8.
58 R. Cloward and L. Ohlin, *Delinquency and Opportunity: A Theory of Delinquent Gangs*, Free Press, Glencoe, 1960.
59 A. K. Cohen, *Delinquent Boys: The Culture of the Gang*, Free Press, Glencoe, 1955.
60 Merton, 'Continuities in the theory of social structure and anomie', pp. 177–9.
61 A. K. Cohen, 'The sociology of the deviant act: anomie theory and beyond', *American Sociological Review*, 30 (1), 1965, pp. 5–14.
62 H. Hyman, 'The value systems of different classes', in R. Bendix and S. M. Lispet (eds.), *Class, Status and Power*, Free Press, Glencoe, 1953, pp. 426–42.
63 Merton, 'Continuities in the theory of social structure and anomie', pp. 170–6.
64 Taylor *et al.*, *The New Criminology*, pp. 106–7.
65 *Ibid.*, p. 108.
66 L. Taylor, *Deviance and Society*, Nelson, London, 1973, p. 148.
67 Horton, 'The dehumanisation of anomie and alienation'.
68 *Ibid.*, pp. 294–5.
69 *Division of Labour*, p. 377.
70 M. D. Krohn, 'A Durkheimian analysis of international crime rates', *Social Forces*, 57, 1978–9, pp. 654–70. Earlier examples of studies with a roughly similar methodological approach, and the same strengths and weaknesses, are: J. P. Gibbs and W. T. Martin, *Status Integration and Suicide*, University of Oregon Press, Eugene, 1964; J. D. Miley and M. Micklin, 'Structural change and the Durkheimian legacy: a macrosocial analysis of suicide rates', *American Journal of Sociology*, 78, November 1972, pp. 657–73; S. D. Webb, 'Crime and the division of labour: testing a Durkheimian model', *American Journal of Sociology*, 78, November 1972, pp. 643–56.
71 Krohn, 'A Durkheimian analysis', p. 660.
72 E. Faris, 'Emile Durkheim on the division of labour in society', *American Journal of Sociology*, 40, 1934, pp. 376–7.
73 J. A. Barnes, 'Durkheim's *Division of Labour in Society*', *Man*, NS, 1, 1966, pp. 158–75.
74 R. D. Schwartz and J. C. Miller, 'Legal evolution and societal complexity', *American Journal of Sociology*, 20, 1964, pp. 159–69.
75 L. C. Freeman and R. F. Winch, 'Societal complexity: an empirical test of a typology of societies', *American Journal of Sociology*, 62, 1957, pp. 461–6.
76 L. S. Sheleff, 'From restitutive law to repressive law: Durkheim's *The Division of Labour in Society* revisited', *Archives Européennes de Sociologie*, 16, 1975, p. 45.

77 T. A. Jones, 'Durkheim, deviance and development: opportunities lost and regained', *Social Forces*, 59 (4), June 1981, p. 1017.
78 *Ibid.*, p. 1020.
79 M. Clarke, 'Durkheim's sociology of law', *British Journal of Law and Society*, 3 (2), Winter 1976, pp. 246–55.
80 R. D. Schwartz, 'Social factors in the development of legal control: a case study of two Israeli settlements', *Yale Law Journal*, 63, 1954, p. 471.
81 H. Wimberley, 'Legal evolution: one further step', *American Journal of Sociology*, 79 (1), July 1973, pp. 78–83.
82 U. Baxi, 'Durkheim and legal evolution', *Law and Society Review*, 8, 1974, pp. 645–51. Schwartz's reply to this conceptual critique was simply to substitute a concept of 'organised repressive sanctions' for the more specific notion of 'police', and re-analyse the data to show that a developed division of labour remained a precondition for this stage of legal evolution: 'Legal evolution and the Durkheim hypothesis: a reply to Professor Baxi', *Law and Society Review*, 8, 1974, pp. 653–68.
83 R. B. M. Cotterrell, 'Durkheim on legal development and social solidarity', *British Journal of Law and Society*, 4 (2), Winter 1977, pp. 241–52.
84 D. Chandler, *Capital Punishment in Canada*, Carleton Library, Carleton, 1976, p. 181.
85 Nisbet, *Emile Durkheim*, p. 30; Wallwork: *Durkheim: Morality and Milieu*, p. 113.
86 Jones, 'Durkheim, deviance and development', p. 1014.
87 Sheleff, 'From restitutive law to repressive law', pp. 16–30.
88 *Ibid.*, p. 22.
89 *Ibid.*, pp. 30–45.
90 S. Spitzer, 'Punishment and social organisation: a study of Durkheim's theory of penal evolution', *Law and Society Review*, 9 (4), Summer 1975, pp. 613–37.
91 *Ibid.*, p. 631.
92 *Ibid.*, p. 633.
93 Cotterrell, 'Durkheim on legal development and social solidarity'; G. Turkel, 'Testing Durkheim: some theoretical considerations', *Law and Society Review*, 13, Spring 1979, pp. 721–38. Turkel's main concern is the epistemological argument that the whole enterprise of empirically testing Durkheim's legal theories is misplaced, for theoretical propositions cannot be tested in isolation from the whole theory within which they are embedded. It seems to me that some of Durkheim's concrete propositions about legal evolution have been adequately falsified in his own terms, as Durkheim himself tacitly conceded. But this certainly does not amount to a discrediting of his overall concerns or theoretical project.
94 *Division of Labour*, p. 387.
95 A recent book by Martin Wright, former Director of the Howard League for Penal Reform argues that making amends to the victim rather than punishing or rehabilitating the offender *per se* should be the goal of criminal justice. He documents the (admittedly rather fragile) growth of such ideas with the rise to fashionability of 'victimology' and positive forms of sentencing such as community service. M. Wright, *Making Good: Prisons, Punishment and Beyond*, Burnett Books, London, 1982.

7. *Durkheim and the study of religion*

1 *Les Formes élémentaires de la vie réligieuse*, Alcan, Paris, 1912, tr. J. W. Swain, *The Elementary Forms of the Religious Life*, Geo. Allen and Unwin, London, 1915.

This was the only one of Durkheim's monographs to be translated into English in his life-time. It is a deplorable translation but since it is still the standard English-language edition it will be used throughout this chapter. The full title will be abridged to *Elementary Forms*.

The best source in English for Durkheim's writings on religion is W. S. F. Pickering, *Durkheim on Religion: A Selection of Readings with Bibliographies*, Routledge and Kegan Paul, London, 1975.

Relevant general studies include E. E. Evans-Pritchard, *Theories of Primitive Religion*, Clarendon Press, Oxford, 1965, ch. 3; D. La Capra, *Emile Durkheim, Sociologist and Philosopher*, Cornell University Press, Ithaca and London, 1972, ch. 6; S. Lukes, *Emile Durkheim, His Life and Work*, Allen Lane, London, 1973, chs. 11 and 23; R. Towler, *Homo Religiosus*, Constable, London, 1974, ch. 4. A fairly old but still interesting and provocative discussion is in Talcott Parsons, *The Structure of Social Action*, McGraw-Hill, New York, 1937, esp. ch. 11. Parsons presents a revised view in 'Durkheim on religion revisited', in C. Y. Glock and P. E. Hammond (eds.), *Beyond the Classics: Essays in the Scientific Study of Religion*, Harper and Row, New York, 1973, pp. 156–80. An earlier account of Durkheim's influence, with very little discussion of substantive issues, is P. Honigsheim, 'The influence of Durkheim and his school on the study of religion', in Wolff, *Emile Durkheim*, pp. 233–46.

In addition, any standard textbook discussion of general sociology or of the sociology of religion is more or less bound to include some consideration of Durkheim's contribution to this field. Towler's *Homo Religiosus* has already been mentioned. Other especially useful references of this kind are J. Bowker, *The Sense of God*, Clarendon Press, Oxford, 1973; A. Giddens, *Capitalism and Modern Social Theory*, Cambridge University Press, Cambridge, 1971, ch. 8; M. Harris, *The Rise of Anthropological Theory*, Routledge and Kegan Paul, London, 1968; Robert Nisbet, *The Sociological Tradition*, Heinemann, London, 1967; B. Wilson, *Religion in Sociological Perspective*, Oxford University Press, Oxford, 1982.

2 *Suicide* of course contains a good deal of discussion of religion – Catholic, Protestant, Anglican and Jewish – but little of it is relevant to the concerns of this chapter.

3 Tr. Pickering, *Durkheim on Religion*, pp. 74–99.

4 The footnotes in question are p. 47 n1 and pp. 208–9 n6.

5 'Essai sur la nature et la fonction du sacrifice', *Année Sociologique*, 2, 1898, tr. W. D. Halls, *Sacrifice: Its Nature and Function*, Cohen and West, London, 1964.

6 For an interesting discussion see G. W. Stocking, 'Matthew Arnold, E. B. Tylor and the uses of invention', *American Anthropologist*, 65, 1963, pp. 783–99. See also Evans-Pritchard, *Theories of Primitive Religion*, and *A History of Anthropological Thought*, Faber, London, 1981, ch. 10.

7 *Année Sociologique*, 12, pp. 33–7.

8 Tr. *How Natives Think*, Geo. Allen and Unwin, London, 1926. Durkheim's review is published in translation in Pickering, *Durkheim on Religion*, pp. 169–73, and in Giddens, *Emile Durkheim*, pp. 246–9. See also chapter 4 of this book on 'primitive mentality'.

9 The definitive dissolution of 'totemism' as a unitary phenomenon is C. Lévi-Strauss, *Le Totémisme aujourd'hui*, Presses Universitaires de France, Paris, 1962, tr. *Totemism*, Merlin Press, London, 1962, repr. Penguin, Harmondsworth, 1969. The Australian research in question was principally W. Baldwin Spencer and F. J. Gillen, *The Native Tribes of Central Australia*, Macmillan, London, 1899, and *The Northern Tribes of Central Australia*, Macmillan, London, 1904.

10 Thus *Suicide* was really only marginally concerned with the title topic, much more with the nature of society, social integration, social regulation, egoism, anomie, etc.

11 An important precursor was the essay written jointly with M. Mauss, 'De Quelques formes primitives de classification' *Année Sociologique*, 6 (1901–2, pub. 1903), tr. R. Needham, *Primitive Classification*, Cohen and West, London, 1963. Needham's introduction to this edition is important.

12 The boundary is hard to draw, as readers of Pickering, *Durkheim on Religion*, will observe.

13 Lukes, *Emile Durkheim*, pp. 31ff, has well described Durkheim's method of arriving at what he takes to be the correct approach by eliminating the incorrect ones. See also n20 below.

14 R. Needham, in *Belief, Language and Experience*, Blackwell, Oxford, 1972, has shown how the notion of belief itself is not a universal category. See also M. Ruel, 'Christians as believers' in J. Davis (ed.), *Religious Organization and Religious Experience*, Academic Press, London, 1982 (ASA Monographs No. 21). For an excellent discussion of the relation between beliefs and practices, see R. A. Rappaport, *Ecology, Meaning and Religion*, Atlantic Press, Richmond, Calif., 1979, esp. pp. 173–243.

15 See esp. A. R. Radcliffe-Brown, *Structure and Function in Primitive Society*, Cohen and West, London, 1952. Radcliffe-Brown's work is discussed in A. Kuper, *Anthropologists and Anthropology: The British School 1922–72*, Penguin, Harmondsworth, 1973, and with a different emphasis in Ian Langham, *The Building of British Social Anthropology*, Reidel, Dordrecht, 1982. (This last is authoritatively reviewed by R. Needham, *Times Literary Supplement*, 12 February 1982.)

16 Obviously this is not to suggest that Durkheim introduced the concept of the sacred into the study of religion! However, it is with *Elementary Forms* that it enters, laden with theory, into the day-to-day vocabulary of anthropological and sociological discussion. For further discussion see pp. 26–9 of this volume.

17 Durkheim elaborated his ideas and clarified his meaning in a series of lectures on pragmatism given at the Sorbonne in 1913–14, published posthumously as *Pragmatisme et Sociologie*, Vrin, Paris, 1955 (tr. as Emile Durkheim, *Pragmatism and Sociology*, ed. J. B. Allcock, tr. by J. C. Whitehouse, Cambridge University Press, Cambridge, 1983). See Giddens, *Emile Durkheim*, ch. 13, and Lukes, *Emile Durkheim*, ch. 24. William James, the philosopher to whom these lectures largely refer, is mentioned in *Elementary Forms* in an epistemological context, p. 417 n1 and n2. See also Pickering, *Durkheim on Religion*, p. 342.

18 See Max Müller, *Oxford Essays*, London, 1856, *Natural Religion*, London, 1889, and other works cited by Durkheim in *Elementary Forms*, p. 72 n7. The reference to the 'dark shadow' cast by language on thought is from 'The philosophy of mythology', appended to *Introduction to the Science of Religion*, London, 1873, pp. 353–61.

19 This has been described as the 'if-I-were-a-horse' school of anthropology: Evans-Pritchard, *Theories of Primitive Religion*, p. 24.

20 See n10 above. Here the procedure is to eliminate the psycho-biological and the cosmic, the residue being without discussion equated with the social.

21 Lévy-Bruhl gradually modified his position over the decade until in his posthumous *The Notebooks on Primitive Mentality*, tr. P. Rivière, Blackwell, Oxford, 1975 (*Les Carnets de Lévy-Bruhl*, Paris, 1949), little or nothing of the original polarity remains. The earlier corpus however represents a defensible position and justly or unjustly remains associated with the name of Lévy-Bruhl.

Evans-Pritchard used the earlier Lévy-Bruhl as a sparring partner in *Nuer Religion*, Clarendon Press, Oxford, 1956. The general thesis has been reformulated by C. R. Hallpike, *The Foundations of Primitive Thought*, Clarendon Press, Oxford, 1979, the most significant modern contribution to the 'primitive mentality' debate. See also this volume pp. 129–35.

22　See n8 above.

23　Paul Bohannan's useful paraphrase. See his article in Wolff, *Emile Durkheim*.

24　See R. Horton, 'Lévy-Bruhl, Durkheim and the scientific revolution', in R. Horton and R. Finnegan (eds.) *Modes of Thought*, Faber, London, 1973, esp. pp. 261ff.

25　By sociologism, sociologistic etc. is meant the unwarranted extension of sociological method and reductive analysis into inappropriate fields; it is a kind of 'sociological imperialism'.

26　'primitivement'.

27　A short study, which has the particular advantage of being written by a scientist, is P. B. Medawar, *Induction and Intuition in Scientific Thought*, Methuen, London, 1969.

28　For a trenchant critique of Durkheim's sociologistic epistemology see R. Needham's introduction to his translation of Durkheim and Mauss, 'De quelques formes primitives de la classification'. See nn44 and 48 below.

29　See *Elementary Forms*, p. 233.

30　Lévi-Strauss, *Le Totémisme aujourd'hui*, p. 128 (cf. Penguin edn, p. 162).

31　Historical and contingent factors are also invoked.

32　See the editors' introduction to R. F. Gray and P. H. Gulliver (eds.), *The Family Estate in Africa*, Routledge and Kegan Paul, London, 1964, pp. 1–33, where the Arusha (who have the ancestor cult) are contrasted with the Sonjo (who do not). Both societies hold the jural rights of the father as central to their political value system; ecological and demographic factors, however, make the maintenance of these rights precarious among the Arusha whereas they confirm them for the Sonjo.

33　See M. E. Spiro 'Religion: problems of definition and explanation', in M. P. Banton (ed.) *Anthropological Approaches to the Study of Religion*, Tavistock, London, 1966 (Association of Social Anthropologists Monograph No. 3); A. L. Stinchcombe, *Constructing Social Theories*, Harcourt Brace, New York, 1968, p. 80; R. Robertson, *The Sociological Interpretation of Religion*, Blackwell, Oxford, 1970.

34　It is discussed in connection with Swanson in Ian Hamnett, 'Sociology of religion and sociology of error', *Religion*, 3, 1973, pp. 1–12.

35　Rappaport, *Ecology, Meaning and Religion*.

36　J. Austin, *How to do Things with Words*, Clarendon Press, Oxford, 1962.

37　Durkheim has been ironically accused of psychologism in his account of the genesis of religious sentiment in crowds: Lévi-Strauss, *Totemism*, pp. 141–2; and Evans-Pritchard, *A History of Anthropological Thought*, pp. 166–7. Durkheim may have read and been impressed by Gustave Le Bon's *Psychologie des Foules*, Paris, 1895; but see Lukes, *Emile Durkheim*, pp. 462f, and fn54; and in any case his reference to crowd psychology is no ground for making the charge. The point has been well discussed in a lengthy review of Evans-Pritchard, *A History of Anthropological Thought*, by R. H. Barnes in *Man*, NS, 17, 1982, pp. 364ff.

38　See D. Martin, 'Towards eliminating the concept of secularization', in *The Religious and the Secular*, Routledge and Kegan Paul, London, 1969.

39 Guy Swanson, *The Birth of the Gods*, University of Michigan Press, Ann Arbor, 1960.
40 The term can in many contexts be assimilated to the 'sacred', though it lacks much of the sense of 'set apart and forbidden'.
41 Not all 'primitive' societies are religious. The point has been forcefully argued by Mary Douglas, *Natural Symbols*, 2nd edn, Penguin, Harmondsworth, 1973, and wittily confirmed by P. Worsley, *The Trumpet Shall Sound*, 2nd edn, Paladin, London, 1970, pp. 300ff. See also note 62 below and text.
42 Cf. J. Goody, 'A comparative approach to incest and adultery', *British Journal of Sociology*, 7, 1956; reprinted in *Comparative Studies in Kinship*, Routledge and Kegan Paul, London, 1969. Goody's analysis depends upon the variations in social rules regarding incest, etc. So long as it was regarded as a universal single phenomenon it seemed to remain within the province of psychology or even biology.
43 Not of course in any crudely empiricist sense.
44 See *Elementary Forms*, Conclusions, chs. 3–4, and Durkheim and Mauss, *Primitive Classification* (see n28 above and n48 below).
45 Swanson distinguishes between the 'primordial conditions' and the 'constitutional arrangements' in the underlying structure of groups. The first correspond to *mana*, and consist of a vast, uncharted and unorganised body of dispositions and potentialities in the participants in a group. These hidden and largely unknown primordial links correspond to the idea that the world is the expression of a 'concretion of latent possibilities'. By contrast, constitutional arrangements are areas of at least partly organized influence, representing the crystallization of purposes springing from the primordial flux. These structures are conceptualized as 'spirits'. It is important to bear in mind that the groups in question, and their 'constitutional arrangements', exist at many levels of magnitude, from (e.g.) a marriage relationship right up to a whole political regime. The methodological hazards in this are noted in the text below.
46 The analogy with the *langue/parole* relationship (F. de Saussure, *Cours de linguistique générale*, Payot, Paris, 1915, tr. W. Baskin, *Course in General Linguistics*, Philosophical Library, New York, 1959) is helpful here, as in much other Durkheimian sociology. The connection is not accidental: see E. Ardener's introduction to his edited volume *Social Anthropology and Language*, Tavistock, London, 1971 (Association of Social Anthropologists Monograph No. 10), pp. xxxivf.
47 In most societies, for instance, the family is 'sovereign' in this sense, whereas the school is not.
48 It should be remembered that Durkheim was not arguing for the vacuous thesis that knowledge arises from the interactions that an individual has with his cultural and natural environment but for the 'strong' if highly vulnerable thesis that social *structure* determines *categories*. See nn28 and 44 above.
49 See Guy Swanson, *Religion and Regime*, University of Michigan Press, Ann Arbor, 1967, where he presents a carefully argued 'retrodictive' account of Reformation changes and continuities in terms of the pre-existing political structures of the states and nations of Europe.
50 See n55 below and text.
51 A comparison can be made with a man standing over a pit holding the two ends of what may or may not be a single chain in each hand, the rest of the chain disappearing into the unseen depths. Durkheim *asserts* that the two ends belong

to the same chain; Swanson tries to cast a light rather further down into the gloom so that we can see the converging curves of the chain and thus have better grounds for accepting that they are part of a single piece.

52 See E. Durkheim, *Rules of Sociological Method*, Collier-Macmillan, London, 1964, p. 8 (tr. of *Règles de la Méthode Sociologique*, Alcan, Paris, 1895).

53 See Burrow, *Evolution and Society*, pp. 7–9, and Hamnett, 'Sociology of religion'. For a robust defence of such an approach from a Marxist standpoint, see S. Feuchtwang, 'Investigating religion', in M. Bloch (ed.), *Marxist Analyses and Social Anthropology*, Malaby, London, 1975.

54 The position is close to that implied in Gray and Gulliver, *The Family Estate in Africa*.

55 The deficiencies can be briefly specified as follows: (a) uncertain basis for the sample of fifty societies; (b) unsatisfactory method of retrieving data from ethnographic records; (c) heterogeneity of those records; (d) imprecision and arbitrariness of operational criteria for placing societies into political categories and (e) into religious categories; (f) failure to confront the theoretical problem raised by the existence of 'exceptions'.

56 Her principal works include *The Lele of the Kasai*, Oxford University Press, London, 1963; *Purity and Danger*, Routledge and Kegan Paul, London, 1966; *Natural Symbols*, 2nd edn, Penguin, Harmondsworth, 1973; *Implicit Meanings*, Routledge and Kegan Paul, London, 1975. See also *Cultural Bias*, Royal Anthropological Institute, London, 1978 (Occasional Paper No. 34), reprinted in *In the Active Voice*, Routledge and Kegan Paul, London, 1982.

57 Natural objects are, of course, on this view as on any other, *used as* symbols, but their meaning is not determined by their 'natural' properties. Moreover, symbols – like the elements of a language – derive their meaning and their capacity to convey 'information' from their position in an ordered system of similarities and oppositions ('distinctive features') and not from what they look or sound like, considered in isolation.

58 One of the earliest as well as one of the most penetrating discussions of *Natural Symbols*, especially from the point of view of religion, is F. H. Pyle, 'The two bodies: social structure and natural symbolism', *Religion*, 1, 1971, pp. 72–7.

59 A second and equally important strand in Mary Douglas's thinking derives from the well-known concepts of restricted and elaborated codes as developed in the work of Basil Bernstein (see esp. his *Class, Codes and Control*, Vol. 1. *Theoretical Studies Towards a Sociology of Language*). It would be impossible to outline Bernstein's work here, and in any case it has much less relevance to the theme of this chapter than the grid/group analysis.

A brief but important comment on the bearing of Mary Douglas's work on liturgical studies has been contributed by Christopher Walsh to K. W. Stevenson (ed.) *Symbolism and the Liturgy I*, Grove Books, Bramcote, 1980 (Grove Liturgical Study No. 23).

60 This is about the nearest either she or her master usually gets to a sociology of conversion, for which, indeed, little in the mainstream literature of the social sciences makes much provision. The phenomenon is not, of course, easily accommodated within the kind of structural determinism typical of the Durkheim school, and where it does appear it is usually (as here) to be found at the fraying edges of the social fabric rather than as part of the pattern. In subsequent essays, Douglas has gone a considerable way towards recognizing and indeed emphasizing the positive role of the actor: *In the Active Voice* contains essays on this theme.

61 Colin Turnbull, *The Forest People*, Jonathan Cape, London, 1961, p. 80.
62 See n41 above.
63 F. Barth, *Nomads of South Persia*, George Allen and Unwin, London, 1964.
64 The reference to 'Bog Irish' should not be misunderstood. They are contrasted, in a similarly deceptive way, with an anonymous group known as 'Londoners', of whom she writes that 'as a Londoner gets drawn more and more into the vortex of industrial society, his religious ideas seem to approximate more and more to those of the pygmy. He believes in spontaneity, friendship, freedom and goodness of heart; he rejects formality, magic, doctrinal logic-chopping and condemnation of his fellow human-beings' (*Natural Symbols*, p. 57). In spite of this – and although she was living in Hampstead at the time – Mary Douglas, who is a Roman Catholic, classified herself as 'Bog Irish' rather than as a 'Londoner'.
65 Douglas makes no bones about equating Catholic sacramentalism with magic, so the reach of this passage is very extensive.
66 Again, see *In the Active Voice*. The quandary is familiar in the 'sociology of knowledge' generally: too often, an implausible determinism is avoided only at the cost of platitude, and vice versa.
67 See above, n28.
68 The discussion has been taken much further in two major articles: J. Soler, 'Sémiotique de la nourriture dans la Bible', in *Annales* 1973, tr. in R. Foster and O. Ranum (eds.) *Food and Drink in History* (Vol. 5 in Selections from *Annales*), Johns Hopkins, Baltimore, 1979, and also in *New York Review of Books*, 14 June 1979; and R. Alter, 'A new theory of Kashrut', *Commentary*, 68 (2), August 1979, pp. 46–52.
69 Lévi-Strauss was born in 1908 and is currently Professor of Social Anthropology at the Collège de France. His principal works are as follows (English editions only are given, with the date of original publication following that of the translation): *The Elementary Structures of Kinship*, Eyre and Spottiswoode, London, 1969 (1949 and 1967); *Totemism*, Merlin Press, London, 1962 (1962); *The Savage Mind*, Weidenfeld and Nicholson, London, 1966 (1962); *Structural Anthropology*, Vol. 1, Basic Books, New York 1963 (1958); *Structural Anthropology*, Vol. 2, Allen Lane, London, 1977 (1973); *Introduction to a Science of Mythology*, Jonathan Cape, London, Vol. 1, *The Raw and the Cooked*, 1970 (1964); Vol. 2, *From Honey to Ashes*, 1973 (1966); Vol. 3, *The Origin of Table Manners* 1978 (1968); Vol. 4, *The Naked Man* 1980 (1971); *Tristes tropiques*, Jonathan Cape, London, 1973 (1955). (The last named was also published in another translation, omitting four chapters, as *A World on the Wane*, Hutchinson, London, 1961.)
70 Of the very considerable literature on Lévi-Strauss and his school only a tiny selection is given, the choice being governed by what is most likely to help readers of this book: C. R. Badcock, *Lévi-Strauss and Sociological Theory*, Hutchinson, London, 1975; Harris, *The Rise of Anthropological Theory*; E. N. and T. Hayes (eds.), *Claude Lévi-Strauss: The Anthropologist as Hero*, MIT Press, Cambridge, Mass., 1970; E. R. Leach, *Lévi-Strauss*, Fontana, London, 1970; E. R. Leach, 'Structuralism in social anthropology', in D. Robey (ed.) *Structuralism: An Introduction*, Clarendon Press, Oxford, 1973; E. R. Leach, (ed.) *The Structural Study of Myth and Totemism* (ASA Monograph No. 5), Tavistock Press, London, 1967; R. Needham, Introduction, to Lévi-Strauss, *The Elementary Structures of Kinship*; D. Sperber, 'Claude Lévi-Strauss', in J. Sturrock (ed.), *Structuralism and Since*, Oxford University Press, London, 1979.

71 The two categories are not, however, symmetrical. The 'sacred' is specified (marked), the 'profane' is residual (unmarked).

72 Once constituted, of course, a symbol can generate other symbols which are not arbitrary (in technical language, they are 'motivated') in respect of the system. Thus 'four' and 'ten' are arbitrary in Saussure's sense, but 'fourteen' as an expression of their sum is motivated.

73 Saussure, *Course in General Linguistics*.

74 An enormous literature exists on structural linguistics and Lévi-Strauss. Lévi-Strauss's own discussion can be found principally in *Structural Anthropology*, Vol. 1, chs. 2–5, and *Structural Anthropology*, Vol. 2, ch. 1. All the works listed in n70 contain references to linguistics. Other secondary discussions include Ardener, *Social Anthropology and Language* (the editor's long introduction is masterly); J. Culler, *Saussure*, Fontana, London, 1976; J. Culler, 'The linguistic basis of structuralism', in Robey, *Structuralism: An Introduction*, ch. 2; E. R. Leach, 'Animal categories and verbal abuse', in E. H. Lenneberg (ed.), *New Directions in the Study of Language*, MIT Press, Cambridge, Mass., 1966; E. R. Leach 'Language and anthropology', in N. Minnis (ed.), *Linguistics at Large*, Paladin, St Albans, 1973.

75 See p. 211.

76 *L'esprit humain*.

77 Chapter 4 of *Totemism* has the English title, 'Towards Understanding'. This obscures the ambivalence of the French 'Vers l'intellect', which means both that and also 'Towards the Intellect'.

78 Lévi-Strauss, *The Savage Mind*. This corresponds to p. 152 of *La Pensée sauvage*, Plon, Paris, 1962.

79 The English presentation of this table contains so many errors as to make total nonsense of the argument. It has been corrected in the text here.

80 *Mythologiques*, Vol. 1, *Le Cru et le cuit*, Plon, Paris, 1964, p. 20: 'Les mythes se pensent dans les hommes, et à leur insu.' J. and D. Weightman's translation (*The Raw and the Cooked*, p. 12) seems to rob this striking and famous phrase of much of its impact ('Myths operate in men's minds without their being aware of the fact').

81 'The centre of the first schemes of nature is not the individual; it is society', Durkheim and Mauss, *Primitive Classification*, pp. 86–7.

82 Pickering, *Durkheim on Religion*, and Towler, *Homo Religiosus*, are works by Anglicans who are to a large extent under Durkheim's spell while remaining ultimately disengaged from him.

83 Something of this is to be found (surprisingly) in Alasdair MacIntyre, *Secularisation and Moral Change*, Oxford University Press, London, 1967, esp. pp. 29ff.

84 Erastianism is the doctrine that subordinates ecclesiastical to secular power.

85 His life's work is his huge *Church Dogmatics*, T. and T. Clark, Edinburgh, 1955–62, but the most pertinent essay in the present context is his introduction to L. Feuerbach, *The Essence of Christianity* (1841), Harper and Row, New York, 1957, pp. x–xxxii.

86 *The Christian Faith and the Marxist Criticism of Religion*, St Andrews Press, Edinburgh, 1970.

87 See his *The Precarious Vision*, Doubleday, Garden City, New York, 1961. He has explicitly repudiated the neo-orthodox position since then: *A Rumour of Angels*, Allen Lane, London, 1969, p. 123, n23.

88 See for example M. Weber, *Sociology of Religion*, Methuen, London, 1965, pp. 46ff.
89 Esp. *Nuer Religion*, and see Lévi-Strauss's discussion of this work in *Totemism*, ch. 4.
90 His principal works include *The Forest of Symbols*, Cornell University Press, Ithaca, 1967; *The Drums of Affliction*, Oxford University Press, London, 1968; *The Ritual Process*, Routledge and Kegan Paul, London, 1969; *Dramas, Fields, Metaphors*, Cornell University Press, Ithaca, 1974 (with Edith Turner); *Image and Pilgrimage in Christian Culture*, Columbia University Press, New York, 1978.
   There is a good discussion of Turner from a specifically 'religious' point of view in Stevenson, *Symbolism and the Liturgy*, pp. 20ff (n59 above).

8. *Assessing Durkheim: classical sociology and modern society*

1 Talcott Parsons, *The Structure of Social Action*, McGraw-Hill, New York, 1937.
2 Talcott Parsons, *The Social System*, Free Press, Glencoe, Illinois, 1955.
3 Alvin W. Gouldner, *The Coming Crisis of Western Sociology*, Heinemann, London, 1971; A. Giddens, *Capitalism and Modern Social Theory*, Cambridge University Press, Cambridge, 1971; Daniel Bell, *The Coming of Post-Industrial Society*, Heinemann, London, 1974.
4 Public lecture, March 1983 at Bristol University; see also his *Central Problems in Social Theory*, Macmillan, London, 1979, and *A Contemporary Critique of Historical Materialism*, Macmillan, London, 1981.
5 Orlando Patterson, *The Sociology of Slavery*, Associated University Presses, London, 1969 and 1975.
6 Lévi-Strauss, 'Race and History', at p. 100.
7 T. H. Marshall, *Sociology at the Crossroads*, Heinemann, London, 1963, ch. 4.
8 Melford Spiro, *The Kibbutz: Venture in Utopia*, Schocken Books, New York, 1963.

Bibliography

Adorno, Theodore (1950), *The Authoritarian Personality*, Harper, New York.
Alderson, J. (1979), *Policing Freedom*, Macdonald and Evans, Plymouth.
Almond, G. and Verba, S. (1963), *The Civic Culture*, Princeton University Press, New Jersey.
Alpert, H. (1939), *Emile Durkheim and His Sociology*, Columbia University Press, New York (republished in 1961).
Alter, R. (1979), 'A new theory of Kashrut', *Commentary*, 68, (2), August, pp. 46–52.
Ardener, E. (ed.) (1971), *Social Anthropology and Language*, Tavistock, London.
Arendt, Hannah (1951), *The Origins of Totalitarianism*, Harcourt Brace, New York.
Arnold, Matthew (1963), *Culture and Anarchy*, Cambridge University Press, Cambridge. (first published 1869).
Asad, T. (ed.) (1973), *Anthropology and the Colonial Encounter*, Ithaca Press, London.
Austin, J. (1962), *How to do Things with Words*, Clarendon Press, Oxford.
Badcock, C. R. (1975), *Lévi-Strauss and Sociological Theory*, Hutchinson, London.
Banks, Olive (1982), 'Sociology of education', see ch. 4 in Cohen (1982).
Banton, M. P. (ed.) (1966), *Anthropological Approaches to the Study of Religion*, Tavistock, London.
  (1967), *Race Relations*, Tavistock, London.
Barnes, J. A. (1966), 'Durkheim's *Division of Labour in Society*', *Man*, NS, 1, pp. 158–75.
Barnes, R. H. (1982), review of Evans-Pritchard (1981), *Man*, NS, 17, pp. 364ff.
Barth, F. (1964), *Nomads of South Persia*, George Allen and Unwin, London.
Barth, Karl (1955–62), *Church Dogmatics*, T. and T. Clark, Edinburgh.
Barton, L., and Meighan, R. (eds.) (1979), *Schools, Pupils and Deviance*, Nafferton, Driffield.
Barzun, J. (1965) (rev. edn), *Race: A Study in Superstition*, Harper Torchbooks, New York.
Baxi, U. (1974), 'Durkheim and legal evolution', *Law and Society Review*, 8, pp. 645–51.
Becker, H. S. (ed.) (1964), *The Other Side*, Free Press, Glencoe.
Bell, Daniel (1961), *The End of Ideology*, Free Press, New York.
  (1974), *The Coming of Post-Industrial Society*, Heinemann, London.
Bellah, Robert (1959), 'Durkheim and history', *American Sociological Review*, 24, December, pp. 447–61.
Bendix, R., and Lispet, S. M. (eds.) (1953), *Class, Status and Power*, Free Press, Glencoe.
Benedict, Ruth (1942), *Race and Racism*, Routledge and Kegan Paul, London.
Berger, Bennet (1960), *Working Class Suburb*, University of California Press, Berkeley.

Berger, Peter (1961), *The Precarious Vision*, Doubleday, Garden City, New York.
(ed.) (1964), *The Human Shape of Work*, Macmillan, New York.
(1969), *A Rumour of Angels*, Allen Lane, London.
Bernstein, Basil, (1971–5), *Class, Codes and Control*, 3 Vols., Routledge and Kegan Paul, London: Vol. 1, 1971; Vol. 2, 1973; Vol. 3, 1975.
(1974), 'Sociology and the sociology of education, a brief account', in Rex (1974).
Birnbaum, Norman (1955), 'Monarchs and sociologists', *Sociological Review*, 3, pp. 5–23.
Blau, Peter (1956), *Bureaucracy in Modern Society*, Random House, New York.
Blauner, Robert (1972), *Racial Oppression in America*, Harper Row, New York.
Bloch, M. (ed.) (1975), *Marxist Analyses and Social Anthropology*, Malaby, London.
Bottomore, Tom (1979), *Political Sociology*, Hutchinson, London.
Bottomore, Tom, and Nisbet, Robert (eds.) (1978), *A History of Sociological Analysis*, Basic Books, New York.
Bourdieu, P. (1971), 'Intellectual field and creative project', in Young (1971).
(1977), *Cultural Reproduction*, Sage, London (translation of Paris, 1970).
Bowker, G., and Carrier, J. (1976), *Race and Ethnic Relations*, Hutchinson, London.
Bowker, J. (1973), *The Sense of God*, Clarendon Press, Oxford.
Bowles, S., and Gintis, H. (1976), *Schooling in Capitalist America, Educational Reforms and the Contradictions of Economic Life*, Basic Books, New York.
Bramson, Leon (1961), *The Political Context of Sociology*, Princeton University Press, Princeton, New Jersey.
Braverman, Harry, (1974), *Labour and Monopoly Capital*, Monthly Review Press, New York.
Bridges, Lee (1973), 'Race relations research: from colonialism to neo-colonialism? Some random thoughts', *Race*, 14 (3), January, pp. 331–41.
Brown, J., and Howes, G. (eds.) (1975), *The Police and the Community*, Saxon House, Farnborough.
Burns, Tom (1962), 'The sociology of industry', in Welford, Argyle, Glass and Morris (eds.) (1962).
Burrow, J. (1970), *Evolution and Society: A Study in Victorian Social Theory*, Cambridge University Press, Cambridge.
Chamberlain, C. W., and Moorhouse, H. F. (1974), 'Lower class attitudes towards the British political system', *Sociological Review*, NS, 22 (4), November.
Chambliss, W. J. (1976), 'Functional and conflict theories of crime: the heritage of Emile Durkheim and Karl Marx', in Chambliss and Mankoff (eds.) (1976).
Chambliss, W. J., and Mankoff, M. (eds.) (1976), *Whose Law, What Order?*, Wiley, New York.
Chandler, D. (1976), *Capital Punishment in Canada*, Carleton Library, Carleton.
Clark, Terry (1968), 'Emile Durkheim and the institutionalization of sociology in the French university system', *European Journal of Sociology*, 9, pp. 37–87.
Clarke, M. (1976), 'Durkheim's sociology of law', *British Journal of Law and Society*, 3 (2), Winter, pp. 246–55.
Cloward, R., and Ohlin, L. (1960), *Delinquency and Opportunity: A Theory of Delinquent Gangs*, Free Press, Glencoe.
Cohen, A. K. (1955), *Delinquent Boys: The Culture of the Gang*, Free Press, Glencoe.
(1965), 'The sociology of the deviant act: anomie theory and beyond', *American Sociological Review*, 30 (1), pp. 5–14.
Cohen, Louis (ed.) (1982), *Educational Research and Development in Britain 1970–80*, NFER-Nelson, Windsor.

Cohen, Percy (1968), *Modern Social Theory*, Heinemann, London.
Coser, Lewis (1960), 'Durkheim's conservatism and its implications for his sociological theory', in Wolff (1960).
(1971), *Masters of Sociological Thought*, Harcourt Brace Jovanovich, New York.
Cotterrell, R. B. M. (1977), 'Durkheim on legal development and social solidarity'; *British Journal of Law and Society*, 4 (2), Winter, pp. 241–52.
Culler, J. (1973), 'The linguistic basis of structuralism', in Robey (1973).
(1976), *Saussure*, Fontana, London.
Dagan, H. (1899), *Enquête sur l'antisemitisme*, Stock, Paris, pp. 59–63.
Dahl, Robert (1961), *Who Governs? Democracy and Power in an American City*, Yale University Press, Yale.
Dale, R. *et al.* (1977), Open University Course E 202, *Schooling and Society*, Unit 18; curriculum and cultural reproduction, the Durkheimian tradition.
Davies, Brian (1976), *Social Control and Education*, Methuen, London.
Davis, J. (ed.) (1982), *Religious Organization and Religious Experience*, Academic Press, London.
Davis, Kingsley (1959), 'The myth of functionalism as a special method in sociology and anthropology', *American Sociological Review*, 24, December, pp. 757–72.
Dawe, Alan (1971), 'The two sociologies', in Thompson and Tunstall (1971).
Dench, Geoffrey (1975), *Maltese in London*, Routledge and Kegan Paul, London.
Douglas, Mary (1963), *The Lele of the Kasai*, Oxford University Press, London.
(1966), *Purity and Danger*, Routledge and Kegan Paul, London.
(1973), *Natural Symbols*, 2nd edn, Penguin, Harmondsworth.
(1975), *Implicit Meanings*, Routledge and Kegan Paul, London.
(1978), *Cultural Bias* (Occasional Paper No. 34), Royal Anthropological Institute, London, reprinted in Douglas (1982).
(1982), *In the Active Voice*, Routledge and Kegan Paul, London.
Downes, D., and Rock, P. (eds.) (1979), *Deviant Interpretations*, Martin Robertson, Oxford.
Draper, T. N. (1969), *The Rediscovery of Black Nationalism*, Viking Press, New York.
Durkheim, Emile (1893), *De la Division du travail social*, Alcan, Paris.
(1895), *Les Régles de la méthode sociologique*, Alcan, Paris.
(1897), *Le Suicide: étude de sociologie*, Alcan, Paris.
(1898), 'L'Individualisme et les intellectuels', *Revue Bleue*, 4th Series, 10, pp. 7–13, translated in Lukes (1969).
(1899), contribution to 'Enquête sur la guerre et la militarisme', *L'Humanité Nouvelle*, May, pp. 50–2.
(1899), Translation of *Emile Durkheim*, 'Notes sur l'anti-semitisme' appears in Dagan (1899).
(1899–1900), 'Deux lois de l'évolution penale', *Année Sociologique*, 4, pp. 65–95, translated in Jones and Skull (1973).
(1900), 'La Sociologie en France au 19e siècle', *Revue Bleue*, 4 (12), pp. 609–13.
(1905), 'Sur l'internationalisme', *Libre Entretiens*, 2nd Series, pp. 17, 27, 30–3, 35, 39–42, 45, 56–7, 147–8, 150, 153, 412, 425–34, 436, 480–4.
(1908), contribution to discussion on 'Pacifisme et patriotisme', Meeting of 30 December 1907, pp. 44–9, 50–2, 66–7; Contained in *Société Française de Philosophie Bulletin*, 8, Paris.
(1912), *Les Formes élementaires de la vie religieuse*, Alcan, Paris.
(1913), reviews of Lévy-Bruhl's, *Les Fonctions mentales dans les sociétiés inferieures*, and Frank Boas's, *The Mind of Primitive Man: L'Année Sociologique*, 12, Paris, pp. 33–7.

(1915), *L'Allemagne au-dessus de tout*, Colin, Paris.

(1915), *Qui a voulu la guerre?*, Colin, Paris.

(1925), *L'Éducation morale*, Alcan, Paris.

(1928), *Le Socialisme*, Alcan, Paris.

(1933), *The Division of Labour in Society*, Macmillan, New York.

(1938), *L'Évolution pedagogique en France*, Presses Universitaires de France, Paris (republished 1969).

(1938), *The Rules of Sociological Method*, Free Press, New York.

(1950), *The Rules of Sociological Method*, Free Press, Glencoe.

(1950), *Leçons de sociologie: physique des moeurs et du droit*, Presses Universitaires de France, Paris.

(1951), *Suicide: A Study in Sociology*, Routledge and Kegan Paul, London.

(1955), *Pragmatisme et Sociologie*, Vrin, Paris.

(1956), *Education and Sociology*, Free Press, Glencoe.

(1957), *Professional Ethics and Civic Morals*, Routledge and Kegan Paul, London.

(1959), *Socialism and Saint-Simon* (edited and introduced by Filloux, J. C.), Routledge and Kegan Paul, London.

(1960), *Emile Durkheim: Essays on Sociology and Philosophy* (edited by Wolff, K.), Ohio State University Press, Columbus.

(1961), *Moral Education*, Free Press, Glencoe.

(1962), *Socialism*, Collier Books, New York.

Durkheim, Emile and Mauss, Marcel (1963), *Primitive Classification* (translated and with an introduction by Needham, R.), Cohen and West, London (translation of *Année Sociologique*, 6, 1901–2 (pub. 1903).

Durkheim, Emile (1964), *The Rules of Sociological Method*, Free Press, New York (pb. edn of 1938 translation).

(1970), *La Science sociale et l'action* (edited and introduced by Filloux, J. C.), Presses Universitaires de France, Paris.

(1976), *The Elementary Forms of the Religious Life*, Allen and Unwin, London.

(1977), *The Evolution of Educational Thought*, Routledge and Kegan Paul, London.

(1983), *Pragmatism and Sociology* (edited by Allcock, J. B., translated by J. C. Whitehouse), Cambridge University Press, Cambridge.

Eldridge, J. E. T. (1971), *Sociology and Industrial Life*, Nelson, London.

Ellwood, C. (1927), 'The development of sociology in the United States since 1910', *Sociological Review*, Keele, 19, p. 31.

Erikson, Kai T. (1962), 'Notes on the sociology of deviance', *Social Problems*, 9, pp. 307–14.

(1966), *Wayward Puritans: A Study in the Sociology of Deviance*, Wiley, New York.

Evans-Pritchard, E. E. (1956), *Nuer Religion*, Clarendon Press, Oxford.

(1965), *Theories of Primitive Religion*, Clarendon Press, Oxford.

(1981), *A History of Anthropological Thought*, Faber, London.

Faris, E. (1934), 'Emile Durkheim on the division of labour in society', *American Journal of Sociology*, 40, pp. 376–7.

Fenton, Charles Stephen (1968), 'The myth of subjectivism as a special method in sociology', *Sociological Review*, NS, 16 (3), November, pp. 333–49.

(1980), 'Race, class and politics in the work of Emile Durkheim', in Unesco (1980).

Feuchtwang, S. (1975), 'Investigating religion', in Bloch (ed.) (1975).

Feuerbach, L. (1957), *The Essence of Christianity* (1841), Harper and Row, New York.

Filloux, J. C. (ed.) (1970), *La Science sociale et l'action*, Presses Universitaires de France, Paris.

Flanders, A. (1970), *Management and the Unions*, Faber and Faber, London.

Foster, R., and Ranum, O. (eds.) (1979), *Food and Drink in History* (Vol. 5 in Selections from *Annales*), Johns Hopkins, Baltimore.

Fox, A., and Flanders, A. (1969), 'The reform of collective bargaining', *British Journal of Industrial Relations*, 8 (2), July, pp. 151–80.

Freeman, L. C., and Winch, R. F. (1957), 'Societal complexity: an empirical test of a typology of societies', *American Journal of Sociology*, 62, pp. 461–6.

Friedmann, Georges (1961), *The Anatomy of Work*, Heinemann, London.

Fromm, Erich (1942), *The Fear of Freedom*, Routledge and Kegan Paul, London.

Galbraith, J. K. (1952), *American Capitalism, the Concept of Countervailing Power*, Hamish Hamilton, London.

(1968), *The New Industrial State*, New America Library, New York.

Gans, Herbert (1962), *The Urban Villagers*, Free Press, Glencoe.

Gerstl, Joel (1961), 'Determinants of occupational community in high status occupations', *Sociological Quarterly*, 2, pp. 37–48.

Gibbs, J. P., and Martin, W. T. (1964), *Status Integration and Suicide*, University of Oregon Press, Eugene.

Giddens, A. (1970), 'Durkheim as a review critic', *Sociological Review*, 18, pp. 171–96.

(1971), *Capitalism and Modern Social Theory*, Cambridge University Press, Cambridge.

(1971), 'Durkheim's political sociology', *Sociological Review*, NS, 19, pp. 477–519.

(1972), *Emile Durkheim: Selected Writings*, Cambridge University Press, Cambridge.

(1977), *Studies in Social and Political theory*, Hutchinson, London.

(1979), *Central Problems in Social Theory*, Macmillan, London.

(1981), *A Contemporary Critique of Historical Materialism*, Macmillan, London.

Gilbert, Michael (1978), 'Neo-Durkheimian analyses of economic life and strife: from Durkheim to the Social Contract', *Sociological Review*, NS, 26 (4), November, pp. 729–54.

Glazer, Nathan, and Moynihan, Daniel Patrick (1963), *Beyond the Melting Pot*, MIT Press, Cambridge, Mass.

(1975), *Ethnicity*, Harvard University Press, Cambridge, Mass.

Glock, C. Y., and Hammond, P. E. (eds.) (1973), *Beyond the Classics: Essays in the Scientific Study of Religion*, Harper and Row, New York.

Gobineau, Le Comte Henri de (1853–5 and 1967), *Essais sur l'inegalité des races humaines*, Firmin-Didcot, Paris, and Belfont, Paris.

Goldthorpe, John H. (1964), 'Social stratification in industrial society', in *The Development of Industrial Societies*, *Sociological Review*, Monograph No. 8, Paul Halmos (ed.), Keele.

(1969), 'Social inequality and social integration in modern Britain', *Advancement of Science*, 26 (128), December, pp. 190–202.

(1974), 'Inequality and the consensus', *New Society*, 10 January, pp. 55–8.

Goldthorpe, John H., Lockwood, David, Bechhofer, Frank, and Platt, Jennifer, (1968–71), *The Affluent Worker*, 3 Vols., Cambridge University Press: Vol. 1, 1968; Vol. 2, 1968; Vol. 3, 1971.

Gollwitzer, Helmut (1970), *The Christian Faith and the Marxist Criticism of Religion*, St Andrews Press, Edinburgh.

Goode, W. J. (1957), 'Community within a community: the professions', *American Sociological Review*, 22, pp. 194–200.

Goody, J. (1956), 'A comparative approach to incest and adultery', *British Journal of Sociology,* 7, pp. 286–305.

(1969), *Comparative Studies in Kinship,* Routledge and Kegan Paul, London (reprinted).

Gordon, Milton (1964), *Assimilation in American Life,* Oxford University Press, New York.

Gossett, T. F. (1965), *Race: The History of an Idea in America,* Schocken Books, New York.

Gouldner, Alvin (1957), 'Cosmopolitans and locals: towards an analysis of latent social roles', *Administrative Science Quarterly,* 2 December, pp. 281–306.

(1971), *The Coming Crisis of Western Sociology,* Heinemann, London.

Gray, R. F., and Gulliver, P. H. (eds.) (1964), *The Family Estate in Africa,* Routledge and Kegan Paul, London.

Gregor, A. James (1974), *Interpretations of Fascism,* General Learning Press, New Jersey.

Hall, Richard (1968), 'Professionalization and bureaucratization', *American Sociological Review,* 33 (1), February.

Hallpike, C. R. (1979), *The Foundations of Primitive Thought,* Clarendon Press, Oxford.

Halsey, A. H. (1970), 'Race relations: the lines to think on', *New Society,* 19 March, pp. 472–4.

Hamnett, Ian (1973), 'Sociology of religion and sociology of error', *Religion,* 3, pp. 1–12.

Hargreaves, David (1979), 'Durkheim, deviance and education', in Barton and Meighan (eds.) (1979).

Harris, M. (1968), *The Rise of Anthropological Theory,* Routledge and Kegan Paul, London.

Hayes, E. N., and T. (eds.) (1970), *Claude Lévi-Strauss: The Anthropologist as Hero,* MIT Press, Cambridge, Mass.

Hinkle, R. C., and Hinkle, G. J. (1954), *The Development of Modern Sociology,* Random House, New York.

Hoefnagels, Harry (1958), 'La "Question sociale" dans la sociologie de Durkheim', *Bulletin de l'Institut de Recherches Économiques de l'Université de Louvain,* 24 (8), pp. 673–703.

Hoffer, Eric (1951), *The True Believer: Thoughts on the Nature of Mass Movements,* Harper and Row, New York.

Honigsheim, P. (1960), 'The influence of Durkheim and his school on the study of religion', in Wolff (1960).

Horton, J. (1964), 'The dehumanisation of anomie and alienation', *British Journal of Sociology,* 15, pp. 283–300.

Horton, R. (1973), 'Lévy-Bruhl, Durkheim and the scientific revolution', in Horton and Finnegan (eds.) (1973).

Horton, R., and Finnegan, R. (eds.) (1973), *Modes of Thought,* Faber, London.

Hubert, H., and Mauss, M. (1898), 'Essai sur la nature et la fonction du sacrifice', *Année Sociologique,* 2, pp. 29–138.

(1964), *Sacrifice: Its Nature and Function,* Cohen and West, London (translated by W. D. Halls).

Hughes, Everett (1958), *Men and their Work,* Free Press, Glencoe.

Hyman, H. (1953), 'The value systems of different classes', in Bendix and Lispet (eds.) (1953).

Jay, Martin (1973), *The Dialectical Imagination: A History of the Frankfurt School and the Institute of Social Research 1923–50*, Heinemann, London.

Jones, T. A. (1981), 'Durkheim, deviance and development: opportunities lost and regained', *Social Forces*, 59 (4), June, pp. 1009–24.

Jones, T. A., and Skull, A. (1973), 'Two laws of penal evolution', *Economy and Society*, 2 (3), pp. 278–308 (translation of Emile Durkheim's 'Deux lois de l'évolution penale').

Kagan, G. (1938), 'Durkheim et Marx', *Revue de l'Histoire Économique et Sociale*, 24 (3), pp. 233–45.

Karabel, J., and Halsey, A. H. (eds.) (1977), *Power and Ideology in Education*, Oxford University Press, New York.

Kedward, R. (1965), *The Dreyfus Affair*, Longman, London.

Kierkegaard, Soren (1962), *The Present Age*, Harper Torchbooks, New York.

Kiernan, V. C. (1972), *The Lords of Human Kind*, Pelican Books, Harmondsworth.

Kornhauser, W. (1960), *The Politics of Mass Society*, Routledge and Kegan Paul, London.

Krohn, M. D. (1978–9), 'A Durkheimian analysis of international crime rates', *Social Forces*, 57, pp. 654–70.

Kuper, A. (1973), *Anthropologists and Anthropology: The British School 1922–72*, Penguin, Harmondsworth.

Kuper, Leo (ed.) (1975), *Race, Science and Society*, Unesco Press and Allen and Unwin, Paris and London.

La Capra, D. (1972), *Emile Durkheim, Sociologist and Philosopher*, Cornell University Press, Ithaca and London.

Labriola, A. (1897), 'Essais sur la conception matérialiste de l'histoire', *Revue Philosophique*, 44, pp. 645–51.

Lacroix, B. (1978), 'Àpropos des rapports entre Durkheim et Marx: de l'analyse de texte à l'analyse sociologique', in *Etudes Offertes au Professor Emerentienne de Lagrange*, Libraire générale de droit et de jurisprudence, Paris, pp. 331–50.

(1981), *Durkheim et le politique*, Fondation National de Science et Politique, Paris.

Langham, Ian (1982), *The Building of British Social Anthropology*, Reidel, Dordrecht.

Le Bon, Gustave (1895), *Psychologie des Foules*, Paris.

Leach, E. R. (1966), 'Animal categories and verbal abuse', in Lenneberg (ed.) (1966).

(ed.) (1967), *The Structural Study of Myth and Totemism* (ASA Monograph No. 5), Tavistock Press, London.

(1970), *Lévi-Strauss*, Fontana, London.

(1973), 'Language and anthropology', in Minnis (ed.) (1973).

(1973), 'Structuralism in social anthropology', in Robey (ed.) (1973).

Leclerc, G. (1972), *Anthropologie et colonialisme*, Librairie Fayard, Paris.

Lederer, Emil (1940), *The State of the Masses*, Norton, New York.

Lenneberg, E. H. (ed.) (1966), *New Directions in the Study of Language*, MIT Press, Cambridge, Mass.

Lévi-Strauss, C. (1961), *A World on the Wane*, Hutchinson, London.

(1962), *La Pensée sauvage*, Plon, Paris.

(1962), *Totemism*, Merlin Press, London, reprinted by Penguin, Harmondsworth (1969).

(1962), *Le Totémisme aujourd'hui*, Presses Universitaires de France, Paris.

(1963), *Structural Anthropology*, Vol. 1, Basic Books, New York.

(1966), *The Savage Mind*, Weidenfeld and Nicolson, London (also published in 1962).

(1969), *The Elementary Structures of Kinship*, Eyre and Spottiswoode, London (also published in 1949 and 1967).

(1970–80), *Introduction to a Science of Mythology*, Jonathan Cape, London: Vol. 1, *The Raw and the Cooked* (1970); Vol. 2, *From Honey to Ashes* (1973); Vol. 3, *The Origin of Table Manners* (1978); Vol. 4, *The Naked Man* (1980); also published: Vol. 1, 1964; Vol. 2, 1966; Vol. 3, 1968; and Vol. 4, 1971.

(1973), *Tristes tropiques*, Jonathan Cape, London.

(1975), 'Race and history', in Kuper (ed.) (1975).

(1977), *Structural Anthropology*, Vol. 2, Allen Lane, London (also published 1973).

Lévy-Bruhl, L. (1926), *How Natives Think*, Geo Allen and Unwin, London.

(1975), *The Notebooks on Primitive Mentality*, translated by P. Rivière (*Les carnets de Lévy-Bruhl*), Blackwell, Oxford (also published Paris, 1949).

Lockwood, David (1964), 'Social integration and system integration', in Zollschan and Hirsch (eds.) (1964).

Lukes, Steven (1973), *Emile Durkheim, His Life and Work*, Allen Lane, London.

Lukes, S., and J. (1969), 'Individualism and the intellectuals', *Political Studies*, 17, pp. 14–30.

Macdonald, Keith, M. (1976), 'A police state in Britain?', *New Society*, 8 January, pp. 50–1.

(1977), 'The forces of social control: "community liaison" by the police', unpublished paper delivered at the British Sociological Association Conference.

McDonald, L. (1976), *The Sociology of Law and Order*, Faber, London.

MacIntyre, Alasdair (1967), *Secularisation and Moral Change*, Oxford University Press, London.

McLellan, David (ed.) (1971), *Karl Marx: Early Texts*, Blackwell, Oxford.

Mannheim, Karl (1936), *Ideology and Utopia*, Harcourt Brace and World, New York.

(1941), *Man and Society*, Routledge and Kegan Paul, London (republished in 1980).

(1950), *Man and Society in an Age of Reconstruction*, Harcourt Brace, New York.

(1952), *Essays on the Sociology of Knowledge*, Routledge and Kegan Paul, London.

Mannheim, Karl, and Stewart, W. A. C. (1962), *An Introduction to the Sociology of Education*, Routledge and Kegan Paul, London.

Marcuse, Herbert (1964), *One Dimensional Man*, Routledge and Kegal Paul, London.

Marshall, T. H. (1963), *Sociology at the Crossroads*, Heinemann, London.

Martin, D. (1969), 'Towards eliminating the concept of secularization', in Martin (1969).

(1969), *The Religious and the Secular*, Routledge and Kegan Paul, London.

Marx, Karl (1971), 'Critique of Hegel's philosophy of right' (1843), in McLellan (ed.) (1971).

Mayo, Elton (1949), *The Social Problems of an Industrial Civilization*, Routledge and Kegan Paul, London.

Medawar, P. B. (1969), *Induction and Intuition in Scientific Thought*, Methuen, London.

Merton, R. K. (1957), 'Social structure and anomie', *Social Theory and Social Structure*, 2nd edn, Free Press, Glencoe.

Merton, R. K., and Nisbet, R. (eds.) (1966), *Contemporary Social Problems*, Harcourt Brace and World, New York.

Michels, Robert (1949), *Political Parties*, Free Press, Glencoe.

Miley, J. D., and Micklin, M. (1972), 'Structural change and the Durkheimian legacy: a macrosocial analysis of suicide rates', *American Journal of Sociology*, 78, November, pp. 657–73.

Miliband, Ralph (1961), *Parliamentary Socialism*, Merlin Press, London.

(1969), *The State in a Capitalist Society*, Weidenfeld and Nicolson, London.

Minnis, N. (ed.) (1973), *Linguistics at Large*, Paladin, St Albans.

Mitchell, M. M. (1931), 'Emile Durkheim and the philosophy of nationalism', *Political Science Quarterly*, 46, pp. 87–106.

Müller, Max (1856), *Oxford Essays*, London.

(1873), 'The philosophy of mythology', appended to *Introduction to the Science of Religion*, London.

(1889), *Natural Religion*, London.

Nandan, Y. (1977), *The Durkheimian School*, Greenwood Press, Westport, Conn.

Needham, R. (1969), Introduction, to C. Lévi-Strauss, *The Elementary Structures of Kinship*, Eyre and Spottiswoode, London.

(1972), *Belief, Language and Experience*, Blackwell, Oxford.

Nisbet, R. (1952), 'Conservatism and sociology', *American Journal of Sociology*, 58, pp. 165–75.

(1962), *Community and Power*, Oxford University Press, New York.

(1965), *Emile Durkheim*, Prentice Hall, Englewood Cliffs, New Jersey.

(1966), *The Sociological Tradition*, Basic Books, New York.

Nordlinger, E. A. (1967), *The Working Class Tories*, MacGibbon and Kee, London.

Ortega, Y., Gasset, J. (1950), *The Revolt of the Masses*, Pelican, New York.

Ottaway, A. K. C. (1953) and (1962), *Education and Society*, Routledge and Kegan Paul, London.

(1955), 'The educational sociology of Emile Durkheim', *British Journal of Sociology*, 3, pp. 213–27.

Papenheim, Fritz (1959), *The Alienation of Modern Man*, Monthly Review Press, New York.

Parsons, Talcott (1937), *The Structure of Social Action*, McGraw-Hill, New York.

(1955), *The Social System*, Free Press, Glencoe.

(1973), 'Durkheim on religion revisited', in Glock and Hammond (eds.) (1973).

Patterson, Orlando (1969), *The Sociology of Slavery*, Associated University Presses, London (also published in 1975).

Pavalko, Ronald (1971), *Sociology of Occupations and Professions*, Peacock Publishers, Itasca, Illinois.

Pearlin, Leonard (1962), 'Alienation from work: a study of nursing personnel', *American Sociological Review*, 27, June, pp. 304–26.

Peyre, Henri (1960), 'Durkheim: the man, his time, and his intellectual background', in Wolff (1960).

Pickering, W. S. F. (1975), *Durkheim on Religion: A Selection of Readings with Bibliographies*, Routledge and Kegan Paul, London.

(1984), *Durkheim's Sociology of Religion*, Routledge and Kegan Paul, London.

Plummer, K. (1979), 'Misunderstanding labelling perspectives', in Downes and Rock (eds.) (1979).

Pope, D. W., and Weiner, N. L. (eds.) (1981), *Modern Policing*, Croom Helm, London.

Pyle, F. H. (1971), 'The two bodies: social structure and natural symbolism', *Religion*, 1, pp. 72–7.

Radcliffe-Brown, A. R. (1952), *Structure and Function in Primitive Society*, Cohen and West, London.

Rappaport, R. A. (1979), *Ecology, Meaning and Religion*, Atlantic Press, Richmond, California.

Reiman, Jeffrey (1979), *The Rich Get Rich and the Poor Get Prison*, Wiley, New York.

Rex, John (1961), *Key Problems in Sociological Theory*, Routledge and Kegan Paul, London.

(1973), 'The future of race relations research in Britain sociological research and the politics of racial justice', *Race*, 14 (4), April, pp. 481–8.

(1973), *Race, Colonialism and the City*, Routledge and Kegan Paul, London.

(ed.) (1974), *Approaches to Sociology*, Routledge and Kegan Paul, London.

Ribington, E., and Weinberg, M. S. (eds.) (1981), *Deviance: The Interactionist Perspective*, 4th edn, Macmillan, New York.

Riesman, David (1953), *The Lonely Crowd*, Doubleday Anchor, New York.

Robertson, R. (1970), *The Sociological Interpretation of Religion*, Blackwell, Oxford.

Robey, D. (ed.) (1973), *Structuralism: An Introduction*, Clarendon Press, Oxford.

Ruel, M. (1982), 'Christians as believers', in Davis (ed.) (1982).

Salaman, Graeme (1974), *Community and Occupation*, Cambridge University Press, Cambridge.

Saussure, F. de (1915), *Cours de linguistique générale*, Payot, Paris (translated by Baskin, W., *Course in General Linguistics*, Philosophical Library, New York (1959)).

Schwartz, R. D. (1954), 'Social factors in the development of legal control: a case study of two Israeli settlements', *Yale Law Journal*, 63, pp. 471–91.

(1974), 'Legal evolution and the Durkheim hypothesis: a reply to Professor Baxi', *Law and Society Review*, 8, pp. 653–68.

Schwartz, R. D., and Miller, J. C. (1964), 'Legal evolution and societal complexity', *American Journal of Sociology*, 20, pp. 159–69.

Sheleff, L. S. (1975), 'From restitutive law to repressive law: Durkheim's *The Division of Labour in Society* revisited', *Archives Européennes de Sociologie*, 16, pp. 16–45.

Shils, E, and Young, M. (1953) 'The meaning of the coronation', *Sociological Review*, 1, pp. 63–81.

Smith, M. G. (1965), *The Plural Society in the British West Indies*, Sangster's Books, and University of California Press, Berkeley.

Soler, J. (1973), 'Sémiotique de la nourriture dans la Bible', *Annales*, Part 4, 28.

(1979), 'The dietary prohibitions of the Hebrews', *New York Review of Books*, 26 (10), 14 June, pp. 943–55.

Spencer, W. Baldwin, and Gillen, F. J. (1899), *The Native Tribes of Central Australia*, Macmillan, London.

(1904), *The Northern Tribes of Central Australia*, Macmillan, London.

Sperber, D. (1979), 'Claude Lévi-Strauss', in Sturrock (ed.) (1979).

Spiro, Melford (1963), *The Kibbutz: Venture in Utopia*, Schocken Books, New York.

(1966), 'Religion: problems of definition and explanation', in Banton (ed.) (1966).

Spitzer, S. (1975), 'Punishment and social organisation: a study of Durkheim's theory of penal evolution', *Law and Society Review*, 9 (4), Summer, pp. 613–37.

Stevenson, K. W. (ed.) (1980), *Symbolism and the Liturgy I*, Grove Books, Bramcote (Grove Liturgical Study No. 23).

Stinchcombe, A. L. (1968), *Constructing Social Theories*, Harcourt Brace, New York.

Stocking, G. W. (1963), 'Matthew Arnold, E. B. Tylor and the uses of invention', *American Anthropologist*, 65, pp. 783–99.

Sturrock, J. (ed.) (1979), *Structuralism and Since*, Oxford University Press, London.

Swanson, Guy (1960), *The Birth of the Gods*, University of Michigan Press, Ann Arbor.

(1967), *Religion and Regime*, University of Michigan Press, Ann Arbor.

Taylor, I., Walton, P., and Young, J. (1973), *The New Criminology*, Routledge and Kegan Paul, London.

Taylor, L. (1973), *Deviance and Society*, Nelson, London.

Thompson, Kenneth, and Tunstall, Jeremy (eds.) (1971), *Sociological Perspectives*, Penguin Books, Middlesex.

Tiryakian, Edward (ed.) (1890), 'The principles of 1789 and sociology', in *The Phenomenon of Sociology*, Appleton Century Crofts, New York, 1971; a translation of Durkheim's review article, *Revue Internationale de l'Enseignement*, 19, 1890.

(1965), 'A problem for the sociology of knowledge: the mutual unawareness of Emile Durkheim and Max Weber', *European Journal of Sociology*, 7 (2).

(1978), 'Emile Durkheim', in Bottomore and Nisbet (eds.) (1978).

(1979), 'L'École Durkheimienne à la recherche de la société perdue: la sociologie naissante et son milieu culturel', *Cahiers Internationaux de Sociologie*, 66, pp. 97–114.

Tocqueville, Alexis de (1945), *Democracy in America*, Knopf, New York.

Towler, R. (1974), *Homo Religiosus*, Constable, London.

Trow, Martin (1977), 'The second transformation of American secondary education', in Karabel and Halsey (eds.) (1977).

Turkel, G. (1979), 'Testing Durkheim: some theoretical considerations', *Law and Society Review*, 13, Spring, pp. 721–38.

Turnbull, Colin (1961), *The Forest People*, Jonathan Cape, London.

Turner, Victor (1967), *The Forest of Symbols*, Cornell University Press, Ithaca.

(1968), *The Drums of Affliction*, Oxford University Press, London.

(1969), *The Ritual Process*, Routledge and Kegan Paul, London.

(1978), *Image and Pilgrimage in Christian Culture*, Columbia University Press, New York.

Turner, Victor, and Edith (1974), *Dramas, Fields, Metaphors*, Cornell University Press, Ithaca.

Unesco (1980), *Sociological Theories: Race and Colonialism*, Unesco Press, Paris.

Van Den Berghe, Pierre (1967), *Race and Racism*, Wiley, New York.

Wallman, S. (ed.) (1979), *Ethnicity at Work*, Macmillan, London.

Wallwork, E. (1972), *Durkheim, Morality and Milieu*, Harvard University Press, Cambridge, Mass.

Watson, J. L. (ed.) (1977), *Between Two Cultures*, Blackwell, Oxford.

Webb, S. D. (1972), 'Crime and the division of labour: testing a Durkheimian model', *American Journal of Sociology*, 78, November, pp. 643–56.

Weber, M. (1965), *Sociology of Religion*, Methuen, London.

Welford, A. P., Argyle, M., Glass, D. V., and Morris, J. N. (eds.) (1962), *Society: Problems and Methods of Study*, Routledge and Kegan Paul, London.

Wilensky, Harold (1961), 'Orderly careers and social participation', *American Sociological Review*, 26 (4), August, p. 521–2.

(1967), 'From religious community to occupational groups: structural assimilation among professors, lawyers and engineers', *American Sociological Review*, 32 (4), August, pp. 541–61.

Williams, Raymond (1968), *Culture and Society*, Penguin Books, Middlesex.

Willis, P. (1978), *Learning to Labour*, Saxon House, London.

Wilson, B. (1982), *Religion in Sociological Perspective*, Oxford University Press, Oxford.

Wimberley, H. (1973), 'Legal evolution: one further step', *American Journal of Sociology*, 79 (1), July, pp. 78–83.

Wolff, K. (ed.) (1960), *Emile Durkheim: Essays on Sociology and Philosophy*, Ohio State University Press, Columbus.

Worsley, P. (1970), *The Trumpet Shall Sound*, 2nd edn, Paladin, London.

Wright, M. (1982), *Making Good: Prisons, Punishment and Beyond*, Burnett Books, London.

Wrong, Dennis (1961), 'The over-socialized conception of man in modern society', *American Sociological Review*, 26 (2), April, pp. 183–93.

Young, M. F. D. (1971), *Knowledge and Control*, Collier-Macmillan, London.

Zeitlin, I. (1968), *Ideology and the Development of Sociological Theory*, Prentice-Hall, New Jersey.

Zollschan, G., and Hirsch, W. (eds.) (1964), *Explorations in Social Change*, Routledge and Kegan Paul, London.

Selected reading

Bottomore, Tom, and Nisbet, Robert (eds.) (1978), *A History of Sociological Analysis*, Basic Books, New York.

Bramson, Leon (1961), *The Political Context of Sociology*, Princeton University Press, Princeton, New Jersey.

Clark, Terry (1968), 'Emile Durkheim and the institutionalization of sociology in the French university system', *European Journal of Sociology*, 9, pp. 37–87.

Clarke, M. (1976), 'Durkheim's sociology of law', *British Journal of Law and Society*, 3 (2), Winter, pp. 246–55.

Coser, Lewis (1971), *Masters of Sociological Thought*, Harcourt Brace Jovanovich, New York.

Cotterrell, R. B. M. (1977), 'Durkheim on legal development and social solidarity', *British Journal of Law and Society*, 4 (2), Winter, pp. 241–52.

Durkheim, Emile (1960), *Emile Durkheim: Essays on Sociology and Philosophy*, (edited by Wolff, K), Ohio State University Press, Columbus.

Fenton, Charles Stephen (1980), 'Race, class and politics in the work of Emile Durkheim', in Unesco (1980).

Giddens, A. (1971), 'Durkheim's political sociology', *Sociological Review*, NS, 19, pp. 477–519.

(1972), *Emile Durkheim: Selected Writings*, Cambridge University Press, Cambridge.

(1977), *Studies in Social and Political Theory*, Hutchinson, London.

Hargreaves, David (1979), 'Durkheim, deviance and education', in Barton and Meighan (eds.) (1979).

Lukes, Steven (1973), *Emile Durkheim, His Life and Work*, Allen Lane, London.

Lukes, S., and J. (1969), 'Individualism and the intellectuals', *Political Studies*, 17, pp. 14–30.

Lukes, S., and Scull, A. (1983), *Durkheim and the Law*, Martin Robertson, Oxford.

Merton, R. K. (1957), 'Social structure and anomie', *Social Theory and Social Structure*, 2nd edn, Free Press, Glencoe.

Pickering, W. S. F. (1975), *Durkheim on Religion: A Selection of Readings with Bibliographies*, Routledge and Kegan Paul, London.

Revue Française de Sociologie (1976), 'À propos de Durkheim', 17 April/June.

Sheleff, L. S. (1975), 'From restitutive law to repressive law: Durkheim's *The Division of Labour in Society* revisited', *Archives Européennes de Sociologie*, 16, pp. 16–45.

Social Forces (ed. Everett K. Wilson) (1981), Special Editor Edward A. Tiryakian, 59 (4), June, Part I.

Swanson, Guy (1960), *The Birth of the Gods*, University of Michigan Press, Ann Arbor.

Tiryakian, Edward (ed.) (1890), 'The principles of 1789 and sociology', in *The Phenomenon of Sociology*, Appleton Century Crofts, New York, 1971; a translation of Durkheim's review article, *Revue Internationale de l'Enseignement*, 19, 1890.

Index

274